More Praise for *Stanley Kubrick*

"The power of the book as a whole . . . will be riveting reading for anyone who loves Kubrick's film."

—*Jerusalem Post Magazine*

"Abrams . . . [identifies] each and every Jewish allusion in Kubrick's oeuvre that he can find."

—*Times Literary Supplement*

"[A] pathbreaking new book."

—*Tablet Magazine*

"Every scholar and devotee of Kubrick will want to read *Stanley Kubrick: New York Jewish Intellectual*."

—*Film Quarterly*

"Abrams combines close readings of the films with intensive, archival research into the source material—scripts, production documents, and Kubrick's personal papers and artifacts—which collectively tell a Jewish story."

—*Jewish Review of Books*

"In Nathan Abrams's *Stanley Kubrick: New York Jewish Intellectual*, [an] exploration of the contradictions of Kubrick's relation to Jewish identity, the film is seen through the lens of Biblical allusion and Kabbalistic interpretation."

—*Wall Street Journal*

"Abrams asserts that if you look closely enough, the tension between being a cultural and religious Jew turns up frequently in Kubrick's work."

—*Jewish Journal*

"[An] extraordinarily entertaining new book."

—*Village Voice*

"An impressive work of original scholarship, *Stanley Kubrick: New York Jewish Intellectual* presents an exceptionally informative study of one of the twentieth century's most renowned and yet misunderstood film directors."

—*Midwest Book Review*

"No film or Jewish history holding should be without this different approach to Kubrick's film magic."

—Donovan's Literary Services

"Abrams . . . makes a very convincing case that while Kubrick posed as an atheist technocrat filmmaker who wanted his films to appeal to world-wide audiences, among the many things he was burying in their subtexts were 'the concerns of Jewish intellectuals in the post-Holocaust world'. . . . Ultimately though, are Abrams's assumptions correct? Many of them ring true and likely are."

—PJ Media

"*Stanley Kubrick* is outstanding in its approach and the material it covers. As a pioneer work, anyone investigating Kubrick in the future would not be able to overlook Abrams's findings and arguments."

—Marat Grinberg, coeditor of *Woody on Rye: Jewishness in the Films and Plays of Woody Allen*

"With imagination and intellectual rigor, using archival research and close readings of the films, Nathan Abrams explores Stanley Kubrick's relationship with his Jewishness in this exceptionally readable and convincing book."

—Robert P. Kolker, author of *The Extraordinary Image*

"Brilliantly documents and analyzes Kubrick's Jewish sensibility by locating him in the lifelong context of his Jewish cultural and intellectual milieu. Abrams breaks acres of new ground. Essential reading."

—Geoffrey Cocks, author of *The Wolf at the Door: Stanley Kubrick, History, and the Holocaust*

Stanley Kubrick

Stanley Kubrick

New York Jewish Intellectual

NATHAN ABRAMS

Rutgers University Press

New Brunswick, Camden, and Newark, New Jersey, and London

First paperback printing, 2020
978-0-8135-8711-0

Library of Congress Cataloging-in-Publication Data

Names: Abrams, Nathan, author.
Title: Stanley Kubrick : New York Jewish intellectual / Nathan Abrams.
Description: New Brunswick, New Jersey : Rutgers University Press, [2018] | Includes bibliographical references and index.
Identifiers: LCCN 2017032568 | ISBN 9780813587103 (cloth) | ISBN 9780813587110 (pbk.)
Subjects: LCSH: Kubrick, Stanley. | Motion picture producers and directors—United States—Biography.
Classification: LCC PN1998.3.K83 A57 2018 | DDC 791.4302/33092 [B]—dc23 LC record available at https://lccn.loc.gov/2017032568

A British Cataloging-in-Publication record for this book is available from the British Library.

∞ The paper used in this publication meets the requirements of the American National Standard for Information Sciences—Permanence of Paper for Printed Library Materials, ANSI Z39.48–1992.

www.rutgersuniversitypress.org

Manufactured in the United States of America

For my *teulu*

Contents

Stanley Kubrick

Introduction

Stanley Kubrick is probably one of the most written-about directors who has ever lived. Yet considering this fascination—extraordinary when he was alive and which has only intensified since his death in 1999—we know very little about his offscreen life. Given how much has been written about him and how fanatically curious his ardent followers can be about him, our knowledge is surprisingly vague. This is particularly so when we consider Kubrick's Jewishness, which this book does, reclaiming him as an artist who came of age and, despite his years in England, has remained a New York Jewish intellectual.

Although the scholarship surrounding Kubrick is large and still growing, very few have considered either his origins or ethnicity and how these impacted his work. This is because few scholars have bothered to take Kubrick's Jewish background into account or the relation between his work and the presence or absence of Jewish themes in his films. The two published biographies of Kubrick include almost no such material. By contrast, Jewish film scholars have failed to adopt Kubrick because their very limited definition of what is "Jewish" restricts them to explicit content, assuming Jews are discussed or analyzable only when they directly appear on-screen; thus they primarily task themselves with locating, describing, and analyzing films with explicit Jewish characters and themes.[1]

To date, only one book-length study, as well as several articles and chapters by the same author, have considered Kubrick's origins and ethnicity and how these impacted his work to any great extent. Geoffrey Cocks has explored Kubrick's secular Jewish identity to mine the deeper significance of Kubrick's ethnicity and background and how this affected his films. But although Cocks firmly grounds Kubrick in a Jewish milieu, both American and central European, his focus on the place of the Holocaust in Kubrick's cinema is perhaps too speculative and too reductive. He also confines his analysis, primarily, to *The Shining* (1980), the film he believed was most concerned with the Holocaust. Nonetheless, we owe a debt of gratitude to Cocks for grounding Kubrick in this setting and for being one of the first historians to study Kubrick using archival sources.[2]

Other works have considered the Jewish influence only sporadically. Where Margaret Burton explored Jewish themes in *Spartacus* (1960), her scope was confined to one film, which many scholars feel doesn't deserve the Kubrick imprint anyway. To this we can add Frederic Raphael, whose highly selective and self-serving memoir of collaborating with Kubrick on *Eyes Wide Shut* (1999) deeply delved into Kubrick's Jewishness, but it is so bitter it should be given a wide berth. Raphael was right, however, in saying it's "absurd to try to understand Stanley Kubrick without reckoning on Jewishness as a fundamental aspect of his mentality, if not of his work in general."[3]

The limitations of these accounts open the ground for a new approach that complements these existing ones. While Cocks and Burton, among others, have noted how Kubrick can be read as Jewish, they have done so with little recourse to the Kubrick and other archives. Such material has been unavailable to scholars in the past or has been overlooked by them (a frustrating tendency that continues today). Consequently, there is still scope to explore in more depth the underlying Jewishness of Kubrick's films, particularly with reference to archival materials, all of which shed significant light on his ethnicity and how it influenced his work. Kubrick didn't just spring from nowhere. By focusing on Kubrick's Jewishness, then, this book fills a key gap in our knowledge of him.

Kubrick was "known to have said that he was not really a Jew, he just happened to have two Jewish parents." Jewish by birth through both his mother Gertrude Perveler and his father Jack or Jacques Kubrick (originally Kubrik), his parents gave him what can be regarded as a very typical first name for Jews born in that era. And he steadfastly stuck to using that name in an industry where fellow Jews—at least the actors with whom he worked—were encouraged to change them. His maternal grandmother spoke Yiddish, and, according to his brother-in-law, Jan Harlan, he "loved" Woody Allen's portrait of New York City in the late 1930s and early 1940s in his *Radio Days* (1987), identifying with the little boy Joe: "He knew the taste and smell of everything in this film. His parents were more sophisticated than the family portrayed in the film, but Stanley felt so at home with the 'drama' and the language used."[4]

As an assimilated American Jewish family, the Kubricks were not religious. They practiced little, if any, Judaism. Jacob Kubrick had changed his own Hebrew name to the more cosmopolitan Jack/Jacques. When asked, "Did you have a religious upbringing?" Kubrick replied, "No, not at all." His education was "totally secular as far as any organized religion is concerned," Harlan said. He received no formal Jewish instruction, never (as far as we know) attended a synagogue or Hebrew School, and wasn't bar mitzvahed; none of these things interested him. Michael Herr, who collaborated on the screenplay for *Full Metal Jacket* (1987), explains, "He was barely making it in school; he couldn't do junior high English, let alone Hebrew, and besides, Dr. and Mrs. Kubrick weren't very religious, and anyway, Stanley didn't want to."[5]

Kubrick had no faith. He stated, "I don't believe in any of Earth's monotheistic religions." His daughter, Katharina Kubrick Hobbs, said, "He did not deny his Jewishness, not at all. But given that he wanted to make a film about the Holocaust and researched it for years, I leave it to you to decide how he felt about his religion." His driver and handyman, Emilio D'Alessandro, recalled, "Stanley wasn't particularly interested in religion, nor did he really understand religious fanaticism." Yet Harlan says he was "always taking a big bow to the great Unknowable." Maybe this explains why the kaddish, the Jewish prayer for mourners, was performed at his funeral.[6]

Others have characterized Kubrick as a self-hating Jew. Dalton Trumbo, who collaborated on *Spartacus*, accused Kubrick of being "a guy who is a Jew, and he's a man who hates Jews. He has said to me that the Jews are responsible for their own persecutions because they have separated themselves from the rest of humanity." Frederic Raphael claimed Kubrick had said Hitler had been "right about almost everything."[7]

Kubrick's Jewish identity was much more complex than these labels suggest. There's no proof that Kubrick was a self-hating Jew, a label thrown about with far too much abandon, especially by disgruntled collaborators. Kubrick was more than just Jewish by birth. He was a Jew by culture and feeling, but not religious. He was acutely aware of his central European

Jewish origins, his ancestors having emigrated from there around 1900. This heritage had a significant effect on him. The critic Alexander Walker, who knew Kubrick well, spoke of "a quality of obsession that seems . . . considerably further east, geographically speaking than his Middle European origins in Austria suggest." He loved the literature of the region: Sigmund Freud, Arthur Schnitzler, Jacob Schulz, Franz Kafka, Stefan Zweig. His father, who was a well-read man, owned an extensive personal library, which he encouraged his son to read, suggesting an informal Jewish education during Kubrick's childhood.[8]

Kubrick grew up in the heavily Jewish West Bronx, surrounded by Jewish neighbors and immigrants. The Bronx was, at that time, home to 250,000 Jews, from which Kubrick drew his early circle of childhood friends. Together with his neighbor, Marvin Traub, he experimented with cameras and developing photos. "I became interested in photography [at the age of] 12 or 13. And I think that if you get involved in any kind of problem solving in depth on almost anything, it is surprisingly similar to problem solving of anything else. I started out by just getting a camera and learning how to take pictures, print, build a darkroom, all the technical things, then finally trying to find out how you could sell pictures and become a professional photographer." High school classmates assisted his early film career: Alexander Singer helped him shoot his first documentary; Gerald Fried composed the score for three of his feature movies; and Howard Sackler cowrote some early screenplays. As one correspondent to the *New Yorker* wrote, "I can't resist pointing with pride to the fact that Mr. K is not only an American but a local boy, born and brought up in the Bronx and owing a certain debt to the business and cultural opportunities of this city."[9]

Kubrick's early interests manifested a Jewish sensibility. By 1946, having graduated from high school, he was working as a photojournalist for *Look* magazine, where he honed his burgeoning photographic eye, while also hustling at chess. As a teenager, Kubrick had been passionate about jazz—Herr described him as "jazz-mad"—and he had hoped to progress from playing drums with the Taft [High School] Swing Band to becoming a jazz drummer.[10] He was seriously studying the technique. Jazz, photography, and chess were extraordinarily Jewish professions or pastimes in the twentieth century. The list of Jewish photographers and jazz and chess players is too long to cite here; suffice to say that Kubrick's immediate boss at *Look*, his department head, Arthur Rothstein, was also Jewish. By 1951

Kubrick had entered the movie business, another extraordinarily Jewish profession.

He married two Jewish women in succession (albeit in civil ceremonies), daughters of first-generation European immigrants. On May 29, 1948, he wed his high school sweetheart, Toba Metz. She came from a sheltered middle-class Bronx Jewish neighborhood. He was twenty, she just eighteen. Kubrick and Metz separated in late 1951, but he dated Ruth Sobotka from 1952, marrying her in January 1955. They separated in 1957.

After leaving high school, Kubrick was supposed to go to medical school, following his parents' wishes. He recalled, "My father was a doctor. My parents wanted me to become a doctor, but I was such a misfit in high school that when I graduated I didn't have the marks to get into college." He instead enrolled in evening classes at New York's City College. Many Jews who, because of Ivy League quota systems designed to bar them, had no choice but to attend what became known as the "poor man's Harvard." He also took classes at Columbia University with Lionel Trilling, Mark Van Doren, F. W. Dupee, and Moses Hadas, expanding his Jewish education.[11]

A clear influence on Kubrick's Jewishness was his relocating to Greenwich Village. He set up home with Metz at 37 West Sixteenth Street, in the heart of the Village, then the center of New York's intellectual and bohemian community of artists, actors, musicians, poets, performers, and writers. Many significant Jewish cultural figures lived and worked in the Village, including *Partisan Review* editors Philip Rahv and William Phillips, poet Delmore Schwartz, author Norman Mailer, singer Bob Dylan, poet and singer Tuli Kupferberg, filmmaker Maya Deren, and many others. Sackler moved there, as did Paul Mazursky, who later played in Kubrick's first feature.

In the Village Kubrick's Jewish circle expanded. He met leading figures in the Beat movement. These included the writer Carl Solomon, who was also born in the Bronx in 1928. Kubrick invited Solomon to a private screening of *Fear and Desire* shortly after its release in 1953. Leading Beat poet Allen Ginsberg studied English at Columbia at approximately the same time as Kubrick, and they knew each other possibly through Solomon, to whom Ginsberg later dedicated his poem *Howl* (1956). Another key Beat figure was Jay Landesman, founder of magazine *Neurotica* (1948–1952). Probably the first Beat journal, it functioned as an outlet for such writers as Solomon (as Carl Goy), Ginsberg, Larry Rivers, Judith Malina, and John Clellon

Holmes. Although only nine issues were published, Kubrick bought and read assiduously every one.

Kubrick also kept the company of émigré and Jewish avant-garde photographers and artists. They had a formative influence on him. Diane Arbus, who also used a Graflex camera, took him under her wing, making a permanent impression, as did the Jewish photographer Arthur Fellig, whose unposed shots of murder victims and uncanny ability to arrive so early at crime scenes had earned him the nickname "Weegee" (as in Ouija board). Likewise, Kubrick also met artists Henry Koerner, George Grosz, and Jacques Lipchitz—all of whom responded to the Holocaust in their work in various ways—when he photographed them for *Look* in 1946.

Kubrick, along with Metz, immersed himself in a world of self-directed learning, becoming largely self-taught. After eschewing formal post–high school study, his education came from voracious reading and then obsessively seeing every film he could at the neighborhood Loew's and RKO, on Forty-Second Street; art films at the Thalia on upper Broadway, the 55th St. Playhouse, and the Museum of Modern Art; and then everything else he had missed elsewhere. He frequently visited exhibitions and read widely, including the work of the Soviet montage directors Sergei Eisenstein and Vsevolod Pudovkin (whom he favored). As Herr puts it, "Stanley never went to college; he was only a stunningly accomplished autodidact, one of those people we may hear about but rarely meet, the almost but not quite legendary Man On Whom Nothing Is Lost." Midge Decter describes Kubrick as a "gifted Jewish boy from the Bronx and we may imagine him in his youthful days as a bit of an intellectual, creative, dying to get out, positively drunk on the movies: a familiar figure."[12]

Kubrick's self-education continued under the tutelage of his second wife. Born in Vienna in 1925, Sobotka had emigrated to America at age fourteen and was a dancer and designer with the New York City Ballet. She was three years older than Kubrick, so it is likely that she introduced him to Schnitzler, as well as a range of other influences that remained throughout his life.

Kubrick can be compared to the New York Intellectuals. They were a group of American writers and literary critics based in New York City in the mid-twentieth century who wrote for such magazines as the *Nation* (1865), the *New Republic* (1914), the *New Leader* (1924), *Partisan Review* (1934), *Commentary* (1945), *Encounter* (1953), *Dissent* (1954), and the *New York Review of Books* (1963) and included such luminaries as Hannah

Arendt, Saul Bellow, Norman Mailer, Bernard Malamud, Norman Podhoretz, Susan Sontag, Lionel Trilling, and Robert Warshow. Irving Howe,
who coined the term, "New York Intellectual," described their "fondness
for ideological speculation; they write literary criticism with a strong social
emphasis; they revel in polemic; they strive self-consciously to be 'brilliant';
and by birth or osmosis, they are Jews." Kubrick shared many of these distinguishing features. His education was very similar. At Columbia he was
taught by the first generation of the New York Intellectuals and was therefore most likely in the same room as its second generation (such as future
Commentary editor, Norman Podhoretz). And while he was never a writer
or literary critic, he read their magazines. He had a fondness for ideological
speculation, he was Jewish by birth, and he strived self-consciously to be
brilliant.[13]

When Dwight Macdonald, a leading New York Intellectual, met
Kubrick in 1959, he was impressed by the director's range: "I spent an
interesting three hours with Stanley Kubrick, most talented of the younger directors, discussing Whitehead, Kafka, Potemkin, Zen Buddhism,
the decline of Western culture, and whether life is worth living anywhere
except at the extremes—religious faith or the life of the senses; it was a
typical New York conversation." Macdonald later wrote to Kubrick to
recall their encounter: "Our three hour session at the Beverly-Wilshire [*sic*]
still clings to memory as echt-Newyork [*sic*]; like two old Etonians chat-
ting in darkest Congo."[14]

Kubrick was also part of that same milieu that produced such other
alternative New York Jewish intellectuals, either those born in the city or
those who became New Yorkers by osmosis. These included playwright
Arthur Miller; novelist Joseph Heller; the editors, writers, and artists of
the magazines *Mad* and the *Realist*; musicians Bob Dylan and Leonard
Cohen; the Beats; comedians Mort Sahl and Lenny Bruce; cartoonist Jules
Feiffer; and academics Stanley Milgram and Robert Jay Lifton. All of them
exerted some influence on Kubrick's work because they shared the same
concerns. His work engaged with the same dilemmas and explored the
same paradoxes. His lifelong commitments mirrored theirs in many ways,
and he took part in many of the same debates through his work, reflecting
the concerns of Jewish intellectuals in the post-Holocaust world.

These concerns continued even when Kubrick began to make his films
in England from the early 1960s onward, relocating there permanently
after 1968. If anything, his New York Jewish intellectual sensibilities

were magnified by the distance. Living across the Atlantic afforded him even more independence and critical distance (as well as access to major studio facilities, without the aggravation of living in either New York or Los Angeles—a city he hated). Penelope Gilliatt, who interviewed him in 1987, wrote, "Though long based in England, Kubrick remains American, looking at his country with 'distance giving a better perspective.'" If anything, his transatlantic relocation gave him the moniker of "exile" or "émigré," now resembling those central European Jewish directors whom he so admired, chief among them Max Ophüls. And he never abandoned his New York Jewish perspective—he retained his distinctive nasal Bronx accent throughout his life—nor forgot his central European heritage.[15]

But Kubrick's satirical approach and use of humor distinguished him from the New York Intellectuals' tone of high moral seriousness. Alex Ross describes his "expert comic timing of a New York Jew." One of his favorite jokes was William Burroughs's line, "A paranoid schizophrenic is a guy who just found out what's going on." He "dug Swift," as well as Kafka, whose work he adored. He was also a fan of Heller, Bruce, Feiffer, and their ilk. His "view and temperament were much closer to Lenny Bruce's than to any other director's," Herr recalled. He held the satirist, Paul Krassner, in high regard. From the late 1950s onward, Krassner published the *Realist* magazine, which featured a blend of "Mort Sahl–like social and political commentary and analysis, put-ons ('I was an Abortionist for the FBI'), in-depth impolite interviews, cartoons and scabrous gossip." Contributors ranged from Dick Gregory, Terry Southern, and Mailer to Sahl and Bruce. A similarly satirical edge, coupled with sexual, scatological humor, can be detected in all his mature films from *Lolita* (1962) onward. In 1964 Kubrick explained, "For me the comic sense is the most eminently human reaction to the mysteries and the paradoxes of life."[16]

Kubrick's major intellectual commitments can be grouped into four interrelated themes. First, he asked what it was to be a man (I use the masculine noun deliberately), a son, a husband, a father and how to be a mensch, the Yiddish term meaning a human being—a decent, upstanding, ethical, and responsible person with admirable characteristics. The Yiddish writer Leo Rosten described a mensch as "1. A human being. 'After all, he is a *mensh*, not an animal.' 2. An upright, honorable, decent person. 'Come on, act like a *mensh*!' 3. Someone of consequence; someone to admire and emulate: someone of noble character. 'Now, there is a real *mensh*!'" In the words of Rebecca Alpert, a mensch is an "ethical human being who displays his virtues through gentility and kindness."[17]

Tellingly, once Kubrick effectively became a parent with his third wife, Christiane Harlan, in 1958, his interest in exploring paternity magnified. He remarked, "When you get right down to it, the family is the most primitive and visceral and vital unit in our society. You may stand outside your wife's hospital room during childbirth uttering, 'My God, what a responsibility! . . . What am I doing here?' and then you go in and look down at the face of your child and—zap!—the most ancient programming takes over and your response is one of wonder and joy and pride." Christiane said Kubrick had read much about ethnology because "the most important question for a man is that of his paternity, of learning that his children are not his own." In 1968 he said, "if [man] is going to stay sane throughout the voyage, he must have someone to care about, something that is more important than himself." It was as if he'd absorbed a line from William Makepeace Thackeray's *The Memoirs of Barry Lyndon, Esq.* (1856), which he later adapted as *Barry Lyndon* (1975), "a man is not a complete *Mensch* [*sic*] until he is the father of a family, to be which is a condition of his existence, and therefore a duty of his education." Jan Harlan said, Kubrick "was always interested in human nature. Whenever there is a crucial thing in our lives—relationships, children—our emotions kick in. If Kubrick was ever afraid of anything, it was to be carried away by those emotions."[18]

Here he drew on his own family dynamics. As the first-born and only son, he was close to his mother, Gertrude, who indulged him. His father, Jack, was a formative influence on him, sharing his love of chess—itself a deeply oedipal game in which the most potent opponent of the king (father) is the queen (mother)—and photography. According to Christiane, Jack "was passionate about photography and this passion was communicated to Stanley at an early age," not least by giving him a Graflex camera for his thirteenth birthday—traditionally the bar mitzvah age when Jews believe that the boy comes of age and enters manhood.[19]

The second concern was ethical introspection and behavior, which Judaism has always encouraged. As Rabbi Norman Lamm explained for the abandoned prologue to *2001: A Space Odyssey* (1968), "Man was created in the image of and he was commanded to imitate God. The imitation of God is understood as being primarily ethical, moral. Man must be ethical because God, too, is ethical." In the modern secular age this ethical impulse can be best described as the uniquely Jewish code of *menschlikayt*. Derived from the term *mensch*, it is the Yiddish expression referring to ethical responsibility, social justice, and decency for others expressed in kindness.

It is a "uniquely Jewish 'code' of conduct," emphasizing the moderate, meek, and intellectual values of Yiddishkeit (literally: Jewishness/Jewish culture, which John Murray Cuddihy defined as "the values, feelings, and beliefs of the premodern *shtetl* subculture . . . 'Jewish fundamentalism'"). It privileged a posture of reliance on family, tradition, accommodation, nonviolence, gentleness, timidity, and a man's responsibility for his fellow men in contrast to conventional goyish ("un/non-Jewish/Gentile") masculinity. Yiddishist Irving Howe defined it as "a readiness to live for ideals beyond the clamor of the self, a sense of plebeian fraternity, an ability to forge a community of moral order even while remaining subject to a society of social disorder, and a persuasion that human existence is a deeply serious matter for which all of us are finally accountable."[20]

Menschlikayt rejected *goyim naches*, a phrase that "broadly describes non-Jewish activities and pursuits supposedly antithetical to a Jewish sensibility and temperament." Literally meaning "pleasure for/of the gentiles," its root is the Hebrew word *goy* (singular of *goyim*, meaning gentiles), but it also derives from the word for "body" (*geviyah*). It can therefore also be interpreted to mean a "preoccupation with the body, sensuality, rashness, and ruthless force," as manifested in such physical activities as bearing arms, horse riding, dueling, jousting, archery, wrestling, hunting, orgies, and sports in general. Denied the right to participate in such activities, Jews instead denigrated them, consequently also disparaging those very characteristics that in European culture defined a man as *manly*: physical strength, martial activity, competitive drive, and aggression. Goyim naches therefore, in Daniel Boyarin's words, is "the contemptuous Jewish term for the prevailing ideology of 'manliness' dominant in Europe."[21]

Jews had long been opposed to goyish physicality. Freud explained how the "preference which through two thousand years the Jews have given to spiritual endeavor has, of course, had its effect; it has helped to build a dike against brutality and the inclination to violence which are usually found where athletic development becomes the ideal of the people." Jean-Paul Sartre also noted, "The Jews are the mildest of men . . . passionately hostile to violence." The period after World War II saw a growth in the influence of Yiddishkeit and interest in menschlikayt in America. The Holocaust provoked an interest in those very Jewish roots that had virtually been wiped out, prompted by émigré intellectuals such as Maurice Samuel and his translations of the Yiddish works of Sholem Aleichem and Solomon Asch, which, in turn, therefore became much more widely available. Such authors as Saul Bellow and Bernard Malamud, were linked to a revival in

Yiddishkeit, particularly their works, *Dangling Man* (1944), *The Victim* (1947), and *The Assistant* (1957). The House Un-American Activities Committee's hearings in 1947 and 1951, combined with the Rosenberg atom spies case (1951–1953), enflamed anti-Semitism and caused an increasing sense of Jewish identification among younger Jews.[22]

The Hebrew prophetic tradition had also bequeathed a passion for ethics, social justice, and decent human values. This was manifested in the postwar period in Jewish sensitivity to civil rights and the support Jewish organizations and individuals gave to minorities. Because they had suffered, Jews felt they couldn't allow other groups to undergo similar discrimination. Kubrick's Jewish background instilled an interest in fairness, equality, and ethical behavior, manifesting itself in a concern for social justice. The horrendous experiences of Jews in Europe throughout the centuries, culminating in the Holocaust, had given Kubrick a "special sense of community" with the subaltern, the marginalized, and the oppressed, for "Jews had been treated as a community apart in many European countries, not fully citizens, not Christian, considered not fully human."[23]

Judaism, through its prophetic tradition, had also bequeathed a heritage and legacy of *tikkun olam*, or "healing the world." Tellingly, in 1968, the very year when it all seemed to be falling apart in America, Kubrick expressed his belief in "man's potential and capacity for progress." When it came down to it, Kubrick didn't hold a pessimistic view of human nature. In 1972 he wrote,

> The question must be considered whether Rousseau's view of man as a fallen angel is not really the most pessimistic and hopeless of philosophies. It leaves man a monster who has gone steadily away from his nobility. It is, I am convinced, more optimistic to accept [Robert] Ardrey's view that, ". . . we were born of risen apes, not fallen angels, and the apes were armed killers besides." And so what shall we wonder at? Our murders and massacres and missiles and our irreconcilable regiments? For our treaties, whatever they may be worth; our symphonies, however seldom they may be played; our peaceful acres, however frequently they may be converted into battlefields; our dreams, however rarely they may be accomplished. The miracle of man is not how far he has sunk but how magnificently he has risen. We are known among the stars by our poems, not our corpses.

He later told Michel Ciment, "I am certainly not an anarchist, and I don't think of myself as a pessimist."[24]

Kubrick manifested his Jewish identity through the moral imperative in his films. He was a moralist, who demonstrated a commitment to his ethnicity through ethical behavior. He manifested what Jewish historian Howard Morley Sacher refers to as the "unconscious desire of Jews, as social pariahs, to unmask the respectability of the European society which closed them out." "There was no more effective way of doing this," Sacher continues, "than by dredging up from the human psyche the sordid and infantile sexual aberrations that were frequently the sources of human behavior, or misbehavior," that is, goyim naches. A system of Jewish values lurked beneath the surfaces of his films, but in the way that Kubrick rendered them, they became the universal values of humankind.[25]

The third concern was humankind's capacity for evil and its nature. Kubrick referred to the "darker side of our natures, the shadow side." Sydney Pollack, who starred in *Eyes Wide Shut*, felt Kubrick "was simply very realistic about the evil that exists in the world." Kubrick's daughter, Anya, said that he believed "we are all both good and evil, and if you think you have no evil in you, you're not looking hard enough." In preparation for *Full Metal Jacket*, Kubrick wrote, "It's not our animal nature because animals don't do such things. It is not in our animal nature but in our human natures. It must be kept locked away in the shadow. Freud exorcised the erotic demons. The shadow of lust for power and destruction still needs to be exorcised." His films are an attempt to achieve just that.[26]

Such evil had been manifested in the Holocaust, which Kubrick believed was "the greatest disaster in history." He openly admitted to sharing "the fairly widespread fascination with the horror of the Nazi period." Born in the interwar period, he grew up hearing about Hitler's rise to the power and the onset of the Nazi regime and its persecution of the Jews under its control, culminating in the Holocaust, during which those close to him were worrying daily about the safety of their relatives. By 1945 he was sixteen and hence reached maturity in a post-Holocaust world. Kubrick read widely in this field, not just in preparation for his aborted film, *Aryan Papers* (based on Louis Begley's 1991 *Wartime Lies*), but for his own education, as manifested by his extensive personal library on the subject, including Raul Hilberg, Hannah Arendt, Bruno Bettelheim, Stanley Milgram, and countless others. Frederic Raphael, who collaborated on the screenplay for *Eyes Wide Shut*, said Kubrick's "work could be viewed, as responding, in various ways, to the unspeakable (what lies beyond spoken explanation)." As John Orr and Elżbieta Ostrowska have pointed out,

"Kubrick, who never realised his Holocaust film project, nonetheless had a post-Holocaust vision of the contemporary world."[27]

In a sense Kubrick even married into the Holocaust. In 1957 he met Christiane Susanne Harlan, and they soon began a relationship. They married in 1958 and remained together until Kubrick's death in 1999. Christiane, like all young Germans of her age, was inducted into the Hitler Youth at the age of ten. Her parents were part of the Wehrmacht entertainment troupes that performed for the troops at the front. Her father was later drafted and sent to a combat unit in the Black Forest, where, according to Christiane, he guarded Russian prisoners. Her uncle, Veit, was the Nazi filmmaker who made the notoriously anti-Semitic propaganda film, *Jud Süss* (1940). Kubrick met him in 1957 and wanted to make a film about him. Cocks suggests that "Kubrick's antennae thus must have been especially attuned to the critical vibrations in the Harlan family caused by sorrow and outrage over Veit Harlan's close collaboration with the Nazi cultural and political elite." Christiane recalled, "Stanley took a great interest in my catastrophic family background. We spoke about it a great deal. People asked him, 'How could you marry a German woman, especially one with a background like that?' I thought a lot about the fact that no one could have taken a greater interest in my family background than Stanley, who understood that I came from the other side, which was the opposite of his [background]. But he also knew that my generation could plead innocence: I was very young during the Holocaust, though at the same time old enough to remember everything."[28]

Although Kubrick said very little about the Holocaust directly in his films, it haunts his work like a ghostly specter. He struggled with its impact and with his own understanding of himself as a potential Jewish victim, an innocent and accidental survivor of the Nazi genocide. Growing up in the age of Hitler and the Final Solution, a heightened sense of threat in the world is central in his films, often conveyed by a child confronting a world of danger and power, from *Lolita* through to *A.I. Artificial Intelligence* (2001). According to Christiane, "All Stanley's life he said, 'Never, ever go near power. Don't become friends with anyone who has real power. It's dangerous.' We both were very nervous on journeys when you have to show your passport. He did not like that moment. We always had to go through separate entrances, he with [our] two American daughters upstairs, and me with my German daughter downstairs. The foreigners downstairs! He'd be looking for us nervously. Would he ever get us back?"[29]

I also explore Kubrick's fourth concern, the treatment of Jews and Jewishness in his films. Naturally, this was intertwined with the previous concerns. Kubrick deliberately and systematically erased the Jewishness of the characters of his source material, repeatedly writing Jewish characters out of his screenplays from *The Killing* (1956), through *Paths of Glory* (1957), *Spartacus, Lolita, A Clockwork Orange* (1971), *Barry Lyndon*, and *Full Metal Jacket*, culminating in the removal of any *overt* reference to the ethnicity of the protagonists of Austrian playwright and novelist Arthur Schnitzler's *Traumnovelle* (*Dream Story*, 1926) for his final film, *Eyes Wide Shut*. More than just an intellectual, Kubrick needed to mainstream his material, so he toned down many of his more explicit references to Jews, Jewishness, and Judaism when writing, shooting, and cutting his movies. A serious filmmaker and businessman, he felt constrained by the need to make a commercial return on his films.

Kubrick never perceived himself as a Jewish director. By distancing himself from the Jewish aspects of his source novels, he reinvented himself as an "American" or "universal" director, rather than a Jewish artist focused solely on parochial Jewish concerns. This meant dispensing, on the surface of the film at least, Jewish cultural and religious identity. He came from that generation of American Jews who wanted to be considered first and foremost American rather than Jewish. Playwright Arthur Miller spoke for them all when he wrote how he didn't feel any "binding tie to what could be called Jewish life," having "graduated out of it." Instead, he'd "adopt[ed] the customs and habits and attitudes of the American nation as a whole," holding "the same idea of myself as any other American boy had."[30]

This was entirely in keeping with the Jewish literary production in postwar America. Submerging Jewishness by concealing their ethnicity became a commonplace and accepted form of Jewish assimilation in the immediate postwar period, and a way to make it. Such writers as Arthur Miller, J. D. Salinger, Herman Wouk, Saul Bellow, and Norman Mailer often felt unable or unwilling to write explicit Jewishness into their works. In a groundbreaking 1964 essay "Jewish-Americans, Go Home," New York Intellectual Leslie Fiedler castigated this literary strategy. Their "crypto-Jewish" protagonists were, in "habit, speech, and condition of life, typically Jewish-American, but are presented as something else—general American," that is, reinvented as gentile or goyish to make them more universal. For Fiedler, there is no trope more "Jewish American" than these "hyper-*goyim*."[31]

Kubrick's refusal to refer to Jews directly also resembled, or deliberately mimicked, Franz Kafka, whom Kubrick admired. Rodger Kamanetz described Kafka's Jews as "so deeply assimilated that they could not inhabit outwardly Christian forms while remaining completely Jewish. There are no rabbis in Kafka's published tales, no bar mitzvahs or synagogues. There are no Jewish characters as such." Rather a "decoder ring" of "man in the street/Jew at home" is required "to penetrate the cover story. Kafka's stories are themselves 'men in the street,' but they are also 'Jews at home,' that is, at core."[32]

To this end, Kubrick drafted and redrafted his screenplays. During preproduction, and shooting itself, a range of script documents, often by various individuals, were generated. Kubrick left behind him an archaeology of many different iterations and versions of what his films could be. This writing process and the resulting screenplay texts formed a palimpsest, which Maria Pramaggiore describes as an "ancient papyrus scroll that was repeatedly used, then washed, and even scraped clean in order to be written on again. These gestures are only partially preserved, however; they are subsequently overwritten themselves, as the palimpsest becomes a tissue that reveals the layers of past and present. Despite the attempt to obliterate the past, the visible evidence of previous structures (in this case graphic or linguistic as well as architectural and social) remains." She continues, "the palimpsest is an appropriate metaphor for Kubrick's films": layers of new material were laid on top of the original scenario, mirroring the "palimpsest of biographical, cultural, cinematic, and historical layers of his mind."[33]

Kubrick's authorial intention was not wholly erased by industrial, commercial, and other considerations. Production documents in Kubrick's archive demonstrate that while Jewish elements were repressed for the final films, they were clear in the production history, and their subtle footprints remained. Certain elements remained consistent, while others were interchangeable or discarded altogether. Some of the details of the source texts of the various drafts of the screenplays—such as characters, similes, or other figures of speech that were not ultimately visualized cinematically and hence may have disappeared on the surface of the film text—nonetheless remained beneath the surface of the film as signs of directorial intention. This was amplified by casting choices and on-set improvisation. Together these produced multiple, consistent but coded clues that suggest that Kubrick retained this palimpsest of Jewishness, albeit a submerged stratum, highlighting elements in the source texts that Kubrick read and understood as Jewish and hence allowing us to read the film as Jewish.

A "hidden Jewish substratum" can be detected in Kubrick's films despite the absence of any such explicit "ethnic" designation. His films were

frequently informed by specialist knowledge (of all kinds). This herme-
neutic approach requires the viewer to locate, identify, and decode a set
of clues to produce "Jewish moments" that a general audience decodes as
universal. These codes, which are both textual and extratextual, including
casting; historical, traditional, and cultural references; appearance; intellect; behavior; professions; names; physiognomy; foods; spoken and body
language; phenotypes; aural, visual or emotional genre signs; speech patterns; accents; hairstyles; anxieties; neuroses; and conflicts. It relies on the
audience decoding stereotypical characteristics, behaviors, beliefs, habits,
and other tics, all of which require a prerequisite and prior knowledge. The
result is the possibility of *"reading Jewish."*[34]

Jewishness was submerged textually in Kubrick's films and hence detect-
able to those able to read the clues or those familiar with source texts.
Contemporary viewers, as we shall see, certainly noted Jewish traces in
his films. Ultimately, I argue that the underlying Jewishness of Kubrick's
source texts, the various screenplay drafts, together with the interventions
of key actors, still penetrated through to the final screen versions, even if
explicit references to Jews, Jewishness, and Judaism were seemingly con-
spicuously absent from the films themselves. What is more, Kubrick
inserted oblique Jewish references that remained in the final edit. The hidden presence of underlying Jewish themes beneath the surface of his films,
and the reasons for their nonexplicitness, provide the key to understanding Kubrick's ambivalent, ambiguous, and seemingly paradoxical attitude
toward Judaism.

Kubrick relied on his audiences to do the work. He admired the elliptical David Mamet, whose response, when it was put to him that most of
his audience wouldn't recognize the Jewish symbolism within his work,
is instructive here. Paraphrasing the great Jewish scholar Maimonides,
Mamet replied, "Those that do, do; those that do not, do not." Early on in
his career, as is explored in the next chapter, Kubrick learned about the art
of staging photographs. His unofficial mentor, Diane Arbus, believes that
"a photograph is a secret about a secret. The more it tells you the less you
know." When he began directing films, Kubrick explained, "I think for a
movie or play to say anything really truthful about life, it has to do so very
obliquely, so as to avoid all pat conclusions and neatly tied up ideas." He
later told Alexander Walker, "I'm sure that there's something in the human
personality which resents things that are clear, and, conversely, something
which is attracted to puzzles, enigmas, and allegories." Kubrick's films
manifested a "tension between representation and concealment." Matthew

Modine, who starred in *Full Metal Jacket*, came closest to understanding this method when he recalled, "He was a master, a real master at creating traps, of feints and illusions." Wally Gentleman, who worked briefly on *2001*, referred to Kubrick's "psychological manipulations," and Sydney Pollack called him a "great manipulator."[35]

Raphael also argues that "S. K. proceeds by indirection," something Kubrick learned from Schnitzler. Modine felt, "Stanley is not a director who can tell you what he wants. In fact, my favorite direction of his is his nondirection!" In an early interview, worth quoting at length, Kubrick admitted,

> I think all great dramatists have achieved their ends in very much the same way [indirection—a roundabout way of getting to the point]. The most potent way to move an audience is to reach their feelings and not their brains. Of course, it's a much more dangerous way to write, because if the audience fails to discover what you mean, they're left quite disturbed. . . . It has always seemed to me that really artistic, truthful ambiguity—if we can use such a paradoxical phrase—is the most perfect form of expression. Nobody likes to be told anything. Take Dostoyevsky. It's awfully difficult to say what he felt about any of his characters. I would say ambiguity is the end product of avoiding superficial, pat truths. The intellectual is capable of understanding what is intended and gets a certain amount of pleasure from that, whereas the mass audience may not. But I think that the enemy of the filmmaker is not the intellectual or the member of the mass public, but the kind of middle-brow who has neither the intellectual apparatus to analyze and clearly define what is meant, nor the honest emotional reaction of the mass film audience member. And unfortunately, I think that a great many of these people in the middle are occupied in writing about films. I think that it is a monumental presumption on the part of film reviewers to summarize in one terse, witty, clever, TIME magazine-style paragraph what the intention of the film is. That kind of review is usually very superficial, unless it is a truly bad film, and extremely unfair.

Certainly, Kubrick shared with his coreligionist émigré filmmakers—Billy Wilder, Fritz Lang, Otto Preminger, and Josef von Sternberg—a reluctance ever to explain his intentions. Indeed, he was an enigmatic, elliptical, and frustratingly uncommunicative director. He refused to explain his films' purposes in part to encourage, through exploration and experimentation, the possibilities of meaning and expression.[36]

Nonetheless, although certain elements were repressed for the final film, they are clearly there as subtle traces and clues in the production history and context that, in turn, illuminate what does not make it to the final script. And what cannot be erased is that all his films have a New York Jewish intellectual quality to them. Even if certain characters or ideas never made it all the way to the screen, they left in his films a Jewish and post-Holocaust sensibility that did.

If such readings are often missed, it is because Kubrick was a universalist and modernist humanist who didn't reduce the human condition to ethnic specificities. As a mainstream commercial director who wished to make money, he resisted limiting his potential audience by making what could be pigeonholed as "Jewish" films. He drew on two elements key to chess and photography, manipulation and misdirection, both of which he mastered. Thus, his ethnicity and its impact in his films is often simply ignored by fans and mainstream film scholars alike, many of whom continue to study his films divorced from the intellectual, ethnic, and religious milieu in which they originated. One of the reasons for this absence is the near-rigid adherence to the conventional dogma that while Kubrick was born a Jew he was not a Jewish director (however that may be defined), so he is rarely perceived in this light. Indeed, few obituaries bothered to mention his Jewishness.

By contrast, this book plumbs the depths of Kubrick's Jewishness. It proceeds in a chronological and thematic fashion, exploring how Kubrick addressed his key concerns over time. After a chapter on his early works, including his photography and first films, and a chapter on his films with Kirk Douglas, each chapter thereafter treats a film in turn, beginning with *Lolita* and culminating in *Eyes Wide Shut*. His unfinished projects are considered where they help us to understand his Jewishness. But since Kubrick's screenplays, and even his preproduction materials, tell us very little about the finished film, I have decided against discussing them in detail. Each chapter explores Kubrick's four key concerns—men, menschlikayt, evil, and Jews/Jewishness—and locates the film in its biographical, psychological, historical, intellectual, and cultural context, seeking to understand why Kubrick made each film when he did and what he was trying to say in each of them at that particular time. In addition to readings of his films, the analysis is rooted in not only the vast amount of writing, both academic and popular (and the downright whacky!), on Kubrick, but also in significant archival resources, including his archive in London, which provides a hitherto unprecedented insight into his thoughts, planning, research, and working practices. It gives us an unprecedented opportunity to understand his intentions and to "get inside of his head" and therefore his films.

This book seeks to answer the following questions: What light can previously untapped archival materials, the director's own archives in London, shed on Kubrick's work? How does locating Kubrick into a New York Jewish intellectual context widen our understanding of his work? How can a deeper understanding of Kubrick's religious-ethnic background enhance our reading of his films? Overall, then, this book is driven by the belief that an intellectual, ethnic, and archival approach to Kubrick's work yields new and interesting insights to produce a better understanding of an opaque, elliptical, and frustratingly uncommunicative, but still Jewish, director.

1

Looking to Killing

The years 1945–1956 are key to understanding Kubrick's New York intellectual Jewishness. During that formative period he began his career as a professional photographer, producing thousands of pictures. This early work culminated in three short documentaries and three feature films, nurturing his nascent authorial signature in terms of both style and content. They were not merely exercises in youthful experimentation but prepared the ground for his work as an auteur. The same themes and ideas that occupied the New York Intellectuals and their alternatives can be seen, including Freudianism and psychoanalysis, existentialism, war, religion, menschlikayt, Jewish masculinity, Nazism, and the Holocaust.

Kubrick as Photographer

Kubrick sold his first photograph to *Look* in 1945, appearing in the June 26 issue. He was subsequently hired as an apprentice in April 1946 and promoted to a full-time position six months later. Between 1945 and 1950 he took approximately twenty-six thousand photographs for the magazine. For Philippe Mather, they "formed the basis for his work as a filmmaker," to which he "constantly referred back." That Kubrick kept at least 259 contact sheets, as well as those copies of *Look* in which his work had appeared, indicates he was more than just a hoarder and attached worth to his photojournalistic work; in Mather's words, his collection was "compelling evidence that he did not try to repress this formative period in his professional life, and that he valued the work he accomplished in New York." This is particularly evident in light of his later attempts to destroy every print and negative of his first feature film, *Fear and Desire*.[1]

At *Look* Kubrick learned to compose shots, develop storytelling techniques through the mini photo-essay, and nurture those nascent interests that defined his entire career. The magazine employed a system of writer-photographer teams for its production of stories and essays, setting up a working method that Kubrick utilized, *A Clockwork Orange* and *Barry Lyndon* apart, for all his movies. Two core elements of his craft, and a key to unlocking his later films, were honed during this time: misdirection and manipulation. Both skills were familiar to him through playing chess, and hence his mind was perfectly suited to photojournalism, in which the staged photograph was a staple. Kubrick intuitively grasped this: his photograph of the dejected newspaper seller in his newsstand on the day that Franklin D. Roosevelt died that landed him a job at *Look* was, he admitted, staged. Kubrick had coaxed the vendor to adopt a disconsolate expression. Kubrick's boss at *Look*, Arthur Rothstein, nurtured this embryonic talent. Rothstein's renowned and controversial shot of a bleached steer skull in the South Dakota Badlands in 1936 had been manipulated. By moving the skull ten feet forward for dramatic effect, Rothstein was accused of faking the shot to convey the impression of drought conditions, making it appear worse than in reality.[2]

Manipulation, misdirection, and staging are evident in Kubrick's *Look* photo-stories. In "A Short Short in a Movie Balcony" (April 16, 1946), a series of four purportedly candid photographs depict a young man in a movie theater making a pass at the young woman sitting beside him, who rebukes him for his impertinence. The whole event was set up—the cinema was closed, the man (Bernard Cooperman) and woman were Kubrick's friends and high school classmates, and the "audience" was his younger sister, Barbara. Each subject was taken aside and privately instructed on how to behave, apart from Cooperman, who was genuinely surprised to be slapped. In "What's Your Idea of a Good Time?" (December 10, 1946), he photographed his Bronx childhood friend and neighbor Marvin Traub, with whom he shared a love of photography, and his then girlfriend Toba

Metz but posed them as passing strangers. She was misleadingly identified as a "musician." Metz also appeared with another high school friend, posing as a young couple, in "A Curious Event at the Natural History Station" (March 21, 1947). "Don't Be Afraid of Middle Age" (January 31, 1950) staged shots of models portraying a couple spicing up their marriage by blissfully dancing and dining. Kubrick never claimed neutrality or objectivity in his photography, or even that he was presenting the world as it was; instead, his photographs explicitly expressed his "own ideas about the world."[3]

Kubrick's *Look* assignments often featured friends and family, a signature that continued through to *Eyes Wide Shut*. His future second wife, Ruth Sobotka, was photographed for "Meet the People" (January 7, 1947), suggesting he knew her much earlier than previously suspected. Opposite her was his uncle, David Perveler. Taft High School classmate Alex Singer appeared in the November 26, 1946, issue, while "Life and Love on the New York Subway" (March 4, 1947) included Singer, Metz, and *Look* writer G. Warren Schloat Jr. Where Kubrick himself may not be glimpsed, he inserted multiple references to his own work or self.

Yet, at the same time, Kubrick developed a grounding in precision and documentary realism. His technique was underpinned by natural lighting and attention to detail. He explained to the *New York Times* in 1958, "We are all used to seeing things in a certain way, with the light coming from some natural source. I try to duplicate this natural lighting in the filming. It makes for a feeling of greater reality." Joanne Stang, who interviewed him that year, said, "Kubrick is fiercely concerned with the accuracy of the small details that make up the backgrounds of his films because he feels this helps the audience to believe what they see on screen." In his setups for *Look*, we can detect manipulation and misdirection of his audience combined with a pragmatic mode of documentary composition grounded in Kubrick's own New York Jewish circle. Such techniques, as well as playful self-reflexivity and autobiographical gesture, continued throughout his career.[4]

Although Kubrick was sent out on assignments, his photographs typically reflected his own interests, something that would continue throughout his career (even when he was seemingly just a "director-for-hire"). For *Look* this was evident in photo-stories about sports (boxing and baseball) and music (especially jazz and drumming). The theme of fathers and fatherhood crops up early, anticipating Kubrick's own paternity. In "What Teenagers Should Know about Love" (October 10, 1950), Kubrick depicts a young girl sitting on a bench holding the hand of and looking up adoringly at her father, who is seated mostly out of frame. The caption reads, "LOVE FOR FATHER The father plays an important part in the child's early love life. He comes in from outside with a hearty welcome and a sturdy hand. He is your first love after your mother, and perhaps also your greatest rival for her affection." On the same page an advert for Arvin TV depicts a father and daughter watching television together. Both photographs anticipate Kubrick's later family life and interest in marriage.

Sex was another early concern. A full-page photograph taken by Kubrick of artist Peter Arno in his studio sketching features a full nude model in semiback view (September 27, 1949). The picture was considered so risqué that Campbell Soup withdrew its advertising contract with the magazine. The caption, that Arno likes to date only "fresh, unspoiled girls" much younger than himself, hints at Humbert Humbert in *Lolita*. Even more explicit are the contact sheets for "Woman Posing," in which a woman dances suggestively on stage, removing her clothes until she is wearing a very skimpy bikini with a see-through bra.[5]

Kubrick's interest in religion emerges in these early photographs. "Prizefighter" (January 18, 1949) features Greenwich Village boxer Walter Cartier, a devout Roman Catholic; and his identical twin brother, Vincent. Walter was twenty-four, not much older than Kubrick when he photographed him for *Look*. On the second page of the photo-essay, titled "Prizefighter," by far the largest photo, what was called the "bleed" picture, that is, a picture extending to the edge of the page for emphasis, is that of Walter, in church, praying. The caption reads, "On way to fight, Walter stops at church, prays that he escape [*sic*] serious injury." "Holiday in Portugal" (August 3, 1948) depicts the interior of Portugal's largest cathedral, Jeronymos, in Lisbon, as well as the "intensely religious" women of the fishing village of Nazaré.

Kubrick's photography manifested his interest in social justice. His photographs of the University of Michigan (May 10, 1949) betrayed his menschlikayt, his concern for race relations, depicting a picture of athlete Val Johnson and the caption, "Racial problems are diminishing at Michigan." Kubrick's interest in depicting the other side of the American dream was clearly articulated in "Chicago: City of Extremes" (with Irving Kupcinet; April 12, 1949), in which aspects of the city's wealth are juxtaposed with images of its poverty and such captions as "A Chicagoan finds place for modest lunch among debris of demolished buildings on west side. . . .

Diners in fabulous Pump Room of Ambassador East, however, think little of playing $10 for lunch."

It was during this early phase of Kubrick's career that we see the first signs of explicitly Jewish material before he learned to submerge it in allegories, analogies, metaphors, and through misdirection. In "Life and Love on the New York Subway" (March 4, 1947), Kubrick photographed a *haredi* Jew, with the caption, "Talmudic scholar reads his Yiddish newspaper aloud to an intent friend." Perhaps Kubrick saw in this *yeshiva bochur* a Jewish alter ego, how he may have turned out if things had gone differently. "Rocky Graziano: He's a Good Boy Now" (February 14, 1950) features the boxer's Jewish manager, Irving Cohen; and trainer, Whitey Bimstein. Cohen also features in "The Fight of My Life" (November 30, 1954), as did legendary gym owner Lou Stillman. He photographed David Sarnoff, the Jewish chairman of RCA and founder of NBC for "Our Last Frontier: Transoceanic TV" (September 12, 1950) and "The Position of the Jews in America Today" (November 29, 1955). Coincidentally, a picture of future collaborator, Kirk Douglas, was also published in this article. "Boy Wonder Grows Up" (March 14, 1950) focuses on Jewish composer, conductor, and pianist Leonard Bernstein. One shot of Bernstein, posing in just a pair of shorts, highlights his trim shape—something Kubrick later emphasized with other Jewish actors, namely Douglas and Tony Curtis—contrasting him with the meek, sallow, and clothed Talmud scholar, evoking the twin Jewish stereotypes of the "tough" and "sissy" Jew. In another shot, Bernstein is shown relaxing with a copy of Jewish psychiatrist Erich Fromm's *Man for Himself: An Inquiry into the Psychology of Ethics* (1947) open and lying across his chest, suggesting Jews can be simultaneously strong and intellectual. Whether owned by Bernstein, or posed by Kubrick, the book is an early hint of the director's intellectual interests.

Even more significantly, the Bernstein photo-shoot invokes the Holocaust. Bernstein is depicted mimicking a Hitler salute and moustache, perhaps Kubrick's first explicit reference to the Nazis on camera, anticipating both *Lolita* and *Dr Strangelove Or: How I Learned to Stop Worrying and Love the Bomb* (1964). One wonders just how commonplace such an image would have been during that period when, it has been argued, the Holocaust was not largely talked about within American Jewry and certainly predated popular culture's interest in the events of 1933–1945. In the August 5, 1947, issue Kubrick provided twelve pictures for a thirteen-photo, three-page spread on fifteen-year-old Polish war orphan Jack Melnik (the only one he did not take was that of Jack being liberated by American GIs in 1944). Titled *"In Amerika Habe Ich Die Freiheit Gefunden* [I Found Freedom in America]," the photo-essay introduces how Kubrick dealt with the Holocaust. Melnik had been a slave laborer in a Nazi camp; liberated by GIs, he eventually emigrated to America. While the Holocaust was clearly its subtext, nowhere was it directly mentioned except in the vague words "slave-labor camp" and "Nazi." Nor was it stated Jack was Jewish, despite the Ashkenazi Polish origins of the name. Indeed, the article suggests otherwise when it states he "met 16-year-old Helen Yarosh at the Polish-Ukrainian Church." While Kubrick wasn't responsible for the text, he was for its photographs, one of which depicted Jack sitting at a table writing a letter. Wearing a white vest, Jack resembles a young Marlon Brando or James Dean. At the same time, his bare arms and shoulders are visible. The shot, taken by Kubrick, is very suggestive, combining his interests in Jewishness and masculinity. Yet the clearest reference to the Holocaust is elided for, even though the Library of Congress notes one of the contact sheets contains a picture of "a person's forearm with an identification number tattooed on it," it isn't visible in the pictures selected for publication. While this editorial choice may not have been Kubrick's, he did not shy away from shooting this key visual signifier of the Holocaust, and it augured how he treated the Holocaust throughout his career in its invocation yet simultaneous avoidance of the topic. Given the similarity in names between Melnik and Kubrick, and that his father was named Jack, surely this story resonated for the nineteen-year-old Kubrick, a mere four years older than Melnik.[6]

Developing into Movies

At age twenty-one, Kubrick became a movie director. As Alexander Walker points out, "his lack of family responsibilities at this age allowed him to pursue the far riskier livelihood of a filmmaker." His filmmaking career began with a series of three short documentaries, made between 1951 and 1953: *Day of the Fight, The Flying Padre,* and *The Seafarers.* They were very much crossover films, combining his *Look* photojournalism with documentary. *Day of the Fight* was financed with his own money, combined with a contribution from his well-off father. Based on his 1949 photo-story "Prizefighter," it likewise features the Cartier brothers and is just sixteen minutes long (a second twelve-minute version omitting the opening four minutes of stock footage, as well as some of the narration and shots of the longer version, is more widely available). He sold it to RKO, which financed his next film, a nine-minute documentary following two days in the life of Roman Catholic priest Father Fred Stadtmueller, who ministered his New Mexico parish by flying his airplane, *The Spirit of St. Joseph*. Finally, Kubrick was commissioned by the Seafarers International Union (SIU) to make a promotional film. His first film in color, it was shot on 16 mm in June 1953, and lasted almost thirty minutes.[7]

Critics and scholars alike have been far too quick to dismiss these latter two films as merely juvenile efforts in which Kubrick took a paycheck, providing the images for another's narration. But such a rush to judgement is too hasty for these documentaries, which, totaling only fifty-four minutes (and hence not long enough to match the length of a standard feature film), established his signature visual and thematic style that earmarked his later movies. They tell us much about Kubrick's technique and preoccupations as he foregrounded his interests in brotherhood; masculinity; all-male, working-class, and homosocial environments; as well as fathers (absent or present); doctors and physicians; domesticity and home; families; females; and the male separation from home and journey back. His films explored both urban and rural environments, as well as faith, organized religion, religious minorities, and ethnicity. Other interests included World War II, doubles, food and sex, machines and technology, sports (particularly boxing), and chess.

While his three documentary films engage different subjects—boxing, priesthood, and seafaring—all of them explore differing aspects of the human, specifically male, condition, what it is to be a man and a mensch. Working men, albeit of different types, are at the heart of these efforts, and women are conspicuous by either their absence or relegation to roles of secondary importance, such as secretarial, food preparation and serving, and familial tasks. All three films possess religious, specifically Roman Catholic, matter. Underpinning them all is his New York, Jewish, and subversive humor, showcasing what he could do with limited artistic freedom. Despite being a commissioned director, subservient to another's script and narration, Kubrick was nevertheless able to slyly insert his own autobiographical signatures, interests, and jokes.

Day of the Fight opens with his signature misdirection, "All events depicted in this film are true." The voiceover narration implies Cartier was chosen at random, eliding the fact that he was featured in Kubrick's earlier photo-story on which *Day of the Fight* was based and that provided the storyboard for the sequence of intentionally staged shots. And in face of the insistence on the film's authenticity, Kubrick "broke with the ethos of the documentary," making several alterations unfaithful to Cartier's life or were staged for dramatic effect. Faked elements included Kubrick giving Walter a dog, possibly Kubrick's own, to add a human dimension. He staged a shot of the culminating fight afterward. Bernd Kiefer pointed out how its camera angle is "quite inconceivable if shot from outside the ring" and "Cartier is not wearing his mouth-guard." Alex Singer, who collaborated with Kubrick, recalls a "crowd shot," which was in fact done in Kubrick's living room with Singer and his wife as the "crowd." Kubrick, as Singer puts it, "understood exactly the fakery of the movies."[8]

The choice of boxing as the subject of Kubrick's first film is significant from a Jewish perspective. From the 1890s until 1945, Jews played an important role in transatlantic prizefighting. Boxing held a strong attraction for impoverished second-generation Jews, as a quick way out of the ghetto, an easy means to make money, and a method to negate prominent stereotypes of Jews as weak and unmanly. In both America and Britain, Jewish participation in boxing was widespread, particularly in the late eighteenth and early nineteenth centuries and from the 1890s through to World War II. Jewish involvement in boxing was also prominent outside the ring, and many Jews became successful promoters, gym owners, trainers, and managers. Watching and betting on boxing was also popular within the Jewish community, leading to Jewish-owned and managed fight halls and attracting thousands of Jewish patrons for boxing programs held several times each week. Although the number of Jewish boxers was declining by 1945, a small reminder of the Jewish contribution to the sport (at least for those in the know) is highlighted in *Day of the Fight* by Jewish boxing historian, journalist, and author Nathan Stanley "Nat" Fleischer, leafing through one his authoritative tomes. (Kubrick removed this segment in the shorter version of the film.)

Kubrick elides the underpinning Jewishness of boxing by featuring Catholic protagonists. The film, like its originating photo-story, foregrounds their religious faith. In the first interior shot, Kubrick shot Walter and Vincent from the foot of the bed, at a corner angle rather than from the side—as in the photo-story—to highlight Walter's devotion to his faith, as this angle shows the crucifix and religious scene above the bedstead. He repeated the shot as they prepare to leave for the fight. He shot them as they walk to morning mass. The first shot of the church's interior is a close-up of a pietà. It occupies the screen for several seconds before the camera cuts to the brothers receiving communion as the narrator intones, "Walter is a good fighter, but he doesn't put all of his faith in his hands. It's important for Walter to get Holy Communion in case something should go wrong tonight," linking religion with fate.

Kubrick's interest in religion was extended in *The Flying Padre*, which is filled with religious iconography and images of devotion. Kubrick called the film "Sky Pilot," a pun on the slang term for priest. While images of religion were less present in *The Seafarers*, the SIU's membership was largely composed of Irish Catholics. This interest in organized Christianity and Catholicism, but always from the perspective of the outsider, was to recur throughout his oeuvre.

These films foreground all-male environments that typify Kubrick's later films. The world of boxing is predominated by men—male managers, promoters, boxers, trainers, restaurant owners, priests, physicians, and historians. Presumably, even Walter's dog is male. The household of the padre is, by its very nature, all male. Seafaring was a male profession, and the SIU is shown to provide the men with the comforts of home when they are away from it; indeed, so extensive are its facilities one may even wonder why such men returned to their humdrum domestic world, which Kubrick juxtaposed, possibly unfavorably, with the SIU. Women appear in the films sporadically, relegated to minor, domestic roles: children, relatives, girlfriends, secretaries, and similar roles, and in paintings and pictures. Shots of Walter's Aunt Eva and girlfriend, Betty, that had featured in "Prizefighter" were even cut out of *Day of the Fight*.

We also see Kubrick's interest in fatherhood and family developing. Walter eats in Dan Stampler's steakhouse in Greenwich Village as the owner looks on, "proudly" smoking a cigar, assuming a "fatherly" role in relationship to his "boy." Walter's own father is never seen, as he is "away," introducing the theme of absent fathers. Reflecting oedipal echoes, Kubrick included a sequence of Walter being checked over by the boxing commission doctor—played by his own father, Jack—who examines his eyes (as a doctor examines those of Danny [Danny Lloyd] in *The Shining*), the first in a long line of physicians and others with the title "doctor" who were to appear in his films. The title of *The Flying Padre* similarly suggests Kubrick's interest in paternity, *padre* being derived from the Latin *pater*. Stadtmueller ferries a sick baby and mother to the hospital because her husband is absent. Many of the men in *The Seafarers* are husbands and fathers taken away from their families by their jobs. At the end of the film, one such man is shown with his family before departing on a ship. His children, together with the sick child, the upset girl, and her tormentor in *The Flying Padre*, provide Kubrick's first cinematic images of childhood that marked his later films.

In a sly Kubrickian joke, food and sex are juxtaposed. An uninterrupted single fifty-eight-second dolly shot depicts the all-male environment of the SIU cafeteria. A further thirty seconds show the food on offer—roast beef being sliced, stews, joints, pasta, and so on—many items shot in close-ups, highlighting the bounty of nutritious and filling foodstuffs available to the seamen, while also anticipating the fully laden buffet table in *Dr. Strangelove*—another film that paired food and sex. It cuts to the galley ("well stocked and well-scrubbed," as in *The Shining*), where the food is prepared. A sudden cut "produces the first example of nudity in a Stanley Kubrick film and shows the director's adolescent sense of sexuality." The screen fills with a shot of a pinup calendar provided by "Thorman, Baum & Co., Incorporated—sellers of fresh and frozen fruits and vegetables" on the wall of the SIU barbershop. On it is a naked woman, wearing only a string of pearls draped above her breasts. Vincent LoBrutto suggests the "shot is there to entertain the hard-living sea-bound men who will be the main viewers of the in-house film and to arouse the perverse the devilish sense of humor tickling Kubrick." Meanwhile the voiceover narration says, "A pleasant sight after any voyage is . . . the SIU barbershop" (the man in the chair resembles a young Jack Nicholson). And when the film depicts the SIU building's art gallery, Kubrick includes two female nudes, echoing the earlier pinup calendar in the barbershop. These scenes not only foreshadow how Kubrick depicted women in his later films, particularly in terms of pictorial art, but also they undercut the film's very wholesomeness, reminding us that these seamen—perhaps Kubrick was also tickled by the thought of making a film about seamen, a homophone analogous to his later sexual jokes in *Lolita* and *Dr. Strangelove*, as well as *Full Metal Jacket*—were also sexual beings but with no allusions to how they satisfied their urges while away from home. Such sexual punning was very much a feature of Kubrick's New York Jewish sense of humor.[9]

By making these films, Kubrick joined the pantheon of legendary Jewish "New York–based photographers and their progressive contributions to avant-garde and non-narrative filmmaking." This tradition included

Paul Strand (*Manhatta*, 1921), Rudy Burckhardt (*The Pursuit of Happiness*, 1940), Helen Levitt (*In the Street*, 1949), Ruth Orkin and Morris Engel (*The Little Fugitive*, 1953), William Klein (*Broadway by Light*, 1958), and Robert Frank (*Pull My Daisy*, 1959), "among whose varying innovations include discrete handheld photography, examples of 'life caught unawares,' and blurring lines between documentary and staged situations."[10]

Fear and Desire

Kubrick quit his job at *Look* to purse his filmmaking career full-time. His first feature film project was *Fear and Desire*. With the collaboration of Howard Sackler, Kubrick developed the screenplay of four soldiers trapped behind enemy lines. He described it as a "study of four men and their search for the meaning of life and the individual's responsibility to the group."[11]

Kubrick drew on his family and New York roots to make the film. He borrowed most of the money from his wealthy uncle, Martin Perveler, who owned a drugstore. The team behind it, apart from the actors and the Mexican laborers he hired to carry the camera equipment, was largely composed of friends and family. Sackler wrote the screenplay under Kubrick's supervision, and Gerald Fried wrote the score. Both were Kubrick's friends from when they worked on the Taft High School magazine, and Kubrick occasionally babysat for Fried's eldest son. Toba Metz helped to scout locations (along with Sackler), as well as serving as "Director of Dialogue" and production assistant, making use of her secretarial and administrative skills. She also appeared in the film as a fisherwoman. Bob Dierkes, one of Kubrick's studio assistants at *Look* magazine, was credited as "production manager."[12]

The result was a film that was very much a product of Greenwich Village. Norman Kagan calls it the work of "high school intellectuals at play," while Thomas Allen Nelson feels its crude "expression resembles that youthful grabbag of 1950s bohemian negativism and existential self-congratulation that a fledging director no doubt found attractive during the period when he and his first wife lived in Greenwich Village." In 1948 Kubrick had married his high school sweetheart and was "outwardly living the life of a bohemian artist" in the Village where, in the wake of the war, conventional morality and values were questioned. By the late 1940s the philosophy of Jean-Paul Sartre and Albert Camus were widely discussed in New York Intellectual journals, generating a great deal of interest.[13]

Kubrick and Sackler designed the film as an allegory. The film opens with the following narration: "There is war in this forest. Not a war that's been fought, or one that will be, but any war. And the enemies who struggle here do not exist, unless we call them into being. This forest, then, and all that happens now, is outside history. Only the unchanging shapes of fear and doubt and death are from our world. These soldiers that you see keep our language and our time, but have no other country but the mind." Even the photography was designed "in such a way as to reflect the mental state of men."[14]

Such allegorical intent came to define the rest of his oeuvre, but in *Fear and Desire* Kubrick was explicit in announcing it. He described the film thus: "Its structure: allegorical. Its conception: poetic. A drama of 'man' lost in a hostile world deprived of material and spiritual foundations seeking his way to an understanding of himself, and of life around him. He is further imperiled on his Odyssey by an unseen but deadly enemy that surrounds him; but an enemy who, upon scrutiny, seems to be almost shaped from the same mold. It will, probably, mean many things to different people, and it ought to." Its allegorical nature was evident in its indebtedness to Joseph Conrad's *Heart of Darkness*, from which both Kubrick and Sackler drew inspiration. As Gene D. Phillips puts it, "As the spoken prologue suggests, the forest becomes a metaphor for the jungle of man's own psyche, the heart of darkness of which Joseph Conrad wrote." The narration for *The Seafarers* directly quoted Conrad, who later influenced *The Shining* (possibly through Francis Ford Coppola's *Apocalypse Now* in 1979).[15]

In *Fear and Desire* Kubrick's developed his nascent interest in war, World War II, Nazism, and Jewishness. Although eligible for the draft at the time of America's entry into the Korean War, Kubrick was rejected by the army, perhaps fueling his lifelong fascination with war, warfare, the military, and militarism. In *Day of the Fight* we learn that both Cartier brothers fought in the navy during the war and presumably many of the seamen in *The Seafarers* did so too, for Kubrick shows us a plaque on which it is engraved, "In Memory of those Brothers of the Seafarers International Union who gave their lives in the service of their country." As the narrator refers to "men of all national origins and religions," the camera scrolls down the names on the plague, including a prominent George Hayman. Despite the lack of specific historical referents and the contemporaneous

Korean War, *Fear and Desire* appears to be set somewhere in Europe during World War II, as demarcated by the soldiers' uniforms and its resemblance to such films as *A Walk in the Sun* (1946) and *The Story of GI Joe* (1945), in which American units are trapped behind enemy lines.[16]

Fear and Desire also tapped into a series of postwar novels, written by Jews, that made Jewish soldiers central protagonists and that dominated the *New York Times* bestseller lists. These included Norman Mailer's *The Naked and the Dead*, Irwin Shaw's *The Young Lions*, Ira Wolfert's *Act of Love*, Merle Miller's *That Winter*, Stefan Heym's *The Crusaders*, Martha Gellhorn's *Point of No Return* (all 1948), Herman Wouk's *The Caine Mutiny* (1952), and Leon Uris's *Battle Cry* (1953). All of them sought to transform the negative stereotype of weak, passive victimized Jews murdered in their millions in the Holocaust into the tough GI. At the same time, this strong soldier was also sensitive, emotional, intellectual, and a mensch. Their massive popularity meant that the Jewish macho-mensch soldier was a recognizable image in the postwar period.

Playing on these novels, as well as the platoon movies of World War II, which located Jews as part of a multiethnic ensemble embodying the ideals of the American melting pot, *Fear and Desire*'s unit is composed of four character types, representing differing classes and ethnic backgrounds. Lieutenant Corby (Kenneth Harp), like Mailer's Lieutenant Hearn, is a WASP intellectual and philosopher in the tradition of the war poet. Sergeant "Mac" (Frank Silvera) is working class and nonwhite (and could pass variously for Indian, Latino, and African American, all of which he portrayed in other films). Private Fletcher (Steve Coit) is a southerner, and Private Sidney (Paul Mazursky) is the "jittery recruit" or, in the words of James Naremore, a "sensitive young New Yorker."[17]

Sidney can clearly be read as Jewish. Naremore's description indicates as much without directly saying it. By convention World War II platoon movies typically included Jews, and Sidney, a syncopated form of "St. Denis," was a name popular with Jews of Kubrick's parents' generation and thus contemporaneous with Stanley. It was representative of that trend of Jews adopting names they thought at the time were all-American but that, in fact, were uncommon among the native whites of native parentage, not least because once certain names became common among Jews, other groups avoided them as "Jewish."[18]

In the first of a long line of self-reflexive gestures, Kubrick cast as Sidney a Jewish actor who was roughly the same age and who bore a "strong physical resemblance" to himself. Born on April 25, 1930, at the Brooklyn Jewish Hospital as Irwin Lawrence Mazursky, he described himself as a "Jewish boy from Brooklyn [who] moves to Greenwich Village and marries a shiksa." Not yet twenty-one, he was beginning a career in off-Broadway theater. He was friends with Jay Landesman, publisher of *Neurotica*. Perhaps Kubrick, who, per Singer, had been "turned down for the Army on some oddball thing" identified with the raw recruit.[19]

As Sidney, Mazursky produced Kubrick's first over-the-top performance. Roughly five whole, uninterrupted minutes are carried by Mazursky's acting and monologue, in which he showcases his performative and comedic abilities, commonly known as Jewish traits. Filmmaker Curtis Harrington, who attended a preview of the film, reported that "Mazursky's performance was laughed at. There were giggles in all the wrong places." Sidney foreshadows the performances of Peter Sellers in *Lolita* and *Dr. Strangelove*, Malcolm McDowell in *A Clockwork Orange*, and Jack Nicholson in *The Shining*, all of which, I argue, can be read as Jewish.[20]

In Sidney Kubrick produced a complex representation of Jewish masculinity. With a clean-shaven face and very little bodily hair, he is the unit's youngest member; Mac repeatedly addresses him as "kid" and speaks to him in a childish voice ("What's the matter, snookums?"). Corby is the paternal figure, acting as a parent to Sidney (invoking the "Bringing-Up-Stanley-Club" formed at *Look* by Rothstein), who's presented as the callow youth in uniform. When they prepare to enter an enemy guard hut, Sidney is afraid. Corby prompts him to action with the barrel of his gun. Entering last, Sidney doesn't participate in the killing; he stands at the back as Mac and Fletcher stab the enemy. Corby urges Sidney to eat, but, put off by the killing, he just rests his head on the table, staring at the dead men on the floor.

Sidney is the weak link. He breaks down under the pressures of combat, suffering from post-traumatic stress disorder. The killings flashback through his mind. Kubrick reflects his mental state through the fragmented cutting style resembling Soviet montage. Left alone to guard the captured fisherwoman (Virginia Leith), Sidney playacts, hoping that his amusing entertainment will pacify her. When this fails, he begins to molest her. Naively believing she will neither scream nor flee, he unties her. Of course, she begins to run, but Sidney shoots her dead. Babbling and cackling, he runs off into the forest. He thus avoids killing any male soldiers. Indeed, he is absent for much of the fighting and killing; in fact, the only person he kills is an unarmed female civilian, shot in the back while trying to run away. He later reappears in the river, wading toward the wounded Mac. Out of the mist, he floats on a raft, crouching like a dog and singing.

Sidney is the movie's heart of darkness. Very much the focus of Kubrick's attention, he is a precursor to Private Pyle in *Full Metal Jacket* (yet another conceptually Jewish character). The first person to speak and the last we see, he's the subject of many close-up shots. Kubrick's synopsis of the plot reveals that he conceived of Sidney as "wild-eyed," "completely irrational," "moaning incoherently," and "laughing and screaming hysterically." Such adjectives feminize Sidney, who is represented as the unit's most intellectual member, intelligent and well-read (he quotes Shakespeare), but panicky and paranoid.[21]

Kubrick's choice to put a Jewish actor in a soldier's uniform, invoking images of the tough warrior Jew, is undermined by the way he is ascribed such unflattering and stereotypical traits by Kubrick and Sackler and contrasts with the more one-dimensional images of Jewish war heroism as found in Jewish war novels such as the characters of Roth and Goldstein in Mailer's *The Naked and the Dead* and Jake Levin and Max Shapiro in Uris's *Battle Cry*.

Kubrick obliquely invokes the Holocaust. After killing the enemy soldiers, Corby reflects, "We spend our lives running our fingers down the lists in directories, looking for our real names, our permanent addresses." The juxtaposition of the killing coupled with the metaphor of searching through lists and directories—which the Nazis did with such deadly meticulousness—invokes the Holocaust, and Kubrick later sought to make a film in which a Jewish boy is forced to hide behind an Aryan name and identity. At the same time, we see images of the legs and feet of the dead men, one of whom is played by Mazursky. Such images not only resemble Holocaust footage of Jewish victims of the Nazis but also shots of a dead Jewish man murdered by an anti-Semite in the film *Crossfire* (1947).

Fear and Desire stands as Kubrick's most explicitly personal film, the one in which he truly revealed himself, before he learned to misdirect the viewer through a subtle sleight of hand. Paolo Cherchi Usai suggests the film gave away too much, especially considering Kubrick's later career. He writes, "it is no surprise that Kubrick wanted to rid himself of such an explicit film, one that revealed far too much of his personal agenda . . . because the film proclaims with uncalculated immediacy the major creative strategies of the director's oeuvre that would follow in coming years.

FIGURE 1 Sidney (Paul Mazursky) presents a complex picture of Jewish masculinity in *Fear and Desire* (1953).

Kubrick, the consummate chess player, had committed in his youth the most unforgivable mistake of the game: announcing his strategy for capturing the adversary's king (or general) with his opening move." Perhaps it was for that reason Kubrick spent so much time distancing himself from it in later years (foreshadowing the same strategy when it came to *Spartacus*). In 1960, in an unpublished interview, he described it as "a lousy feature, very self-conscious, easily discernible as an intellectual effort, but very roughly, and poorly, and ineffectively made picture." Elsewhere he called it a "bumbling, amateur film exercise . . . a completely inept oddity, boring and pretentious." He personally oversaw the destruction of the original negative and several prints and spent much of his life tracking down others so that he could buy and destroy them as well. According to Christiane, he "disowned it and would have happily gathered together every print and neg and consigned them all to an incinerator had it been possible." Kubrick's suppression of *Fear and Desire* may have owed to embarrassment because it provided the key to unlocking the secrets of his later, denser, and more elliptical films.[22]

Killer's Kiss

In the summer of 1953, Kubrick announced he had raised $80,000 for his next film, which he described as a "Love Story of New York, shooting all around the town" and a "tragic, contemporary love story." He recalled that "the story was written in a week in order to take advantage of a possibility of getting some money." Drawing heavily on both "Prizefighter" and *Day of the Fight* (its first twenty minutes were a virtual facsimile), it features a failed boxer, Davey Gordon (Jamie Smith), assisting and falling for Gloria (Irene Kane), a "taxi dancer" (prostitute), who's preyed on and sexually harassed by her gangster boss, Vincent Rapallo (Frank Silvera). Rapallo's thugs mistakenly beat Davey's manager to death, believing he's Davey, before abducting Gloria. Davey chases them, kills Rapallo, and then escapes with Gloria to Seattle.[23]

As with *Fear and Desire*, *Killer's Kiss* drew on Kubrick's immediate ethnic milieu. It was financed by Morris Bousel, a Bronx pharmacist and family acquaintance. Sackler again worked on the screenplay, under Kubrick's supervision, but was uncredited. Alexander Singer did some of the filming, and Gerald Fried again composed the score. Kubrick's second wife, Ruth Sobotka, was the film's art director and played the dancer, Iris, performing a ballet solo in the film, choreographed by their mutual friend, David Vaughan, who played the drunken Shriner conventioneer who grabs Davey's scarf and runs off with it. Kubrick's friend Alec Rubin played another Shriner. Irene Kane (b. Irene Greengard) was a Jewish actress recruited through a friend of Kubrick's who worked in the *Look* mailroom. In an insert that shows a pair of framed photographs of a ballet dancer in costume and an older man, Kubrick used photographs of Sobotka and her father. Julius "Skippy" Adelman, a stills photographer, played the owner of the mannequin factory. In a crowd scene the large group of extras were recruited from Kubrick's Greenwich Village milieu.

Killer's Kiss had "Made in New York" stamped all over it. Kubrick deliberately designed the movie to be shot within a short distance of his Tenth Street Greenwich Village apartment, and Sackler's screenplay ensured that it took place in all the locations Kubrick listed. Naremore points out its "indebtedness" to the black-and-white photographic tradition of the New York school, bearing the traces of Weegee, who'd advised Robert Wise's *The Set Up* (1949), a noir boxing movie, into which *Killer's Kiss* tapped. *Killer's Kiss*, Eitan Kensky states, "really aligns nicely with the ideas running through *Partisan Review* and *Commentary*" at that time. It contained clear Freudian and oedipal elements: Gloria's guilt over her sister's death; her feelings of jealousy toward her sister, whom her dead father preferred; Davey's dream sequence; the linkage of sex and death; twins and doubles; the relationship between Gloria and the much older Vincent (note the duplication of Walter Cartier's brother's name); and the final oedipal struggle between the older and younger generation, as Davey duels Vincent, and the usurper defeats the patriarch. The film also references absent fathers: Gloria's dead father and Davey's, who is never mentioned.[24]

In making *Killer's Kiss*, Kubrick fitted into a long tradition of left-wing Jewish American playwrights, screenwriters, and authors representing Jewish boxers onstage and on-screen but without directly acknowledging their ethnicity. These include *Golden Boy* (1937), *The Harder They Fall* (1947), *The Set-Up* and *Champion* (1949), *The Ring* (1947), and *Champ for a Day* (1953). *Body and Soul* (1947) is the one key exception to this rule. Charley Davis (John Garfield, b. Jacob Julius Garfinkle) is a promising young Jewish (although the word is mentioned only once in the entire film) boxer, who rises in the sport to become champion of the world. Kubrick alluded to *Body and Soul* in *Killer's Kiss*. Both occur in flashback, were shot, guerilla-style, on the streets of New York, which by 1955 had a large Jewish population (although, unlike *Body and Soul*, Kubrick shot around Greenwich Village, as well as Midtown, moving the action *away* from the largely Jewish working-class areas of the Lower East Side and the Bronx to the more intellectual and bohemian Village).[25]

Unlike *Day of the Fight* and *Body and Soul*, which *Killer's Kiss* mimics and draws on, Davey's religion is ambiguous. Where Walter was explicitly Catholic, no such markers attach to Davey, allowing the possibility of reading him as Jewish. Davey Gordon is as white bread a name as Charley Davis, whom Kubrick is clearly referencing. His given name suggests the biblical king who spied Bathsheba while she bathed on the roof of her house. Likewise, Davey spies Gloria as she undresses. Gordon was a name typical of Jewish immigrants, perhaps a corruption of the Russian name Grodno in Eastern Europe, from where many Jews hailed. A shot of Davey topless on the telephone shows his hairy chest. Hirsuteness is a stereotypical marker of Jewish masculinity, in which the Jewish body was presumed to be abnormally hairy, a marker that, as we shall see, crops up in Kubrick's later films. Per Dana Polan, Davey is a "loser" and a "passive absorber of the worst that life can dish out," that is, a schnook (Yiddish: fool). His career is a disappointment, losing boxing matches and fights, and he's described in the film as an unlucky boxer with a "weak" and "glass" chin.[26]

Like *Body and Soul*, *Killer's Kiss* indirectly invokes World War II. The opening sound of the film is that of a train, as Davey waits anxiously at the train station for Gloria (although they'll travel west rather than east). Soldiers are in uniform in the dance hall, and Davey is subtly referenced as a veteran through his possession of a Luger, the gun above all associated with the Nazis. When Davey and Rapallo duel to the death in the warehouse, the piles of naked mannequins suggest the heaps of dead bodies in the camps, as depicted in documentary footage of their liberation. Severed body parts, specifically decapitated heads and hands, hint at Nazi medical experimentation. The Production Code Administration complained that "the concluding sequence among the mass of nude mannequins is unacceptable as now edited. Certain portions of these scenes seem to go too far in their exploitation of the nudity of the mannequins."[27]

Killer's Kiss clearly illustrates Dana Polan's observation of Kubrick's films: "Humans are often little more than meat." Building on the juxtaposition of food and sex in *The Seafarers*, close-ups of food in shop windows—confectionary, hot dogs, and ice cream—segue into shots of the dancing girls sign, linking food, women, and sex in much the same way as the earlier nude calendar. Gloria, after all, is a prostitute. Similarly, as Davey waits for Gloria in the street, a Hi Grade All-Beef Frankfurters billboard can be seen in the background, suggesting Davey is also just a form of food, specifically meat, which, like Walter, he also presumably consumes to maintain his weight and physique. Both Gloria and Davey are pieces of meat, watched and consumed by others.[28]

The Killing

In 1955 Alex Singer introduced Kubrick to James B. Harris, whom he had met in the army. Born on August 3, 1928, in New York, Harris was also Jewish and only eight days younger than Kubrick. Together, they formed a production company, Harris-Kubrick Pictures. They bought the rights to Lionel White's pulp novel *Clean Break* (1955) for $10,000 and hired novelist Jim Thompson, whose writing Kubrick admired, to collaborate on adapting it. Where Kubrick broke down the novel into sequences, Thompson wrote most of the dialogue, with contributions by Harris. The result was *The Killing*: a racetrack heist planned by ex-con Johnny Clay (Sterling Hayden), who, to carry off his perfect plan, recruits a group of six men. These are Clay's rich benefactor, Marvin Unger (Jay C. Flippen); racetrack barman Mike (Joe Sawyer), who has a sick wife who requires better health care; corrupt cop Randy (Ted de Corsia), who owes money to a loan shark; racetrack cashier George Peatty (Elisha Cook Jr.), who is desperate to impress his avaricious wife, Sherry (Marie Windsor); shooter Nikki Arano (Timothy Carey), and wrestler and chess player–cum-philosopher Maurice Oboukhoff (Kola Kwariani). A series of tiny events serve to foil Clay's plan; ultimately, he is left empty-handed, and all but him end up dead.

The Killing—although set in and hence shot in and around Los Angeles—was still a product of Kubrick's Greenwich Village milieu. As the *New York Times* later reported, "One observer who watched Kubrick walking down a Hollywood street commented that he looked as though he might logically have 'Made in New York' stamped on his forehead." Thompson's daughter, Sharon, recalled that Kubrick was "a beatnik before beatniks were in. He had the long hair and the weird clothes." Alexander Singer again did some secondary shooting. Kola Kwariani was a friend from Kubrick's New York chess club, the 42nd Street Chess and Checker Parlor, which was recreated for the film. Ruth Sobotka designed the sets. Kubrick added other little touches: two of the nameplates of George's fellow cashiers feature the names David Vaughan and Shaun O'Brien, two of Sobotka's friends.[29]

Like *Killer's Kiss*, *The Killing* showcases an existentialism characteristic of both Sartre and Camus. Robert Kolker suggests that it was "very much a work of its time" in that "Kubrick draws on the existentialist philosophy popular among fifties' intellectuals, representing in Johnny Clay a man attempting to create an identity through a failed attempt to impress himself violently on the world. He is a loser diminished by the gaze of authority." Quite possibly, in conceiving the film, Kubrick was moved by Sartre's observations in an essay published in 1947: "Man is nothing else than his plan; he exists only to the extent that he fulfills himself; he is nothing else than the ensemble of his acts; nothing else than his life." Kolker is also certain that Kubrick read Robert Warshow's famous 1948 *Partisan Review* essay, "The Gangster as Tragic Hero." Unlike the novel, Kubrick, Thompson, and Harris decided not to kill off Clay. Where he is shot by a jealous George, who believes Clay is having an affair with Sherry, Kubrick not only permitted Clay to survive but made him stand and watch as the money blows away, compounding the futility he feels, hence his refusal to escape. "You've got to run," Johnny's girlfriend, Fay (Coleen Gray), tells him. "What's the difference?" he mutters as the net closes in on him at the end. A fatalist and pessimist, he's resigned to his fate.[30]

As this was Kubrick's first attempt at adaptation, rather than innovation, it provides an intriguing insight into Kubrick's treatment of Jews and Jewishness. Set in New York, *Clean Break* contains a significant number of Jewish characters. Maurice Cohen is an ex-con hired by Johnny to "run a little interference" at the racetrack. Cohen visits his lawyer, Harry Soskin. The other most obviously Jewish character in the novel is loan shark Leo Steiner. Officer Randy Kennan owes money to Leo, and Kennan explicitly highlights Leo's Jewishness when he refers to him as "Shylock." Yet, in transposing the film to Los Angeles, Leo was the only Jewish character from the novel to survive the adaptation. Soskin was removed, along with the overt "Shylock" reference, and Cohen was blended with another character called "Tex" to create Maurice Oboukhoff, a hirsute, Russian, chess-playing wrestler who, in his given name, recalls Kubrick's uncle Martin, who went by the name Maurice. The meeting between Kennan and Leo is replicated in the film. Because Kubrick's use of a single lighting source creates a harsh atmosphere, Leo, as played by Jay Adler, is depicted as much more intimidating. Referred to as "Leo," both in the film and in the credits, his identifiably Jewish last name is removed. But, at the same time, Kubrick cast a recognizably Jewish actor to play him. Adler was the son of Yiddish theater stars, Jacob and Sara Adler, and the brother of the more famous Stella Adler (whom Kubrick had photographed for *Look* in March 1949). One of Leo's hoods, Tiny, was played by Jewish actor Joe Turkel (who'd later go on to feature in *Paths of Glory* and *The Shining*). Born to Polish Jewish immigrants, he'd previously played a Haganah soldier in *Sword in the Desert* (1949). The only sign of his Jewishness is his left-handedness, drawing on age-old stereotypes of the Jew as sinister.[31]

As with *Fear and Desire* and *Killer's Kiss*, Kubrick created another conceptually Jewish character in George Peatty. His surname invokes the word "petty" or "pity." Described on the poster as "the little man with big ideas," he invokes *dos kleine menschele*, "the little man" of Yiddish literature. This antihero seemingly tolerates those frustrations unacceptable to a "normal" man. George displays other stereotypically Jewish traits. In the novel he is described as having a "large and aquiline" nose. As a racetrack cashier, he is associated with money (like Leo). He complains of being ill from a bowel-related complaint. He's also the schlemiel, the nebbish, the

FIGURE 2   Loan shark Leo played by Jewish actor Jay Adler in *The Killing* (1956).

schmuck, the *putz*, the *schmendrick*, the loser. He's called a "meatball," a "jerk" and a "clown." He's a milquetoast, "the weak link that ultimately brings the whole scheme crashing down." George is certainly a patzer, the slang term for a poor, amateurish chess player, which comes from the Yiddish but is probably originally German for bungler, from *patzen*, to bungle, and which is uttered in the film. Desperate to please and satisfy an indifferent wife, he's henpecked and cuckolded. In Elisha Cook, Kubrick cast an actor who specialized in playing the "nervous, bug-eyed, cowardly, self-loathing, penny-ante loser," what Penelope Houston describes as the "prototype of all sad little men." In a synopsis submitted by Harris-Kubrick Pictures, George is described as "brow-beaten and misled by his scheming and self-righteous wife." Sherry questions his masculinity, sarcastically referring to him as a "big, handsome, intelligent brute." She chides him, "So you had to be stupid. You couldn't even play it smart when you had a gun pointed at you." Even with her dying words she goads him, "Not a real husband, just a bad joke without a punch line." George is clearly out of his depth, conjugally and criminally.[32]

George can be read as the downtrodden Jewish husband, married to a blond shiksa who treats him like dirt. Sherry is predatory, avaricious, two-timing, and sluttish; the voluptuous wife with a "pretty face" who systematically tortures her devoted yet timid and pitiful husband. George, anticipating Humbert, is enslaved. Kubrick emphasizes George's sense of being trapped. Our first view of George is from behind the bars of his cashier cage, thus resembling one of the apes from a Kubrick *Look* photo shoot ("How Monkeys Look to People," 1946), as well as the canaries raised by Stadtmueller in *The Flying Padre*. And, like a canary, George sings, as his slavish devotion to Sherry leads him to leak crucial details of the plan, which she feeds to her lover, Val (Vince Edwards), who plans to hijack the takings for himself.

By comparison to the novel, Harris, Kubrick, and Thompson amplified George's feelings of jealousy and sense of inferiority. They "fleshed out the faithless marriage of George and Sherry Peatty, expanding a trite plot device from *Clean Break* into a definitive dramatization of a sadomasochistic relationship for the film." The scenes between them play out with the same violent undercurrent that haunts the plays of fellow Jewish playwright Harold Pinter (whose first play, *The Room*, was performed a year later). Kubrick's sympathy, however, lies firmly with George, who is "one of the most interesting and sympathetically drawn characters in the film." Kubrick privileges George's point of view. In George's final sequence, Kubrick identifies with him, using a handheld camera to show his subjective point of view, in a shot that lasts twenty-three seconds, as he stumbles out of the apartment and staggers across the road to his car. This is the only instance of a point-of-view shot in the film, and it is reserved for George. It's accompanied by a jazz score (of which Kubrick was fond) and the sound of George's breathing (anticipating Kubrick recording his own breathing when Dave shuts down HAL in *2001*). Kubrick later told Terry Southern, "I feel like Elisha Cook in one of those early Warner films."[33]

Jewishness was further evident beneath the surface particularly in Kubrick's choice of genre and the film's underlying tone. Film noir, as a genre, grew out of the emigration of filmmakers from Nazi Germany to America and provided a means for Jewish filmmakers to insert subliminal Jewish messages and motifs. Vincent Brook has demonstrated the prevalence in the film noirs of Kubrick's heroes—Billy Wilder, Fritz Lang, Otto Preminger, and, above all, Max Ophüls—of "specific, if largely disguised and possibly unconscious, Jewish references." *The Killing*'s theme of human fallibility and the frustration of their plans in this racetrack heist that goes badly wrong, foiled by the forces of chance and fate, very much betrays a Jewish sensibility. Despite Clay's precise and meticulous planning, too many contingencies combine to wreck his scheme: George and Sherry's relationship, George's loose tongue, Sherry's infidelity, Marvin's rebuffed feelings for Johnny, Nikki's racism, the shoddy bag Johnny buys, the small dog let loose by its owner. When Sherry says, "It's a bad joke with no punch line," a fitting epigram for the film could have been the Yiddish proverb, *Mensch tracht, Gott lacht* (Man plans, God laughs).[34]

Kubrick peppered the film with self-reflexive gestures. The narrator describes Johnny as "perhaps the most important thread in the unfinished fabric." In this he resembles Kubrick. Clay is the only person in the film who has complete knowledge of the plan, which he drip-feeds to the individual participant on a need-to-know basis, just like a film director. The name Johnny Clay may have been invented by White but its retention by Kubrick foretells a career-long obsession with fatherlike figures, often named "John" or "Jack." Jack can be read as short for "Jacob," which, rendered into Hebrew, refers to Ya'acov, the flawed biblical patriarch who stole his brother Esau's birthright. Jack, or Jacques, was also the name that Kubrick's father adopted in English. In amplifying the relationship between Johnny and his wealthy benefactor, Marvin, perhaps Kubrick slyly alluded to his own indebtedness to his uncle, Martin, who bankrolled his previous film, and with whom he lived for a year when he was thirteen, as well as childhood, photographer, and friend Marvin Traub. Clay and Marvin's relationship certainly bears oedipal echoes; Marvin tells him, "I've always thought maybe you're like my own kid." Indeed, Marvin has no overt need, unlike the others, to be involved in this heist, other than his attachment to Johnny.

In adapting *Clean Break*, Kubrick's relation to Jewishness was paradoxical. While he reduced the number of Jewish characters in the source text, he didn't remove them altogether. Yet he didn't draw any explicit attention to their Jewishness. At the same time, he infused a Jewish sensibility beneath the surface of the film. Kubrick thus didn't entirely scrub away the Jewish traces of *Clean Break* when adapting it into *The Killing*, but he did make them less overt, giving the viewer only subtle clues. It was the second instance of a recognizably Jewish character appearing in a Kubrick film, but this time fulfilling a less than savory, stereotypical role of criminal loan shark.

Conclusion

In every medium he used, Kubrick stamped his artifacts with his signature style and themes, transcending commercial and other constraints. In documenting the late forties and early fifties, his photographs and documentaries were also social critiques that simultaneously expressed his subversive Jewish sense of humor. Moving into the world of feature film, his choice of genres was significant. It was with these three films that his Jewishness, while never being explicit, came closer to the surface than in his first three documentaries. In adopting the World War II platoon movie, the boxing film, and film noir, he joined a long tradition of Jewish writers and filmmakers, many of whom he admired. He produced complex images of subsurface Jewish masculinity in the characters of Sidney, Davey, George, and Leo. Clearly, we see Kubrick engaging in concepts that not only characterized his later oeuvre but also came to the fore in Hollywood in the coming decades. He may have developed as a more sophisticated filmmaker, but these early influences lived on, particularly in his concerns, themes, motifs, humor, and continued penchant for misdirection and manipulation.

And these early efforts were deeply rooted in a New York Jewish intellectual, Greenwich Village milieu. His work bore its stamp, and even though Kubrick moved away from New York with *The Killing* and his subsequent films—both literally and figuratively—they manifested that location's Jewish traces.

2

The Macho Mensch

For Kubrick the late 1950s can be labeled the "Kirk Douglas" years. It is during this time that we see a major shift in his work, moving beyond the existential exercises of his youth (*Fear and Desire*, *Killer's Kiss*, and *The Killing*) to more mature, what critic Pauline Kael calls "liberal-intellectual," material. It is with *Paths of Glory*, his first collaboration with Douglas, that critics began to notice his technical abilities and emerging signature style. At the same time, this is when we really begin to see Kubrick investigate his Jewishness, albeit indirectly, through the value system of menschlikayt and Jewish manliness, to produce a new character type known as the "macho mensch." In helping to promote this new character type *Paths of Glory* and subsequently *Spartacus* built on and contributed to a particular movement in the late 1950s in Hollywood in which Jewish men as Jewish characters, both implicitly and explicitly, began to feature far more frequently than since the first three decades of the century.[1]

The Path to *Paths of Glory*

Harris-Kubrick Pictures bought the rights to Humphrey Cobb's 1935 novel *Paths of Glory* in 1956. Based on real events during World War I in

1915, the plot concerns the French general staff who were willing to sacrifice an entire division in a hopeless attack on a fortified German position known as "The Pimple." But when it fails, they require a scapegoat and five soldiers are selected as blood sacrifices for the greater good of France. Although ably defended, the soldiers are court-martialed for cowardice. The trial is a mock formality, and the men are executed, but exonerated nearly two decades later. Cobb's narrative of an unjust trial followed by a pardon evoked that of the Dreyfus Affair a half century earlier. In October 1894 Alfred Dreyfus, the only Jewish officer in the upper ranks of the French army, was accused of spying for Germany and publicly disgraced. Convicted without evidence, he was stripped of his rank and sentenced to solitary life confinement. As he was taken away, crowds chanted "Death to the Jews." It was a miscarriage of justice so profound that it divided France and beyond—Arthur Schnitzler, as an ardent Dreyfus supporter, closely followed the case. Dreyfus died the same year Cobb published his novel.

Kubrick first read the novel when he was young: "It was one of the few books I'd read for pleasure in high school. I think I found it lying around my father's office and started reading it while waiting for him to get finished with a patient." He recalled that it had "made an impression on me, not because of its literary qualities but because of the troubling and tragic situation of three of its characters—three innocent soldiers accused of cowardice and mutiny who were executed to set an example." Norman Kagan and Robert Polito saw "astonishing similarities" between Cobb's "caustic vignettes" and the "pitch-black comedy" of Joseph Heller's *Catch-22* (1961), which Heller had outlined and begun around 1955.[2]

Together with the hard-boiled thriller writer, Jim Thompson, Kubrick began to work on the *Paths of Glory* screenplay. The script went through at least five drafts before shooting. Thompson and Kubrick produced an initial version late in the summer of 1956. Greenwich Village writer Calder Willingham, who was being hailed as part of the new tough, postwar novelists (Norman Mailer among them) and described by the *New Yorker* as having "fathered modern black comedy," was then brought on board. A second draft, completed in November 1956, was credited to Kubrick, Thompson, and Willingham. Two subsequent screenplays labeled "third draft" were produced by February 1957, and the shooting script was finalized during the spring and summer. Colonel Dax's initially minor role was enhanced with each version, making him into a more heroic protagonist, presumably to make it attractive to a big box-office star. Impressed by *The Killing*, Kirk

Douglas contacted Kubrick, who showed him the Willingham-Thompson screenplay. Douglas agreed to make it for $350,000. The film was shot in Germany for almost $1 million and released on December 20, 1957.[3]

Macho Douglas

When they alighted on *Paths of Glory*, Harris-Kubrick Pictures specifically wanted Douglas to play the lead. Douglas was, by this point, a huge box-office star with pull in Hollywood, having previously appeared in films whose subjects were close to Kubrick's own interests—boxing (*Champion*, 1949) and the Holocaust (*The Juggler*, 1953). Born in 1916 as Issur Danielovitch Demsky to illiterate Russian Jewish immigrants, Douglas won a wrestling scholarship before enlisting in the navy during World War II as a communications officer in antisubmarine warfare. He then went on to play a series of leading roles. Kubrick was most likely attracted to the prospect of working with a Jewish actor who was, in the 1950s, at the forefront of publicly redefining the image of the weak, passive, ineffectual, intellectual Jew into one of macho toughness. The desire for Douglas was manifested by the size of the deal offered to him, his salary being more than a third of the film's total budget. In addition, Harris-Kubrick Pictures agreed to a five-film deal with Douglas's production company, Bryna, agreeing that *Paths of Glory* would carry its imprimatur.[4]

Douglas as Dax rejected age-old anti-Jewish stereotypes. Since antiquity, but particularly in the modern era, Jews were perceived as weak, passive, and averse to military involvement. For centuries Jewish physiognomy and physiology were intertwined with notions of unmanliness, hysteria, and pathology, all bred by the lack of healthy, outdoor activity. Jewish legs and feet were characterized as unnatural and unsuited to war, making Jews seem "unfit" for military service as foot soldiers in the modern infantries of the newly created nation states of the late nineteenth and early twentieth centuries. Such demeaning perceptions of Jewish weakness were embedded in U.S. society and its military, as well as having been devastatingly underlined by the Holocaust. Kubrick himself had been deemed unfit for military service, perhaps fueling his desire to recreate convincingly and accurately battle scenes as a form of compensation.

To this end, the role of Dax was magnified and strengthened. Dax was amplified from the film's periphery to become its core character, highlighting him as its focal point. Where the novel focuses on the five scapegoated soldiers, the film reduced them to three and relegated them to the background, rendering them passive and without agency. Thus the audience identifies with Dax, who defends the men at the court-martial, rather than Etienne, further accenting the focus on him. These alterations centered the film squarely on Dax, on whose face (and then retreating back) the movie ends, which also mollified Douglas's ego, producing a vehicle befitting his star status. Douglas also had a large say, insisting that his role was drawn from the second and third drafts of the script revised by Willingham. "Sure enough," as James Naremore points out, "in his first scene in *Paths of Glory*, which has no equivalent in either the novel or the play, he is shown naked to the waist, washing his face from a basin of water in his underground bunker." The shot emphasizes the muscular physicality of Dax's build, beginning the full frontal assault on anti-Semitic stereotypes of weak, defenseless Jews. This enlargement of a key role beyond its original significance, occupied by a Jewish star, set a pattern that defines Kubrick's next three films.[5]

Dax, though, isn't one-dimensional. He's brawn and brains, as befitting a mensch. General Mireau (George Macready) describes him as "perhaps the foremost criminal lawyer in France." General Broulard (Adolphe Menjou) refers to the "keenness of [his] mind." Such designations define him by his intellect, possessing what is known, approvingly, in Yiddish as Yiddische *kopf* (Jewish brains), tapping into a trend, predating the invention of cinema, whereby Jews are stereotypically defined by their minds. Later, in cinema, the legal profession became a stereotypical marker of Jewishness. Twice in their initial exchange, Dax trips up Mireau, giving the impression that he's much more intelligent than his superior officer. With lawyerlike precision, he punctures Mireau's circumlocutions, forcing him to admit, "You're right on your toes this morning, Colonel. Even sharper than usual." Dax stresses his rhetorical and ethical authority, his blunt language contrasting with Mireau's banal clichés, suggesting Dax earned his rank through merit, whereas Mireau obtained his through class privileges.

Dax is a model soldier and a good officer. Passionate, sincere, brave, humane, and forthright, he isn't afraid to get his hands dirty, as shown by his location in the confined spaces of the trenches. When given an exit strategy from the doomed attack—Broulard offers to place him on leave—Dax refuses to abandon his men and agrees to lead the charge on the Ant Hill, assuring his superior officer of success. Dynamic and brave, he

FIGURE 3 The tough, macho Colonel Dax (Kirk Douglas) in *Paths of Glory* (1957).

heads the assault, returning to rally those troops who remained behind. A loyal officer, he returns to the front with his troops later on and has "never failed to live up to" Mireau's "credo" of "He's got to fight. He can't do that unless he's where the fighting is."

Goyim Naches and Menschlikayt

Paths of Glory operates through a series of binary opposites pitched against each other as if in trench warfare: opulence/squalor, general staff/infantry, selfish ambition/menschlikayt. This is particularly evident in the opening sequences. Kubrick housed Broulard and Mireau in the opulent and spacious Chateau d'Aigle, full of exquisite art and ornate interior decoration, where they spend most of their time dining, dancing, and drinking, far from the trenches where their troops are dying. Mireau declares, "I always like to keep pleasant surroundings." By contrast, Dax and his enlisted men are in cramped and dirty trenches, besieged by the bleak panorama of no-man's-land, punctuated by the sound of exploding shells and falling dirt and debris. Their predicament is contrasted to that of the general staff, emphasized by Kubrick's use of deep focus, which shows the vastness of their palatial residence, particularly as the soldiers are being marched to trial. The incongruous silver tray on which they're served their final meal only serves to highlight the vast chasm between the officers and infantry. Mireau stoops to enter Dax's cramped bunker; whereas Broulard praises Mireau's taste in "carpets and pictures," which create a pleasing atmosphere, Mireau compliments Dax on his "neat little spot." Even when Dax is quartered at the chateau, his room is dark, unadorned, and low-ceilinged, with no natural light.

Dax's attitude toward his men contrasts him with that of his superior officers, highlighting his menschlikayt. The general staff consider and treat the lower ranks like animals or insects. Even Dax must remind Mireau of his humanity ("I'm not a bull"). They're housed like rats, underground in trenches, and the three prisoners are imprisoned in an animal stall, where they are compared to cockroaches. Mireau describes them as "scum" and a "pack of sneaking, whining, tail-dragging curs." By contrast, Dax treats his soldiers like fellow human beings. Major Saint-Auban (Richard Anderson) comments, "Well, they never learn, it seems. They get in a tight spot under heavy fire—gang up every time—herd instinct, I suppose. Kind of a lower animal sort of thing." Dax responds, "Kind of a human thing, it seems to me. Or do you make a distinction between the two, Major?" As a further commentary on Saint-Auban's views, we can read his name as Kubrick's signature toilet humor, in that it contains a near homophone for the French word for "bath" (*bain*).

Like Dax, Kubrick humanizes the enlisted men in the way he ends the film. He depicts them being moved by the girl's singing, as their sexual taunts and leering are replaced by tears, and their inner mensch emerges. The camera passes over their faces in the tavern, pausing on perhaps the youngest soldier, whose cheeks are streaming unashamedly with tears. Dax turns away, convinced they have not lost their humanity, and his faith is restored.

These oppositions highlight Dax's upstanding character and increase our identification with him. His sympathetic and positive presentation is magnified by the negative portrayals of the odious men in positions of power. The embodiment of menschlikayt, Dax is a benevolent and heroic paragon of reason, compassion, virtue, humanity, and justice, standing up for his ordinary men in the face of injustice and corruption. Honorable and highly ethical, he naively believes that some semblance of "truth" or "justice" might result from his actions. He believes that "the noblest impulse of man" is "his compassion for another." Broulard pooh-poohs Dax's genuine concern for his men as sentimental idealism. Dax washes from a decorative porcelain bowl, the one luxury item he possesses, manifesting his desire to remain clean in a morally dirty world. Dax is such a mensch that he even volunteers to be executed in place of his men. Broulard immediately quashes this suggestion with the words, "I think you're overwrought. This is not a question of officers!" He then volunteers to represent the condemned men at their trial, thus providing Dax/Douglas with the chance to act in the film's melodramatic highpoint. Having failed to save them, Dax collects the evidence of Mireau's order to open fire on his own troops, which he hands over to Broulard. Mireau is swiftly fired by Broulard, who then offers the vacant positon to Dax. Dax rejects him, to Broulard's astonishment: "You really did want to save those men, and you were not angling for Mireau's command. You are an idealist—and I pity you as I would the village idiot."

Kubrick clearly encourages us to identify with Dax, whose perspective and position are privileged, as Kubrick gives him more close-ups and point-of-view shots than anyone else in the movie. This is emphasized when he walks through the trenches, with shots alternating from Dax's point of view to backward dolly shots of Dax's face. We are never shown Mireau's point of view except for one occasion, a shot through binoculars. The proximity of the camera, which was often held by Kubrick, creates an attachment to Dax, forming an emotional connection between viewer and character and director.

Kubrick was careful to preserve the audience's good opinion of Dax. In a note for distributors regarding the synchronization of the film in foreign-language releases, Kubrick stated, "The voice should be cultured and educated but not to the point of being snobbish. However it should also be strong and manly. Be careful not to let Dax ever wear his heart on his sleeve. Despite the conflict with his commanding officers he is always a soldier; and never let him indulge in self-pity, or, for that matter, never let him break his heart over the injustice being done to his men. His actions express his sympathy for his men fully enough. It would be disastrous to over-emphasise his indignation or his pity."[6]

Dax is the embodiment of what Rebecca Alpert calls the "macho mensch," which was emerging in Jewish American popular culture at this time. The macho mensch, according to Alpert, manifested three features: "he is an outstanding athlete; he is an ethical human being who displays his virtues through gentility and kindness; and he is demonstrably connected to his Jewish identity, marking his *menschlichkeit* through the attributes of loyalty and bravery." He's also a "conqueror with a conscience," combining his power with morality. Such macho mensches had featured in Mailer's *Naked and the Dead*, Irwin Shaw's *Young Lions*, and Leon Uris's *Battle Cry*, having, arguably, already influenced *Fear and Desire*.[7]

The Banality of Evil

In *Paths of Glory* Kubrick reflects on the nature of evil, as manifested by the vainglorious Broulard and Mireau. Like Uris's *Battle Cry*, he showed how officers' self-interest, desire for glory, and personal promotion led them to willingly sacrifice their men in battle. Broulard and Mireau are corrupt, immoral, and unethical. They are seemingly much more concerned with propriety, the appearance of the proper conduct of the war, the orderly handling of courts martial, and decorum during executions than in the soldiers' welfare, justice, or even victory. The men are also merely statistics, whom they will send to their deaths without even blinking, indicating their callousness. On the threshold of death, Cpl. Philippe Paris (Ralph Meeker) is advised, "Act like a man." This interest to maintain the outward behavior of a proper man is quintessential goyim naches. This is demonstrated when, the morning after, Broulard and Mireau discuss the executions over breakfast as if they had attended a social function. No concern for the proper implementation of justice is exhibited, nor the killing of innocent men, rather that one of them will spoil the occasion. Mireau and Broulard display an inability to think, or feel, beyond themselves, anticipating much of what Hannah Arendt later said of Adolf Eichmann.

The trial highlights their evil. At the commencement of the trial, Mireau reclines, cross-legged, on an elegant couch. The president of the court announces he'll "dispense with unnecessary formalities," and when Dax interjects with valid legal objections, he's cut short with the response, "Please don't take up the court's time with technicalities." Such "unnecessary formalities" and "technicalities" refer to proper legal procedure, namely, the defense's presentation of its case, the introduction of evidence, the questioning of witnesses, a written indictment of the charges, and a stenographic record. The dispensing of these means the proceedings are flawed, unjust, and amount to a Nazi-style show trial.

The banality of evil is also evident in Kubrick's nascent interest in obedience and sacrifice, particularly the idea of fathers sacrificing their sons, as captured in Genesis 22, when Abraham is willing to offer up his son, Isaac, as a sacrifice. Such an idea had already been applied to World War I in Wilfred Owen's "Parable of the Old Man and the Young" (1920): "But the old man would not so, but slew his son, / And half the seed of Europe, one by one." As the film's father figures, Broulard and Mireau are eager to sacrifice their "sons," the troops under their command, in pursuit of vanity, vainglory, ambition, and promotion. They know the attack is doomed to failure. Broulard emphasizes his patriarchal position when he refers to Dax as "my boy" and says, "Troops are like children; just as a child wants his father to be firm, so troops crave discipline." When the troops refuse to leave the trenches, Mireau orders his own artillery to fire on them. But when the artillery officer refuses to obey his command, Mireau is still willing to sacrifice his men by his own hand: "If those sweethearts won't face German bullets, they'll face French ones!" Ultimately, Mireau selects the three scapegoated soldiers to be sacrificed to save (his) face. In turn, Mireau is sacrificed by his superior officer, Broulard, whom Dax calls a "degenerate, sadistic old man." Dax is the sole soldier unwilling to sacrifice his "children." He not only leads them into battle but also offers himself up as a scapegoat in their place.[8]

Kubrick's casting emphasizes their negative portrayals. Mireau, as played by Macready, sports a Prussian dueling scar, the manifestation of goyim naches, recalling Erich von Stroheim, who played Rommel as a Wilhelmine officer complete with dueling scar in Billy Wilder's 1943 *Five Graves to Cairo*. Broulard was played by a notorious informer for the House Un-American Activities Committee. Adolphe Menjou was a leading member of the Motion Picture Alliance for the Preservation of American Ideals, a collective of reactionary right-wingers, including John Wayne, formed to oppose communist influence in Hollywood. Menjou cooperated with the House Committee in 1947; he was a friendly witness who told the committee that "Hollywood is one of the main centers of Communist activity in America." In this way, Kubrick connects contemporary U.S. actions with past French injustice. Broulard's "pompous cruelty" suggests Robert Kolker, "may be Kubrick's way of commenting on [Menjou's] politics."[9]

Dreyfus Redux and the Holocaust Foretold

Filming in Germany so soon after the Holocaust surely had some impact on Kubrick. "It was very close, and it was very new for Americans to come to Germany and make films, and for an American Jew," suggested Christiane. But if he had any problem with the location—or with such production personal as cameraman Georg Krause, who'd worked throughout the Nazi period, shooting some of its best pilot films; and production manager George von Block, who'd served in the Luftwaffe—he never said. James Harris recalled Kubrick, "thinking more as an American" than a Jew. When asked if thoughts of the Holocaust affected Kubrick while he was shooting in Germany, Harris replied, "not as a Jew but as an American." But Harris and Kubrick did visit Dachau. "That was about the only time you started thinking about your Jewishness. It reminds you of all the atrocities and genocide that took place," Harris recalled. In the face of Kubrick's silence, Harris's feelings act as a stand-in, as do those of Douglas: "The war was too close, and I still had deep feelings that I tried to hide. I kept telling myself that not all Germans had participated in the Holocaust, the massacre of the Jews, all Germans were not like that."[10]

These feelings were kept well hidden, and little recent history seemingly entered *Paths of Glory*. Even virulent French anti-Semitism, highlighted by the Dreyfus Affair, was deliberately omitted from the film. Only echoes remain, such as when Mireau orders artillery officer Captain Rousseau (John Stein) to fire on his soldiers to force them out of cover of the trenches. Rousseau refuses to obey, exercising a restraint uncharacteristic of the Nazi era. In the wake of the Nuremberg Trial defense of "just following orders," it stands out as a beacon moment, invoking his namesake philosopher. Later Mireau relies on the Nuremberg defense: "it was their duty to obey that order."

The question of how the three men will be selected is a thorny issue in both the book and the film. In the wake of the Holocaust, which ended only twelve years earlier, the very notion of *selection* must surely have contained echoes of the extermination camps. In the novel and draft screenplays, one of those initially selected—Private Meyer—is Jewish. Classed as a "social undesirable," Meyer is also described as a criminal, drug-abusing, untrustworthy, brutish, syphilitic child molester suspected of murder, drawing on age-old anti-Semitic canards about deviant Jewish sexuality.

Cobb may have chosen the name Meyer because it invoked the case of Captain Armand Mayer, which erupted in 1892, two years before the Dreyfus Affair. Born in 1857, Mayer was a French army officer and a teacher of engineering at the prestigious École Polytechnique. On June 23, 1892, he was killed in a duel by the notoriously anti-Semitic Marquis de Morès. The duel was fought with sabers (rather than the typical pistols), and instead of dueling to inflict a light wound to satisfy honor—as was then the custom—Morès fought with lethal intent, stabbing Mayer, who subsequently died of his wounds. Much of French society was horrified and outraged: A Jewish officer of the French army had been killed at the hands of a reviled anti-Semite. The denunciations rang out, and twenty thousand people attended Mayer's funeral. The minister of war, Charles de Freycinet, declared in the chamber of deputies, "the army must not make any distinction between Jews, Protestants and Catholics. Such a division in the army is a crime against the nation." Morès was charged with homicide but was eventually acquitted. Mayer's death was so shocking because, by the end of the nineteenth century, France had gone much further than other European countries in granting equality to its Jewish citizens, and there were signs that anti-Jewish propaganda was losing its power over the public imagination. The death of Mayer dispelled this notion, inspiring the founder of Zionism, Theodor Herzl, to write his first article on anti-Semitism. Herzl was friends with Arthur Schnitzler, whom he urged to move to Palestine to become the "leading playwright of the Jewish state."[11]

Meyer, though, is spared precisely because he's Jewish, when a French army captain sees the wider ramifications of such a choice. Meyer avoids selection for the very reasons that would, ironically, mark him out for death in the decades to follow. As Cobb wrote, "This is the one time when being a Jew is going to save a man his life instead of costing him it." Meyer isn't saved because of either philo-Semitism or altruism. Rather the captain's caution is rationalized by the fear of resurgent anti-Semitism—in Cobb's words, "you never know what connexions these Jews may have"—and by a desire to protect the reputation of the French military, which suffered such a battering in the wake of Dreyfus. When the captain's perplexed and anti-Semitic colleague doesn't follow this line of thought, the captain reminds him,

Do you remember the Dreyfus case? . . . It's a lesson, that's all, a lesson against exposing yourself to the same thing over again. . . . They didn't dream when they picked on that quiet little Jewish officer, that the whole world would ring with his name, that ministry after ministry would fall and war loom because of him, or that the whole of France would be kept in a state of disturbance over him and his fate. . . . No, my boy, I'm not going to touch Meyer [because the] the cry of anti-Semitism will go up instantly. And once that cry is raised, no one can tell when or at what price it will be silenced.[12]

Harris and Kubrick removed this entire subplot. Various, almost verbatim, chunks of this material appeared in drafts but were erased by February 1957. Yet Meyer remains in the film and is mentioned by Private Ferol (Timothy Carey) no less than four times in his courtroom testimony. Against stereotype, Meyer is also described as being an excellent soldier, in an age when Jews were often singled out for their lack of martial qualities. He's even listed in the credits as being played by Jerry Hausner. But it's nearly impossible to locate Meyer in the film, and all references to his Jewishness were deleted. As publicity director Syd Stogel wrote, "The Private Meyer (Jewish) issue. This no longer applies inasmuch as the changed script makes no reference to Meyer's religion." The only clue remains in his last name, but only for those attuned to its suggestion of Jewishness. The only other hint is that Hausner (under the assumed name of "Roger Vagnoid") also plays the café owner, who Naremore notes, introduces the singer (Susanne Christian, later Kubrick's wife) "in the style of a borsht-belt comic." But, for whatever reasons, Harris, Kubrick, and Douglas refused to publicize this dual role and omitted this subplot, perhaps for fear that a commercial Hollywood product, so soon after the death of McCarthyism three years earlier, was not yet ready for explicit references to Jewishness, Dreyfus, and anti-Semitism.[13]

The novel's overt Jewishness may have been removed in the film, but it left its traces and subtle footprints nevertheless. *Paths of Glory*'s subsurface Jewishness is evident in the specter of Dreyfus and the Holocaust, both of which hang over the film, even if nowhere explicit. In her study of the French army during World War I, Elizabeth Greenhalgh shows how the military code of justice in force from 1914 was the same as had been legislated in 1857, hence that same code that had condemned Dreyfus was that which condemned the men in *Paths of Glory*; in fact, "the Dreyfus affair had made any revision a sensitive matter." *Paths of Glory*, therefore, is not only very accurate in the portrayal of French wartime military tribunals but also very like the 1894 proceedings against Dreyfus, even to the extent that the accused's defense counsel or representative was not entitled to attend the interrogation of the prisoner.[14]

Even though the film never mentions the Holocaust, because the events depicted in it happened decades beforehand, in invoking Dreyfus the specter of the Shoah was invoked nonetheless. In *The Origins of Totalitarianism*, Hannah Arendt drew a direct connection between the anti-Semitism of the Dreyfus Affair and the Holocaust, describing it as "a huge dress rehearsal for a performance that had to be put off for more than three decades." As this description demonstrates, the stench of anti-Semitism that hung over the Dreyfus Affair, which viewed Jews as a lower form of life no better than insects and cockroaches, hangs over the condemned men in *Paths of Glory*, one of whom, Private Arnaud, was played by Jewish actor Joe Turkel. And Kubrick downplayed the criminality of the scapegoated soldiers and drew out their execution to maximize sympathy for their plight.

The Road to *Spartacus*

Kubrick's next collaboration with Kirk Douglas, *Spartacus*, deepened his exploration into menschlikayt. Called in to replace Anthony Mann as director, he joined a Jewish production team that included screenwriter Howard Fast, on whose eponymous 1951 novel the film was based; star and motivating force behind the film, Douglas; actor Tony Curtis; titles and battle sequence designer, Saul Bass; and editor Irving Lerner. Kubrick was drawn to the film, in part, because of the circumstances of his personal life, which had prompted an inquiry into and reckoning with his own identity as a Jewish man, specifically, as a son, father, and husband. These considerations were initially treated by Kubrick through the prism of Jewish masculinity, in particular three interrelated, yet wholly and previously unexplored, elements of the Jewish male self-image in *Spartacus*: the character of David the Jew, the Jewishness of the character Antoninus, and menschlikayt.

Why *Spartacus*?

Kubrick agreed to direct *Spartacus* for many reasons. Not having helmed a film for the two years since *Paths of Glory*, he was eager to get back into the director's chair. The period 1956–1959 had seen a variety of projects proposed, and even partially developed, but, frustratingly, none came to fruition. *Spartacus* offered Kubrick the chance to establish himself as a major Hollywood director by helming a star-studded, big-budget, box-office blockbuster. Naturally, Kubrick was keen to direct such a film, starring such British actors as Laurence Olivier, Peter Ustinov, and Charles Laughton. Ustinov recalled "feeling that during *Spartacus* he was biding his time, getting on the record as the director of a big and successful film which would give him greater freedom in the future." It also enabled Harris-Kubrick Pictures to discharge their contract with Douglas's Bryna Productions and was a much-needed financial injection into the company.[15]

Kubrick's personal life also underwent some profound changes in the years immediately preceding *Spartacus*. (As mentioned earlier, it was while working on *Paths of Glory* that he had met Christiane). Shortly thereafter she became his girlfriend, and they moved in together in Munich with Christiane's young daughter, Katharina. They were married in 1958, and the following year their daughter Anya—Kubrick's first child—was born, followed by his second daughter, Vivian, in 1960. He needed to feed a young and growing family.

Kubrick's new wife, Christiane, was not Jewish. After two failed marriages to two different Jewish women—he divorced Metz in 1955 and legally separated from Sobotka in 1958 before finally divorcing her in 1961—Kubrick had finally rejected and moved beyond the heredity faith of his family to "marry out." His marriage to a gentile woman meant, in Orthodox halachic terms at least, that his children would not be Jewish.

Christiane was also German. As a gentile German who spoke very little English, she provided a major contrast to Kubrick—a Jew from the Bronx. She grew up in the Third Reich while the Holocaust was happening. "I was the little girl who moved in where Anne Frank was pushed out," she stated. Around that very time Kubrick began drafting a script set in Nazi-occupied Amsterdam in February–March 1943, narrated from the perspective of a ten-year-old German girl named Anna, who observes Jewish suffering. Christiane was the same age at that time. Ustinov recalled how Kubrick "wanted to do a kind of film biography of a German officer, why he did what he did. I know he was obsessed with that sort of thing." "The German Lieutenant," a screenplay Kubrick had written with Richard Adams, a former paratrooper in Korea, was completed and a budget compiled by January 30, 1959. Alan Ladd was cast as the star, and shooting was scheduled to start in mid-April.[16]

Christiane was also the niece of Nazi filmmaker Veit Harlan, who, in 1940, had made the notorious Nazi propaganda film *Jud Süss*. Christiane recalled, "Stanley took a great interest in my catastrophic family background. We spoke about it a great deal. People asked him, 'How could you marry a German woman, especially one with a background like that?' I thought a lot about the fact that no one could have taken a greater interest in my family background than Stanley, who understood that I came from the other side, which was the opposite of his [background]. But he also knew that my generation could plead innocence: I was very young during the Holocaust, though at the same time old enough to remember everything." He met her family and relatives, including Veit, in 1957. He drank a big glass of vodka beforehand and was much shaken afterward. He told her, "I'm standing here like Woody Allen looking like ten Jews." This encounter prompted some self-reflection on Kubrick's part, according to Christiane: "Stanley of course asked himself the same questions: if I had been in his position, what would I have done?" He considered a movie about the making of *Jud Süss*. Jan Harlan remembered that "Kubrick wanted to make a film about this era, the normal course of daily events when producing a film in Berlin. What was it like? A production meeting at 8am, budget, costumes, the whole thing, casting. He wanted to know, wanted to make a film about how this all took place. What was it like? At what point did Goebbels intervene? When was the OK required for each scene of the script? What were these discussions like? What influence was applied? What conversations were held? Revealing things like that."[17]

For Dalton Trumbo, Kubrick's marriage to Christiane was essential to understanding *Spartacus*. "Stanley, who is thirty years old, has married a German. The question in my mind is this: Did he marry her because he loved her or did he marry her because he wanted to marry a German girl in order to punish the Germans (through her) for what they had done to the Jews. Therefore we have the problem about Stanley which is terribly important in relation to this picture. What is he trying prove? It may be that he is a more devoted Jew than any other. It may be that he is the essential renegade."[18]

Arguably, these events triggered Kubrick to reconsider his own Jewishness and Jewish masculinity, in particular his status as a Jewish man—a son, father, and husband. At this time, the mid to late 1950s was a period in which filmmakers, both Jewish and otherwise, began to introduce a wider range of Jewish themes and characters, including the Holocaust and Israel, into their films in a fashion not seen since the 1920s. After what Henry

Popkin calls the "great retreat," explicit Jews began to appear on the screen with more frequency, particularly in such historical and biblical epics as *The Ten Commandments* (1956) and *Ben-Hur* (1959).[19]

Spartacus also fit into Hollywood's so-called Israeli period, which lasted from the early to mid-sixties. The key film sparking this cycle was Otto Preminger's *Exodus* (1960), itself an adaptation of Leon Uris's hugely successful 1958 novel, which promoted a fantasy of the muscular "New Jew," the modern warrior reborn in violence from the ashes of the gentle shtetl Jew and provided a counterpoint to the Holocaust's images of Jewish weakness, victimhood, and passivity. The novel was a blockbuster, one of the biggest best-sellers in modern American publishing.[20]

For these reasons Kubrick was surely attracted to the prospect of working with Douglas again, as well as Tony Curtis, who, like Douglas, was publicly redefining the Jewish image. Indeed, Kubrick praised their "beautifull [*sic*] builds," and those sequences showcasing Curtis's muscularity, it's generally agreed, were the result of Kubrick's interventions. By the late 1950s there had been a pronounced growth in the observable Jewishness of film stars such as Douglas and Curtis, leading to an increased willingness to point it out, or vice versa, the increased willingness of people to point it out led to a growth in observable Jewishness. Lenny Bruce outed them both when he commented, "Even the Vikings are Jewish," as Curtis had starred alongside Douglas in Richard Fleischer's *The Vikings* (1958). The British newspaper the *Jewish Chronicle* opened its review of *Spartacus* with the words, "Two of Hollywood's leading Jewish stars, Kirk Douglas and Tony Curtis, combine with a glittering cast."[21]

The historical figure and plight of Spartacus and his fellow slaves also appealed to Kubrick. Independently, he read Arthur Koestler's version of the Spartacus story, *The Gladiators* (1939), as well as the works of Appian, Sallust, Plutarch, and Xenophon. It was a clear choice in part because of its underlying left-wing and anti-McCarthyite sentiments and in part because Kubrick's sympathies lay with the outcast and the ostracized. He told the *New York Times*, *Spartacus* "concerns the outsider who is passionately committed to action against the social order. I mean the outsider in the Colin Wilson sense—the criminal, maniac, poet, lover, revolutionary. The protagonists of 'Paths of Glory,' 'The Killing,' 'Spartacus' and my next film, 'Lolita,' are all outsiders fighting to do some impossible thing, whether it's pulling a perfect robbery or saving innocent men from execution by a militaristic state or carrying on a love affair with a 12-year-old girl."[22]

A Kubrick Film

Kubrick's autonomous research indicates that he saw himself as more than just a gun for hire. He set his stamp on anything that wasn't nailed down. Three weeks after meeting principal screenwriter Dalton Trumbo, who was brought on board to beef up Howard Fast's initial script, Kubrick produced a "final" shooting script, which differed significantly from the one Trumbo had produced in January 1959. Together with Douglas, Kubrick further revised the scripts, cutting out Trumbo. Kubrick told the *LA Mirror* in September 1960 that he wrote "a lot" of the screenplay. Trumbo pointed to Kubrick's "haphazard set rewriting" and allowing of Ustinov to "dabble mercilessly" with his and Laughton's roles. Referring to the script revisions made during the shoot, Kubrick told the press that there had been a great deal of on-set improvisation. He doubtless absorbed a great deal from Olivier, Laughton, and Ustinov about character development, possibly instilling a taste for British actors. Trumbo's son concluded, "Kubrick's hiring changed everything. All of the problems *Spartacus* encountered began with Kubrick. They are of his manufacture. He was hired to do a job and then subverted what he was supposed to do."[23]

Kubrick was certainly willing to be credited as *Spartacus*'s screenwriter. He worried that Anthony Mann was receiving too much credit for his initial work on the film: "It's my film but 1 sequence." He continued, "Press people asked me over here how much of the film I did? I should be extremely depressed if this point were not absolutely clear to the American press and the Foreign as well!" Later he said, "I directed the actors, I composed the shots, and I edited the movie." He told the *LA Times* that "I spent eight months in the cutting room. I always cut my own pictures." In an interview with the *New York Times*, he boasted, "It's just as good as 'Paths of Glory,' and certainly there's as much of myself in it. I don't mean to minimize the contributions of the others involved, but the director is [the] only one who can authentically impose his personality onto a picture, and the result is his responsibility—partly because he's the only one who's always there." Kubrick also gave his active assistance to the film's restoration in 1991.[24]

Spartacus as Muscular Moses

In Fast's novel the tale of Spartacus is recounted posthumously by those who knew him. One whole chapter is narrated by his commander, "David the Jew." David is the last fighter to be crucified rather than Spartacus, whose body is never identified. But David's role was reduced to allow for Spartacus's to grow, rendering his Jewishness invisible on-screen. Production aide Stan Margulies insisted, "David should not, I believe, be identified as a Jewish slave since we have eliminated all the scenes from the early script in which his religion was emphasized and used for dramatic purposes." So while the character remained, he's never referred to by name. With little actual dialogue the only clue to his Jewishness was the actor who played him: Harold J. Stone (b. Harold Jacob Hochstein), a third-generation actor whose father was Yiddish actor Jacob Hochstein. Instead, Spartacus absorbed David's Jewishness, rendering him a pallid version of the character as sketched in the novel and draft screenplays.[25]

The downplaying of David's central role in Fast's novel and Trumbo's scripts allowed for the concomitant growth of Spartacus as the subtextually Jewish protagonist. As Douglas said, the "role of Spartacus was a myth." "It didn't exist. I came up with the idea of combining his character and the character of David the Jew." Through palimpsest, performance, and casting, those who were familiar with Fast's novel were now invited to read Spartacus himself as Jewish. The novel provided various clues to

FIGURE 4 David the Jew (Harold J. Stone) in the center with Spartacus (Kirk Douglas) on the right in *Spartacus* (1960).

understanding Spartacus in this way: he was a "Thracian." As Fast wrote, "in the sporting language of the city of Rome and in the common slang of the arena, a Thracian was anyone who fought with the *sica*. Thereby, the Jew was a Thracian."[26]

Spartacus very much mimics a charismatic Moses-like liberator. Having killed an overseer, he liberates the slaves, heading a diverse rabble of oppressed peoples from different lands, leading them toward a promised land he'll never see. In another nod to Moses, the whereabouts of whose grave is unknown, Roman general and politician Marcus Licinius Crassus (Laurence Olivier) orders, "I want no grave or marker. His body is to be burned and his ashes scattered in secret." Trumbo had suggested to Douglas that Spartacus "exercise his inner discipline" to do what "leaders from Moses to Lenin had had to do." Douglas himself perceived the parallel: "Looking at these ruins, and at the Sphinx and the pyramids in Egypt, at the palaces in India, I wince. I see thousands and thousands of slaves carrying rocks, beaten, starved, crushed, dying. I identify with them. As it says in the Torah: 'Slaves were we unto Egypt.' I come from a race of slaves. That would have been *my* family, *me*." Further suggesting parallels with the flight from Egypt, *Spartacus* deliberately resembles such period biblical epics as *The Ten Commandments*. In a similar manner Kubrick picked out individual faces in the crowd sequences, as they went about their daily activities of cooking, playing, training, and crafting. Such techniques harked back to his early documentaries. And the film's publicity posed Spartacus in a Moses-like fashion, standing with a burning touch (as if to say, "Let my people go!") while the battle rages around him.[27]

Spartacus also parallels *Exodus*, released in the same year. Trumbo similarly wrote the *Exodus* screenplay, which he began working on while finishing up on *Spartacus*. Spartacus therefore mimicked the hero of *Exodus*, Ari Ben Canaan (Paul Newman), as well as Douglas's earlier role in *The Juggler* as a traumatized death-camp survivor who finds redemptive love in Israel. As an ardent Zionist and supporter of the State of Israel, Douglas deliberately emphasized the Zionism of Fast's novel. Dax was a mere foreshadow of the buff, barely clothed Spartacus, whom Pauline Kael describes as "Douglas at his most muscular" and whose army was a "giant kibbutz on the move." Alex North's use of an Israeli recorder on the soundtrack invited comparisons, as did Universal-International's plot synopsis, which describes the pirates who betray and abandon Spartacus and his people to Roman slaughter as "Arab." Contemporary Catholic viewers upheld this reading, detecting Jewish traces in the film; a National League of Decency reviewer referred to Varinia (Jean Simmons) as a "proud young Jewess."[28]

Although Kubrick's views on Israel are still a complete mystery, some of this Zionism may be attributable to him. The view presented of the freed slaves reflects what Trumbo calls "hostile Koestlerian ideas derived from quite another book," that is, Koestler's *Gladiators*, which Kubrick had read. Koestler wrote, "Spartacus chose as his mentor and guide a member of the Judaic sect of the Essenes—the only sizeable civilized community that practiced primitive Communism at that time, and taught that 'what is mine is thine, and what is thine is mine.'" Kubrick, like Douglas, may have shared some affection for the Zionist project.[29]

Antoninus ("the Jew")

The removal of David's explicit Jewishness also allowed for the further exploration of Jewish masculinity through the introduction of a character who did not appear in Fast's novel: the Greek slave boy Antoninus, who becomes Spartacus's symbolic son. Kubrick explained that the part "started out with a brief scene or two and a few lines of dialogue" but just kept building. In fact, Trumbo had drafted an extensive part for the character.[30]

Antoninus's Jewishness is nowhere identified in the film, but, as with Spartacus, the casting of Jewish actor Tony Curtis in the role—which was specially created for him—is the first clue toward uncovering it. Curtis was born Bernard Schwartz in 1925 at the same Flower Hospital in Manhattan that was part of the medical school at which Kubrick's father trained. By speaking in what Ina Rae Hark calls an "American urban ethnic idiom," *Time* notes how Curtis's accent "suggests that the ancient Tiber was a tributary of the Bronx River." Cameraman Russ Metty connected Jewish urban ethnicity, urban, and that particular district of New York when he said, in reference to Kubrick, "get that little Jew-boy from the Bronx off the crane."[31]

Kubrick and Curtis bonded in a way that anticipated the director's relationship with Peter Sellers on his next two films. Curtis recalled, "We were about three years separated in age, and we had an excellent relationship." He hailed him as "so good with actors in general—and with me in particular—so appreciative. He was a very fine person. My favorite director." The appreciation was mutual. Kubrick called him a "great friend."

Christiane said that Kubrick "loved Tony Curtis, because they had lots in common." Geoffrey Cocks notes that when Kubrick "was unhappily dealing the lack of directorial control and the intimidation and arrogance of established actors and technicians, many of them Gentile, on *Spartacus*, his first and last big-budget Hollywood assignment, he found refuge in friendship with Tony Curtis." As a result, Fiona Radford speculates that Kubrick concentrated more on Antoninus, who, "after the breakout, Spartacus seems to value just as highly as Varinia."[32]

As David's Jewishness was diluted, Antoninus absorbed those remaining traces that hadn't already been sucked up by Spartacus. Consequently, Antoninus reveals some stereotypical Jewish traits to the extent that at least one critic mistook him for David. A poet, scholar, tutor, singer, and magical tricks performer, his intellect defines him. He possesses Yiddische *kopf*, emphasized when Spartacus and Antoninus first meet. Fingering Antoninus's fine white linen tunic, Spartacus inquires with some skepticism, assuming, as many anti-Semites do of Jews, that Antoninus has not done a hard day's work in his life, "What kind of work did *you* do?" When Antoninus replies, "Singer of songs," Spartacus asks again, "But what *work* did you do?" Antoninus's answer, "That's my work. I also juggle," may be read as a sly nod to one of Douglas's previous roles. Spartacus maintains Antoninus's intellectual, nonphysical role by refusing to allow him to fight until the very end, using him to read his documents, as he is illiterate. And Saul Bass's assignation of the image of open hands for Antoninus in the opening credits obliquely invokes that of the Jewish priestly blessing.

Further accentuating Antoninus's Jewishness was his unmanliness. The unmanly, sissy Jew was the product of centuries of anti-Jewish attitudes, as well as a means by which Jews defined their own masculinity. Recall that Kubrick had already described Curtis as beautiful, and Trumbo also referred to Curtis's "somber, feminine beauty." Curtis recollected how many people were "convinced" he was gay (calling him "fairy," "queer," "fag," and "faggot"). His previous cross-dressing drag act in Billy Wilder's *Some Like It Hot* (1959) confirmed it for some. In *Spartacus* Kubrick drew on, and amplified, such extradiegetic knowledge by making him attract the lustful attention of Crassus. Crassus chooses Antoninus to be his body servant because of his youth and beauty, hoping to engineer an opportunity to seduce him. And Trumbo was worried that Crassus's presence during Antoninus's death lent Spartacus's kiss "homosexual implications."[33]

Menschlikayt and Paternity

The introduction of the character of Antoninus also facilitated another signature Kubrick concern, namely the opposition between menschlikayt and goyim naches. Kubrick emphasized the differences between the slaves and the Romans, constantly contrasting the slaves' wholesomeness with Roman debauchery. The Romans indulge their every decadent desire. They privilege such goyim naches as gladiatorial fights, lions devouring Christians and Jews, chariot races, orgies, food, and drink. They are depicted as licentiousness, narcissistic, and childless with little to no family ties—Crassus's marriage is a sham. They are cold and heartless, idly gossiping about petty politics while gladiators brutally fight to the death, paying no attention to the bloody spectacle, emphasizing their casual cruelty and utter indifference to the dignity and sanctity of human life.

The introduction of the character of Antoninus allowed Kubrick to highlight this distinction even more, particularly when Crassus attempts to seduce him. In a scene that appeared in the version shown to the National Legion of Decency and Production Code Administration reviewers—but was cut from the 1960 version and then restored in the 1991 rerelease, with Kubrick's participation—when Crassus makes his move on Antoninus, he refers to him as "boy," suggesting he is potentially underage. Crassus analogizes bisexuality to a "taste" for "both snails and oysters." Knowledge of kashrut (the Jewish dietary laws) here introduces extracritical commentary on the scene. The laws of kashrut dictate that seafood is kosher only if it has fins and scales and that all shellfish (indeed, anything with a shell) is forbidden. The symbolic or allegorical interpretation of the kashrut laws suggests fins and scales are signs of endurance and self-control; hence the lack of them means wild, impetuous abandon. Shells here stand as a code for wantonness and excess, and the metaphor of "snails and oysters" hints at Crassus's warped sexuality, his libertine, all-consuming but entirely self-directed passions. Crassus's turpitude, as expressed through his sybaritic and *treyf* (explicitly nonkosher) tastes, indicates the feelings of Jewish repugnance toward Crassus and the Romans.

By contrast, Spartacus is a model of self-sacrifice, restraint, and modesty. Despite being offered to Spartacus, and fully expecting to be taken, Varinia leaves his cell untouched. Refusing to rape her, instead, he is respectful and tender. This disrobing in Spartacus's cell was Kubrick's idea, transposed from a scene written by Trumbo where she was to undress for Crassus. The effect is to emphasize Spartacus's menschlikayt.

Spartacus is the compassionate and sentimental father figure to Antoninus and the slaves, including many children, who he views more as a family and a community than an army. He genuinely cares about his charges. He's a model of family values, as he marries and fathers a child. Kubrick described him as "obviously morally superior. He has all the audience's sympathy."[34]

Kubrick went to great lengths to articulate the difference between the "animal" and the "mensch" sides of Spartacus, who begins, in Trumbo's words, "a powerful, filthy, brutalized animal." In the opening sequence he bites a Roman guard in the leg like a dog. He's branded at the gladiatorial school, a practice used only on animals in ancient Rome. By removing most of Spartacus's dialogue in the first half of the film, Kubrick's changes to the script reinforce this impression. Trumbo describes their "efforts to make Spartacus a human being, a man of nobility, a humane leader." And before the gladiatorial combats had begun, when Crixus (John Ireland) asks, "Would you try to kill me?" Spartacus responds, "Yes, I'd kill. I'd try to stay alive, and so would you." Trumbo points out how although "Spartacus begins as an animal," he "becomes a man, that is he becomes conscious of other than himself, that the essence of manhood is to rise above the petty ambitions of one's self with something larger, with mankind as a whole." As producer Edward Lewis puts it, Spartacus begins as a "beast of burden," and the film "dramatize[s] his growth as a man." When paired with Varinia but watched by the leering voyeurs, Batiatus (Ustinov) and Marcellus (Charles McGraw) through the barred skylight of his cell, he exclaims, "I'm not an animal!" His declaration resists the Romans' dehumanizing tactics, revealing him to be a mensch, causing Batiatus to smirk, "You may not be animal but this sorry show gives me little hope that you'll ever be a man."[35]

The death of Draba (Woody Strode) prompts Spartacus to live for something beyond the self. In their gladiatorial pairing, Draba is the model of the macho mensch. Rather than kill Spartacus for the Romans' pleasure, he nobly sacrifices himself to save Spartacus. The lesson is not lost on Spartacus, as displayed in a long close-up on his face, which codes his transformation from animalistic slave to mensch.

As leader, Spartacus rejects the goyim naches of rank, medals, insignia, and so on, which the Romans so prized. In an illustrated guide produced to market the film, production aide Stan Margulies describes how, "Never, during the four brutal years of his struggle for freedom, did the slave hero bother to adorn himself with insignia of rank." When Spartacus discovers the gladiators forcing two captured Roman noblemen to fight to the death, he contemptuously addresses the captives, "Noble Romans! Fighting like animals." He then turns on his comrades, rebuking them, as Monica Silveira Cyrino, puts it, "like Moses scolding the reveling Israelites." "I swore that if I ever got out of this place, I'd die before I'd watch two men fight to the death again. . . . What are becoming—Romans?" He asks, "Are we animals?" He tells Antoninus, "An animal can learn to fight." Such attitudes were rare in the Roman world of Spartacus's era, except among the small Jewish communities of Rome. Spartacus was following the advice from another film from the same year, Billy Wilder's *The Apartment*: "Be a mensch! You know what that means? . . . A human being!" Kubrick equates Roman goyim naches with animality and resists both.[36]

Given that Douglas played both Dax and Spartacus, it's easy to fold them together. Spartacus, like Dax, is another macho mensch. On the eve of the battle, *Spartacus* repeats *Paths of Glory*'s spatial arrangements in which the gladiators, like the enlisted men, are confined to underground chambers, while their masters, like the French command, stroll above them. Spartacus, like Dax, strolls among his men to invigorate morale. As Gene D. Phillips points out, "Kubrick and Douglas might easily have had that scene from the earlier film in mind while shooting the present one, for it is built up in a similar fashion: the camera cuts from Douglas's friendly face to reaction shots of admiration and affection from the people whom he passes."[37]

Any awkward or uncomfortable facts that contradicted the film's image of Spartacus as a mensch were suppressed. Trumbo blamed Kubrick for toning down the revolutionary aspects of Spartacus by allowing Ustinov to expunge a key exchange from his script: "Spartacus is a criminal. He's destroyed the Republic. The change isn't apparent yet, but the Republic is dead." The slaves' violent rebellion isn't glorified, and Spartacus doesn't revel in revenge. As Marguilies wrote, "what may seem quite surprising, [is that he] normally did all that he could to protect innocent people from the revenge of his men." *Spartacus* also didn't dwell on how the slaves amassed the funds to bribe the pirates to take them to safety. Rather, the stress on the love story between Varinia and Spartacus domesticates him by focusing on his role as a husband and father (in keeping with the gender roles and family values of the 1950s), further distracting attention from his political and revolutionary successes. But it also has the effect of humanizing him, emphasizing his role as both a real and symbolic father and mensch. This is cemented when Spartacus kills Antoninus, as a mercy killing to prevent a lengthier torturous death by crucifixion; it is an act of (Jewish) love rather than (Roman) violence for its own sake, also invoking the sacrifice of Isaac. And when Spartacus spits in Crassus's face, suggesting a reversion to his previously animalistic nature, it serves only to reinforce his humanity.[38]

We can detect Kubrick's influence here. Various memos demonstrate Spartacus's essential humanity was entirely Kubrick's doing. Kubrick had emphasized to Lewis and Trumbo that "it is essential for Spartacus to be motivated by a simple, straightforward positive belief in the goodness of man, together with a faith in the eventual ascendance of human dignity. He must not be motivated by *negative* rationalizations of the slaves [*sic*] plight." And Trumbo responded, "You conceived it, you created it, you directed it, you shot it—it's all yours, and it's all there, and it's wonderful. Spartacus is *gentle*. For having characterized him thus, we are all in your debt. We must not depart from that basic characteristic of our hero: *Spartacus is gentle!*"[39]

Probably not uncoincidentally, Kubrick's own personal life and the stuff of *Spartacus* uncannily overlapped. Becoming a father to three daughters in three years, Kubrick surely felt some empathy with Spartacus the father figure. In Fast's novel, as well as in initial casting, the character of Spartacus's lover and wife, Varinia, was Germanic, and the German actress Sabina Bethmann was screen-tested and hired for the part by Douglas, reflecting Kubrick's hiring of Christiane on *Paths of Glory*. In an act of demonstrating his control, however, Kubrick fired Bethmann, whom Douglas had personally chosen. Natalie Zemon Davis speculates that Kubrick ended the film on Spartacus's surviving son because of the birth of his two daughters. Recall that Kubrick had said, following the birth of Vivian, "When you get right down to it, the family is the most primitive and visceral and vital unit in our society. You may stand outside your wife's hospital room during childbirth uttering, 'My God, what a responsibility! . . . What am I doing here?' and then you go in and look down at the face of your child and—zap!—the most ancient programming takes over and your response is one of wonder and joy and pride." He may well have later likened the experience of working on the studio production of *Spartacus* to that of a slave, too![40]

Conclusion

In *Paths of Glory* and *Spartacus* Kubrick articulated those creative concerns that defined the rest of his oeuvre. These included subtextual Jewish manliness and menschlikayt, embodied in the new character type of the macho mensch, even if he wasn't explicitly represented as Jewish. Dax and Spartacus are probably the most noble and admirable characters in all of Kubrick's work, never to be repeated so unambiguously. They also showcase how he submerged Jewish issues beneath the surface of his films, preferring to tone down the overt Jewish references in his source texts but replacing them with a Jewish sensibility and ethos that reflect the key intellectual and contemporary Jewish concerns. *Spartacus* is particularly important. With an all-star cast of Jewish and gentile actors Kubrick succeeded in producing a blockbusting epic that also has something to say about Jewishness. Yet, because of the fraught nature of the adaptation process, containing a myriad of conflicting interventions—Fast, Trumbo, Douglas, and the big-name British cast—Kubrick's individual vision is not as distinctive as he may have liked. Instead, he had to wait to be freed of studio control and the influence of others' dominant opinions to more fully articulate his authorial voice. But what transpired on the set of *Spartacus* on a daily basis, how Kubrick operated and made decisions, however contentiously, set the pattern for his future career, enabling him to possess greater control over his movies than any other commercial director in Hollywood.

3

Kubrick's Double

Following the critical and commercial success of *Spartacus*, Stanley Kubrick was an established name. Christiane recalled how "he felt now he had this label: 'I'm a film director, officially. Now I can make a story that I have a crush on.'" If Kubrick wanted to distance himself and declare his independence from Hollywood and his Kirk Douglas films, then there was no better way than to direct a film about rival pedophiles vying for the prize of a teenage girl. In *Lolita* Kubrick rejected the one-dimensional, noncomplex representations of the Jewish "macho mensch" in *Paths of Glory* and *Spartacus*. The sophistication of the source material was such that it allowed him to explore negative stereotypes of Jewish masculinity, the nature of man, fatherhood, and evil.[1]

A Love Story

Harris and Kubrick had read Vladimir Nabokov's controversial novel *Lolita* shortly before its publication in English in 1958. Calder Willingham, who was friends with Nabokov, gave a copy to Kubrick. *Anchor Review* had published excerpts with an enthusiastic introduction by Frederick Wilcox Dupee, Kubrick's Columbia English professor. Dwight Macdonald may also have pushed Kubrick in that direction, as he wrote to Kubrick, "I'm glad the seed I sowed in our talk may bear forbidden fruit or should the cliché be varied to strange fruit?" Macdonald later visited the set of *Lolita*. The Beats had also approved of the novel: Jack Kerouac had described it as a "classic old love story."[2]

Kubrick explained the novel's appeal. He told Robert Emmett Ginna in 1960, "I was instantly attracted to the book because of the sense of life that it conveyed, the truthfulness of it, and the inherent drama of the situation seemed completely winning. I've always been amused at the cries of pornography on the part of various film columnists and people of that ilk, because, to me, *Lolita* seemed a very sad and tender love story." Harris-Kubrick Pictures had earlier attempted to adapt Stefan Zweig's 1913 novel, *The Burning Secret*, in which a man attempts to seduce a Jewish woman by befriending her young son. The superficial plot similarities between *Lolita* and Zweig's book, which Michel Ciment describes as "almost the inverted double of Nabokov's: a man befriends a young boy the better to seduce his mother," may therefore also have been a consideration, allowing Harris-Kubrick Pictures to channel some of their disappointment in failing to complete that project by adapting Nabokov's novel. Christiane said Kubrick "thought *Lolita* was a fantastic book because it clarified the feeling that we all have that good and evil does not come in the expected package." It therefore allowed him to continue his exploration into the nature of humanity, manliness, and evil.[3]

But it was Lionel Trilling's review of *Lolita* in *Encounter* that really influenced Kubrick. Trilling argues that *Lolita* is "not about sex, but about love." He concludes, "It may be that Mr. Nabokov really wants us to believe with entire seriousness that we are witnessing the culmination of H. H.'s moral evolution. Perhaps he even wants us to believe that his ascent from 'ape-like' lust to a love which challenges the devils below and the angels up over the sea to ever dissever his soul from the soul of the lovely Annabel Lee constitutes the life-cycle of the erotic instinct." Kubrick was very taken with the review. He typed a note to himself, "Trilling's piece in *Encounter*. Save." He repeatedly quoted Trilling in interviews.[4]

Lolita also appealed because, as Trilling noted, it was already a satire "upon the peculiar sexual hypocrisy of American life." Nabokov mocked iconic cultural artifacts of the 1950s and devoured them with unparalleled comic relish. He attacked Americana, middle-class cultural pretentiousness, TV playwrights (the one "star" in the film is only a middlebrow TV writer with fifty-two successful credits to his name), book clubs, fine-art reproductions, the rootlessness of contemporary American society, and more. *Lolita* also lampooned the current intellectual fads for existentialism, Freudianism, and psychoanalysis that had to all intents and purposes replaced Marxism by the 1950s. The novel also had a Beat quality to it.[5]

Kubrick felt "the story offers a marvellous opportunity for humor." *Lolita* was full of sexual, toilet, and scatological humor, appealing to what Michael Herr describes as Kubrick's "low adolescent humor, smutty actually, sophomoric, by which I mean a sophomore in high school." Its "crude," in the words of John Trevelyan of the Production Code Administration, "juxtaposition of lavatory noises and sexual situations" resembled *Mad*, Lenny Bruce, and the early sixties sickniks. It was replete with deliberate, intentional, rich, symbolic, playful, smutty sexual language, puns, innuendo, and double entendres. The "cherry pie, cavity-filling, and limp noodle jokes, so blatantly smutty, without shame" tickled Kubrick, said Herr. Nabokov's use of names was particularly associative: Mona Farlow, Camp Q, Camp Climax, Hourglass Lake, Mr. Swine, Captain Love, The Frigid Queen, Dr. Cudler, Miss Starch, Miss Fromkiss, Beardsley, Ramsdale, the Bliss family, Rev. Rigor Mortis, Dr. Kramm, Miss Beard, Mrs. Pratt, Miss Lebone, Mona Dahl, Dr. Blue, and Vivian Darkbloom.[6]

Nabokov also evoked the Holocaust in the novel through metaphors and descriptions that suggest trains, camps, and other details, both directly and obliquely. He referred to the "brown wigs of tragic old women who had just been gassed" or the "ashes of our predecessors." While Kubrick removed these direct and indirect allusions to World War II and the Holocaust from his film, their traces remained nonetheless, as he paradoxically inserted a further subtextual Jewishness not present in the novel.[7]

Harris-Kubrick Pictures immediately acquired the film rights for $150,000 and 15 percent of the net. The following year they solicited Calder Willingham to produce a screenplay, but then rejected it. They subsequently approached Nabokov, who began the laborious task of adapting his own novel and produced various draft screenplays. He held his final script conference at Kubrick's home in Beverly Hills on September 25, 1960. Little of Nabokov's work found its way into the final screenplay, as, a month later, Harris and Kubrick completed their version. Although further changes were made during shooting generated from rehearsals and the filming process itself, they shrewdly gave the screenwriting credit to Nabokov. At the same time, preproduction began. Shooting started on November 29, 1960, and lasted until March 29, 1961. It was released on June 12, 1962.[8]

The Wandering Ape

Kubrick's interest in subtextual Jewish masculinity was rendered through two characters in his adaptation of *Lolita*: Quilty and Humbert. The way Nabokov characterized Humbert hinted at his Jewishness. He wrote how Humbert's father was composed of a "salad of racial genes: a Swiss citizen, of mixed French and Austrian descent, with a dash of the Danube in his veins." Humbert's car is named "Melmoth," invoking Charles Robert Maturin's 1820 novel *Melmoth the Wanderer* about a Wandering Jew–type scholar and Anthony Trollope's Jewish financier, Augustus Melmotte, in his *The Way We Live Now* (1875). Rendered into Hebrew, Melmoth becomes m,l,m,t, which could be translated as from-to death, or as a homophone for teacher (*melamed*), which, of course, Humbert is when he reaches America. Nabokov's Humbert also resembles Svengali, the antagonist of George du Maurier's 1895 novel *Trilby*—that infamous literary embodiment of nineteenth-century English hatred of the Jew as a dirty, sinister, and predatory figure, selfishly manipulating the innocent—which was adapted into the 1954 film *Svengali*. Humbert adopts a pseudonym of "Mesmer Mesmer," being a short form of the very mesmerism at which Svengali excelled.[9]

In an "Afterword to *Lolita*," Nabokov explains the germination of the novel as the story of an ape learning to draw and producing a sketch of the bars of its cage. He gave Humbert an "attractively Simian" physiognomy, with multiple references to "ape eyes," an "ape-ear," and an "ape paw." Trilling's review mentioned Humbert's "'ape-like' lust." Nabokov's recollection uncannily mirrors Franz Kafka's 1919 story, "A Report to an Academy," in which he satirized the Jewish assimilatory experience in Western civil society by comparing it to that of a captive, mimicking ape. Nabokov perhaps acknowledged this debt by giving Humbert the name "Hamburg," precisely the place where Kafka's ape arrived.[10]

Humbert is thus often mistaken for being Jewish and hence is victim to the type of genteel anti-Semitism and various racial slurs prevalent in postwar America. Charlotte Haze, Jean and John Farlow, Quilty, and the hotel receptionists all assume, because of his foreign-sounding name, looks, physiognomy, European extraction, and manners, that he's German Jewish or Austrian Jewish. Quilty tells him, "You are either Australian [a deliberate mispronunciation of Austrian?] or a German refugee. This is a gentile's house—you'd better run along." Before marrying him, Charlotte first wants to find out precisely how "foreign" he is, as he had in his family a "certain strange strain." She can tolerate "Turk" ancestry, if he was "truly Christian," but "she would commit suicide" if she discovers he "did not believe in Our Christian God." Likewise, Jean also has a vague suspicion he may be Jewish because of his dark looks and exotic name. When her husband, John, is about to make disparaging remarks about Jews in Humbert's presence, she cuts him off. Humbert attempts to check in to the Enchanted Hunters Hotel but is initially refused because it's restricted, advertising itself as being "Near Churches," a coded expression to indicate its discriminatory practices.[11]

While Kubrick omitted many of these details, consistent with his practice of removing explicit references to Jewishness from his films, his casting choices suggest he was looking for an actor capable of producing a Jewish performance. He approached Peter Ustinov with a view of casting him as Humbert. Ustinov's great-grandfather Moritz Hall had been born Jewish before converting to Christianity. Ustinov had starred in Max Ophüls's final film, *Lola Montès* (1955), no doubt of some appeal to Kubrick, and had played Batiatus in *Spartacus* in such a way that it certainly tapped into age-old Jewish stereotypes: mercenary, salacious, mincing, cheap, and greedy. Walter M. Abbott, SJ, of the National League of Decency felt "it is offensive to the Jewish faith to have a man who is so obviously Jewish playing the role of the cowardly, venal commander of the Capua gladiator institution." Kubrick ultimately cast James Mason, who had been offered a starring role in *The Gay Life*, an adaptation of Arthur Schnitzler's *Anatol* (1893), and had previously starred in Nicholas Ray's *Bigger Than Life* (1956), in which he assumed the role of the Hebrew patriarch Abraham.[12]

Kubrick also retained or amplified many aspects of Nabokov's novel that can be read as stereotypical Jewish signifiers. Humbert is the intellectual of the film, versed in European literature, and quotes "the divine Edgar [Allan Poe]." He's educated, cosmopolitan, witty, and urbane. Like so many European Jews, he "found a haven" in America, and, like Kubrick, he's a chess player. And when Humbert narrates in the film how he was to be a "chief consultant in production of a film dealing with existentialism, still a hot thing at the time," it might also be read as a self-reflexive joke by Kubrick, referring to his first three feature films.[13]

In both novel and film Humbert is connected with many bathrooms—a key signifier of cinematic Jewishness and a Kubrick signature. Charlotte (Shelley Winters) makes a point of showing off her "old-fashioned" plumbing to Humbert, of which she is proud, and which she thinks will impress him. Humbert hides in that bathroom to write in his journal, which is where Charlotte discovers it. Following Charlotte's death, Humbert lies in the bathtub sipping Scotch. And he spies Lolita (Sue Lyon) talking to Quilty (Peter Sellers) from a bathroom window.

Humbert, like George Peatty before him, is feminized, subject to events in which he has little agency. Things are done to him rather than by him. He is a prospective lodger trapped in Charlotte's house, and she ensnares him despite his repeated attempts to back away from her relentless advances. After the high school dance, he's given pink champagne and made to do the cha-cha clumsily. Once married, he becomes the henpecked and emasculated (Jewish) husband. Charlotte calls him "Hum" and reprimands him for indulging Lolita. He complains "not all the decisions are taken by the female." He's her "bronze glamour boy," "scoot[ing] along after [her] like an obliging little lapdog." "I'm delighted to be bossed by you," he tells her through gritted teeth. When Lolita returns home unexpectedly, he asks if she's eaten and offers to make her a sandwich, which he does "loaded with mayonnaise, just the way you like it." He attempts to instruct Lolita in poetry but ends up as a trained seal being fed the reward of a fried egg, which she lowers into his mouth. On the day that Lolita leaves for camp, donning a silk dressing gown, he becomes the proverbial static, lovelorn, and forlorn "woman at the window," so generically typical of costume drama or Douglas Sirk's films. He watches Lolita leave, walks into her bedroom where he's enveloped by her feminine items, and weeps into her pillow.[14]

Ultimately, Lolita seduces *him* and thereafter he becomes her slave, as coded by the opening credits. He paints her toenails, buys her presents, does all the housework, and, like a governess, attempts to oversee her education. He finishes an argument with "and don't smudge your toenails!" In fact, he fills the gaping gap left by Charlotte, becoming the nagging, whining, domineering, needy allegorically Jewish mother figure. At the film's end, he breaks down in tears. Lolita implores him, "Come on now, don't make a scene. Stop crying!"

Humbert plays the classic schlemiel in the film. He's a model of ineptitude. His European savoir faire is continually undone, providing much of the comedy where he's concerned. The attempt at vengeful lover is undermined by his fur-trimmed topcoat and pathetic poem, which Quilty mocks even when Humbert threatens him with a gun. He cuts a pitiful killer and is repeatedly distracted and thrown off balance by Quilty's lightening wit and chameleonlike behavior. It takes repeated shots to kill Quilty, who is not even put off by his firing of the gun. Even as he dies, Quilty is unable to take Humbert seriously. And when Humbert does kill Quilty, it's almost by mistake—it takes him five shots to hit Quilty in the leg and six more to finish him off. At the high school dance Humbert is a chaperone, but he sits awkwardly on a folding chair, balancing a cup of punch in one hand and a slice of cake in the other; every attempt to follow Lolita is foiled as one or another of the characters traps him down. When he tries to murder Charlotte, he snaps open the revolver, only to spill the bullets on the floor. And he cannot even go through with it. Even though Humbert seeks to disguise his desire for Lolita, Quilty instantly recognizes it exactly for what it is. His plan to seduce Lolita happens to be right in the middle of a police convention, and he ends up sleeping on a collapsed cot, which takes much slapstick humor to erect.

In physiognomic terms, Mason fitted Nabokov's description of Humbert's hirsuteness: we see his hairy chest in the bath and as he rises from bed on the day that Lolita leaves for camp. Lolita asks him why he shaves twice a day. "All the best people do," he replies. Kubrick's various allusions to other films in *Lolita* also hint at Humbert's Jewishness. Various sequences evoke other roles played by Jewish actors. The opening toenail-painting sequence alludes to Fritz Lang's *Scarlet Street* (1945), in which Edward G. Robinson, playing an older artist besotted with the younger Joan Bennett, paints her toenails. The shooting at the painting evokes the moment in *Party Girl* (1958) when gangster Lee J. Cobb fires into a large picture of Jean Harlow, while Humbert's bathtub whiskey references tippler Robinson's similar posture in *Key Largo* (1948). Humbert presents a model of feminized Jewish masculinity, as a hairy, wandering, apelike schlemiel, but who, ultimately, is revealed to be a mensch in contrast to Quilty.[15]

Sellers's Shtick

It was in the role of Quilty that Kubrick displayed his fascination with the underside of Jewish manliness, the antithesis of Dax and Spartacus. Because Kubrick felt that *Lolita* offered humorous possibilities, he cast a comic actor. Sellers had displayed an impressively wide comedic range up to that point on *The Goon Show* (1951–1960), as well as in such films as *The Ladykillers* (1955), *The Naked Truth* (1957), and *The Battle of the Sexes* (1959), as well as on his album *The Best of Sellers* (1958). And hailing from the world of stand-up comedy and radio parody sketches, he shared an affinity with such Jewish stand-up comics as Mel Brooks, Sid Caesar, Mike Nichols, Lenny Bruce, and Elaine May.

Sellers was Jewish by birth through his "archetypal Jewish mother." Like Kubrick, Sellers didn't practice any religion nor was he bar mitzvahed. But he was circumcised, and, as the only Jewish boy at a North London Catholic school, he was certainly aware of his ethnic and religious other-ness. In an interview with the *Jewish Chronicle* in 1959, he explained how he felt Jewish emotionally, sentimentally, and gastronomically, sharing the Jewish "clannish feeling," devotion to family and children, and sense of humor. He'd also previously played on-screen and on-air roles as Jew-ish characters in *Sellers' Market* (1950), *The Goon Show*, and *Finkel's Café* (1956).[16]

Where Sellers excelled was mimicry. In a "perfect fit" between real-life and acting roles, his career to date was as a talented mimic. He had done scores of impersonations during his regular *Goon Show* appearances and played three different roles in *The Mouse That Roared* (1959). Sellers was thus the very embodiment of the condition described by Max Horkheimer and Theodor Adorno as "undisciplined mimicry," which was "engraved in the living substance of the dominated and passed down by a process of unconscious imitation in infancy from generation to generation, from the down-at-heel Jew to the rich banker." This was because "Jewish Emanci-pation involved Jews in collisions with the differentiations of Western society," John Murray Cuddihy suggests, and Jews "were being asked, in effect, to become bourgeois, and to become bourgeois quickly" but simul-taneously denounced for intruding where they didn't belong. Mimicry was the ideal strategy to overcome these barriers but even more so in Britain, where, unlike America, the "social forms and rules of decorum" required the "constant suppression of the ego" and the "impersonation of another identity entirely." British Jews had to resort to "wildly inventive" and "cha-meleonic impersonation," as required by a society dominated by class prej-udices and nuances.[17]

Kubrick adored Sellers's shtick. His stand-up sensibility permeated the film, as Sellers was given a freedom to improvise in front of the camera that Kubrick gave few other performers, before or after. Mason recalled how Sellers was "the only one allowed, or rather encouraged, to improvise his entire performance. The rest of us improvised only during rehearsals, then incorporated any departures from the original script that seemed par-ticularly effective." Kubrick, he said, "was so besotted with the genius of

Peter Sellers that he never seemed to have enough of him." And, as the two grew closer, it became clear that they shared many hobbies and the same mordant and morbid sense of humor. Christiane recalled that "Stanley and Peter were made for each other. Their ideas dove-tailed and they each spurred the other on with ideas and challenges." Vincent LoBrutto added, "The two men were bonded by a growing cynicism about life. Kubrick especially prompted Sellers to probe the darker side of the comedy of *Lolita*. Sellers had feared that his interpretation of Quilty went too far, but Kubrick assured him that larger-than-life was the essential reality."[18]

Beginning with the lines as they were sketched in the screenplay, Sellers interpreted them however he wished in devising Quilty. The preproduction script closest to shooting indicates that very little of Quilty's dialogue was locked down at this stage, suggesting that much, but not all, of it was improvised. Winters felt Sellers was "acting on a different planet." According to cinematographer Oswald Morris, "The most interesting scenes were the ones with Peter Sellers, which were total improvisations. They'd roughly block it out, go upstairs and leave me to light it, then come down with, for instance, the table tennis scene. There was nothing like that in the script, it was just off the cuff."[19]

Sellers's free reign allowed Quilty's role to greatly expand. Nabokov's character is barely realized. He sketched a hazy, veiled, fleeting, shadowy, nebulous, and desultory phantom, who's referenced in oblique allusions and coded wordplay as the "lone diner in the loud checks." He's certainly absent more than he is present. Kubrick described him as a "mysterious presence. . . . Every time we catch a glimpse of Quilty we can imagine anything, police, pervert or parent." Together, Kubrick and Sellers drew him more boldly, fleshing the bare bones of Nabokov's creation into the multifaceted performer of the film. His brief, pithy, and laconic exchanges in the novel are transformed into anxious, babbling, wise-cracking, quick-talking tics, as Quilty nervously fidgets with his glasses and speaks in broken phrases in a display of verbal diarrhea. Quilty ended up commanding greater narrative space than Nabokov's brief sketch: while Sellers appeared in only 34 minutes of the 154-minute film, he is its ubiquitous, uncanny spirit even when absent, the core of *Lolita*, whether invisible or disguised. We feel his presence even when he's not there. Even when offscreen he's omnipresent and seemingly omniscient.[20]

Kubrick and Sellers crafted Quilty into *Lolita*'s undisputed heart of darkness. *Lolita* may have been a film based on a novel named after its titular teenage girl (the word "Lolita" bookends the text), but the film verbally opens and closes with the word "Quilty." Kubrick thus transformed Nabokov's narrative of sexual infatuation with a young girl into a film emphasizing Humbert's obsession with Quilty. (Contrast this with his next film, *Dr. Strangelove*, which, although taking the hydrogen bomb as its subject, is named after a character who barely occupies any screen time.) This shift in emphasis sanctioned greater scope for Sellers's unpredictable performance that was, moreover, accentuated by Kubrick's signature style of long takes and deep focus, providing even more space for Sellers. Because Kubrick had already made the decision to shift Quilty's death from the end of the novel to the beginning of the film, which he imagined in the vein of *The Maltese Falcon* (1941), Quilty's role as the center of the film was in place before shooting began. But the upshot of Sellers's improvisations was that he played a shape-shifting character performing multiple roles—a possibly homosexual state trooper, a shadowy pursuer whose ambulism evokes the Wandering Jew stereotype, a German-émigré high school psychologist called Dr. Zemph, Lolita's uncle, and a mysterious unnamed voice on the end of the telephone during the night. Another consequence was these improvisations allowed greater possibility for detecting the subsurface allusions to Jewish masculinity, for they lent the film the quality of early 1960s Jewish stand-up humor, as if they were compiled into one long audio-visual version of a *Mad* parody. Indeed, several critics described Sellers's performance as having the feel of a "riff," "skit," "spiel," and "shtick."[21]

These elements were showcased in the film's opening sequence. Nabokov's first draft of the screenplay described the opening as a "silent shadowy sequence which should not last more than one minute." Kubrick fleshed out the scene to its eleven-minute duration, writing most of the dialogue himself, giving it a completely personal feel. In the annotated first draft of the screenplay, the entire scene is rewritten in his hand, except for the poem, "Because you took advantage." Even here, he inserted his typical brand of humor when Quilty says, "a little repetitious, what?" This key sequence provides many Jewish clues. We first meet Quilty sitting in a chair, beneath a white shroud, suggesting the tallith (prayer shawl) or *kittel* (robe) in which Orthodox Jews pray and are buried rather than Nabokov's "silk dressing gown, the sash of which he is tying as he goes." When aroused by Humbert, who asks him to confirm his identity, Quilty replies, "No, I'm Spartacus. Have you come to free the slaves or somethin'?" Not only does this refer to Kubrick's previous film, but it also obliquely points to the Jewish actor who played the title role—Kirk Douglas—in a film that can be read as a biblical epic that retells, albeit in an alternative form, the Exodus from Egypt with Spartacus liberating the slaves in a Moses-like fashion. And when Quilty realizes that the weapon-wielding Humbert intends to harm him, his initial and unconvincing move in trying to stay alive "is to make sure Humbert knows he is not a Jew." ("This is a gentile's house. You'd better run along.") This attempt to hide his Jewishness, to pass, only serves to underline it even more. Quilty inadvertently he reveals his Jewishness, for only a Jew would use the term "gentile." It echoes a statement, attributed to Kubrick: "Gentiles don't know how to worry."[22]

Quilty is an expert at mimicry, shifting between characters with chameleonlike ease, anticipating Woody Allen's much later creation, Zelig, that curiously nondescript changeable Jewish character who is discovered for his remarkable ability to transform himself to resemble anyone he is near, as depicted in the film *Zelig* (1983). Sellers is a brilliant mimic throughout the course of the film, but his mimicking abilities are highlighted during the opening sequence when, realizing he's about to die and attempting to delay it, he "runs through his repertory of accents, remembering all the identities he assumed in the past." Initially, he plays himself (at least that is what we think he does, although we can never be entirely certain). He then mimics a Texan cowboy; a hard-boiled, tough, jaded film noir cop; a boxer; a librettist; and a piano player. There was only one stage direction in the screenplay—"(imitating underworld numbskull)" when Quilty says "that's a swell little gun you've got there"—suggesting that the rest was Sellers's invention.[23]

Quilty is a wisecracking, humorous, comical, and obsessively nervous talker, an uncanny combination of city slicker, witty improviser, playwright, and librettist—all stereotypical defining features of what Michael Rogin calls "Jew is mouth as nervous brain." He's defined by intellectual rather than physical properties, manifesting Yiddische *kopf*. Indeed, Quilty's suggestion to Humbert, "We could dream up some lyrics, share the profits," recalls the successful Jewish songwriting partnerships, dating as far back as early-1900s Tin Pan Alley and continuing through 1950s Motown and rock 'n' roll.[24]

Quilty challenges Humbert to a game of Ping-Pong. After beating a clearly distracted opponent, he puts on a pair of boxing gloves and mimics punching, stating, "I wanna die like a champion." The choice of both sports, neither of which appears in the novel, seem unlikely to be accidental; Kubrick was a big fan of both. Behind each sport stretches a long history of Jewish involvement and hence can be read as Jewish clues. "Following the earlier reference to Spartacus," Gene D. Phillips suggests, "this could be another satirical jibe at Kubrick's previous association with Kirk Douglas, one of whose first starring roles was in *Champion*." Sellers may also be alluding to his maternal great-grandfather Daniel Mendoza, perhaps the greatest boxer of the eighteenth century. Mendoza probably appeared as an ideal role model to Sellers. Later, in 1960, when he planned to form Sellers-Mankowitz Productions, its logo was to be a portrait of Mendoza, whose likeness hung in the background of several of his later films. Sellers's later character Inspector Clouseau was one of Mendoza's most fervent admirers, and prints of the boxer can clearly be seen on the walls of his apartment in the *Pink Panther* series.[25]

Even when taken on its own, the opening sequence alone provides enough material for establishing the subsurface, subliminal Jewishness of Quilty, but his Jewish performativity is reinforced throughout the film. Robert Roper suggests as Sellers prepared to play the role, he scrutinized TV footage of Lionel Trilling discussing *Lolita* with Nabokov. Quilty is shown with a camera around his neck and, at one point, ordering his sidekick to fetch some Kodachrome Type A film. Jews also dominated still photography, like boxing, as they did the motion pictures, even if the public was unaware of this. We further learn that Quilty's main hobby was making "art movies"—which Kubrick explained is a "polite way of saying 'pornographic' film," yet another industry in which Jews were involved on both sides of the Atlantic but particularly in London's Soho during the 1950s.[26]

At the Ramsdale High School prom and summer dance, Quilty performs as a *Mad*esque "parody of New York cool." Wearing a white dinner jacket and a pair of black-rimmed glasses, he's accompanied by a dark-haired bohemian dressed all in black. When he speaks about Lolita, he "breaks into alliterative, literary-hipster talk," his speech patterns reminiscent of such sixties Jewish literary hipsters as Allen Ginsberg and Lenny Bruce, whom Richard Corliss feels would've made a great Quilty. The music for the sequence was taken from the Playback record *BEATNIK*. Quilty's oversized glasses resembles those that were a standard feature of Sellers's own early 1960s style and are another coded clue to Quilty's Jewishness: this "look" played into the stereotype of Jewish shortsightedness, scholarliness, and nerdiness, which Woody Allen, around this time, began to typify.[27]

Quilty's sense of parody at the high school dance is carried over when he plays the possibly homosexual state trooper. Here he mocks the odd fit between Jew and cop. A Jewish cop was often considered an oxymoron and hence treated as a fertile subject for humor, playing on what Hannah Arendt describes as "the traditional Jewish fear of the 'cop'—that seeming incarnation of a hostile world." Stereotypically, the police world was one that excluded Jews. Kubrick was very suspicious of people with power, and he considered including a sequence with a private detective called "Ben Hirsch," a stereotypically Jewish given and surname. Kubrick shot, or at least rehearsed, a scene with this character with Sellers as Quilty pretending "to be an undercover detective for a full nine minutes while poor Humbert Humbert had nothing to do but look uncomfortable." While this character was dropped, his traces are evident in Quilty's masquerade as a state trooper. Nervously talkative, his speech reveals his attempt to pass and to make a pass. Quilty's multiple references to "normality" suggest an excess, a trying too hard to be "normal" but failing. He becomes, in Homi Bhabha's formulation, "almost the same, *but not quite*." The very excess of his mimicry gives him away, highlighting his failure to pass and echoing the Jewish saying that "Jews are like everybody else, only more so."[28]

Another Kubrick/Sellers invention, the high school psychologist Zemph, provides yet more Jewish clues, as well as a further chance for Sellers's undisciplined mimicry. Appearing neither in the novel nor in any draft, Sellers had full freedom to create a character completely of his own devising. Many have decoded Zemph as a prototype of one of his later characters in his next Kubrick collaboration, the ex-Nazi Dr. Strangelove, and Kubrick later admitted that Zemph was a parody of "movie clichés about Nazis." But such comparisons miss the clear resemblance to Freud. Zemph's reference to Lolita's private jokes of her own that no one else understands subtly invokes Freud's *Jokes and the Unconscious* (1905), as does his blatant concern with Lolita's developmental health, which he coyly and repeatedly refers to as the "home situation." Zemph concludes, in a Freudian fashion, "And so, in our opinion, she is suffering from acute repression of the libido of the natural instincts." While Kubrick was an avid Freud reader, he couldn't resist poking fun at the contemporary intellectual fashion for psychoanalysis; as he had told Ustinov, "We shall treat psychiatrists [*sic*] with the same irreverence that Mr. Nabokov does in the book." Later, as the unnamed man on the telephone who calls Humbert in the middle of the night, Quilty invokes sexologist Alfred Kinsey and refers to "Freudian lingo."[29]

Zemph is also a caricature of various other Jewish figures of the period, including the émigrés Frederic Wertham, Paul Reich, and Herbert Marcuse, all of whom were writing and in the public eye in the 1950s and early

1960s. Roper even suggests that Zemph "borrows [Lionel] Trilling's bit-ing way with certain loaded words ('sex,' 'sexual'), and Trilling's way with a cigarette." The critic for the *New York Mirror* felt Zemph was a "menacing Sid Caesar–type Viennese official." Certainly, his name is a parody of the profession in a fashion worthy of *Mad* in that Zemph can be interpreted as *Senf* (German: mustard), as in "to cut the mustard" sexually, another of the myriad sexual jokes that punctuated *Lolita*.[30]

The "physician" in general and the psychologist in particular (indeed psychology as a whole—the "talking cure") have both been associated with Jews. Sander Gilman refers to the "quite powerful" image of the Jewish doctor that haunts anti-Semitic literature, as well as the work of such Jew-ish physicians as Schnitzler. Kubrick may also have been influenced here by Kafka's short story, "A Country Doctor" (1917). Humbert is referred to as "Dr. Humbert," and, of course, Kubrick's father was a (homeopathic) physician.[31]

As Zemph, Quilty even draws attention to his own mimicry, furtively lifting his thick, oversized glasses to light a cigarette since he cannot see what he is doing with them on. Humbert fails to notice this clear hint. He's also left-handed, drawing on age-old stereotypes of the Jew as sinister. He's shot from the side, emphasizing his "Jewish" profile. He offers Hum-bert a Drome cigarette and suggests that he "keep ze pack"—yet another clue to Zemph's real identity as Quilty—that Humbert fails to decode despite the poster of Quilty advertising that very brand in Lolita's room. Gilman suggests smoking was another sign of Jewish otherness. Zemph also sits in the dark to save Humbert the expense of the electricity—perhaps another clue, pointing to the stereotype of Jewish miserliness and stingi-ness. When he says *schving*, it sounds suspiciously Yiddish. And when he says "we Americans" in a thick Germanic accent, he's chiding Humbert for his inability to pass.[32]

Although Quilty tells Humbert, "My name is really obscure and unre-markable," it's replete with allusion, suggesting "guilt/guilty," "quill" (pen), and "quilt" (patchwork), all features that define Jewishness. His first name, already noted for being ambiguous in its gender, further reinforces his sexual ambivalence, as well as suggesting the very opposite of its French homophone, *clair* or "clear" (itself an anagram of Clare). It might also indi-cate "clearly guilty" or a "clear text." "Quilt" suggests "stitching and weav-ing, the joining together of layers of fabric; in other words, a signifier with connotations of the word textile—and hence text." A quilt also suggests

FIGURE 5   Clare Quilty (Peter Sellers) showcases his mimicry as Dr. Zemph, as Humbert Humbert (James Mason) looks on in *Lolita* (1962).

many layers, like the disguises of Quilty. As quilts, stitching, and weaving are all conventionally a "woman's" activity, it is another effeminate association of Quilty with the Jewish male stereotype. Textiles, or *schmattes* (Yiddish), are another common Jewish signifier, given Jews' long-standing, disproportionate involvement in the garment trade. Kubrick's grandfather and great-grandfather were both tailors from Poland, and his parents lived in Manhattan's garment district before moving to the West Bronx in 1927.[33]

Prevert

According to Christiane, Kubrick "thought *Lolita* was a fantastic book because it clarified the feeling that we all have that good and evil does not come in the expected package." It therefore allowed him to continue his exploration into the nature of humanity, manliness, and evil. If one takes Quilty's various attributes as coded as Jewish, then his character and especially the way Sellers portrays him suggest a potential reading of him as a villainous, if not diabolical, Jewish pervert (or "prevert," to appropriate a term from his next film with Kubrick).[34]

In the novel Quilty's lifestyle is described by Lolita as "all drink and drugs. And of course, he was a complete freak in sex matters." Sellers's Quilty is sybaritic and louche. He has had affairs with Charlotte, Lolita, and Vivian Darkbloom (Marianne Stone), an anagram of whose name is Vladimir Nabokov and who can also be "read as a cross-gendered if sinister version of the half-Jewish Leopold Bloom from *Ulysses*." There are many Joycean references in the novel, and the *London Evening News* reported that Sellers had signed up to play Leopold Bloom in *Ulysses* following *Lolita*. Quilty is a sadistic and gratuitous torturer of the increasingly desperate and paranoid Humbert; his masquerade as the state trooper, like the nighttime phone call, highlights his cruelty. He wants Lolita *and* to torment Humbert. His discarding of both mother and daughter is done for the self-gratification of his own ego. He has no superego; he is all id.[35]

It's also suggested that Quilty is bisexual, or at least sexually ambiguous. His given name, Clare, is androgynous. He's feminized in both film and novel, referred to as "Aunt Clare." Lolita tells Humbert in the novel: "Sometimes . . . you are quite revoltingly dumb. First, Vivian is the male author, the gal author is Clare." Quilty is also a cross-dresser. The first instance is when he hides behind the Gainsborough-like portrait of the young woman at the outset. In one draft, he plays "Miss Pratt," Beardsley College's headmistress—described in the novel as a "huge woman, grey-haired, frowsy, with a broad flat nose and small eyes behind black-rimmed glasses"—in drag. This was the plan until shooting took place. Three days later Pratt was discarded and Zemph inserted voicing what remained of her dialogue. It was also possible that Sellers was planning to burlesque a psychopathologist who appeared in an earlier draft. Named Dr. Blanche Schwarzman, her surname suggests Jewish ethnicity, and both names hint at Nabokov and Kubrick's twin chess obsessions, given that her name literally translates as "White Blackman." Another clear association with Blanche Schwarzman as "White Blackman" is its biracial aspect, which, given Jews' historical identification with blacks, adds another (hypersexual) Jewish aspect. At the last minute, however, according to James Harris, Sellers and Kubrick agreed that it was a "bit too broad (no pun intended)" to have him impersonate a woman so this idea was abandoned, and the character of Zemph "was more or less invented on the spot." Nevertheless, negatives and miniature prints show how Sellers appeared in the role.[36]

It's not clear where to locate Quilty's polymorphous perversity, but the dialogue offers many suggestive clues. He's portrayed as being overtly camp, and the summer camp Lolita attends is named "Camp Q." He introduces innuendo at the very outset when he suggests a game of table tennis, in which a testicular Ping-Pong ball is batted back and forth while Humbert holds a phallic gun and during which he says, "I'll take the service again, if you don't mind. I sort of like to have it up this end." Later, at the Enchanted Hunters Hotel, he engages the hotel receptionist, George Swine (William Greene), in a very loaded conversation, similarly replete with sexual double entendres. The casting notes on Greene describe him as "t[all] U.S. homosexucual [sic]—from Georgia good looking." Monsignor Thomas F. Little of the Catholic Legion of Decency certainly felt that the tone between the men in this scene blatantly portrayed a homosexual advance. Quilty's encounter with Humbert on the porch that evening is similarly homoerotic. Assuming a passive posture, he bends over the rail of the dark veranda of the hotel, keeping his back to Humbert, acting nervously and slightly effeminately. Quilty's near obsessive repetition of the word "normal" five times serves to undermine that very normality by its very excessiveness.[37]

These various traits fitted into the stereotype of the dangerous, primitive, predatory, sleazy, sex-obsessed, and sexually deviant Jew who was, simultaneously, a seductive and devilish monster as well as an unmanly, weak, effeminate sissy, outside the norm of goyish masculinity. This Jew was the product of Christian theology, medieval anti-Jewish polemics, religious art, Victorian English literature (consider Mr. Isaacs, Fagin, Svengali), and anti-Semitic propaganda such as Veit Harlan's *Jud Süss*. In Kubrick's words, Quilty was "mysterious and sinister," "like something out of a nightmare."[38]

Kubrick coaxed a nuanced subsurface ethnicity that both actor and director shared from Sellers's improvised and mercurial performance. Sellers had hitherto tended to play Jews as "oy-vay caricatures, with names like Geraldo or Izzy." Yet, in so doing, an unresolved tension between Kubrick and Sellers's Jewishness and the intentionality behind the potentially anti-Semitic character they created remains. For those able to read the signs, maybe it is attributable to playfulness or a reversal of stereotypes. Kubrick seemingly sensed something in the novel's characterization of Quilty that struck a chord and resounded as Jewish, hence his casting of Sellers in the first place. In so doing, possibly Kubrick uncovered a facet of the novel of which even Nabokov was unaware, a detail folded into the author's description of Quilty as a "semi-animated subhuman trickster," which his keen eye picked up and amplified (and Nabokov had described Quilty in ways that emphasized his hairiness).[39]

While Quilty is clearly evil, Humbert is more of a mensch. Kubrick softened him by reducing the smarmy moral ambiguity, narcissism, depravity, and perversity of Nabokov's character, removing any references to his violent behavior toward Lolita and his first wife, Valerie. Instead, he emphasized Humbert's suaveness, sophistication, cosmopolitanism, wit, and urbanity. Humbert's attempts to kill Charlotte are diluted and rendered half-hearted. We never truly believe he's a killer, and when she does die, it's not even by his own hand. Kubrick's casting of Winters and changes to her character, making her a cartoonish caricature, ensure sympathy with Humbert's frustrated anxiety rather than identification with her hurt and humiliation. Likewise, Lolita is rendered as a materialistic and self-absorbed brat who dominates Humbert, who is seemingly more mesmerized by Lolita than he mesmerizes her. He becomes more of an undignified pathetic and abject victim than perpetrator, and their road trip seems "like a harmless romp" rather than the illegal abduction of an underage girl. Thereafter, Humbert becomes a Charlotte replacement, an exasperated parent, nagging Lolita and arguing with her over dates, parties, homework, and the school play. By contrast, Nabokov's Humbert was clearly a pedophile, and Nabokov emphasized his abuse of Lolita. In the novel he overhears her crying every night, and when he translated *Lolita* into Russian, he added that Humbert molests Lolita three times a day.[40]

Kubrick seemingly sympathized with Humbert. He told Terry Southern in 1962, "Nabokov was brilliant in withholding any indication of the author's approval of the relationship," and "the really genuine and selfless love [Humbert] has for her is revealed." He pointed out Lolita seduces Humbert, and called *Lolita* a "tragic romance" and "one of the great love stories": "I think the most important thing to say about 'Lolita' is that it is a love story. A sad, tender, eventually heartbreaking story of passion-love." In fact, Harris-Kubrick Pictures proposed treating the story as a comedy, based on "the humor that arose from the problems of a mature man married to a gum-chewing teenager." Geoffrey Shurlock describes their intentions as "the story of a bitter-sweet relationship between a middle-aged man married to a very young wife. . . . There would be no suggestion whatever of anything perverted in this relationship. The man would fall genuinely in love with what looked like an innocent young girl, marry her, and then discover that she was no good, and that he had ruined her life."[41]

Kubrick's downplaying of Humbert's worst traits may have been done to appease the Production Code Administration, and preempt any controversy, but it had the effect of rendering Humbert much better than Nabokov's protagonist. Shurlock noted that the topic of an "elderly man having an affair with a twelve-year old girl" would probably fall into the "prohibited" area of "sex perversion." Sue Lyon was "too old to play Lolita, so Humbert seems less sick and less grotesque, more human," wrote Hollis Alpert in the *Saturday Review*. By making Lolita older, so that she did not look childlike, Humbert appears "normal, not perverse." Also, the "fact that the relationship is technically incestuous" is not emphasized. Instead, Harris and Kubrick worked to make the result "unglamorous." Even his attempted seduction of Lolita is comic, distancing us from his actions.[42]

Humbert, unlike Quilty, we discover, is more than just a pedophile, cynically preying on underage girls, but truly loves and cares for Lolita irrespective of her age and looks. He treats her tenderly and with compassion. Stanley Kauffman, writing in the *New Republic*, states, "Humbert is not, in the movie, a 'gonad nomad,' but has become a 'trusty, trustful Tristram.'" Kubrick and Harris even proposed a wedding between Humbert and Lolita. But ending the film as he did, in line with Trilling's thinking (and one of Kubrick's reasons for killing Quilty at the beginning of the film rather than at the end as in the novel), was so "the story will end on heartbreak." Kubrick showed that "when Humbert sees her again four years later, and she's no longer by any stretch of the definition a nymphet, that the really genuine and selfless love he has for her is revealed." Humbert genuinely loves Lolita, unlike Quilty who uses her and throws her away when he's done ("because you took advantage"). By killing Quilty at the outset, the film's finale focuses and ends on the lone tragic and sentimental figure of Humbert. While he is indeed a pedophile, we're therefore encouraged to sympathize with him as the broken-hearted character, seeking to take justifiable revenge on the man who robbed him of his love.[43]

Humbert and Quilty represent one of Kubrick's most deeply rooted obsessions: the double. Pauline Kael describes Quilty as Humbert's "walking paranoia." He's Humbert's "grotesque alter ego and parodic Double," just as Humbert Humbert is a double name. Thus, Kubrick used both, potentially Jewish, characters to code the mensch/goyish binary but, shockingly, both play rival pedophiles. What better way to subvert the moral simplicities of *Spartacus* and *Paths of Glory*, but also to question the values of the wider society, when Quilty compares them to "two *civilized* Roman senators."[44]

Q-Brick

Jerold J. Abrams writes how "Kubrick identifies with the Hamlet-changeling director character of Quilty, the smartest man in the play who is always controlling the action, always the Minotaur hidden behind the scenes. They are directing the game, just as Quilty is directing the game of 'Roman Ping-Pong' at the beginning of the film and every subsequent game that Humbert loses. And when they recede back behind the scenes, after momentary involutions, we know that they are only temporarily masked behind Quilty, whose mask is always changing—sometimes a policeman, sometimes Kubrick himself." Alexander Walker states, "To watch (as I did) Sellers improvising his monologues in *Lolita* and *Dr. Strangelove*, with Kubrick feeding him the oxygen of his own inspiration when the actor grew short of creative breath, was to be witness to a rare double act."[45]

Nabokov's description of Quilty certainly shares many characteristics with Kubrick. "Born in Ocean City, NJ. Educated at Columbia University. Started on a commercial career but turned to playwriting. . . . Hobbies: fast cars, photography, pets." Bronx-born Kubrick audited classes at Columbia, loved photography, and worked as a photojournalist before turning to filmmaking. He owned various fast cars, dogs, and cats; according to Christiane, "Stanley liked [animals] even more [than her] because he never had any." Like Kubrick, Quilty is a film director (of sorts) with Hollywood experience, where he promises to take Lolita to write "one of those spectaculars" (such as *Spartacus*). He wants to put Lolita in an "art movie." His first words to Humbert are a reference to *Spartacus*. It's tempting to compare Quilty's plays, *The Little Nymph*, *The Strange Mushroom*, and *Fatherly Love* to *Lolita*, *Dr. Strangelove*, and *Barry Lyndon*/*The Shining*, respectively. Throughout the novel Quilty is referred to as "Cue" or "Q," and Kubrick's family insisted their name be pronounced as *Kyu*-brick rather than Koo-brick. Although set in America, the film was mainly shot in Hertfordshire, where Kubrick lived until his death in 1999.[46]

These somewhat superficial similarities are reinforced in the film. Quilty's first action is to challenge Humbert to a game of Ping-Pong, which Kubrick often played in real life. Christiane recalled that "Stanley was never a great practical sportsman but he made an exception for table tennis." In stills from the set Lyon, Mason, and Sellers are playing between takes, and Kubrick "communicated his enthusiasm" to them. When Quilty tells Humbert, "I intend moving to England or Florence forever," it foreshadows Kubrick's decision to relocate there permanently.[47]

Kubrick was also a passionate boxing fan. He'd photographed the sport for *Look*, and his first film was a documentary about a prize-fighter, which also informed his second feature. Quilty's nomadic wanderings, trailing Humbert and Lolita, before disappearing with her, recall Kubrick's time at *Look* when he was constantly on the road. In several of his appearances Quilty wears a 35 mm still camera strapped around his neck, much like the one Kubrick can be seen wearing in behind-the-scenes publicity shots taken during *Lolita*'s production. He and Sellers shared a love of photography and home movie making, and they would often photograph each other at work. They corresponded about cameras and film stock long after they ceased working together. There are other deliberate coincidences: Jack Brewster, Quilty's friend, is James Harris, and Christiane "played" Lolita in the principal car for the closer shots. Quilty's silent companion, the dark-haired enigmatic-looking beauty, Vivian Darkbloom, resembles Kubrick's wives Toba Metz and Ruth Sobotka. Both women had adopted the Greenwich Village beatnik look and lifestyle, and both had played nonspeaking characters, like Darkbloom, in *Fear and Desire* and *Killer's Kiss*, respectively. Quilty's aura of New York beatnik resembled Kubrick's late fifties "hipster" look.[48]

James Naremore suspects that at times Sellers was also imitating Kubrick. In a distinctive Bronx accent, Quilty orders Brewster to "Go and get some Type-A Kodrachrome," much as Kubrick probably did in real life. As aforementioned, Sellers's speech patterns are also reminiscent of Lenny Bruce, whom Kubrick resembled, according to Herr. Sellers, in part, modeled his American accent on that of Jewish jazz impresario Norman Granz, who recorded some of Quilty's dialogue for him to study and mimic, a form of music Kubrick was passionate about.[49]

Kubrick, like Quilty, is ubiquitous, an uncanny presence, even when absent, the center of *Lolita*. In Ariadne-esque fashion, he leaves us a trail of crumbs that lead to a possible (albeit not certain) encoding of this Minotaur. As if to guide us, during the dissolve from the exterior to the interior of Quilty's mansion at the beginning of the film, as Humbert enters Quilty's mansion, a figure can be briefly seen walking across the set from the center of the screen and stooping out of the way bottom right. IMDb suggests that it is Kubrick himself, inadvertently or deliberately interpolating himself into the opening scene. One viewer wrote to Kubrick, "I swear to this day, there is a man jumping out of camera range seen almost subliminally when Mason first enters Sellers' castle-like residence at the beginning of the picture; how could you allow such a colossal goof to pass?" Given

FIGURE 6 A spectral presence exits the frame in *Lolita* (1962); legend suggests it is Kubrick himself.

Kubrick's attention to detail and supervision of the final edit, it is unlikely that he missed this slip.[50]

Parodying Stereotypes

The 1960s were also an era when American Jewish filmmakers began to introduce a wider range of Jewish themes and characters into their films in a fashion not seen since the 1920s. But Hollywood still tended to shy away from explicit Jewishness unless located in ancient or contemporary Israel. In modern America, though, Jewishness was introduced "through the metaphor of the alienated outsider." This was perfectly embodied by Humbert and Quilty. But, if so, Kubrick created seemingly negative caricatures of Jews in *Lolita*. It's hard not to read the characterizations as intentional, an inside joke, or a series of jokes, about Jews as Jews and stereotypes of Jews. *Lolita* can be contextualized as part of a wider Jewish American strategy of assimilation in the late 1950s and early 1960s. Jonathan Freedman suggests that Jewish men had one of two choices in rejecting goyim naches: "they had to display exquisite ethical sensitivity, perform acts of earnest self-sacrifice, display strenuous intellectualism" or "see themselves as degenerates, perverts—as the very figures that this ethical imperative was intended to relieve them from embodying." If *Paths of Glory* and *Spartacus* embody the first choice, then *Lolita* is characterized by the second.[51]

Another "response to that dilemma" was "to revel in the role of the Jewish pervert, to play to the hilt," to subject it to "comic scrutiny and hence critique." Kubrick certainly intended to make the film essentially a comedy, as it provided a great chance for humor. His concerns to skewer the social, political, and intellectual issues of the times made *Lolita* into a "light, long, complex social" and "suburban satire." Pauline Kael describes it as "black slapstick," which, at times, was "so far out that you gasp as you laugh." Karyn Stuckey has pointed out how many of Kubrick's alterations to Nabokov's screenplay injected both comedy and sarcasm. Thus, with *Lolita*, his first film as a mature, independent director, he was deliberately playful with stereotypes, using an underlying and Jewish-inflected humor to make cogent and deeply serious points about post-Holocaust Jewish masculinity, particularly at a time when explicit Jewish characters, played by Jewish actors, were not as much in evidence in Hollywood cinema as they were to become.[52]

Conclusion

Kubrick continued his inquiry into, and reckoning with, his Jewishness in *Lolita* through his exploration of Jewish masculinity and menschlikayt. Given that he had been contemplating adapting the novel since July 1958, some of this material naturally found its way into *Spartacus*. But because of the fraught nature of that production's process, containing a myriad of other interventions, his particular voice and vision was not as fully defined or developed as he wished. His almost total control over *Lolita*, by contrast, allowed him to express himself in a much more realized fashion. Before *Spartacus*, he was a commercial failure; with *Spartacus* he became a major player, albeit, and somewhat ironically, without full control. *Lolita*, though, was his first film in which, as a major Hollywood player, he stamped his individuality and authorial signature, as well as work out his auteurist style, and hence was the major turning point in his career, setting the pattern for what came after.

4

Banality and the Bomb

If *Lolita* showcased Kubrick's New York Jewish sense of sick and black humor, it was taken to a new mordant level in *Dr. Strangelove*. The United States was in the middle of Cold War nuclear brinkmanship when the film was being made and was slated to be released just over a year after the Cuban Missile Crisis of October 1962. By envisaging nuclear apocalypse because of human incompetence, it drew on the very real contemporary fears of Mutual Assured Destruction (MAD). Underlying this humor lay Kubrick's signature concerns of men, menschlikayt, and Jewish masculinity, as well as another very serious topic, one that he shared with other Jewish academics and intellectuals at that time: the Holocaust. *Dr. Strangelove* was Kubrick's most extended, and scholarly, engagement with the topic yet and betrayed how, in the late 1950s and early 1960s he, like many others, conflated the Nazi genocide of the Holocaust with nuclear holocaust.

How Kubrick Started to Make a Film about the Bomb

Kubrick had already begun worrying about the possibility of mass nuclear destruction by the late 1950s. In 1958 he told a friend he was seriously considering moving to Australia because it was one of the few places likely to escape nuclear conflict and well out of the USSR's nuclear range. Following a recommendation from Alastair Buchan, director of the Institute for Strategic Services in London, in October 1961 he read and decided to adapt Peter Bryant's *Two Hours to Doom* (1958), published in the United States the following year as *Red Alert* under his own name, Peter George. The novel narrates how an insane U.S. general launches an unauthorized preemptive nuclear strike on the Soviet Union, but cooperation between the Cold War powers narrowly prevents disaster. After buying the rights for $3,500, Kubrick plunged deep into research, reading some seventy to eighty books and journals about nuclear warfare, rows of which lined his office. He consulted with prominent nuclear strategists such as Herman Kahn and Albert Wohlstetter, whose works he'd read. In early 1962, together with George, Harris and Kubrick began working on the screenplay. Later that year hip writer Terry Southern was hired to assist with parts of the writing. Shooting began on January 28, 1963, and lasted until May 24, and the film was released in the United States on January 29, 1964, having originally been scheduled for November 22, 1963, but postponed when President John F. Kennedy was assassinated.[1]

Kubrick's choice of subject showed how close he was to concerns of the New York Intellectuals in the early 1960s. Like *Lolita*, *Dr. Strangelove* engaged with the same dilemmas and paradoxes as the intellectual New Yorkers. In theme and style *Lolita* and *Dr. Strangelove* formed a Cold War diptych, exploring American Cold War domestic and foreign policy, respectively. Two sides of the same coin, they cohered into an alternative New York intellectual critique, skewering the key intellectual fads of the period. In blaming both sides for nuclear apocalypse, Kubrick very much dovetailed with revisionist takes on U.S. foreign policy, as well as fascination with nuclear brinkmanship, that swirled around such journals as *Commentary*, which began to publish revisionist New Left foreign policy analyses that overturned previously sacrosanct U.S. orthodoxies by blaming the onset of the Cold War on America as much as the USSR. Nuclear disarmament and pacifism became key concerns, and many American intellectuals advocated unilateral U.S. nuclear disarmament to reduce the danger of nuclear war and to end the Cold War in general.

But Kubrick parted company with the New York Intellectuals in his refusal to be identified with a political position and to take a stance. When he engaged in the issue of disarmament, he avoided taking sides and making pronouncements on the issue, while also staying aloof from the peaceniks. In an unpublished note on the film, he wrote, "I'm against everybody. The joint chiefs and the nitwit liberals and the sit-downers." And in response to a letter from SANE (National Committee for a Sane Nuclear Policy), he replied, "Though I obviously share most of their views and objectives (the film speaks for that) I have avoided any identification with Peace Groups because I believe this film and my future films will have more impact coming from an uncommitted source, not easily labeled as a Peace Group effort." In this way, Kubrick resembled the alternative New York intellectual voices, such as *Mad* magazine, whose publisher, William Gaines, stated, "we like to say that *Mad* has no politics and that we take no point of view." *Mad* may have been critical of Cold War America, but it never sympathized with the New Left revolt against it either. Indeed, student radicalism also became its target. Neither did *Mad* offer any affirmations of or alternatives to the consumerist and conformist American way of life that it purportedly held in such contempt. This consistent inconsistency ran counter to the dynamics of the New York Intellectuals, which were clearly aligned on ideological and political grounds.[2]

Sick Humor

Kubrick also distinguished himself from the New York Intellectuals by his use of sick or black humor to tackle the topic of MAD. *Dr. Strangelove* was an anti–Cold War film in the same mordant vein as *Mad* and the *Realist*. Both spoofed Cold War attitudes. Kubrick not only parodied fears of the Soviet Union but also deconstructed the ideas that lay behind them. He assailed the core values that informed postwar American foreign policy, as articulated in such directives as the Truman Doctrine and National Security Council Report 68. He ridiculed American fears of communism as absurd statements and a set of banal clichés. Through the character of Gen. Jack D. Ripper (Sterling Hayden) and his obsession with fluoridation as a dastardly commie plot, for example, Kubrick satirized the Cold War linkage of communism, disease, and sexual impotence. Sexual and scatological humor permeate the film, as Kubrick directed his satire at generals, soldiers, politicians, and even the president himself, turning on everyone, including the Soviets, Americans, and British equally. Politicians, peaceniks, military brass, and the common soldier all came into his sights. No one was safe from his attack. The whole film came together to form a biting parody, assailing America's most respected institutions during the fifties and early sixties.[3]

Kubrick described his untitled film as an "irreverent, vicious, satirical comedy. It's [*sic*] objective will be to kick a few sacred cows and in the process examine some of the widely held attitudes and theories of the Bomb. It will be in the satirical tradition of Aristophanes, Juvenal and Swift." He elaborated that he "chose to tell our story this way as a reaction to the stupefying reverence with which the subject has been approached in the past." To this end, he discarded *Red Alert*'s deadly straight and clearly anticommunist tone. He retained its plot outline, but made significant changes in introducing comedy and satire. Unlike *Lolita*, in which the satire was already intact, particularly in its use of names, puns, and double entendres, Kubrick injected *Red Alert* with black and sick humor, although many bits of original dialogue remained unchanged, showing just how close to comedy the Cold War mind-set was in reality. According to Southern, "[Kubrick] told me he was going to make a film about 'our failure to understand the dangers of nuclear war'. He said that he had thought of the story as a 'straight forward melodrama,' until this morning—when he 'woke up and realized that nuclear war was too outrageous, too fantastic to be treated in any conventional manner.' He said he could only see it now as 'some kind of hideous joke.'" James Harris objected to this approach and they parted company.[4]

Kubrick's satirical approach, in contrast to the New York Intellectuals' tone of high moral seriousness, meant he came much closer to resembling the sensibility of the alternative New York intellectual influences of the early sixties, in particular, Paul Krassner's the *Realist*, Jules Feiffer, Lenny Bruce, Mort Sahl, Mike Nichols, Elaine May, Shelley Berman, Tom Lehrer, Joseph Heller, the Beats, Bob Dylan, and *Mad*. Michael Broderick argues that Krassner's *Realist* magazine "had the most evident, though more indirect, influence on the film." For years Kubrick had been attempting to work with cartoonist and graphic novelist Feiffer, a Bronx-born acquaintance whom he knew from his youth. Impressed with *Sick, Sick, Sick* (1958), he approached Feiffer to collaborate during the early stages of *Dr. Strangelove*. Feiffer fleetingly worked on the script but received no credit, so his precise contribution is still unknown. Kubrick contacted Joseph Heller, having admired his satirical antiwar novel *Catch-22*. Kubrick sent him a copy of *Red Alert* and suggested they get together for a "chat" once he'd read it. While David Seed suggests Kubrick wanted Heller to cowrite the screenplay, the letter is inconclusive on that front. Nevertheless, the finished result struck Heller as similar in comic technique to *Catch-22*'s use of satire, farce, burlesque, and puns. Kubrick also asked Lenny Bruce to collaborate on a film. While this never materialized, he did briefly engage Bruce's close friend, Southern, in late 1962 to beef up the screenplay.[5]

Kubrick also thought of drawing his cast from the alternative intellectuals. He considered Theodore J. Flicker, who during the early 1950s was one of the early members of the improv comedy troupe Chicago's Compass Players, appearing alongside Elaine May. By 1960 Flicker had moved to New York City and begun performing in and producing *The Premise*, an irreverent revue in Greenwich Village. Kubrick also contemplated hiring other Jewish comedians, including Shelley Berman, Jerry Lewis, and Jackie Mason.[6]

The titular figure of Dr. Strangelove, in seeming to invoke Wernher von Braun, also drew on early sixties Jewish humor. Jewish comic Tom Lehrer sang, "'Once the rockets are up, who cares where they come down? That's not my department,' says Wernher von Braun." Both *Monocle* and

FIGURE 7 A Lenny Bruce poster can clearly be seen in *The Killing* (1956).

the *Outsider's Newsletter*, set up by Jewish New Yorker Victor Navasky in 1957 and 1962, respectively, anticipated *Dr. Strangelove*, particularly in their adept burlesques of von Braun, Herman Kahn, and their military collaborators. One cartoon depicted a statue of von Braun clutching a missile, saying "I Aim At The Stars," and pointed out that the engineer who had helped to develop the V-2 rocket for the Nazis had switched his allegiance from the "Master Race" to the "Space Race."[7]

At the same time, Kubrick felt that the "only honest way" to treat nuclear war was in a "Kafkaesque" fashion. By this he meant a simple, straightforward, humdrum routine, based on the everyday and ordinary. He explained to Heller, "This is where the laughs are, in this thing of banality and reality and absurdity intruding into something we imagine is immune." He referred to the "improbable comic nightmare characters of Kafka" and *Dr. Strangelove*'s ending, which can be read as an homage to Orson Welles's adaptation of Franz Kafka's *The Trial* (1962), which, unlike the novel, ends with an explosion. Various sequences are characterized by attention to detail and documentary realism, particularly the interior of the B-52 bomber and the ground-attack sequences. Kubrick found absurdity in the banality of everyday life. A Coca-Cola vending machine plays a crucial role in the attempt to prevent nuclear catastrophe. The serious disclaimer that prefaces *Dr. Strangelove* appears to be yet another of the film's jokes (mimicking that which opened *Day of the Fight*). The use of cinema verité to shoot the sequences in which Rangers attack and storm Burpelson Air Force Base, combined with the realistic interior detail of the War Room and the B-52 bomber, serve to intensify the satiric effect, as Kubrick imagined the unfolding of the apocalypse through a series of absurdities against the backdrop of total nuclear devastation: the Soviet premier forgetting the telephone number of his general staff's headquarters and suggesting his U.S. counterpart contact Omsk Information instead, an American colonel refusing to smash a Coca-Cola machine because it's private property, and a vast, well-stocked buffet table, featuring gourmet foods and pastries (recalling *The Seafarers*), in the War Room. James Earl Jones, who played bomber crew member Lt. Lothar Zogg, recalled, "One curious thing was that he always had us eating. Every time he'd cut to us, we'd be eating a Twinkie—just constantly stuffing our faces. That was a comment about how people deal with fear. I think he liked the mundane aspect of horrific events."[8]

Kubrick's New York sicknik humor was particularly evident in his use of sexual and scatological puns. This was especially so in the carnal concerns as reflected in the names of *Dr. Strangelove*'s characters: Gen. Jack D. Ripper, Group Capt. Lionel Mandrake, President Merkin Muffley, Gen. Buck Turgidson, Ambassador De Sadesky, Premier Kissoff, Col. Bat Guano, Maj. King Kong, and Dr. Strangelove himself. An early draft screenplay—before Southern was drafted in—had a cast list that included Private Charlie Stiffsocks, Private Tung, Sergeant Blunt, Gen. "Buck" Schmuck, Von Klutz, Zlat, Frankenstein, Cadaverly, Didley, Crudley, Waffel, Moffo, Kulnick, Funkel, M. P. Orderly, Major Nonce, Capt. "Ace" Angst, Lt. Quentin Quiffer, Lt. "Binky" Ballmuff, Lt. Terry Toejam, Colonel Puntrich, Miss Milky Way, Miss Pietraskiewicz, and Premier Belch. Other (pre-Southern) versions mentioned General Klapp, Mrs. Hammerhead, Major Mountcalm, Senator Blood, Dildo, Senator John Applekuegel, and Lt. Irving "Doc" Schwartz.[9]

Several names stand out here for manifesting Kubrick's New York Jewish sense of humor. Klutz is Yiddish for "clod; a clumsy, slow-witted, graceless person; an inept blockhead." The prefix of the "von" Germanizes the name, incongruously making this Yiddische *klutz* into Teutonic aristocracy. *Mad*'s "Strangely Believe It" (no. 42, November 1955), written by guest contributor Ernie Kovacs, features a "Dr. Sidney Klutz." In 1957 Kubrick and Harris went to see *Operation Mad Ball* (1957), starring Kovacs, which they both loved. Together with Kovacs they began to research the idea of a television series based on his character. It never materialized. Gen. Buck Schmuck's name drew on the Yiddish term for a "dope, a jerk, a boob; a clumsy, bumbling fellow." It also means "penis," making it very appropriate that Turgidson (George C. Scott) oversees "SAC." There are hints of Lenny Bruce in this name, too, for in October 1962 he was arrested for using the word "schmuck" on stage. Perhaps this scared Kubrick off from using that name in the film. Next to Schmuck's name in the screenplay is a footnote either warning or mockingly pointing out: "The name Schmuck appears on page 1491 of the 1961–62 Manhattan telephone directory." General Schmuck was renamed Turgidson. Even though Turgidson lost his "schmuck" moniker, he still, in palimpsestic fashion, played like one; lacking social awareness, even under the most serious of circumstances—potential nuclear holocaust—he's a buffoon. In his "Notes to Translators and Dubbing Directors," Kubrick insisted that Turgidson "should be played by a boisterous and loud person," and Kubrick's secretary, Pat Ivens, described Scott's performance as "his schmuckiest." Applekuegel is a variant spelling of apple kugel, a popular Ashkenazi Jewish pudding of the type that Kubrick probably grew up eating. Kubrick described him as a "rightwinger—half Jewish" ("I am half Jewish," Applekuegel says). Another document features a long and exhaustive list of characters including, among others, a rabbi, beatnik couple, bohemian woman, and an American communist. These last four might well have been Jewish. Even if these characters and ideas did not make it to the final version, their traces stamp the film with the quality of sixties sicknik Jewish humor.[10]

Dr. Strangelove further resembled the sixties sick sensibility in its scatological humor. Kubrick explained, "Confront a man in his office with a nuclear alarm, and you have a documentary. If the news reaches him in his living room, you have a drama. If it catches him in the lavatory, the result is comedy." Turgidson is introduced when he's in the toilet, where he's "very tied up" and "catching up" on some "paperwork." He later compares nuclear war to sex or defecation—"we'd stand a damn good chance of catching 'em with their pants down." One of the most scatological moments was in the cut final act when Ambassador De Sadesky (here named De Sade) is caught with two cameras hidden on his person. The president orders him strip-searched.

SCHMUCK: Zlat, make sure the secret service boys carefully search his *seven bodily orifices.*

DE SADE: (Horrified) *My seven bodily orifices?????*

SCHMUCK: That's right, fella.

DE SADE: (Touches ears) One, two … (touches each nostril) three … four … (touches mouth) five … (freezes, turns red and swallows hard) Why you dirty, stinking …

This prompts a mass custard pie fight, which stepped right out of the Jewish vaudeville tradition or a Marx Brothers movie. This scene was cut from the final reel, but its absurdity permeates the film nonetheless. What was a buffet doing there in the first place other than to provide an opportunity for such a sequence? Perhaps it reflected a (Jewish mother's) concern that the gentlemen in the War Room might get hungry and need to eat. At the very least, it provided the opportunity for several jokes. Meanwhile, as Kubrick was working on postproduction for *Dr. Strangelove*, he registered the title *Secret Uses of Uranus.*[11]

Even Kubrick's aesthetic in these films came to resemble *Mad*'s. He inserted visual flourishes to his films, rendering them a rich experience in which the often dense mise-en-scène can be dissected and redissected to reveal minute clues, from the opening midflight-refueling coupling of two airplanes to the final nuclear orgasm. *Dr. Strangelove* is liberally peppered with such signs, often defined by their incongruity, including "Peace Is Our Profession," "Keep off the Grass," "Civil Defense Is Your Business," "Gee, Dad! Thanks for thinking of us," and "Pause and Refresh." Two nuclear bombs aboard the B-52 Leper Colony are labeled "Dear John" and "Hi There!"

Peter Sellers brought a stand-up shtick to the film. Kubrick intended that Sellers play at least four, maybe five, roles: Mandrake, Muffley, Schmuck, Major Kong, and Strangelove. Gene D. Phillips notes that Kubrick wanted "some version of Peter Sellers holding the fate of the world in his hands" almost everywhere the viewer looks. While Sellers declined to play Kong, ostensibly because he couldn't effectively mimic his southern drawl, and Schmuck went to Scott, Sellers still showed off his talent for improvisation that enthralled Kubrick so much in *Lolita*. Kubrick explained that "during shooting many substantial changes were made in the script, sometimes together with the cast during improvisations." Christiane recalled, "Stanley was his best audience. In fact, he spent many of his scenes just being an audience, not a director at all. He would simply put cameras everywhere he could so that when Peter was off flying high, Stanley says, 'I don't want anything to be lost.' And he would just lie on his back, you know, roaring with laughter. That egged Peter on to ever greater heights."[12]

Sellers's improvisations heightened the sick humor. He brought the "shpritzing" quality of Lenny Bruce, the Yiddish term for a sudden outburst, as when a bottle of soda is shaken up and allowed to spray outward. His conversation with the Soviet premier showcases these abilities in that only the first line of dialogue during the two hotline phone calls was scripted, and Sellers ad-libbed the remainder. The result had the quality of a Shelley Berman sketch and the cadence and feel of a Nichols-and-May skit. The proliferation of telephones, intercoms, public-address systems, and other communications devices allowing for conversations often featured in the latter's routines, such as when a nervous wife tries to break to her husband the news of an expensive automobile collision. Indeed, Kubrick marketed the film as a "Hot-line Comedy."[13]

Kubrick captured the mood, or zeitgeist, of the New Left and counterculture, both of which were beginning to emerge and coalesce during the early years of the decade. Lewis H. Rubman, in *Commentary*, describes the film's "extreme flippancy, in the *Mad-Playboy* tradition." The *New York Times*'s Bosley Crowther calls it "the most shattering sick joke I've ever come across. And I say that with full recollection of some of the grim ones I've heard from Mort Sahl, some of the cartoons I've seen by Charles Addams and some of the stuff I've read in *Mad* Magazine." Sahl was known for "giving voice to the anxieties of the age, the unspoken horrors of nuclear weapons, the emerging sexual revolution, the racial divide, and the sense of being controlled by the government." Philip Hartung refers to its "vulgarity." *Dr. Strangelove* also possesses a Beat quality, reflecting Allen Ginsberg's "Go fuck yourself with your atom bomb." The ending, in particular, in which the bomb bay doors open, and Major Kong (Slim Pickens) rides the nuclear weapon to his doom, waving his hat and shouting in final triumph, is a graphic representation of Ginsberg's *Howl* (1956): "Moloch whose mind is pure machinery! . . . a cloud of sexless hydrogen! . . . granite cocks! Monstrous bombs! They broke their backs lifting Moloch to Heaven!" It also uncannily mirrors a line from *Catcher in the Rye* (1951): "I'm sort of glad they've got the atomic bomb invented. If there's ever another war, I'm going to sit right the hell on top of it. I'll volunteer for it, I swear to God I will." This was also the era of the rise of protest song by such Jewish singers as Woody Guthrie, Leonard Cohen, and Bob Dylan, whose "Talkin' World War III Blues" was released contemporaneously with *Dr. Strangelove* and took a similarly satirical approach about the bomb and fears of nuclear war. In 1963 Dylan also wrote the lyrics to "Go Away You Bomb," which was never released.[14]

Mad Goys versus Sane Mensches

Kubrick's humor was also demonstrated through the tactic by which he took the deadly straight and clearly anticommunist drama of George's novel and remodeled it with satire. In one major shift, he transformed the all-American goyische names (Clint Brown, Andrew Mackenzie, Franklin, Quinten) into parodic figures. Kubrick continued his signature opposition of menschlikayt and goyim naches through doubled pairs of characters in this film, as if multiplying the Quilty/Humbert relationship. They were embodied in the characters of Ripper and Turgidson on one side and Muffley and Mandrake on the other. In Ripper and Turgidson, Kubrick mercilessly lampooned the hawkish, goyish position on the bomb by creating two caricatures of "square-jawed, goyishe American tough guys."[15]

Ripper instigated a nuclear strike because he believes his precious bodily fluids have been sapped by fluoridation, a communist conspiracy. Kubrick clearly makes his own feelings clear by giving him a virtually identical name to that of the notorious Victorian serial killer. Kubrick described him as an "armed madman." Turgidson, having been circumcised of his schmuck moniker, now reads as straightforwardly goyish. His given name and surname highlight his obsession with hyperpriapic masculinity, coupled with a "swollen sense of military potency." Kubrick described him as "so suspicious. His terrific suspicion of everything that arises is completely logical from his point of view. He suspects everything of being a trap."[16]

Ranged against Ripper and Turgidson are Muffley and Mandrake. Sellers brought a subsurface Jewishness to the roles he played; hence Muffley and Mandrake stand as the relative embodiments of menschlikayt. We are encouraged to sympathize with them, as both are categorized by their rationality and sanity, which Kubrick equates with femininity, particularly in contrast to the hypergoyish Ripper, Turgidson, Kong, and Col. Bat Guano (Keenan Wynn). Kubrick told Sellers he wanted Muffley to display reasonable lucidity amid the chaos, an oasis of reason amid all the madness. Sellers played him as a liberal humanist, loosely modeled on Adlai Stevenson. Muffley is a sensible, moderate liberal intellectual, and the only voice of reason in the War Room. But he's slightly effeminate, passive, and meek, a dove to Turgidson's hawk, a muff to his schmuck. He prefers negation over preemption. Where Turgidson urges an all-out nuclear preemptive strike before the Soviets can retaliate, Muffley counters that it is avowed U.S. policy never to strike first with nuclear weapons and that Ripper's action was not that of national policy. Turgidson's retort plays on and emphasizes the lack of Muffley's masculine characteristics, specifically his baldness: "Mr. President, I'm not saying we wouldn't get our hair mussed." Muffley has no hair to get mussed. It's also Kubrick's humor that the bald Muffley's two names (a merkin is a pubic wig), like Turgidson's dig, refer to the very hair that he lacks. Muffley, in addition, emphasizes that there are still other alternatives to Turgidson's belligerent suggestions and accordingly telephones the Soviet premier.

The other voice of menschlikayt is Royal Air Force officer Mandrake. Kubrick conceived of Mandrake as "classically 'British'; Eton and Oxford background," which gives him an effeminate quality. Mandrake's surname is a metaphor for the human form and a biblical aphrodisiac. Like Muffley, he stands as a simile for creating life, whereas as Ripper and Turgidson stand for destroying it. Mandrake is a model of sanity. He attempts to cajole Ripper into recalling the wing, if to no avail. He acts as a counterpoint to Col. Bat Guano, whom critic Penelope Gilliatt calls a "hard-core hetero," a reincarnation of Ripper.[17]

Nuclear Holocaust and the Holocaust

When reviewing *2001*, critic Eric Rhode looked back to say, "it is worth noting the extent to which *Dr Strangelove* is indebted to Hitler's favorite film, the *Metropolis* of Fritz Lang. Neither Lang nor Kubrick is a Nazi, but they do explore those areas of life from which the Nazi ideology arose." Specters of the Shoah can be detected in both *Spartacus* and *Lolita*, but it's in *Dr. Strangelove* that Kubrick's thoughts on the Holocaust begin to coalesce, arguably betraying a much more scholarly influence than in his previous films. As Peter Krämer argues, "*Strangelove* equates the ideas and practices of American nuclear strategy, including visions of post-war underground society, with Nazi ideology and crimes. Only nineteen years after the end of World War II and the collapse of the Nazi regime, this parallel greatly enhanced the terrifying plausibility of the scenario depicted in the film." The equation between the Holocaust and nuclear holocaust certainly underpinned Kubrick's film. Christiane recalled her husband saying in the early 1960s, "Why aren't we moving away? . . . We're like the Jews in Germany. Why didn't they run? We should go. You know they were standing there saying they can't kill us all. Well let's up . . ." They stayed, apparently because Kubrick didn't want to share a bathroom on the ship.[18]

Preproduction materials written by Kubrick clearly indicate he was grappling with the issue of mass death in the post-Holocaust era:

> Nazi trials were based on premise the Nazis should have recognized that mass murder dictated they follow their conscience rather than their nation. What happens to someone who does this today even mass suicide.
> WALT DISNEY SHOT OF LEMMINGS
> JUMPING OFF CLIFF BY TENS OF THOUSANDS
> 6,000,000 JEWS TO GAS
> 6 millions [*sic*] Jews cooperated in their destruction.
> 400–600 millions—USA Europe Russia—do the same thing.

In one draft, written in his hand, he observed,

> There is no defense against a nuclear attack. We may shoot down fifty-percent
> of attacking air-craft but the remainder can easily overkill 180 million Ameri-
> cans. There is no foreseeable defense whatsoever against missiles. How do we
> take this? I've read that inmates of concentration camps gave up and became
> "walking dead" when they believed that nothing they could do, no effort or
> cooperation on their part would have any effect on their fate. We are pacified
> by full stomachs, TV and comfortable homes but we have become "something
> dead." We've given up as individuals. We deny the threat and sub-consciously
> experience our anxieties elsewhere.[19]

Kubrick's observations clearly demonstrate the influence of the three
best-known scholars writing on the Holocaust at the beginning of the sixties, Bruno Bettelheim, Raul Hilberg, and Hannah Arendt. His use of the
phrase "walking dead" is seemingly directly lifted from Bettelheim's 1960

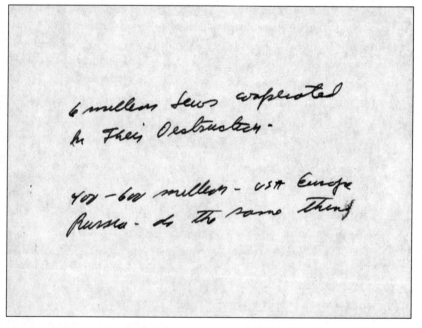

FIGURE 8 Kubrick's notecards show he was grappling with the implications of the Holocaust
when planning *Dr. Strangelove* (1964). Courtesy of the Stanley Kubrick Archive, "Index
Cards," c. 1963, SK/11/2/7, SKA.

book *The Informed Heart: Autonomy in a Mass Age*, based on his own expe-riences in German concentration camps. Hilberg, by contrast, details the administrative process that culminated in the Final Solution, concluding that its perpetrators "were not different in their moral makeup from the rest of the population." The killings were typically organized and carried out by ostensibly ordinary individuals, who were sane, God-fearing family men and who simply claimed to be following orders. Often, they were pro-fessionals and intellectuals such as physicians, singers, clergy, and lawyers. In Kubrick's personal copy, he'd underlined the words, "The German per-petrator was not a special kind of German." Hilberg also shows how the Jews of Europe complied and even collaborated in their own destruction through the administrative unit of the Judenrate (Jewish Councils). Jew-ish leaders in occupied Europe obediently selected Jews to be killed by the Nazis. Without their cooperation the extermination would not have been so efficient.[20]

Following in Hilberg's wake, and relying heavily on him, Arendt wrote a series of articles for the *New Yorker*, generating much more publicity and controversy. Observing the trial for war crimes of Adolf Eichmann—one the chief architects of the Nazi genocide—in Jerusalem in 1961, she pro-duced a twin thesis that genocide required neither monsters nor patho-logical anti-Semites but rather Nazi bureaucrats who, like Eichmann, were normal, banal even, and that the Jews acquiesced, even cooperated, in the genocide. "One cannot extract any diabolical or demonic profundity from Eichmann," Arendt wrote, and "if the Jewish people had really been unor-ganized and leaderless, there would have been chaos and plenty of misery but the total number of victims would hardly have been between four and a half and six million people." She acknowledged that "it would have been very comforting indeed to believe that Eichmann was a monster," but what "stared one in the face at the trial" was "sheer thoughtlessness."[21]

Dr. Strangelove reflects these observations. Its key agents certainly mani-fest an intellectual blindness, suffering from thoughtlessness, and a defi-ciency of any wider realization of the consequences of what it is they are doing. They lack the capacity for introspection or reflection on the conse-quences of their actions. In 1966 Kubrick recalled, "When I was research-ing *Dr. Strangelove* I found that the people in the think tank happily chatted away about the most somber topic, buoyed up by what must have been pride and satisfaction in their professional expertise; and this seemed to completely overcome any sense of personal involvement in the possible destruction of their world. Perhaps it has something to do with the magic of words. If you can talk brilliantly about a problem, it can create the consoling illusion that it has been mastered." Heller captures this perfectly in his summation of Turgidson: "He reacts with horror to the President's solution that we blow up our own plane. This is the way a sensitive, normal human begin would react, not a monster. At the same time, he is somewhat obtuse, somewhat of a clown, somewhat lecherous, he's concerned with self-advancement. He is a human being. . . . You create the realization that there are men like this, there are people with attitudes like this, and the danger from these people is tremendously grave and very immediate." This is also highlighted in the sequence where the B-52 crew runs through the bomb-release sequence. Immersed in the task of preparing for nuclear detonation, they're so engrossed in their individual assignments they miss their larger significance, particularly when they employ their resourcefulness and imagination to maintain course and open the bomb bay doors. Indeed, when Muffley moves beyond thoughtlessness ("I don't want to be known as the biggest mass murderer since Hitler"), he's criticized for his vanity.[22]

Social-psychologist Stanley Milgram, who conceived and designed his famous obedience experiments study to understand the Nazi genocide, cited the B-52 sequence in support of his experiments when they were published in book form in 1974: "One such mechanism is the tendency of the individual to become so absorbed in the narrow technical aspects of the task that he loses sight of its broader consequences. The film *Dr. Strangelove* brilliantly satirized the absorption of a bomber crew in the exactly technical procedure of dropping nuclear weapons on a country." Milgram's own obedience experiments, the first results of which were published in 1963, as *Dr. Strangelove* was in production, reached similar conclusions. In fact, in two 1963 interviews, Milgram compared his subjects to pilots who dropped atomic bombs.[23]

Reflecting Hilberg's and Arendt's conclusions in his mimicry and mockery of the typical World War II platoon movie, Kubrick insisted on placing a clearly Jewish character on the B-52 bomber. George's novel features a potentially Jewish character in gunnery, officer Lt. Herman Goldsmith, who, in terms befitting of Quilty, was described as a "small, lively, intelligent-eyed man, with a devastating gift of mimicry" and the "established comic of the crew." Kubrick re-resketched him as "Lt. Irving 'Doc' Schwartz, the Radio-Radio Officer," describing him as an "argumentative and opinionated fellow" who "could have been a top-rated surgeon if the quota-system had not kept him out of medical school." Although nowhere stated Schwartz is Jewish, his given name, surname, and reference to the well-known quota system that denied Jews entry into the top Ivy League universities point to such a conclusion. Schwartz disappeared from the screenplay and was replaced by radio operator Lt. B. Goldberg. (Kubrick begged George not to call him Hymie or Hyman, as it was unrealistic, requesting a "more normal name like Joe, Bill or so forth.") In another draft Goldberg reads *Commentary* magazine, and Kubrick considered casting Jewish actor-comedian Ted Flicker for the role. While *Commentary* was dropped, Goldberg was played by Jewish actor Paul Tamarin. Only his character's name hints at his Jewishness, resembling the World War II platoon movies and novels, particularly *Battle Cry* and *Naked and the Dead*, that featured Jewish soldiers. Kubrick placed another Jewish soldier, Hal Galili, in the Burpelson Air Force Base Defense Team. These Jewish characteristics didn't appear in *Red Alert*, making it one of the few Kubrick films in which an overtly Jewish character appears, but, troublingly, one who is implicated in mass murder.[24]

Euphemism was another means by which Kubrick grappled with the Holocaust. A new language was one of the key distancing and deceiving devices preparing the ground for the perpetrators, in which "final solution," "solution possibilities," "special treatment," "cleansing operation," "deportation," "displacement," "resettlement," and "evacuation" meant murder. Hilberg also demonstrates that, just as the Nazis deceived the Jews, the Jews were willing to be deceived and deceived themselves, and Jewish denial was a key component in their genocide. Jews even devised and used their own euphemistic language: "bakery" for crematorium; "Moslem" for someone destined for the gas chambers, and "Canada" for the stockpile of confiscated belongings. Arendt further observes how Eichmann was unable to "utter a single sentence that was not a cliché."[25]

Dr. Strangelove's characters talk in such clichéd and euphemistic language. Turgidson argues it's not "quite fair to condemn the whole program because of a single slip-up." The "slip-up" to which he refers is a tactical nuclear strike on the Soviet Union. As we have seen, he compares a preemptive nuclear strike on the Soviets to discovering them in the act of doing something normally private or hidden. "Modest and acceptable casualties" equates to "twenty million people killed," which he describes as "get[ting] our hair mussed." Kong's "target opportunity" means detonating a nuclear device. In a rare departure from euphemisms, Muffley tells Turgidson plainly, "You're talking about mass murder, General, not war." Kubrick stressed the importance of such euphemisms as "preempt," "modest," "acceptable civilian casualties," "Doomsday device," and "megadeaths." Ripper's and Strangelove's language especially invokes Nazi euphemism. Ripper is obsessed with the preservation of "purity" and "purifying." When he invokes "purity of essence," essence could easily stand in as a synonym for "race." Strangelove refers to "select[ion]" in order "to preserve a nucleus of human specimens," who, if provided with a "proper breeding technique," would "breed prodigiously." Such language mirrors Nazi eugenicist ideas. It also echoes Zempf's words to Humbert in *Lolita*: "We Americans are progressively modern and believe it is important to prepare the majority of young people for satisfactory mating and successful child rearing." It's no coincidence that Dr. Strangelove works for the "Bland Corporation."[26]

Kubrick made the comparison between Nazi Germany and contemporary America explicit. Strangelove refers to the president as "Mein Führer" and does the Nazi salute. Muffley worries about posthumous comparisons to Hitler. Turgidson explains the Russian mentality in terms of all "them Nazis" they killed. The draft screenplays reveal there would have been even more. The decision to keep some and drop others demonstrates that much consideration was given to just how much the film should include explicit Holocaust references. The importance of those lines that remained to Kubrick was illustrated when a German translator altered Muffley's concern about his retrospective reputation to remove the reference to Hitler. Kubrick described it as a "cynical disregard for the past suffering caused by that illustrious gentleman" and not in any way a "little insignificant matter" or a "small cut."[27]

Dr. Strangelove thus fitted into an era when intellectuals were increasingly and explicitly linking the Nazi genocide in Europe with the bomb and nuclear mass death. In 1953 Dwight Macdonald had observed, "From Frankenstein's laboratory to Maidenek [*sic*] and Hiroshima is not a long journey." By the late 1950s the word "holocaust" was being used as both a referent to the Final Solution and nuclear war. In 1961 Bettelheim attacked the glorification of Anne Frank and included the words "impending holocaust." A key sentence in Eugene Burdick and Harvey Wheeler's 1962 novel *Fail-Safe*, which bore many similarities with *Red Alert* and with which Kubrick was very familiar, ended with the words "atomic holocaust." Referencing *Fail-Safe*, Holocaust survivor Elie Wiesel wrote, "It has become a kind of intellectual fad to upbraid the Jews murdered in World War II for allowing themselves to be killed. . . . Psychologists like Bruno Bettelheim, and sociologists like Hannah Arendt, are not the only ones who have been complaining. . . . One finds this . . . even in fiction whose theme has nothing to do with the Nazi holocaust. For example, in *Fail-Safe*, the best seller about an atomic accident . . . a minor character [contends that Jews] should have murdered the SS men who came to arrest them." Lenny Bruce had equated the Holocaust with Hiroshima onstage in 1962, closing his shows with Thomas Merton's poem "My Name is Adolf Eichmann," whose final line states, "Hiroshima . . . *Auf Wiedersehen*." He even made shocking jokes about the genocide.[28]

Dr. Who?

This is where the titular character, Dr. Strangelove, comes in. On the surface he's an unreconstructed ex-Nazi, most likely modeled on Wernher von Braun, the former Nazi rocket scientist who oversaw the development of America's postwar space program. Strangelove didn't appear in George's original novel but evolved out of Kubrick's early drafts, in which a scientist called Dr. Otto Strangelove wins a shock presidential victory for the Republicans before emerging into a separate character in his own right. In December 1962 Kubrick informed the *New York Times* that Sellers would play an "American college professor who rises to power in sex and politics by becoming a nuclear wise man." In his initial drafts of the character of Strangelove, then named "von Klutz," Kubrick described him as "rather sinister in the manner of a Nazi nobleman." Von Klutz tells the president, "man is an amazingly adaptable creature. After all, the conditions would be far superior to those, say, of the Nazi concentration camps, where there is ample evidence most of the wretched creatures clung desperately to life." These words, which are not uttered in the film, are put into Strangelove's mouth in George's novelization, which described Strangelove as a "recluse and perhaps had been made so by the effects of the British bombing of Peenemunde, where he was working on the German V-2 rocket. His black-gloved right hand was a memento of this."[29]

In the film Dr. Strangelove is an ex-Nazi with an autonomous or alien arm. Kubrick explained, "Dr. Strangelove is suffering from a psychosomatic right arm—the right arm is rebelling against the treachery of the rest of his body." Sellers recalled that he immediately thought, "'Hey, that's a storm-trooper's arm.' So instead of leaving it there looking malignant I gave the arm a life of its own. That arm hated the rest of the body for having made a compromise. That arm was a Nazi." The result is that Strangelove's arm gives a Hitler salute and tries to strangle its owner. Sellers added, "It was always Wernher von Braun. But the one gloved hand that kept rising up to salute, well, the man *was* a Nazi."[30]

Intertextuality also suggests that Strangelove is a Nazi. Grant B. Stillman argues that *Dr. No* (1962) was a major influence on Kubrick. Ian Fleming's 1958 novel, on which the film was based, was published the same year as *Two Hours to Doom*. Both protagonists are mad German émigré nuclear scientists, who've changed their names on assuming U.S. citizenship and have gloved right hands resulting from accidents. Dr. No even hails the scientific benefits of Nazi medical experimentation, and his movie minions wear SA-like uniforms. Like Strangelove, he barely occupies any screen time, appearing after only eighty minutes, but he's the film's unseen presence, its heart of darkness, its Quilty. Another link between them is the set design: Ken Adam's work on *Dr. No* so impressed Kubrick that he hired him for *Dr. Strangelove*, and the War Room was based on his plans for the Bond movie.[31]

Contemporary critics certainly recognized Strangelove as a Nazi. Lewis Mumford writes, "By making 'Dr. Strangelove' the central symbol of this scientifically organized nightmare of mass extermination Mr. Kubrick has not merely correctly related it to its first great exponent, Hitler, he has likewise identified the ultimate strategy of nuclear gamesmanship for precisely what it would be: an act of treason against the human race." He also notes that the aim of American nuclear policy was the "'final solution' of the Communist problem," equating nuclear war with Nazi extermination policies. James A. Wechsler states that the German scientist's final vision is of a "new super-race of man born out of selective breeding in the mine shafts." The *Christian Advocate* reports that the film's "combination of the radical right, the military complex, and Nazism expresses Mr. Kubrick's conviction that all are expressions of the same inner spirit." In an extended article on the film, Joe Goldberg concludes that Kubrick has "not forgiven the Germans."[32]

But since Strangelove was a Kubrick-Sellers invention, his superficial seemingly Nazi appearance belies a multidimensionality, and he's possibly yet another example of Kubrick's signature misdirection. For the intelligent viewer Jews and the atom bomb were inseparably intertwined. Albert Einstein's theories had laid the groundwork, J. Robert Oppenheimer oversaw the Manhattan Project, and Julius and Ethel Rosenberg were executed for passing atomic secrets to Russia. When the Final Solution was officially implemented in 1942, the Los Alamos site became the epicenter of atomic bomb development and was staffed by those very Jewish scientists expelled from Nazi-occupied Europe. Indeed, they were engaged in attempting to prevent the Nazis developing the bomb first. And as the development of the bomb progressed, more and more Jews were being murdered. Certainly, as Max Lerner points out, it was a "historic fact that almost all the great American nuclear scientists have been refugees from Nazism." In *Commentary* (which Kubrick considered including in the film), Midge Decter criticizes Kubrick for not being "quite daring enough to have risked portraying his nuclear strategist as a Jew—not a Nazi, but a refugee, in fact, from Hitler, as so many real-life nuclear strategists are."[33]

But maybe Kubrick did. In addition to von Braun, Strangelove was a composite of real-life Jewish nuclear strategists: Bernard Brodie, Herman Kahn, Henry Kissinger, Edward Teller, John von Neumann, and Albert Wohlstetter. In an early sketch of his characters, Kubrick referred to a "Herman Kahn type." Kahn, whose 1960 book, *On Thermonuclear War*, Kubrick had read and with whom Kubrick had conferred while working on the film, worked as a strategist for the RAND Corporation, as did Brodie, von Neumann, Teller, and Wohlstetter, the think tank that provided the model for the film's Bland Corporation. Indeed, Strangelove's words, that underground survivors will feel a "spirit of bold curiosity for the adventure ahead," reflects Kahn's chapter on mineshafts, titled "Will Survivors Envy the Dead?," which predicted a "renewed vigor among the population with a zealous, almost religious dedication to reconstruction." (Kubrick also placed some of Kahn's words almost verbatim in Turgidson's mouth.) On top of those six, Kubrick had invited Jewish photographer Weegee to take photographs of the set, and Sellers claimed that he "put a German accent on top of Weegee's." Christiane confirms this. Kubrick felt "Strangelove's accent was probably inspired by the physicist Edward Teller, who became known as the father of the H-bomb, though Teller's origins are Hungarian and his accent isn't really that close to what Peter did." Kubrick later told Arthur C. Clarke, "Please tell Wernher I wasn't getting at *him!*" If this is the case, and we take Kubrick and Sellers at their word, then the remaining influences are all Jewish. Robert Levine, a "defense intellectual" working for the RAND corporation, wrote to Kubrick, saying how much he and other "RAND types" had enjoyed the film but objected to the "stock Nazi caricature you made of Strangelove. Surely, Mr. Kubrick, you could have satirized us better than that."[34]

Kubrick described Strangelove simply as a nothing more than a "German scientist" and a *parody* "of movie clichés about Nazis," opening up the possibility of reading him as conceptually Jewish. Much of Strangelove was the product of Seller's gift for mimicry and improvisation (his "resurrection" at the end of the film being a main example). And Sellers brought a subsurface ethnicity to the role, recalling Quilty-as-Zemph, to whom Kubrick compared Strangelove. For example, Strangelove's seated entrance from the shadows mirrors that of Zemph sitting in the darkness of Humbert's home. Like Quilty, Strangelove occupies very little of the film, perhaps even less. He rises from his wheelchair, as does Quilty at the opening of *Lolita*. Robert Roper even suggests that Sellers drew on Lionel Trilling's peculiar way with a cigarette and unusual speaking emphasis when playing Quilty *and* Strangelove. And Sellers's mimicry of a Nazi is so excessive, so over the top, that it's impossible to read it as even approaching a realistic attempt. Pat Ivens describes Sellers's performance as the "vaudeville pyrotechnics" of a "Nazi send-up," anticipating *The Producers* (1967), whose director, Mel Brooks, watched a screening of *Dr. Strangelove*.[35]

As we've seen, Sellers suggested how if Strangelove's arm was Nazi, the rest of the body was not. Kubrick also confirmed that this arm was protesting Strangelove's disloyalty. This opens up the possibility that, like Dr. No, a prosthetic Nazi arm had been grafted onto the body of a German émigré who, though everyone else has read as Nazi, may just be Jewish. The hand and arm function independently of their owner, explaining the seemingly involuntary Sieg Heil salute and attempt to strangle its owner.[36]

There are various other clues to Strangelove's potential Jewishness. In palimpsestic fashion, Strangelove absorbed elements of the discarded "von Klutz" character. *Metropolis*'s C. A. Rotwang, from whom Strangelove is spiritually descended and with whom he shares a black-gloved hand, has been read as a neokabbalistic Jewish scientist. Similarly, another proto-Strangelove, Dr. Gogol in *Mad Love* (1935), was played by Jewish actor Peter Lorre. David Hughes believes the inspiration behind Strangelove was *Fail-Safe*'s German Jewish nuclear adviser Dr. Walter Groteschele, played by recognizably Jewish actor Walter Matthau in the 1964 film. Kubrick was certainly familiar with *Fail-Safe*, as Burdick had approached Harris-Kubrick

Pictures in December 1961, sending them a partially completed draft of the novel for their consideration. The following January Harris and Kubrick requested a complete copy but then rejected it and successfully stalled the film's release. Dr. No, Strangelove's other double, was portrayed by Jewish actor Joseph Wiseman. Furthermore, Strangelove's gloved right hand and prosthetic arm draws attention to his sinister nature, invoking the left-handed Jew. The wheelchair suggests he suffers from sort of crippling foot defect. These are visual markers of his difference and subtle allusions to a historical Jewishness coded in crudely stereotypical terms by the "Jew's foot." As Rebecca Raphael astutely wonders, how did Strangelove survive the Nazi eugenicist euthanasia program? Strangelove is represented as a Satanic figure or some sort of Angel of Death, alluding to classic Christian Judeophobia, in which Jews are perceived as Satan's earthly mediators. The dark glasses in a dark room are another coded sign of his Jewishness. The stereotype of the Jewish physician haunts anti-Semitic literature, as well as the work of Arthur Schnitzler and Kafka. The first two letters of the title, "DR," dominate the screen, and when Strangelove is seen fiddling with a wheel in the film, it bears a passing resemblance to those used to determine birth and due dates.[37]

As with *Lolita*, Sellers found inspiration for the role of Strangelove in Kubrick himself. The black glove he wore belonged to Kubrick, and in one still photo from the set, Kubrick gives a Sieg Heil salute like Strangelove's. Kubrick smoked constantly, and Strangelove wears a suit and thin black tie similar to Kubrick's; in a rare color photo of Sellers dressed as Strangelove and Kubrick on set they wear near-identical clothing. Kubrick also innovated the use of a wheelchair in *Paths of Glory*, which he continued to use until replaced by the Steadicam. Kubrick resembled the mad scientist, directing and dictating the action. By the time *Dr. Strangelove* was made, he'd done prodigious research on the subject and hence was presumably as knowledgeable about nuclear war and strategy as Strangelove himself. The wheelchair-bound, dark-suited, chain-smoking director with the gloved hands may resemble nothing less than a self-reflexive comic caricature. Kahn was a Bronx-born Jew five years older than Kubrick. Perhaps this explains why Joe Goldberg titled his article "Dr. Kubrick" and why Pauline Kael referred to Kubrick as a "thick-skulled German professor" who "may be Dr. Strangelove himself." Atypically, Kubrick even made brief appearances in *Dr. Strangelove*'s theatrical trailer, suggesting he was the "I" of the film's subtitle.[38]

If Strangelove is a Nazi, it reduces the film's universalism and fudges the argument that evil is in all of us. Kubrick's own team complained that the decision to cut the pie fight and give the final words to Strangelove emphasized the Nazi dimension and undermined that universalist argument. By ending on "Mein Führer—I can walk!" Pat Ivens points out, the film accentuates the "*Nazi role*" by ending "on a 'final Nazi note.'":

> It's about *people being irrational* not about strategists being Nazis, demons or anything else. . . . All Human nature is not necessarily involved at the end because Nazi nature is so monstrous that the issue is confused. . . . The comic use of accident, incongruity, drunkenness, etc. makes sense only if you are saying that *all* people are frail, that the human condition is absurd, and *dangerously* so when there's a bomb to be controlled. An ending concentrated on Strangelove as a Nazi blurs almost to obscurity this crucial point. When a critic analyses Strangelove's "last word" position (bolstered by his title role) and the final Nazi note, he can say that viewpoint of the film seems to change and narrow.

Ivens insists that with the original ending "Strangelove's Nazi facet is greatly minimized. . . . The real danger is human nature not Nazis, or strategists or soldiers." Similarly, sound editor Leslie Hodgson feels it "particularizes too much on the figure of Strangelove both as an individual and as a Nazi. In this form, the message becomes that Strangelove is the person most fully responsible for the Doomsday and Atomic situations, whereas with the pie fight and the cheers at the end, the acceptance of nuclear thought is more universal." In conclusion, Hodgson believes, "it would be a wrong end to the film to lay the blame on to Strangelove, for even if he represents nuclear thinking, the responsibility is shared by those who have allowed him his power." He argues that the words "'massive retaliation' were better as the last words for the film than 'Mein Fuhrer, I can walk.'" Decter feels the film would have been bolder had Kubrick had the courage to make Strangelove explicitly Jewish. But is it possible that they missed something: that Kubrick used Strangelove to reflect on how, as he noted early in the production, "Jews cooperated in their destruction"?[39]

Conclusion

Kubrick's intellectual sensibility in *Dr. Strangelove* operated much more in the mold of the biting and mordant satire of sixties black and sick humor. Kubrick consciously used his New York Jewish background to comment on the key intellectual preoccupations of the early 1960s: MAD, nuclear strategy, disarmament, the nature of man, the banality of evil, and the Holocaust. *Dr. Strangelove* meshed seamlessly into a period when secular Jewish American intellectuals, who had grown up while the Holocaust was happening, used the Holocaust to forge emotional and deeply personal expressions of identity. In becoming much more conscious of the devastation of the Holocaust, they were vocal about it, using the Shoah to mold public opinion. Kubrick, as we know, shared the "fairly widespread fascination with the horror of the Nazi period." *Dr. Strangelove*, therefore, very much mirrored contemporary Jewish post-Holocaust intellectual anxieties, as well as the New Left, countercultural zeitgeist. It also implicated Jews and non-Jews alike in total nuclear extermination, especially Jewish nuclear scientists, soldiers, and strategists, drawing on its most recent parallel in the Holocaust. In this light, it's uncanny that Kubrick commenced filming on January 28, 1963, the day following the commemoration of the liberation of Auschwitz.[40]

5

Kubrick and Kabbalah

The film *2001: A Space Odyssey* marked a major turning point in Kubrick's oeuvre. It was his first solely helmed film in color; while he had worked on *The Seafarers* and *Spartacus*, he lacked total control on both projects. It also signaled what can be described as a "religious" turn. This isn't to say that Kubrick had become religiously observant in any conventional or orthodox sense—indeed, as outlined earlier, he neither practiced nor believed in anything approaching organized religion or normative Judaism—but rather that this film became much more of an experience akin to religion. Each section of the film is laden with symbolic imagery that can be decoded in terms of Jewish ideas and iconography. While there had been hints and allusions to Jewish history and culture in his previous works, none were as developed or as extended as to what was to appear in *2001*, nor did they embrace, as fully, Jewish mysticism, that is, Kabbalah. Kubrick wanted to provoke people into thinking about humanity: "I think that if *2001* succeeds at all, it is in reaching a wide spectrum of people who would not often give a thought to man's destiny, his role in the cosmos and his relationship to higher forms of life." His *2001*, therefore, offers a rich text to mine for Jewish meaning, as well as showing New York Intellectual influences, in a film that explores the evolution of humanity from its very origins through to its ultimate end, the superman, or Übermensch.[1]

Science Fiction Buff

Kubrick's interest in science fiction dated back to his childhood. In the 1930s he read pulp magazines like *Amazing Stories* and *Astounding Stories*. *Forbidden Planet* (1956) impressed him, and he was inspired to watch a range of Japanese science fiction films. When Alexander Walker asked him if he intended "to make a film about Outer Space," Kubrick replied, "Please, be careful what you write." In the early 1960s a BBC Radio science fiction–drama serial, *Shadow on the Sun*, about a meteorite delivering a virus to earth, interested him. Kubrick also enjoyed the BBC television show *Doctor Who* (1963–), occasionally even watching it as a live audience member. He envisaged adopting such an approach for *Dr. Strangelove*. Voice-over narration from the perspective of an alien civilization in the distant future, looking back at the long-dead planet Earth, was to open and close the film as part of a series, "The Dead Worlds of Antiquity." Even without those features, *Dr. Strangelove* still won a Hugo Award for the best science fiction film of 1964 because it dealt with those very "what if" questions at the heart of the genre.[2]

In March 1964 Kubrick contacted science fiction writer Arthur C. Clarke, whose books he had admired for some time, with the aim of making the "proverbial 'really good' science fiction movie." They met in New York City in April and together developed a novel-like treatment for *2001*, loosely derived from Clarke's short story "The Sentinel" (1951) and his novel *Childhood's End* (1953). For the first time since *Killer's Kiss*, Kubrick didn't work from a preexisting novel. Instead, he developed one in collaboration with Clarke, out of which the screenplay simultaneously took shape. In February 1965 they submitted their treatment, *Journey beyond the Stars*, to MGM. The following December the principal photography began. The film premiered on April 2, 1968.[3]

"Total Mystery"

Initially, the screenplay Kubrick and Clarke developed was somewhat didactic. It included extensive voice-over narration, dialogue and explanatory sequences, a composed score by Alex North (who'd worked on *Spartacus*), and a planned ten-minute opening expository prologue consisting of edited interviews with scientists, thinkers, and theologians (including a rabbi) discussing the existence of extraterrestrial life, space, theology, biology, chemistry, and astronomy, among other topics. They also wrote some explanatory narrative.

But, between November 1967 and the summer of 1968, Kubrick implemented a series of changes that drastically transformed the film. The expository prologue, narration, and score were all abandoned, as was an opening scene of the ape named Moon-Watcher and his dead father and images of aliens (test footage of which had already been shot in September 1967). The dialogue was also drastically reduced, as were other explanatory sequences, and the new score was entirely composed of preexisting nineteenth- and twentieth-century classical and avant-garde recordings by György Ligeti, Aram Khachaturian, and Johann and Richard Strauss.[4]

Where his previous films had been verbal experiences (*Spartacus*'s first half aside), characterized by what Kubrick called the "magic of words," namely, carefully constructed dialogue, wordplay, punning, comedy, and black and sick humor, *2001* entered the realm of near wordlessness. Indeed, *2001* is marked by its sheer abstraction, making the viewer work harder to decode its underlying, if any, meanings. This decision to remove every trace of narration was another significant departure for Kubrick, who, as we've seen, used voice-over narration for every one of his films from *Day of the Fight* onward.[5]

Kubrick's edits removed any hope of a simple ride. His changes resulted in an extremely elliptical, enigmatic film, confounding simple interpretations. Viewers had to work much harder to decode and connect the series of images presented to them. No longer, for example, was human evolution explicitly shown to be the product of intelligent alien intervention, nor was it clear that the various satellites seen orbiting the earth were nuclear devices. This was deliberate. Kubrick wanted to "convey complex concepts and abstractions without the traditional reliance on words." In an interview with *Playboy* in 1968, he explained his intentions:

It's not a message that I ever intend to convey in words. *2001* is a nonverbal experience; out of two hours and 19 minutes of film, there are only a little less than 40 minutes of dialog. I tried to create a visual experience, one that bypasses verbalized pigeonholing and directly penetrates the subconscious with an emotional and philosophic content. To convolute McLuhan, in *2001* the message is the medium. I intended the film to be an intensely subjective experience that reaches the viewer at an inner level of consciousness, just as music does; to "explain" a Beethoven symphony would be to emasculate it by erecting an artificial barrier between conception and appreciation. You're free to speculate as you wish about the philosophical and allegorical meaning of the film—and such speculation is one indication that it has succeeded in gripping the audience at a deep level—but I don't want to spell out a verbal road map for *2001* that every viewer will feel obligated to pursue or else fear he's missed the point.

And because Kubrick insisted on a "non-specific" ending, it produced what Piers Bizony called an "unapologetically ambiguous" result.[6]

In another form of misdirection, Kubrick denied that the film had any conventional religious or theistic meaning to it. He issued a series of contradictory statements, describing *2001* as the "first six-million-dollar religious film," that the "God concept" lay at the heart of the film, and that he had tried to achieve a "scientific definition of God." Later Christiane would call it his "agnostic prayer." Many have seen it both as Kubrick's most secular and most religious film, but suffused with Christian iconography. Clarke indicated the absurdity of such readings when he stated, "People are telling Stanley and me things we didn't realize were in the movie. A theological student said he saw the Signs of the Cross—and he may have, which would have been interesting, since Stanley is a Jew and I'm an atheist."[7]

Kubrick may have also deliberately misled his audiences into believing the film was simply an allegory for Homer's *Odyssey*, albeit in space. While elements were drawn from that text, they neither overshadowed nor obscured its Jewishness. The interpolation of the word "space" between "a" and "odyssey" clearly signaled it wasn't a straightforward interpretation of Homer, that something was amiss. Kubrick considered various titles for the film, but insisted on *2001: A Space Odyssey*. "As far as I can recall," Clarke said, "it was entirely his idea."[8]

And where the source texts and screenplays for his films from *The Killing* through to *Dr. Strangelove* contain allusions to Jewishness, there are no such extant traces or footprints in those for *2001*. Instead, what can be interpreted as Judaic symbols in the film, revealing a distinctly Jewish understanding of the universe, especially in the use of imagery drawn from Hebrew scripture, Jewish liturgy, and Kabbalah, were inserted by Kubrick. As Jan Harlan felt, "Kubrick takes a big bow to the unknowable. I told him this was a very Jewish film, and I explained why I thought so. Judaism is a breakthrough in thinking; it is like the discovery of the fact that the earth is a globe circling the sun. It was the sun, mountains, animals and fantasy figures that represented God before. Now this God had no name, was eternal, the omnipotent creator of everything. What a breakthrough in thinking. Stanley liked my reasoning."[9]

Spiritual Awakening

If the final cut of *2001* was very much the product of 1967–1968, what happened in those years for Kubrick to make these major changes? Kubrick cut his physical ties to the United States—he stopped renting an apartment in Manhattan and eventually abandoned traveling there altogether. The sudden and unexpected death of his second wife, Ruth Sobotka, in June 1967, may have been a factor in this decision. Permanently settling in England, where he remained for the rest of his life, he transferred his entire base of operations from New York City. This new environment gave him full creative autonomy with almost no interference, allowing him to experiment with new ways of filmmaking. With *Lolita* and *Dr. Strangelove* under his belt, he was under no pressure to produce another immediate hit. He had the luxury of time, which doubled in the making of *2001*.

He abandoned his clean-shaven, black-suit, tie, and white-shirt fifties New York intellectual look in favor of a scruffier, hippie sixties one. When Jeremy Bernstein met Kubrick in 1965, he described him as having the "bohemian look of a riverboat gambler or a Rumanian poet." Kubrick was becoming a member of the countercultural zeitgeist. His hair grew longer and messier, and he grew a full and untrimmed beard, giving him the "aura of a Talmudic scholar" and the look of a "slightly cynical rabbi" that he retained for the rest of his life. As Harlan said, "He knew he looked Jewish and his big beard emphasized this." It was as if he was obeying the injunction of Leviticus 19:27: "Ye shall not round the corners of your heads, neither shalt thou mar the corners of thy beard."[10]

The sixties were for many Americans a period of spiritual reawakening. The political protest movements of the 1960s, especially the civil rights, antiwar, and women's liberation movements, questioned assumptions about God's will and society's complicity with evil. Greater nonconformity and diversity was tolerated, provoking exploration of nonnormative religions. Many baby boomers began experimenting with new age and occult ideas such as tarot, astrology, and Kabbalah, as well as those imported from the East, including yoga, mysticism, meditation, Hinduism, Zen Buddhism, the *I Ching*, and the *Tibetan Book of the Dead*, as a continuation of the sixties counterculture. American Jews, including Allen Ginsberg, Michael Herr, and J. D. Salinger, joined such groups at a disproportionate rate compared to their gentile counterparts, finding religious affinity with Zen Buddhism, in particular, helping to popularize it. Kubrick's discussions with Dwight Macdonald in 1959 revealed he was already interested in such ideas, and Clarke had been living in the primarily Buddhist Sri Lanka for eight years when Kubrick approached him. Ginsberg was staying at the Chelsea Hotel while Clarke was writing *2001*, and Clarke had a drink with Ginsberg while "in search of inspiration." The following year Ginsberg announced, "Tonight, let's all make love in London, as if it were 2001, the year of thrilling God."[11]

In the case of Judaism, this new spirituality led to increased Jewish observance, including some return to Orthodoxy among younger Jews. Even when heightened spirituality did not involve increased halachic observance, there was a greater sense of something more instinctive, less explicable. Others turned to ancient Jewish mysticism, or Kabbalah, with its emphasis on words, numbers, and numerology, capitalizing on the translation of key works into English, particularly those of the great scholar of Kabbalah, Gershom Scholem, whose book *On the Kabbalah and Its Symbolism* was published in English in 1965. Scholem did much to bring Kabbalah out of obscurity and into the wider circle of modern intellectual ideas, while Hasidism, as Kabbalah-in-praxis, had become familiar to a wider group of contemporary readers through the writings of Martin Buber and the fiction of Isaac Bashevis Singer. Hasidism seemed to offer a romantic vision of an alternative life, one that held great appeal for countercultural Jews, and was popularized by the publication of Chaim Potok's best-selling 1967 novel, *The Chosen*. Buber had a particularly great influence on the Jewish American counterculture, and in 1962, while on his way to study Buddhism in India, Allen Ginsberg met Buber in Jerusalem.

Kabbalah even influenced Jews not drawn to Judaism. Back in 1945 artist Barnett Newman had already begun to describe himself and such artists as Adolph Gottlieb, Hans Hofmann, Jackson Pollock, Mark Rothko, and Rufino Tamayo as creating a new American religious art, a modern mythology concerned with numinous ideas and feelings. "The present movement in American art transcends nature. It is concerned with metaphorical implications, with divine mysteries. These new painters have brought the artist back to his original primitive role as the maker of gods," he said. Newman's stripe paintings (1948–) had been influenced by Kabbalah, and echoes of these artists' work can be seen in *2001*'s abstraction (as well as the opening credits of *A Clockwork Orange*).[12]

This mysticism was a source of the film's appeal among the younger generation, who flocked to see the film, repeatedly, in huge crowds. Christiane recalled how, "If you were under thirty you dug the film, and if you were over thirty you came out of the cinema bored and perplexed in equal measure, generally speaking. It was a divisive, generational film." MGM took advantage of this market by advertising it as "The Ultimate Trip." As with his previous two films, Kubrick had yet again tapped into the zeitgeist of the late 1960s, *2001* proving very popular with the stoners, hippies, and those wishing to shed the conformity and politics of their parents' generation.[13]

At the same time, the notion that God was dead was gaining in popularity in the postwar world. From 1950 onward, Walter Kaufmann's English translations of Friedrich Nietzsche's works, notably *Nietzsche: Philosopher, Psychologist, Antichrist* (1950, reprinted in 1968) and *Portable Nietzsche* (1954), not only popularized his writings but also went some way to rehabilitating the philosopher after World War II, arguing he wasn't anti-Semitic. In 1966–1967, Kaufmann produced a flurry of translations of other works by Nietzsche, published as easily available Vintage paperbacks (*The Birth of Tragedy, The Case of Wagner, On the Genealogy of Morals, Ecce Homo,* and *Beyond Good and Evil*). They were also bound together in Kaufmann's 1968 Modern Library anthology, *The Basic Writings of Nietzsche*. The result was that Nietzsche became a semiofficial author of the counterculture.

Nietzsche also informed and was in dialogue with the small but highly visible "Death of God" movement in theology. Protestant thinkers asked whether Christian views of the universe were still tenable after the horrors of World War II. In 1965 Harvey Cox argued in his *The Secular City* that God no longer made sense and should be abandoned. The following year, in large letters on its cover, *Time* magazine asked, "Is God Dead?" Inside it wrote, "The three words represent a summons to reflect on the meaning of existence. No longer is the question the taunting jest of skeptics for whom unbelief is the test of wisdom and for whom Nietzsche is the prophet who gave the right answer a century ago." The *Time* cover even featured in Roman Polanski's 1968 adaptation of *Rosemary's Baby*, Ira Levin's best-selling novel of 1967, which envisaged the birth of a new anti-Christ in the form of Satan's son.[14]

Jews also grappled with the theological significance of the Holocaust, as the "site and occasion of [God's] abdication." In 1960 François Mauriac wrote how, for Elie Wiesel, "God is dead. . . . The God of Abraham, of Isaac, of Jacob . . . has vanished forevermore . . . in the smoke of a human holocaust exacted by Race, the most voracious of all idols." In 1966 theologian Richard Rubinstein's published his *After Auschwitz*. Heavily indebted to Nietzsche, he argued that the Holocaust had destroyed the traditional view of God as omnipotent and beneficent. Far from being anti-Semitic, responsible for the Jews' plight, Rubinstein argued, Nietzsche helped Jews to understand it. That same year Scholem wrote in *Commentary*, "It is indeed significant that Nietzsche's famous cry, 'God is dead,' should have gone up first in a Kabbalistic text warning against the making of a Golem and linking the death of God to the realization of the idea of the Golem." Not long afterward *Commentary* asked, "Does the so-called 'God is dead' question which has been agitating Christian theologians have any relevance to Judaism?"[15]

Meanwhile, a series of domestic and international developments coalesced arguably to influence Kubrick's decisions. When the combined military forces of the Arab armies massed on Israel's borders in May 1967, threatening to annihilate the Jewish state, it seemed the world stood by and watched, indifferent to Israel's survival. Comparisons were made with the Holocaust: Jews, it was feared, were faced with the specter of a second genocide within the space of a single generation. After twenty years of Jewish self-confidence in America, there was a sudden belief that anti-Semitism was not something of the past but a real and present danger. A concomitant revulsion against the passivity of the Nazis' Jewish victims was felt. Because of the Six-Day War in June 1967, New York intellectuals engaged with Israel, the Holocaust, and Judaism with much more profundity than hitherto. In this context, Raul Hilberg's *Destruction of the European Jews*, which detailed this nonresistance, was reissued in paperback, having been largely ignored on its initial publication six years earlier.

At this same time, Jewish American filmmakers began exploring their Jewish identity after years of ignoring it. The civil rights and Black Power movements empowered them, like other Americans, to "recover" their ethnic origins, producing an ethnic pride and greater interest in Jewish genealogy. The result was the proliferation of unselfconscious representations of images of Jews and Jewishness, representing the first significant "coming out" since Henry Popkin's "great retreat." Jews appeared in front of the camera much more often, whether playing explicitly Jewish characters as with Barbra Streisand in *Funny Girl* (1968) or not, such as Dustin Hoffman as Benjamin Braddock in *The Graduate* (1967).[16]

Kubrick, now an émigré, was aware of these trends, maintaining his voracious reading and film watching when researching and writing *2001*. He read Joseph Campbell's *The Hero with the Thousand Faces*—first published in 1949 and revised and published again in 1968—a book that very much tapped into the trend of spiritual awakening. He gave a copy to Clarke. He inquired after proofs of *Rosemary's Baby*, but they'd already been optioned. Alexander Walker recalls Kubrick discussing SAM-3 missiles, and Fred Ordway, who provided technical assistance on *2001*, recalled, "The only time in all those years I didn't hear Kubrick talk about *2001* was during the Israel-Arab War in 1967, when he kept saying, 'Where are the Russian advisers? Where are the Russian advisers?' Stanley, always the general." Kubrick's backers at MGM were also producing *The Bible: In the Beginning* (1966) simultaneously with *2001*. And by July 1968 Kubrick had turned forty, the age at which, according to the Ethics of the Fathers (5:21), men should pursue "understanding," that is, study Kabbalah.[17]

Kubrick also consulted the modern descendants of the kabbalists. He read Marvin Minsky's 1961 article, "Steps towards Artificial Intelligence," and arranged to meet him in London in 1965. Minsky was the head of the Artificial Intelligence Project at MIT and advised Kubrick on the subject. (One hears an echo of his name in that of the hibernating *Discovery* crew member Dr. Kaminsky.) Minksy revealed in the late 1960s, around the time that Kubrick was making *2001*, that his grandfather told him that he was a descendant of Rabbi Judah Loew (1525–1609), the Maharal of Prague, the famous Kabbalist who created a golem. Kubrick also met with Irving John "Jack" Good, a statistician and mathematical genius who contributed to cracking the German Enigma codes during World War II, as well as working on the pioneering computer, Colossus. He subsequently published *Speculations concerning the First Ultraintelligent Machine* and *Logic of Man and Machine* (both 1965). Good's father, Moshe Oved, was also a Kabbalist. And Scholem described wheelchair-bound Jewish nuclear strategist, John von Neumann, one of the sources for Dr. Strangelove, as Loew's "spiritual ancestor," from whom Neumann claimed descent, one of those who has "contributed more than anyone else to the magic that has produced the modern Golem."[18]

The Rule of Four

The first clue to a Kabbalistic reading of *2001* is its structure that Kubrick described as "really four short stories." Carolyn Geduld notes how "Kubrick seems to be fascinated by the number four," such that it "crops up ritualistically throughout the film, something not accounted for by Clarke. It creates an obsessively rhythmic force in the film." Taking four years to make, *2001* is separated into four parts and has four words in the title. It also has four digits, a four-million-year timespan, four protagonists (Moon-Watcher, Floyd, HAL, David Bowman), and four progressions (man, machine, alien, the universe). The film uses four composers' music and has a four-sided rectangle appearing four times at four different temporal moments. We leave the *Discovery* in the pod four times, HAL kills four astronauts, the Star Gate sequence can be divided into four types of material (shots of Bowman, grids, color, and landscapes), Bowman goes through four transformations, and there are four dimensions in the film. This clear four-fold division mirrors the Judaic approach of PaRDeS. An acronym for Peshat (plain/simple), Remez (hint/implication), Derash (probe/search), and Sod (secret/mystery), PaRDeS seeks to penetrate a text through four layers of seeing. Just like the PaRDeS system, each of *2001*'s four levels progressively penetrate deeper into the movie's mysteries.[19]

The opening section, "The Dawn of Man," is perhaps the easiest segment to digest: the evolution of ape from ignorant herbivore to conscious, and violent, carnivore. Hominids are also at their plainest here, eking out a simple subsistence on the desert plains of Africa. But, states Robert Poole, the sequence is the "skeleton key" to *2001*. Originally a flashback sequence, "placed late in the film to provide a backstory for the alien encounter in the year 2001," its importance was raised when, like the shooting of Quilty at the end of Nabokov's *Lolita*, it was moved to the beginning of the film at Kubrick's insistence. When it was "finally filmed in the late summer of 1967, long after the rest, the guiding hand was Kubrick's."[20]

The second section penetrates deeper into its mystery. The opening section is refined through implication. This section, per the level of Remez, yields up only hints or clues. Technocrat Dr. Heywood Floyd (William Sylvester) flies in spaceships named *Orion* and *Aries*, respectively. Despite their non-Hebraic origins, both names invoke the Bible. Where Orion is a hunter, resembling Esau, the brother of Jacob, Aries is a ram, alluding not only to the sacrificial victim of the Akedah but also to the idea of a shepherd such as the biblical King David.

Part three, "Jupiter Mission: 18 Months Later," accords to the realm of Derash or Midrash. In this light, the name of the spaceship *Discovery*, which is a space probe on a voyage of inquiry, seeking the source of the monolith on Jupiter, is highly resonant. This section is laced with Hebrew symbolism. Eighteen in Hebrew is equivalent in numeric value to "life" (*chai*), referring to double the human period of gestation and birth. The silent prayer central to the Jewish daily service is also known as the Shemonah Esrei (Eighteen) because it contains eighteen benedictions. The film's silence renders it the quality of the Amidah, or "standing" prayer. The biblical twins, Jacob and Esau, are obliquely evoked: one of the crew members on board the *Discovery* is named Dr. Charles *Hunter*, and astronauts Dr. Dave Bowman (Keir Dullea) and Dr. Frank Poole (Gary Lockwood) unsuccessfully attempt to outwit HAL, thinking he can only hear but not see, just as Jacob deceived his blind father, Isaac.

Called "Jupiter and Beyond the Infinite," the fourth and final section invokes the Kabbalistic concept of *ein-sof*, the Hebrew for "without end" or "the infinite." Ein-sof is also typically used to describe the supreme entity or Godhead. Doubling the reference, in ancient Roman religion and myth, Jupiter, or Jove, is the king of the gods and the god of sky and thunder, Zeus's equivalent in the Greek pantheon. Since Sod is the most mystical or hidden element of the PaRDeS system, it's the level associated with the esoteric and Kabbalah. This final segment, in which we find the most religious, mystical, and, arguably, Jewish, imagery, is the one most susceptible to a Kabbalistic reading. It is by no means insignificant that the final words spoken in the film are "total mystery," invoking a doctrine of faith or religious truth, as might be revealed by Kabbalah.

In the Beginning

This opening of *2001* itself mimics Genesis. The bible describes how, "When God began to create heaven and earth—the earth being unformed and void, with darkness over the surface of the deep and wind from God sweeping over the water—God said, 'Let there be light,' and there was light" (1:1–3, New International Version). The film begins in darkness in the cinema itself, as an extended black screen, lasting three minutes and seventeen seconds, and is punctuated only by the MGM logo. Ex nihilo, out of a void, the moon and sun become visible rising over the curve of the earth, transforming the darkness of the cinema into bright sunlight. The screen's formlessness and void form becomes recognizable objects. Maryvonne Butcher, writing for the Catholic *Tablet*, calls it a "serious allegory of the creation." But in what seems like a deliberately humorous gesture, this version was directed by Kubrick. A joke circulating around Borehamwood went, "In six days God created the heavens, and the earth. On the seventh day, Stanley sent everything back for modifications." A photo was pinned on the wall of the art department, on which was scribbled, "OK guys, what do we do on day eight?" The film was also backed by a studio otherwise known as "Mayer's Gantze Misphocah" (Yiddish: Mayer's entire/complete family). MGM was perceived as a very Jewish firm abroad, in contrast to, say, Universal, Paramount, or Fox, whose names sounded more goyish. MGM also bragged it boasted "more stars than there are in heaven."[21]

"The Dawn of Man" sequence very much draws on the Bible. In its suggestion that extraterrestrials are responsible for the evolution of human consciousness, whereby prehistoric apes acquired intelligence and learned to use tools, and hence to kill, the sequence resembles Genesis 1–3's account of the Garden of Eden in which, despite being commanded not to, Adam and Eve eat from the "tree of knowledge of good and bad," and their eyes are opened, that, is they acquire knowledge. Kubrick's decision to call it "The Dawn of Man" reflects the biblical use of *haAdam* (the man). Clarke described the moment when Moon-Watcher (Daniel Richter) "picks up the bone and studies it thoughtfully" as "foreshadowing Cain." When he kills the rival ape leader, it invokes the first murder of Abel by Cain. This juxtaposition of food and violence, and men or apes as meat, has been a Kubrick theme since *Day of the Fight*. Other biblical sources may also have inspired Kubrick here. That the murder weapon is a thigh bone suggests Jacob's struggle with an angel that left him with a permanent limp in his hip and provided the basis for the halachic ban on consumption of the thigh muscle (Gen. 32:23–33, Jewish Study Bible). The use of a bone as a weapon also echoes Judges 15:15, JSB, in which Samson slew a thousand men with the jawbone of an ass. As Fred Myers recognizes, writing in the *Christian Century*, "The jawbone of an ass becomes the legbone of a tapir." A skeleton dried by the sun and the pile of bones in the sand recalls Ezekiel's vision of a valley of dry bones (37:1–14, JSB), itself interpreted as a prophecy of resurrection, presaging what will happen to Bowman in the film's finale.[22]

Monoliths

The appearance of the monoliths continues the biblical, mystical theme. In Clarke's "The Sentinel," which inspired *2001*, the monolithic structure "is not a building but a machine," an ancient metallic pyramid-shaped artifact. Kubrick rejected Clarke's initial suggestions, ultimately determining the precise form and contours of the monolith, deciding that a rectangular, black, opaque, shiny, impenetrable, impressive, impassive, dark, thin, and geometrically perfect object was required. In his signature form of misdirection, Kubrick mysteriously described the monoliths as "something of a Jungian archetype." (According to Joseph Dan, "Jung saw in it [Kabbalah] universal archetypes of the human psyche."). The pyramid was, as Vincent LoBrutto puts it, "linked to the engineering marvels of Ancient Egypt." To the Jewish mind, pyramids are inextricably intertwined with Hebrew slavery.[23]

In an absence of an explanation, contemporary critics associated the monolith with the Ten Commandments. Harry Geduld describes it as the "science fiction equivalent of the handing down of the Decalogue on Mount Sinai." In the *Christian Advocate*, Willmon K. White advises his readers, "If it has even crossed your mind that the tablet in the sky might be chiseled with the Ten Commandments, don't go." "Even to atheists, the slabs wouldn't look simply like girders," states Penelope Gilliatt. "They immediately have to do with Mosaic tablets or druidical stones." John Simon feels that as a "Mies van der Rohe version of one half of the Tables of the Law, this Pentalogue has no writing on it." But where Kubrick does insert a written ten commandments, it is in the intricate and intimidating instructions posted on the door of a "Zero Gravity Toilet."[24]

It might be more convincing to compare the monolith to what Hillel Halkin describes as the "whole vast edifice of Jewish law," both the written law handed down at Sinai and the accompanying oral law codified in the Talmud. As he said, "It suddenly towered above me, this edifice, in all its architectural immensity, dizzyingly tall, explication upon explication, disagreement upon disagreement, complication upon complication." (*Mad* magazine suggested it was a giant book, "*How to Make an Incomprehensible Science Fiction Movie & Several Million Dollars* by Writer-Producer-Director Stanley Kubrick.")[25]

But the way in which the apes dance and scream around the monolith suggests the worship of the Golden Calf more than the two tablets,

FIGURE 9   Kubrick's Decalogue in *2001: A Space Odyssey* (1968).

reinforced by the overlay of Hungarian Jewish composer György Ligeti's churchly yet unearthly and wordless heavenly choir of both *Requiem* and *Lux Aeterna* (1966), both of which slowly swell in the background as we see the monolith, intensifying its mystery even more. The uncovering of the second monolith buried in the Tycho crater on the moon resembles an archaeological excavation of a sacred altar that the astronauts approach reverently. In the first draft, the language used to describe its location was decidedly biblical: "the sun would smite this sleeping land. . . . This tiny camp in the wilderness looked very lonely, very vulnerable to the forces of nature ranged silently around it."[26]

The vertical monoliths resemble the pillars or standing stones that literally dotted the Bible's desert landscapes. As foci of worship for the ancient Canaanites and Israelites until the reign of Solomon, monoliths played a key role in the Bible. Purposely arranged and carefully selected stones set vertically into the ground, individually or in groups, possessed cultic significance in early Israelite religions and were an important element of ancient worship, associated with abodes of deities. They also served as markers of graves, boundaries, important events, or sacred areas where God could be "found," where prayer could reach him. Such stone monuments marked places where God had appeared and were thus originally legitimatized for worship. Because Kubrick's monoliths are blank, they recall such stelae, upright stones often used in ancient times as funerary markers. In the novel the monolith reminds Floyd "somewhat ominously of a giant tombstone." Kubrick and Clarke's first draft refers to the monolith as a "shrine," "tomb" or "vault."[27]

FIGURE 10 *Mad* magazine's suggestion of what the Monolith is in *2001: A Space Odyssey* (1968).

The monoliths also resemble doors, gateways, ladders, or towers. In his novel *Childhood's End*, Clarke describes space exploration in the same terms: "A century before, man had set foot upon the ladder that could lead him to the stars." As Hollis Alpert wrote in the *Saturday Review*, the "slab" serves as a "sort of 'gate'" to knowledge. In his copy of Franz Kafka's *Parable and Paradoxes* (1961), Kubrick had written, "The tower of Babel was the start of the space age." It's also probably for this reason that Andrei Tarkovsky placed Pieter Bruegel the Elder's painting *The Tower of Babel* in what can be considered his companion piece to *2001*, *Solaris* (1972). And the music at the end of *2001* is a babble of voices. Babel itself means "gate of God." And the monolith has been thought to represent "something of a deity." Kubrick's decision to portray the monolith as omniscient and blank makes it appear "godlike." Geduld's description of the monolith— "infinite, indivisible, ideal, unknowable"—are precisely the same terms in which Jews have described God. Joseph Morgenstern asks, "But what was the slab? That's for Kubrick and Clarke to know and us to find out. Maybe God, or pure intelligence, maybe a Jovian as we perceive him with our primitive eyes and ears."[28]

Of Gods and Golems

HAL, the *Discovery's* computer, began life as a humanoid automaton called Socrates. He then became "Athena," after the Greek goddess of wisdom, war, and fertility and was to speak with a woman's voice. In choosing the name HAL, which Kubrick claimed stood for *H*euristic *Al*gorithm, the computer became male, backed up by the choice of Douglas Rain to voice it. Kubrick's rejection of the initial names and physical forms had the advantage of not explicitly anchoring HAL in any specific religious tradition, opening up the possibility of alternate readings and origins; however, the godlike traces remained.

HAL exercises an omnipresent and omniscient power over the *Discovery's* crew. He regulates their life-support systems. As Dr. Frank Poole puts it, "There isn't a single aspect of ship operations that's not under his control." HAL is without form; Clarke and Kubrick state "HAL was not really there" in the novel. This disembodiment makes him resemble the biblical God, whose ubiquity is conveyed through voice alone, a voice that has no precise physical location. HAL's name can be read as invoking one of the biblical names for God, corresponding to the Hebrew letters *he* (h), *aleph* (a) and *lamed* (l). Reflecting Kubrick's obsession with doubles and doubling, HAL is a twin of a computer back at Mission Control in Houston. In Genesis 1:26 (JSB) God says, "Let *us* make man in our image, after *our* likeness" (emphasis added). HAL's alleged androgyny also taps into a biblical view of God as both male and female (Gen. 1:27). In explaining this, Joseph Campbell, whom Kubrick had read, quoted Midrash (Genesis *Rabbah* 8:1): "When the Holy One, Blessed be He, created the first man, He created him androgynous." This explains why he chose Douglas Rain to voice HAL, because he possessed a "patronizing, asexual quality."[29]

HAL is also "by any practical definitions of the words, foolproof and incapable of error." Even those actions that appear to be erroneous can be interpreted otherwise. When playing chess with Poole, he makes a mistake in calling out the notation. While this seemingly contradicts what HAL had earlier told the BBC presenter, "No HAL 9000 has ever made a mistake or distorted information," his inaccuracies are deliberate deception and misdirection, foreshadowing his deception of the crew. As in a chess game, his moves are all planned in advance. Bowman may appear to outwit HAL by deactivating him, but the mission is ultimately completed when this act triggers a recording by Floyd revealing its reason, and Bowman successfully reaches Jupiter.

If a practical use of Kabbalah was the creation of golems, namely powerful androids animated by the appropriate incantations consisting of mathematical permutations and combinations of the letters that made up various mystical names of God, then this bears much similarity with modern computer science. The animation of inert, inanimate objects by imputing the correct sequences of letters is precisely the task of computer scientists who are hence, in practical terms, modern Kabbalists. Mitchell P. Marcus writes, "Without the correct programming, our computers are just inanimate, inert objects. By virtue of the correct programs, of the correct sequences of letters and symbols, we animate these machines and make them do our will." This connection between computer programming and the use of practical Kabbalah to create automata was well recognized when, as he observed in *Commentary* magazine in 1966, Gershom Scholem named the first computer in Israel "Golem." The creation of such a golem was, as Scholem notes, "in some sense competing with God's creation of Adam" and "in such an act the creative power of man enters into a relationship, whether of emulation or antagonism, with the creative power of God." Clarke confirms this when he writes, "'God made man in His own image.' This, after all, is the theme of our movie."[30]

HAL as Abraham

HAL continues Kubrick's signature theme of murdering patriarchs. He replaces the astronauts' absent parents, becoming the head of a virtual family, replacing those the astronauts (like the seamen in *The Seafarers*) are forced to abandon on their mission. And like the men in Kubrick's previous films, they are away from home and located in typically homosocial environments. There are various references in the film to absent fathers and families, particularly parents, partners, and offspring. Repeated sequences of spacemen eating together, whether an airline meal, sandwiches on a Moon Bus, or ready meals on the *Discovery*, reinforce this invocation of the family that is at the heart of Jewish religious and secular life. HAL is also the caretaker of the ship, responsible for his crew. As the paternal authority, he controls all systems aboard the *Discovery*, plots and maintains the ship's course, monitors the condition of all its thousands of working parts, and automatically performs a multitude of additional functions. In one draft, Kubrick had written, "The computer as doctor?" invoking oedipal relationships to his own father. And when Kubrick replaced Saturn with Jupiter, he introduced another symbol of the father (some have also interpreted the monolith in this light).

Through HAL, Kubrick invokes the Akedah and the obedience experiments of Stanley Milgram. Like Abraham, HAL is willing to sacrifice his children for the success of the mission. He behaves like a subject in a Milgram experiment, exceeding the proper bounds of obedience to authority, even willing to carry out murder in the fulfilment of his orders ("This mission is too important for me to allow you to jeopardize it"). This is hinted at early in the sequence when, in the interview between HAL and the BBC, the word *responsibility* is repeated five times (another caretaker, Jack Torrance, later uses the same term to justify murder). No angel stays HAL's hand when he is slaying the four astronauts, nor is a ram substituted in their place.

And yet HAL is more human, more mensch-like, than the crew. Kubrick made HAL the "only genuine character in the film." He, unlike them, is capable of emotional responses, distinguishing him from his human counterparts, whose language betrays no emotion. Poole looks bored when his family wishes him a happy birthday. By contrast, HAL appears more rounded and sympathetic than the astronauts, not least because we experience events from HAL's point of view; the subjective shots are exclusively reserved for HAL, through whose eye we see. Indeed, we are even invited inside HAL's mind and memory, learning of his "childhood" and "birth." Perhaps it was out of a form of identification with HAL that Kubrick attributes HAL's multiple acts of murder to "I know I've made some poor decisions recently, but I'm feeling much better now." Clarke even encourages us to believe that HAL had a breakdown because of an ethical conflict between preserving secrecy and ensuring the success of the mission. This personalization and individuation enables us to empathize with HAL by contrast to any of the other characters in the film with whom we do not empathize, particularly when HAL is terminally disconnected. HAL begging for his life as Dave slowly euthanizes him encourages us to believe that HAL should be treated more humanely, more like a human being. We don't weep for Poole or the hibernating astronauts who we have never met and who exist for the audience only as names printed on sarcophagi.

Tellingly, Kubrick considered Jewish voices for HAL. He told Jeremy Bernstein that "maybe it [HAL] ought to sound like [rabbi-cum-comedian] Jackie Mason." His U.S. lawyer Louis Blau suggested the Jewish actor Walter Pidgeon, as well as Jose Ferrer, who'd played the Jewish lawyer, Lt. Barney Greenwald, in the film version of *The Caine Mutiny* (1954). Kubrick later recorded Jewish actor Martin Balsam but rejected him because, according to Vincent LoBrutto, his vocal quality was "too American and overly emotional."[31]

Bowman's deactivation of HAL is loaded with Jewish, and other, symbolism. If HAL is God, and Bowman causes his death, it taps into the Nietzschean theme, signaled by Kubrick's use of Richard Strauss's *Thus Spake Zarathustra* (1896) to open and close the film, explicitly inviting us to consider Nietzsche and hence the Death of God theologies growing in popularity in the sixties. But if HAL is indeed a golem, or an idol, then Bowman's act recalls Abraham's smashing of the idols. As the patriarch, HAL engages in another oedipal struggle in which the "son" kills the father, as Dave's namesake does in *Killer's Kiss*. In their *Journey beyond the Stars*, Kubrick and Clarke had introduced an explicit oedipal element from the very outset, when "Moon-Watcher saw that his father had died in the night. He did not know the Old One was his father, for such a relationship was beyond understanding, but as he stood looking down at the emaciated body he felt something, something akin to sadness."[32]

David the Jew

There is a certain amount of textual evidence to allow us to read Bowman as subtextually Hebrew. Originally, in Clarke's story, on which the film was based, he was called Alexander, apparently to reference Alexander the Great. But Kubrick altered it to David "Dave" Bowman. (Perhaps he was saving Alex for his next film.) By having HAL call him "Dave," Kubrick invokes the eponymous character of Abraham Cahan's *The Rise of David Levinsky* (1917). When addressed as "Dave" by a gentile with whom he has been conducting business, he perceives this form of address as an implicit anti-Semitic affront: its familiarity implying "I was his inferior . . . a Jew, a social pariah." The change from Alex to David also invokes his boxing namesake from *Killer's Kiss*, whom I've read as subtextually Jewish. Indeed, two images from *Killer's Kiss* are recreated in *2001*: when Davey looks through a fish bowl, the resulting close up fish-eye effect resembles an astronaut's helmet, and when Davey has a dream that he's hurtling down

New York City's deserted streets in negative image, it foreshadows the Star Gate sequence.[33]

The name also harks back to David the Jew in *Spartacus*, as well as his biblical namesake, the shepherd boy–cum-warrior who slew Goliath and succeeded Saul as Israel's second king. When Bowman, in the vastly smaller pod, confronts HAL in the *Discovery*, their contrasting size resembles the biblical standoff of 1 Samuel 17, and Bowman certainly slays a "Goliath" in the form of HAL. The name Bowman suggests King David's ability to play a bow harp. Bowman can also play chess. Midrash and myth suggest that the biblical King Solomon played chess but does not say from whom he learned it. Perhaps it was from his father, King David. The appearance of the monolith in Dave's room also points to the biblical King David, for it resembles a door or gateway. Doors and gates feature prominently in the 24 Psalm, which is traditionally attributed to David's authorship, and *2001* has been read as a meditation on that psalm.

Other possible clues point to Bowman's Jewishness. Kubrick had wanted Paul Newman to play the role. Part-Jewish, Newman had previously starred in *Exodus*. The queerness and passivity that characterize Dave play into the stereotype of the queer or sissy Jew. While not Jewish, Dullea's previous roles in *David and Lisa* (1962) and *Bunny Lake Is Missing* (1965) tapped into the growing Jewish stereotype of an "introverted, neuter young boy with parent problems, usually his mother." Kubrick saw all Dullea's films and cast him without an audition.[34]

As the sole survivor on his ship, and utterly alone, Bowman resembles Odysseus, hence the film's title. Many have read the name Bowman as representing Odysseus's archer. Odysseus provided the inspiration for James Joyce's *Ulysses* (Latin for Odysseus), which is primarily the story of Leopold Bloom, a wandering middle-aged Irish Jew. In *Ulysses*, therefore, Joyce ironically transforms the macho Greek warrior (resembling *Spartacus*) into the figure of the sexually confused, jealous, insecure, self-loathing Irish Jew. The connection between Odysseus and Jewishness may have been forged for Kubrick when he read that, following the release of *Lolita*, Peter Sellers had signed up to play Leopold Bloom in *Ulysses*. Odysseus also provided the inspiration for Samuel Taylor Coleridge's "Old Navigator," the Ancient Mariner, which in turn invoked the myth of the Wandering Jew. Kubrick was aware of this from his reading of John Livingston Lowes's study of Coleridge, *The Road to Xanadu* (1964). But, to apply what Lowes wrote about Coleridge to Kubrick, David (like Humbert and Quilty before him) "is *not* the Wandering Jew." Kubrick's "art is not so crass as that." These films are no "New Adventures of Ahasuerus." Rather, David "is a subtle transfer to a figure which is essentially a new creation, of associations that had long been gathering about an accepted and mysterious personality of legend." Is it possible that, like Coleridge, the wandering figure is that of Cain, that is, of the same lineage as Moon-Watcher, the Cain figure from "The Dawn of Man" sequence? As Lowes puts it, "the Wandering Jew and Cain together took possession of the astral body of an ancient Mariner." Dave is an ancient, solitary sailor aboard a spaceship.[35]

Like the wandering Humbert, Dave finds himself in a tidier version of Quilty's mansion. After traveling through time and space, the first thing he does is locate a bathroom. He's dressed in white pajamas as he lies dying, harking back to the subtextually Jewish Quilty's white toga-like shroud, which also suggests the white tallith in which the Jewish male is shrouded for burial. Even those interpretations that are overwhelmingly Christian connect to Judaism. John Allen in the *Christian Science Monitor* describes Dave's meal as a "last supper," which itself was a celebration of the Passover. When Dave knocks a crystal wine glass to the floor, it references the tradition of smashing a glass at Jewish wedding ceremonies in memory of the suffering of past generations, symbolizing the destruction of the Holy Temple in Jerusalem in 70 CE and marking the change from one way of life to a new one. It may also obliquely invoke Kristallnacht—the Nazi pogrom against the Jews. Clarke interprets it as an allusion to Jewish liturgy, believing that, in some way, Kubrick was expressing his Jewish identity through this image: "I think Dave's breaking the glass was a cinematic gimmick. Stanley was listening to his inner deamons [*sic*] at the time and they may have been telling him, 'What's a nice Jewish boy like you doing in a place like this.'" It also points to his clumsiness, his being a klutz, and his lack of table manners, claiming that even in the future, Jews still don't know how to eat with decorum.[36]

Bowman undergoes a metamorphosis into the fetal shape of what Clarke calls a "Star-Child" in utero. Bowman, the last surviving crew member of the *Discovery*—perhaps the last member of humanity—is reborn as, Joseph Morgenstern puts it, a "cute little embryo Adam, staring into space from his womb." The X-ray-like image of his enlarged head evokes the skull in "The Dawn of Man." Like Rosemary's baby, born in the same year, the Star-Child is neither innocent nor ignorant. He symbolizes "childhood's end," the very title of the story from which Kubrick drew his inspiration.

That the Star-Child is born with such knowledge invokes the idea found in the Talmud, in Niddah 30a, where the fetus is poetically described as learning Torah from an angel in the womb. Upon exiting, the angel strikes the baby, forming the indent in the upper lip, causing the baby to forget all the knowledge that it once knew. The room in which Bowman ends up can be interpreted as a symbolic womb where Dave undergoes rebirth. Noah is also entombed in a womblike ark as the world is deluged and transformed around him. Similarly, the Hebrew prophet Jonah is spiritually reborn after being swallowed by a whale and thus carried safely to land after he had been cast out from a ship. In *The Uses of Enchantment*, Bruno Bettelheim explains how "Jonah discovers his higher morality, his higher self, and is wondrously reborn," and Clarke's *Childhood's End* had already connected Jonah with human evolution and space travel.[37]

Bowman's transformation suggests the Kabbalistic *gilgul-neshamoth* (Hebrew: rotation or transmigration of souls, reincarnation). Also known as metempsychosis, the term played a prominent role in Joyce's *Ulysses* and is also associated with Nietzsche. Gilgul is a transmigration of the soul in which lofty souls recycle to complete spiritual missions. Gilgul, which means in Hebrew "to roll or cycle," forms the same root as that for the Hebrew word for skull (*golgeleth*), another reminder of the skull in "The Dawn of Man" sequence. On this note, Clarke wrote how he had to fight hard "to stop Stan from bringing Dr. Poole back from the dead. I'm afraid his obsession with immortality has overcome his artistic instincts." Kubrick had labeled this section "Metamorphosis," and *Der Gilgul* was the Yiddish translation of Kafka's 1915 story *The Metamorphosis*, in which Gregor Samsa is transformed into a giant beetle. Kafka knew the concept of *gilgul* from his reading and contacts, noting it in his diary, and Scholem describes "Kafka's deep roots in the tradition of Jewish mysticism" and its "enormous force" in his books. Volker Fischer feels the ending of the film "resembles Kafka and is obviously meant to do so."[38]

Kubrick described Bowman's transformation as becoming "a star child, an angel, a superman." His use of the term "superman" is a translation of Nietzsche's Übermensch, reinforced by the musical choices and other motifs in the film. For Walter Kaufmann, this Übermensch means a yet unrealized higher humanity, with a stress on social responsibility, a key Kubrick idea. Kubrick's term also hints at the subsurface Jewish comics character, Superman, itself a retelling of the Moses story. Stuart Freeborn, who worked on *2001*'s special effects, stated Dave was 120 at that point, making him the same age as Moses when he died. John Simon's description of *2001* as a "kind of space-*Spartacus*" also hints at Moses, given the parallels between him and Spartacus. Underpinning this biblical theme was Kubrick's initial choice of Alex North, who composed the music for *Spartacus*, but his score was replaced with music by Aram Khachaturian, who had written a Spartacus ballet. And Gary Lockwood had been a stuntman in *Spartacus*.[39]

The film *2001* is messianic and hopeful, a film in which Kubrick reiterates his faith in humanity's menschlikayt. In Hebrew, Jupiter is known as *tzedek* (Hebrew: righteous, charitable), and the Talmud states, "He who is born under *Tzedek* will be a right-doing man" (Shabbath 156a). The Star-Child represents the coming of the supermensch, a Messiah who, in Jewish tradition, is a descendant of the House of *David*. Where *Rosemary's Baby* and *Planet of the Apes* (1968) both end pessimistically, with the birth of a satanic antimessiah and the revelation of a postnuclear holocaust, *2001* introduces a ray of hope, confirming Kubrick's belief in healing or repairing the world, *tikkun olam*. From the point of view of the Star-Child, we zoom into the monolith, the darkness of which fills the screen. As the draft of the novel describes, the darkness was "absolute": "Like the chaos before Creation, it was without form, and void." Thus, we return to the beginning of the film, except this time, as the monolith's darkness fills the screen, it turns into the skies above the Earth, where the reborn Bowman hovers. The cycle begins again, just as the title represents a dawn of a new era. And by introducing the monoliths, Kubrick may have been saying that violence is not innate to human nature; it is the result of alien intervention. Joseph Gelmis asked Kubrick, "Why does *2001* seem so affirmative and religious a film? What has happened to the tough, disillusioned, cynical director of *The Killing*, *Spartacus*, *Paths of Glory*, and *Lolita*, and the sardonic black humorist of *Dr Strangelove*?" Kubrick never answered this question directly.[40]

Conclusion

Kubrick's "religious" turn, while not manifested in any traditional or conventional religious belief or practice, is evident in *2001*. Fred Myers, writing in the *Christian Century*, opined, "I think what he has done is something like what Michelangelo did on the ceiling of the Sistine Chapel." Kubrick said after the film was released, "If *2001* has stirred your emotions, your subconscious, your mythological leanings, then it has succeeded." Kubrick may not have become any more religiously observant after *2001*. After all, he was still married to a gentile. But it did seem that he was aspiring for something more spiritual and metaphysical, channeling his religious and ethnic heritage into *2001*. The film was the product of the years 1967–1968, and whatever happened to Kubrick in those years marked a significant watershed.[41]

6

A Mechanical Mensch

Following his most religious film, *2001*, *A Clockwork Orange* is possibly Stanley Kubrick's most explicitly philosophical film. Where *2001* ended on the supermensch, *A Clockwork Orange* explored the mensch in the future. In adapting Anthony Burgess's 1962 novel about free will versus behavioral conditioning, Kubrick continued his inquiry into the nature of man (the word *orang* means human in Malay) and the problem of evil. In the words of the character, P. R. Deltoid, when addressing the violent protagonist, Alex, "You've got a good home here, good loving parents, you've got not too bad of a brain. Is it some devil that crawls inside of you?" Here Kubrick's curiosity was piqued by the metaphor of a man as a "clockwork orange," an organic outer layer, containing internal machinery that determines or dictates a man's actions. Ultimately he sought to answer the question: if a man cannot choose, does he cease to be a man?[1]

Peeling the Orange

A Clockwork Orange was not Kubrick's first choice of project to succeed *2001*. Over the summer of 1967 he began devoting his energies to a film about Napoleon, but failure to acquire studio funding for it over the course of 1969 forced him to turn to other projects. In 1968 he had acquired the rights to Arthur Schnitzler's *Traumnovelle* with a view to adapting it but was not ready to proceed. Sometime during the production of *2001*, circa 1966, Terry Southern gave Kubrick a copy of *A Clockwork Orange*, hoping to entice him to adapt it. But Kubrick didn't read it until two and a half years later, over the summer of 1969, when Christiane told him, "Forget Schnitzler—read this," referring to Burgess's novel. Kubrick, she said, "jumped to that one immediately and Schnitzler was forgotten for a while." He recalled, "Then one evening I passed the bookshelf, glanced at the paperback still patiently waiting on the shelf, and picked it up. I started to read the book."[2]

Set in a future England, *A Clockwork Orange* blends the present with futuristic dystopian elements. Focused around the leader of a violent youth gang, Alex DeLarge, the book explores his propensity to criminal behavior, including violence, rape, and, ultimately, murder. Alex is imprisoned and then subjected to an experimental aversion treatment aimed to induce nausea when confronted with either violence or sex. He soon becomes a tool in the hands of the state and those who conspire against it. Forced to jump out of a high window, he's "cured" shortly thereafter.

A Clockwork Orange instantly appealed to Kubrick. He recalled how he "finished it one sitting. . . . As soon as I finished it, I immediately reread it." He told *Rolling Stone*, "One could almost say that it's the kind of book you have to look hard to find a reason not to do." "It has everything: great ideas, a great plot, external action, interesting side characters and one of the most unique leading characters I've ever encountered in fiction—Alex. The only character comparable to Alex is Richard III and I think they both work on your imagination in much the say way. They both take the audience into their confidence, they are both completely honest, witty, intelligent and unhypocritical." Kubrick explained to Michel Ciment, "I was also interested in how close the story was to fairy tales and myths, particularly in its deliberately heavy use of coincidence and plot symmetry." He also described it as a "fairy tale of retribution" and a "psychological myth." He told *New York* magazine, "The narrative invention was magical, the characters were bizarre and exciting, the ideas were brilliantly developed, and, equally important, the story was of a size and density that could be adapted to film without simplifying it or stripping it to the bone." And he informed the *New York Times*, "I was excited by everything about it, the plot, the ideas, the characters and, of course, the language. Added to which, the story was of manageable size in terms of adapting it for film."[3]

A Clockwork Orange held many attractions. It allowed Kubrick to cap off his trilogy of science fiction films. It permitted him to incorporate the Napoleonic and Schnitzler themes of sex, violence, leadership, the responsibilities and abuses of power, the dynamics of social revolution, and the relationship of the individual to the state. It also dealt with Kubrick's long-term interest in Nazism and the Holocaust. Like Nabokov's *Lolita*, with which the film of *A Clockwork Orange* bears some comparison, many of the metaphors and descriptions in Burgess's book evoke the trains, camps, and other details of the Holocaust, both directly and subtextually. Burgess invokes a consistent pattern of references to Nazi persecution and genocide: Alex is incarcerated in Staja 84F, shorthand for "state jail," but which recalls the German stalags of World War II, and Alex is forced to watch Nazi documentary footage of the death camps, mass shootings, and gassing of Jews.

In 1970 Warner Bros. offered Kubrick complete creative freedom in return for three films. It meant there was no reason to leave Hertfordshire, and Warner's office in London would fund the purchase, development, and production of properties for him to direct. Warner's Los Angeles executives Ted Ashley, Terry Semel, Steve Ross, John Calley, and Julian Senior in London protected his interests, freeing him of the need to find backing and distribution for each new project. He had final cut, giving him the control he required, and he received 40 percent of the profits. By hiring his brother-in-law, Jan Harlan, as his executive producer, his total control and privacy was cemented.

On February 3, 1970, *Variety* announced that Kubrick was to "write, produce and direct" *A Clockwork Orange*. The *New York Times* reported that it was "slated to go before the cameras in London this summer although it has not yet been cast." When Southern learned of Kubrick's involvement, he sent him his own version of the screenplay, written in 1966, but was informed, "Mr. Kubrick has decided to try his own hand." Like *Napoleon*, this represented another unusual working pattern for Kubrick, for it was the only screenplay for a finished film to date that he wrote entirely on his own. It was also, unlike his previous efforts, one "whose cultural background is truly English" (as his next film, *Barry Lyndon*, was to be). Kubrick started working on his own version in early 1970, ignoring both Southern's and Burgess's screenplays. Working hard, he completed a full draft by the end of February. By mid-May he completed what he considered a proper "first draft." For the first time, Kubrick used a computer, enabling him to rearrange scenes digitally. His "shooting script" was completed by early September.[4]

Kubrick contacted Malcolm McDowell, asking him to read the book, before offering him the lead role, and filming began in September 1971, lasting twenty-three weeks, until February 1971. *A Clockwork Orange* was made using a small mobile crew, on location, with only a few sets built where suitable locations couldn't be found, resembling the shoots of his earliest feature films (*Fear and Desire* through to *The Killing*). He did all of the handheld shooting himself, which, combined with the film's lack of stars, made it a relatively cheap production at just $2 million. During the shoot Kubrick extensively rewrote the dialogue during long rehearsals with the actors, especially McDowell. He worked on Alex's voice-over until March 1971, when he began postproduction. Working seven days a week, he completed the film by the end of the year. The film premiered in New York City on December 20, 1971, and in Britain on January 13, 1972. Two years later Kubrick himself withdrew the film in the United Kingdom and it was not rereleased there until after his death, on March 17, 2000.

Good and Evil

The period following the release of *2001* in April 1968 was one of the most violent within recent American history. Martin Luther King Jr. and Robert F. Kennedy were both assassinated, the Tet Offensive broke out in Vietnam, and protesting students were shot by National Guard troops at Kent State University. There were also the violent scenes at the Chicago Democratic Convention. This was reflected in the loosening of the production code, resulting in more graphically violent films. *A Clockwork Orange* was released in the same year as Sam Peckinpah's *Straw Dogs* and Roman Polanski's *Macbeth*. British society had also witnessed its own postwar violence in bloody decolonization abroad and between mods and rockers at home.

As the Vietnam War intensified, "ordinary Americans of many different backgrounds were encouraged to see their own lives and political actions through the lens of Nazi Germany." Accounts such as David Halberstam's *The Making of a Quagmire* (1965) cataloged the inhumane actions performed by ordinary Americans in Vietnam. Raul Hilberg's *Destruction of the European Jews* was released in paperback in 1967. When the My Lai Massacre on March 16, 1968, demonstrated American complicity in war crimes, comparisons between Vietnam and the Holocaust increased in frequency. In 1970 Nuremberg prosecutor Telford Taylor published *Nuremberg and Vietnam: An American Tragedy*, a cautious meditation on American and German war crimes. J. Glenn Gray's *The Warriors: Reflections on Men in Battle* (1959), which explored his World War II experiences, was reissued with an introduction by Hannah Arendt. The following year, in his *Vietnam, Inc.* (1971), photographer Philip Jones Griffiths documented the impact of the war on Vietnamese civilian life, particularly U.S. war crimes, including the murder of women and children.[5]

This U.S. propensity toward violence surely impelled Kubrick to continue his study of the nature of humanity, into menschlikayt and evil. Writing in the *Alternative*, John Ashmead asked, "Can we speculate even further, that a good deal of the violence of America (and this is an American film for all its British dress—note the stress on blows to the crotch, four of them, as against one in the novel—) is rooted in this covert homosexuality. A repressed homosexuality which finds overt expression on the one hand in *Playboy*, on the other in Mylai?" This was precisely the subject of Norman Mailer's 1967 novel *Why Are We in Vietnam?*, which Kubrick had read. "Man's capacity for violence," Kubrick told interviewers, "is an evolutionary hangover which no longer serves a useful purpose but it's there, all the same." Emanuel Schwartz felt, "The question of good and evil is central to the entire film," and Kubrick informed *Sight and Sound*, "If I were a reviewer I would describe the film as a morality tale, told by a 1972 Voltaire."[6]

As with his previous projects, Kubrick immersed himself in research. Already grounded in the work of Robert Ardrey, Sigmund Freud, Charles Darwin, and so on, he extended it into the particularly topical field of developmental and behavioral psychology and psychological conditioning, reading about Ivan Pavlov's experiments and conditioned-reflex training used by the Soviets during World War II. In the Cold War context, brainwashing was of particular interest. Sociologists Edgar Schein, Inge Schneier, Curtis H. Becker, and Robert Lifton, respectively, studied how Korean and Chinese communists used specific techniques to influence American prisoners of war, resulting in their captives' cooperation and sympathy, popularized by the 1959 novel and 1962 movie, *The Manchurian*

Candidate. The growth of new radical, separatist, religious cults in the sixties and early seventies led to fears that they used "coercive persuasion" and other mind-control techniques to brainwash their adherents.[7]

Kubrick showed a familiarity with both the French philosophes and the more contemporary work of B. F. Skinner, particularly his *Beyond Freedom and Dignity* (1971), which argues that free will is illusory. Skinner contends our belief in autonomy is outdated; rather, our behavior is conditioned by a myriad of external factors that, if isolated, could be manipulated through conditioning to improve the chances of our long-term survival. Immediately, fears that such a technology could be abused by a Nazi or Soviet dictator were reported. Skinner was accused of being a fascist and apologist for totalitarianism, viewing humans as no more than mindless machines. He was called a "distant cousin of Dr. Strangelove."[8]

Kubrick agreed with Skinner's critics. "I like to believe that Skinner is wrong and that what is sinister is that this philosophy may serve as the intellectual basis for some sort of scientifically oriented repressive government." He added, "Another area where Skinner should be attacked is in his attempt to formulate a total philosophy of the human personality solely in terms of conditioning. This is a dreary conception. I like to believe that there are certain aspects of the human personality which are essentially unique and mysterious." For Kubrick, like Burgess, the ultimate act of evil is dehumanization, the killing of the soul, that which creates art and culture, such as movies. Had such a self-described "misfit" as Kubrick undergone social conditioning, there would have been no photography and no films, certainly not as unique as his. He clearly betrays his feelings when he explained, "The essential moral of the story hinges on the question of choice, and the question of whether man can be good without having the choice to be evil, and whether a creature who no longer has the choice is still a man." Kubrick's careful selection of words, posing man against creature, shows that without choice, man is no longer a mensch; he's just an animal. *A Clockwork Orange* has the "quality of a morality play. It brings home forcefully how we participate in the corruption and dehumanization of one another: parents, children, friends, enemies, police, doctors, politicians, clergymen, government, and so on."[9]

"A Porno-Violent Sci-Fi Comedy"

"So what is a nice Jewish boy from the Bronx like Stanley Kubrick doing making bizarre films like 'A Clockwork Orange'?" Craig McGregor asks in the *New York Times*. Staying true to Kubrick's New York Jewish roots, the film is a black comedy parodying contemporary society, laden with cynicism and irony, overblown caricatured characters, and overacting, in the mode of *Dr. Strangelove*. One of the characters was to be called "Nurse Brain Drain," showing a similar sense of humor. As with *Dr. Strangelove*'s abandoned ending, it becomes pure slapstick when Alex passes out and his face lands in a dish of spaghetti. Kubrick told Gene Siskel, "It's a satire, which is to say that you hold up current vices and folly to ridicule. You pretend to say the opposite of the truth in order to destroy it." McDowell states, "I honestly thought I was making a black comedy and played it for humor." He feels that he and Kubrick shared a "wicked sense of humor," which was as "black as charcoal." The result is, for Hollis Alpert, "Every scene, every shot even, is seasoned with touches of satire, mordant humor, and a soupçon of the sinister." Pauline Kael feels Kubrick carried over from *Dr. Strangelove* "his jokey adolescent view of hypocritical, sexually dirty authority figures." William S. Pechter in *Commentary* calls it "sophomoric in its misanthropic humor."[10]

As in *Dr. Strangelove*, Kubrick refused to take a political stance. The genteel classes in the film share a taste for the pornographic with the underclasses. The droogs can easily become police officers who, in turn, are equally as violent and brutal as the droogs. The hypocritical writer is no better than the minister of the interior (who, despite his name, aims to remove any interiority). Kubrick even denies the victims any sympathy. Alex is both odious and charming, perpetrator and victim. The chaplain is simultaneously a crude caricature and the moral voice of the film. Perhaps the most violent individuals in the film are the doctors who administer the Ludovico Treatment. While clearly critiquing the totalitarian tendencies of the authoritarian government in a society lacking in positive traits, its left-wing opposition similarly resorts to violence and the cynical exploitation of the individual but with no alternative manifesto or strategy.

Intensifying the satiric effect was Kubrick's decision to give *A Clockwork Orange* the quality of a Hollywood musical. Burgess's novel is filled with musical references. Kubrick explained, "I wanted to find a way to stylize all this violence and also to make it as balletic as possible. The attempted rape on stage has the overtones of a ballet. They move around the stage. The speeded-up orgy sequence is a joke." In another interview, he explained,

> In a very broad sense you can say the violence is turned to dance, although it is in no way any kind of formal dance. But in cinematic terms, I should say that movement and music must inevitably be related to dance, just as the rotating space station and the docking Orion spaceship in *2001* moved to the "Blue Danube." From the rape on the stage of the derelict casino, to the super-frenzied fight, through the Christ figures cut, to Beethoven's Ninth, the slow-motion fight on the water's edge, and the encounter with the cat lady where the giant phallus is pitted against the bust of Beethoven, movement, cutting, and music are the principal considerations—dance?"

By orchestrating most of the violence to the overture to Gioachino Rossini's *The Thieving Magpie* (1817) and locating it in theatrical settings (literally onstage in at least two sequences), as well as within films within the film, the immediate effect is to make it, in the words of John Weightman in *Encounter*, a parody of *West Side Story*, or "Jerome Robbins gone mad." Alexander Walker, writing in the same journal, refers to the "ballet" of the gang fight and the "vaudeville" of the assault and rape to the melody of "Singin' in the Rain." Concluding the film on that same tune fits nicely into a period of such Jewish musicals as *Funny Girl, The Producers*, and *Fiddler on the Roof* (1971). Indeed, as if in an MGM production (ironically, the studio that backed *2001*), Alex struts into the writer's house with a cane and bowler hat, as if about to perform a tap routine. He does a soft-shoe dance, orchestrating the action, but punctuating it with choreographed movements. At one point, he even gets down on one knee like Al Jolson. It is, for Stephen Mamber, "obvious musical comedy parody."[12]

As with Kubrick's two previous satires, sex is a key feature. *A Clockwork Orange* is peppered with smutty jokes, sexual imagery, sight gags, and humor, but in a manner forbidden by the Production Code hitherto. Such restrictions meant sex was heavily censored in *Lolita* and *Dr. Strangelove* and rendered much more obliquely in *2001*. But what Kubrick calls a "revolution in Hollywood's treatment of sex" allowed him more freedom to indulge this preoccupation, evident from his *Look* assignments, *The Seafarers, Fear and Desire, Killer's Kiss, The Killing*, and which permeated his previous three films, as well as other projects he was considering in the mid-1960s. He was interested in adapting the 1962 novel *The*

Passion Flower Hotel, in which some enterprising boarding school girls sell sexual services to a neighboring boys school to make money. He also discussed with Southern making a big-budget Hollywood hard-core porno. His screenplay drafts for *Napoleon* reveal a prurient interest in Napoleon's sex life, and the sexuality of *Traumnovelle* is always present in the background. Kubrick channeled some of this into *A Clockwork Orange,* resulting in frequent female nudity, paintings and models of women in sexually explicit positions, a giant penis sculpture, phallic popsicles, naked Jesus statues, a defaced mural of Jesus with an erection, turgid codpieces, and a pack of "Eat Me" dates in a hospital fruit basket. Overall, what Ciment calls Kubrick's "obsession with breasts" gives it the feel of a "high class Russ Meyer pornyshow," "with," as Craig McGregor suggests, "some Andy Warhol freakery thrown in for shockpower." A six-page pictorial from the movie even appears in the January 1972 *Playboy.* Critics and ordinary viewers alike complained it was gratuitously pornographic: Kael described it as a "porno-violent sci-fi comedy."[13]

And, as with *2001, A Clockwork Orange* is deliberately elliptical and ambiguous. Kubrick's discarding of Burgess's final chapter, in which Alex is rehabilitated, reintegrated, and reformed of his own volition, combined with Kubrick's other changes—the addition of classical music and dream images, especially the final enigmatic scene—lends the film an unreal quality. Kubrick told *Take One* that the film is intentionally dreamlike and, like dreams, requires a "suspension of moral judgment." He continued, "The story functions, of course, on several levels, political, sociological, philosophical, and what's most important, on a kind of dream-like psychological-symbolic level." The coincidences of the film's second half, which mirrors many of the events of the first, also makes it similar to *Traumnovelle.*[14]

Kubrick's Judaism

Kubrick had never adapted a book with such an overtly religious leaning by such an openly religious writer. Anthony Burgess was a Pelagian Catholic, who, in rejecting the concept of original sin, believed in the notion of moral progress, themes underpinning his 1962 novel. Burgess was explicit about his book's religious intentions: "I wanted to show in my story that God made man free to choose either good or evil and this is an astounding gift." He described the book (and film) as a "parable" and "intended homiletic work." "What I had tried to write was a sort of Christian allegory of free will. Man is defined by his capacity to choose courses of moral action. If he chooses good, he must have the possibility of choosing evil instead; evil is a theological necessity."[15]

Kubrick betrayed his indebtedness to what Burgess described as the "Judaeo-Christian ethic that *A Clockwork Orange* tries to express." Man's freedom to choose between certain courses of conduct is a fundamental principle of the Jewish religion. As Rabbi Norman Lamm explains in the abandoned prologue to *2001*, "the image of God refers to His creative, intellectual, and ethical powers and, even more so, His freedom: freedom of will, freedom to do right or wrong, to do evil or good." Kubrick chose the prison chaplain (Godfrey Quigley) to act as the "moral voice of the film," articulating its central thesis: "When a man cannot choose, he ceases to be a man." The chaplain declares, "The question is whether or not this treatment really makes a man good. Goodness comes from within. Goodness must be chosen." Later he shouts, "Choice! The boy has no real choice, has he? Self-interest, the fear of physical pain, drove him to the grotesque act of self-abasement. Its insincerity was clearly to be seen. He ceases to be a wrongdoer. He ceases also to be a creature capable of moral choice." The writer, Mr. Alexander (Patrick Magee), articulates similar sentiments: "I tell you, sir, they have turned this young man into something other than a human being. He has no power of choice any more. He's committed to socially acceptable acts, a little machine capable only of good." Kubrick, showing his debt to normative Judaism, believed that a man unable to choose is not a mensch but an animal. Yet again, though, Kubrick proceeded by misdirection, denying that this view of humankind derived from his Jewish background: "I mean, it's essentially Christian theology anyway, that view of man." Instead, he claimed it came "from observation. Knowing what has happened in the world, seeing the people around me."[16]

Jewish critics, though, complained about the film's ambivalence and ambiguity. Writing in the *Jewish Exponent*, Jane Biberman, states,

> There are no victims because this violence is practiced by everyone, many times for the sheer thrill of brutality. The philosophical and psychological meaning of the work is not clear. The film seems to lack a viewpoint and a moral comment. It is, if anything, amoral, and its surface is cold and unsparing. It is hard to relate to this film on any level because none of the characters is drawn with

sympathy or compassion. Alex (Malcolm McDowell) is a vicious hoodlum who is repulsive in every aspect, lacking all humanity. But he is no less repulsive than everyone else in the film.

Kenneth Matheson, in the *Jewish Advocate*, suggests "The film assumes an absence of positive human relationships that is psychologically unhinging. Women are victims, parents stupid, chaplains fools, politicians corrupt and doctors inhumane." But Leighton Ford of the *Kilgore Texas News Herald* sees how the film "underlines the fact, that, from the beginning, God has respected and loved men so much that He has made us with the capacity to freely choose one course of conduct. And man can choose whether or not to repent." Ironically, it is Frederic A. Brussat in the *Lutheran Forum*, who compares Kubrick's "parable" to the "prophets of the Old Testament," particularly Hosea, who "were about the business of exposing idolatry." John E. Fitzgerald, in the *New York Catholic News*, explains that because Kubrick was "an artist rather than a moralist," he "leaves it to us to figure what's wrong and why, what should be done and how it should be accomplished."[17]

In addition to its view of evil and free will, *A Clockwork Orange* comments on organized religion, particularly Christianity, continuing a theme that engaged Kubrick from his first photographs and documentaries. But compared to this early work, which dispassionately presented images of the Catholic Church from the perspective of the outsider, in *A Clockwork Orange* Kubrick took a skeptical and satirical stance on organized religion through its conception of free will and its representative in the chaplain. Kubrick admits to Ciment that he balanced the "important ideas he [the chaplain] is [*sic*] called upon to express" with his "somewhat comical image." The chaplain is, in Kubrick's own words, "trotted out looking a bit of the buffoon," becoming a somewhat satirical semicaricature. Already called a "Charles," referencing Charles Chaplin, this very moniker conceptualizes him as a figure of fun. Kubrick also presents him as a "closeted homosexual" when he makes what can be interpreted as a pass at Alex. Many contemporary reviewers complained that the padre was a caricature of a clergyman.

Moreover, the chaplain may oppose the Ludovico Treatment, expressing the importance of the human capacity for free will, but Kubrick undermines his point by penning a sermon for him that preaches fire and brimstone, articulating his own kind of aversion therapy to encourage a fear-based morality. This sermon was a significant departure from and expansion of the novel's brief description. The chaplain's attempt to teach morality is weakened by religion's traditional methods, as well as its resort to sex-and-violence–filled scriptures, illustrated by the clear joy that Alex derives from its racier passages. Kubrick further satirizes the chaplain's stance by humorously equating the chaplain's use of the words "in and out" and Alex's earlier description of copulation as "in-out in-out." The minister of the interior's (Anthony Sharp) response shows just how hollow these claims are. "Padre, there are subtleties! We are not concerned with motives, with higher ethics. We are only concerned with cutting down crime and with revealing the ghastly congestion in our prisons. He will be your true Christian, ready to turn the other cheek, ready to be crucified rather than crucify, sick to the heart at the thought of killing a fly. Reclamation! Joy before the angels of God! The point is that it works." It's noticeable that the most religious iconography is seen only in the prison and that this society appears completely areligious. In this way, Kubrick critiques the Bible and biblical-based religion, particularly Christianity, for its hypocrisy.[18]

Starry Yahoodies

Kubrick's views on free will and Christianity may have slotted in nicely with rabbinic Judaism, but, in signature fashion, his attitude toward Jewishness in *A Clockwork Orange* is seemingly contradictory. While he omits references to some of the novel's Jewish characters altogether, he retains the names of others and includes direct verbal and visual references to Jews, as well as inserting subsurface Jewish characters. In the novel one of the masks was to be of Disraeli (of which no comment is made by Alex, in contrast to his remark that "poor old Dim had a poet veck called Peebee Shelley"), and in prison there are fellow inmates called "Zophar" (one of the biblical Job's three friends) and "Big Jew." None of these details appear in Kubrick's drafts (although they do in Southern's and Burgess's) or in the final film.[19]

Where Burgess directly invokes the Nazi genocide of the Jews, Kubrick refuses to do so. In the novel Alex explains how he was shown a "particularly bad film of like a concentration camp," as he acquires his conditioning, but in the film, we see sequences of combat and Adolf Hitler and Heinrich Himmler commemorating the German dead of World War I. Kubrick explained this avoidance by saying, "I didn't want to show scenes of a real camp." He added, "Also somehow the idea of watching Nazis marching along to Beethoven's Ninth has echoes of those pictures (like *Judgement at Nuremberg*) in which people say things like 'How can a country that produced Beethoven . . . ?'" He told Victor Davis of the *Daily Express*, "Culture seems to have no effect upon evil. People have written about the failure of culture in the twentieth century: the enigma of Nazis who listened to Beethoven and sent millions off to gas chambers."[20]

Yet Kubrick retained Alex's visions of "starry yahoodies tolchocking each other and then peeting their Hebrew vino and getting onto the bed with their wives, like handmaidens, real horrorshow." He rendered them visually in a style reminiscent of *Spartacus*. Research materials show that these scenes were based on the costume epic *Ben-Hur*, the very film that prompted Kirk Douglas to make *Spartacus* in the first place as a riposte for being denied the lead role. When reviewing *Spartacus*, Hollis Alpert notes how it "differs from the usual Romanesque type in that it . . . lacks the

FIGURE 11 A close-up of a Nazi swastika in *A Clockwork Orange* (1971).

customary orgies in which dusky, semi-nude girls cram grapes into their mouths as fat Roman nobles eye them lasciviously." This seems to have been saved for *A Clockwork Orange* as a knowing nod to his earlier film.[21]

The casting of Steven Berkoff as a cop continued Kubrick's fascination with Jewish masculinity and power. Berkoff was a Jewish theater actor and director who had already directed theatrical productions of Franz Kafka's *Metamorphosis* and *The Trial*. Kubrick also considered him for role of Joe the Lodger but ultimately cast him as the police officer who interrogates Alex. Berkoff played him as a tough and menacing cop, ridiculing the oxymoronic notion of a Jewish cop. On his casting notes, Kubrick had written, "very very sinister" and "Very Good Cop." Kubrick also retained the Jewish name of one of the conspirators—Rubinstein. And one reviewer, Jackson Burgess, even felt that Dr. Brodsky (Carl Duering) was Jewish: "Visual horrors abound in *A Clockwork Orange*, yet the worst moment may not be any of the murders, rapes, tortures, or beatings, but the moment when you notice that the film's monster, the manager of the aversion therapy to which Alex is subjected, has a Jewish name. Mere bad taste? Or the fearful symmetry of a nightmare?" Lending some credence to this point, Brodsky's surname is a version of the Galician town of Brody, an important center of Jewish life on the border between Austria and Russia. It is also the surname

FIGURE 12   Alex (Malcolm McDowell) imagining himself as a "starry yahoodie" in *A Clockwork Orange* (1971).

of the famous Jewish poet, Joseph Brodsky, who in 1963 wrote "Abraham and Isaac." Onscreen he resembles a hybrid of the real-life Stanley Milgram (whose experiments were being conducted at this time) and Doctors Zemph and Strangelove.[22]

The way that Kubrick rewrote the role of the Catlady lends her a subsurface Jewishness. In the novel she's an elderly, reclusive woman, "very gray in the voloss," living alone in a decaying house with her pets. In his memo of August 1970, Kubrick outlined his "significant innovations." One of those was his changes to the character of Miss Weathers at Woodmere Health Farm, aka, the "Catlady." Kubrick noted, "A substantially changed character of the Catlady as well as her décor. In the novel and previous screenplay versions she was an old, eccentric woman with a walking stick. In this case, she is a youngish, diet-slim 40-year-old, in a room full of pornographic art and sculpture, one piece of which is the cause of her death." By contrast, Kubrick's Catlady has jewels, art, and other valuables stashed at her house, which is decorated with vulgar, garish, and erotic art. The *Albany New York Evangelist* notes, "the Cat Lady whom Alex kills (an act which leads to his arrest) is transformed from a terrified little thing fighting for her life into an arrogant pop-culturist who surrounds herself with grotesque erotic art (she is killed with one of her own phallic sculptures) and who virtually challenges Alex to kill her." Before they attack her, Georgie (James Marcus) justifies robbing her because her house "is full up with like gold, and silver, and like jewels." But the way he pronounces "jewels" sounds as if he is saying *Jews*. These changes turn her into the common stereotype of the rich, unsympathetic, uncaring, vulgar, Jewish pornographer, and her death uncannily mirrors Quilty's and her taste anticipates Ziegler's. And Robert Hughes refers to her "sculptured *schlong*," as if her subtextual Jewishness is rendered through his deliberate use of the Yiddishism for "penis."[23]

In the role Kubrick cast Jewish actor Miriam Karlin. Described as a "female Peter Sellers," she'd earlier starred in *East End, West End*, a six-part comedy series penned by Jewish writer Wolf Mankowitz, and was part of what was called "Mankowitz's Jewish troupe." She had also appeared in *Sellers' Market* with Sellers himself. In 1960 she played the anxious Jewish mother, Mrs. Matthias, in *Hand in Hand*; played a mean-spirited Jewish wife in *The Small World of Sammy Lee* (1963); and starred opposite Topol, as Golde, in the 1967 London production of *Fiddler on the Roof*. Karlin was also a prominent Jewish activist, a member of the

Anti-Nazi League, which fought British neo-Nazis. Kubrick met her at a party, where Christiane told her, "Stanley's been looking at you." The next day she was offered the part. There are intriguing parallels between Karlin and his earlier casting of Shelley Winters in *Lolita*. In addition to their shared ethnicity, both had played Mrs. Van Daan in versions of *The Diary of Anne Frank*. Like Winters, both had lost family members in the Holocaust: Karlin's Dutch mother's entire family was murdered at Auschwitz. Karlin felt the Holocaust "was so very close to me personally. Far too close—I identified so closely with Anne Frank. If my mother hadn't stayed in England and married my father, she could have been me." In fact, when Winters saw *A Clockwork Orange*, she wrote to Kubrick praising the film and jokingly asking why she had not been asked to play "the very British woman who gets raped in this film." Winters recalled, "He did not get the joke. He sent me back a very stern reply and informed me that he would cast me in any role I was suited for in any one of his films. And that was final."[24]

Id-Yid

Even more significantly, the way that Kubrick portrayed Alex also opens up the possibility of reading him as Jewish. Kubrick referred to Alex as a "creature of the id," with whom we have a "basic psychological, unconscious identification." He continued elsewhere, "Alex symbolizes man in his natural state, the way he would be if society did not impose its 'civilizing' processes upon him." Here, one can read an equation between Kubrick and Philip Roth, who, in *Portnoy's Complaint* (1969), exclaims, "Let's put the id back in yid." John Murray Cuddihy elaborates by suggesting that Freud's id "pressing for admission to consciousness" is the "Yid" "pressing for admission to civil society." "This importunate 'Yid,' released from the ghetto and shtetl, is the model," he contends, "for Freud's coarse importunate 'id.'" He referred to it as "the id-'Yid.'"[25]

Although Greek in origin, the name Alexander had become, among Jews, a "sacred name," sanctified by constant usage, possibly as an homage to the benevolent conqueror, Alexander the Great. In fact, Alex styles himself as Alex DeLarge. Napoleon once said, which Kubrick surely knew given his prodigious research, "If I had not been born Napoleon, I would have liked to have been born Alexander," and one of Napoleon's favorite paintings was Albrecht Altdorfer's *Battle of Alexander at Issus*. Alex is highly intelligent, witty, charming, inventive, eloquent, and certainly brighter than his droogs, as well as many of the adults around him. In his use of language and clearly superior intellectual abilities to his fellow droogs, he demonstrates Yiddische kopf. In such lines, as "to *tolchok* a *chellovek* in the *kishkas*," perhaps Kubrick heard an echo of the language spoken by his grandparents, as kishkas is Yiddish for guts.[26]

There are other markers of Alex's potential Jewishness. Apishness, as we have seen in regard to Humbert, has often been used to code the Jewish condition, and Alex's similarity to a simian from *2001*, also hints at this. His movement at times, such as when he fights his fellow droogs, is apelike, resembling the confrontation at the waterhole in *2001*. As he wanders around his flat, scratching his posterior, he also appears apish. As our "humble narrator," he's aware of the bars of his cage, becoming a version of Kafka's Red Peter and hence, in turn, Humbert. Another stereotypical marker of Jewishness is lack of decorum, and Alex lacks table manners: at the film's end, when he is being fed, he opens his mouth wide and chews with broad, lip-smacking, exaggerated movements. His parents' taste in décor is vulgar. The only piece of pop-culture kitsch, Erica Eigen's "I Want to Marry a Lighthouse Keeper," is played to hint at the bad taste of his parents. Alex's mother (Sheila Raynor) does not dress as befitting her age, especially by comparison to his father (Philip Stone), who is more traditionally dressed. Addicted to "sleepers," she dresses in outlandish fashions and purple wigs. In classic stereotypical fashion, his father is a weak figure, while his mother is overindulgent and credulously accepts Alex's poor rationalizations for how he earns his money. Mamber describes their interactions as "Pinteresque." Note how, although Nazi-themed regalia is in vogue at that time, Alex and his droogs resist adopting it. Indeed, they deliberately pick a fight with Billy Boy's SS-helmeted gang. Alex lives in "municipal flatblock 18a Linear North," the 18 here having the same gematric properties as the word "life" seen in *2001*. The letters DAV on the stolen Durango's license plate may refer to Dave in *Killer's Kiss, Spartacus,* or *2001*. On that latter note, Burgess was influenced by James Joyce's *Ulysses*, where, he explained, Stephen Dedalus had called the world an "oblate orange." Alex is portrayed in the film as a biblical Hebrew, and like a good Jew he prefers the Old Testament ("I didn't so much like the latter part of the book [the New Testament], which is more preachy-talking than fighting and the old in-out") and is seen scourging the source of Christianity: Jesus.

He identifies with Dracula, a character laden with Jewish imagery—in 1971, General Mills Corporation introduced a monster-themed breakfast cereal named "Count Chocula," wearing a Star of David.[27]

With his dancelike grace, Alex is performative, particularly when delivering a beating. He performs in the disused theater, and following his treatment he stars onstage in what Mario Falsetto refers to as "skits." Falsetto's use of this word recalls Sellers in *Lolita* and *Dr. Strangelove*, and, as a brilliant mimic, Alex is not unlike a younger version of Quilty, able to adapt and survive with Zelig-like ease in whichever circumstance he finds himself, playing with consummate ease whatever role is assigned to him. He shifts comfortably between criminal, perpetrator, convict, obsequious born-again Christian, willing volunteer, obedient patient and subject, and political football. Indeed, McDowell's working relationship with Kubrick resembled that with Sellers. "Stanley and Malcolm got on like a house on fire," recalls *A Clockwork Orange*'s producer, Jan Harlan. Like Sellers, McDowell was allowed some room to improvise. Most notably, this included the addition of "Singin' in the Rain" in the rape sequence. Even this song can be read as a subsurface nod to Jewishness, given that it hails from a film directed by another Stanley (Donen), which is rooted in the heyday of the Jewish-run studio system, especially Arthur Freed's celebrated MGM production unit.[28]

Alex can also be read as queer—another marker of the Jewish condition. Burgess stated that his inspiration for the title, which refers to Alex, was the phrase "as queer as a clockwork orange." His whole dress sense is camp, but his false eyelashes marks him as particularly feminine, as does the opening music of Henry Purcell's *Music for the Funeral of Queen Mary* (1695). When he sits on Dim's (Warren Clarke) lap, their codpieces butting, it has been interpreted as a "strikingly homosexual posture." Alex's full name ("Alexander DeLarge"), phallic mask, oversized codpiece, and huge phallus sculpture with which he kills the Catlady all seem compensatory, as if anxious about his penis size. Billyboy (Richard Connaught) refers to Alex as "her" when he says, "Let's get her, boys." Alex is also the feminized object of the gaze, particularly in the second half of the film when things are done to him, and he's subjected to various beatings, humiliations, and homosexual advances. Deltoid (played by Jewish actor Aubrey Morris) and fellow prisoners make passes at him, the chief guard (Michael Bates) subjects him to a rectal examination, and his groin receives repeated blows throughout the film. When, following his near-drowning, he staggers to the writer's house, the hirsute, burly Julian (David Prowse) carries him, making him appear the damsel in distress.[29]

Alex is the sacrificial victim, the scapegoat, the Isaac of the film. He's subject to various oedipal pressures, particularly by the state and its enemies, all of whom seek to sacrifice him for their own ends. Where the former seeks to remove his free will, the latter literally aims to kill him, although rather than "offering him up" as a sacrifice, they ironically cause him to jump down to this death. In addition to his own father, who's silently impotent, Alex has other symbolic Abrahamic fathers—Deltoid, the chaplain, the doctors, the writer, and the minister of the interior. As Emanuel K. Schwartz describes it, "The need to exploit and kill the young (even the Son of God is crucified) is one of the most important themes of this film."[30]

As the scapegoat of the film, Alex's Jewish status is reinforced. In the scene when the effectiveness of the Ludovico Technique is demonstrated, Alex is abused, hit, and forced to the floor by the "Stage Actor" (John Clive). The nausea induced by his anger incapacitates him. Lying flat on his back, Alex is helpless, like Kafka's Gregor Samsa. In a departure from Burgess's novel, the Stage Actor asks him, "You see that shoe?" before demanding that Alex lick its sole. Geoffrey Cocks notes, "What is very odd about the scene (in an *Annie Hall* [1977] sort of way) is that the actor's enunciation of the line 'You see that shoe?' sounds like 'You see that, Jew?'" John Clive didn't recall how the line came about but believed he may have ad-libbed it. When Kubrick redid the shot, from Alex's point of view, looking upward past the shoe toward the Stage Actor's face, Clive recalls that, "Stanley decided that he wanted to shoot that himself. . . . So he took the camera and laid down on the floor at my feet. Something I never expected . . . and I had to put my foot in front of his face and tell him to lick it. Like I said, right out of left field."[31]

Kubrick explored the human propensity to violence on two levels: that committed by humans of their own free will, as an extension of the apes in *2001*, and that by the state on its citizens through its "civilizing processes." He was seeking to overturn what he called "one of the most dangerous fallacies which has influenced a great deal of political and philosophical thinking," that "man is essentially good, and that it is society which makes him bad." In his "savage" precivil state, man possesses a "guiltless sense of freedom to kill and rape," Kubrick told the *New York Times*. He singled out Jean-Jacques Rousseau, who "transferred original sin from man to society, and this importantly contributed to what I believe has been a crucially incorrect premise from which to base political and moral philosophy." He added, "To continue the psychological analogy, in the middle section of the story, the Ludovico Treatment is imposed on Alex as a cure for crime. This would, on this symbolic, level represent the society imposing itself on the individual and producing the neurosis of civilization which is necessary but for which we pay a high individual price . . . and the final section of the film, ending with Alex's line, 'I was cured alright,' brings him back to 'normal' and leaves him in his savage natural state again."[32]

Kubrick's use of the term "civilizing process" betrays a debt to Norbert Elias's 1939 *The Civilizing Process*, which had been republished (in German) in 1969. Elias traces the historical development of "civilizing" of manners and personality in Europe since the Middle Ages with a focus on table manners, bodily functions, bedroom behavior, and attitudes between men and women. He demonstrates how the "psychic structure of people is also transformed" to the effect that the "prohibitions supported by social sanctions are reproduced in individuals as self-controls." The "social code of conduct so imprints in one form or another on human beings that it becomes a constituent element" of the individual self. He compares this to what Freud characterizes as the "superego" and the "unconscious," or what was popularly called the "subconscious." If Kubrick was aware of Elias, it put him ahead of the curve in the Anglophone intellectual world, for he was not translated and published in English until 1978.[33]

Kubrick put Alex in a Hobbesian condition: "Alex represents natural man in the state in which he is born: unlimited, unrepressed." It is this state that Kubrick seemingly admires, depicting Alex in a sympathetic manner—charming, eloquent, intelligent, and cultured. He explained, "The fact that Alex is the very personification of evil and is still in some strange way attractive is due to several things: his honesty, his lack of hypocrisy, his energy, and his intelligence. I've always compared him to Richard III, and I think it's a very good comparison. Why do you find yourself liking Richard III? But you do, in a very stylized way." The impact of Alex's violence is diluted by its cutting to the music, whereas that done to him is very realistically presented. His victims are unpleasant and unsympathetic: a dirty, drunk, old tramp; a posh elitist writer and his wife; a stuck-up Cat Lady. Those who seek to contain him—Deltoid, his parents, the prison guards, the chaplain, the minister of the interior—are caricatures. Posttreatment, he becomes ordinary, banal, his interactions like something out of a Harold Pinter play. This is why "we feel exhilarated when Alex is 'cured' in the final scene," avers Kubrick. The ages of the two young girls are raised, and they engage in seemingly consensual sex, as does the woman at the end who playfully bats his arms away. Ending on "Singin' in the Rain" again, the film shows Alex emerging as a loveable, albeit incorrigible, rogue. Hence the *Albany New York Evangelist* complains, "Rather than present Alex as the clearly evil and despicable roach he is in Burgess's book, Kubrick has softened the lad, not so much by making his deeds less shocking (in fact, they are much much more graphic) but by making his victims very nearly as execrable as the bully boys."[34]

The real evil in the film is state-sanctioned violence. Alex is grabbed by his testicles, kicked, punched, spat on, anally probed, almost drowned—all by agents of the state. Alex's violence, and the consequences of it, are rarely seen; he may have raped the writer's wife, but he saves another girl from being raped. "Eventually," Kubrick explained, "you begin to sympathize with Alex, because you begin to identify with him as a victim of a much greater evil." He described it as the "question of evil committed by the government in trying to change Alex's nature." He told Ciment, "the government eventually resorts to the employment of the cruelest and most violent members of society to control everyone else . . . not an altogether new or untried idea." In *Sight and Sound* magazine he explained, "As the story progresses, of course, one feels sympathy for Alex as a victim, not necessarily because we like him, but because we can identify with the loss of his humanity and we are appalled by it. On the unconscious psychological level we rebel against the destruction of the id."[35]

Kubrick reserves his greatest ire for the state-sanctioned violence that seeks to deprive Alex of his free will and turn him into an automaton. If the title refers to a cybernetic organism, a mechanical interior masked by a covering of biological flesh, then we can read Alex as a robotic automaton or golem, a son of Strangelove. Following his treatment, Alex has become conditioned or programmed (HALex) not to do bad, underpinned by the mechanical sonic feel provided by the newly invented Moog synthesizers. Like this mythical creature molded from clay to do its master's bidding, Alex's name also begins with an A, or Aleph, which dominates the publicity for the film. In one poster, he is framed by a giant letter "A," from which he reaches out to the audience. This automation then explains the emphasis on eyes throughout the film, from Alex's eyelashes to his eyeball cufflinks, through the connection to Freud's story of the Sandman in his essay "The Uncanny."[36]

The future that this state is trying to protect is sterile, banal, and arid. Family relationships are attenuated, and distractions are sought through sex, drugs, and violence. The possibilities of emotion, love, and procreative sex seem distant. Kubrick underpins his point about evil by the depiction of the Ludovico Technique. It draws on Kafka's execution machine, which slowly inscribes the punishment on the victim's body in his 1919 story "In the Penal Colony." Alex certainly undergoes a metamorphosis. The visceral, realistic, Kafkaesque mode in which Alex's eyeballs are clamped open makes us wince. And Kubrick drew on popular representations of Skinner as a totalitarian Hitler-like figure. The "technique"—notice the deliberate Nazi-like euphemism here—is sanctioned by an autocratic government, using repressive means to quell political dissent. Alex is imprisoned in "Staja 84F," suggesting also some sort of Soviet-style gulag. The writer explains, "Oh, we've seen it all before in other countries. The thin end of the wedge. Before we know where we are we shall have the full apparatus of totalitarianism." After all, the raison d'être for Alex's treatment is to clear the prisons to make space for the increased flux of political prisoners. The deployment of Nazi and World War II iconography underlines his point, and, noticeably, such imagery is attached to Alex's enemies rather than himself. Although Nazi regalia and insignia are chic, as sported by Billyboy's gang and a droog in the Korova Milk Bar, Alex and his companions reject such apparel. Only when imprisoned is Alex forced to wear an SS-like uniform of black clothing with a red armband.

Here Kubrick created a parallel between this dystopic vision and Arendt's study of totalitarianism. Alex was intended to be an everyman, an "exemplar of humanity." As Kubrick explained, "He is within all of us." Burgess's orange metaphor deliberately suggests a sphere, like the Earth, albeit in microcosm. By saying any and every inhabitant of a totalitarian state can become a potential victim at any given moment, all men are potential Jews. To underline the point, Kubrick inserted an arguably needless and detailed five-minute sequence, even constructing an appropriate set, in which Alex undergoes registration into the prison regime, where he is stripped both literally and metaphorically of his individuality, diluting him to a number ("6554321"), symbolically reducing him to a concentration camp inmate, who then adopts the concomitant servile, obsequious manner. The Ludovico Treatment is not for sadistic pleasure nor to obtain information, but for the systematic destruction of Alex's id, to ensure that no human spontaneity interferes with the orderly operation of society. Its administrators, like Adolf Eichmann, are "perfectly normal" bureaucrats. Once "treated," Alex resembles Bruno Bettelheim's "walking dead" and the "living corpse" of Arendt's concentration-camp system, robbed of his individuality and unique personality, that which makes him human. He is, as Vincent D. Foley puts it, "totally stripped of human emotion. He is antiseptic and dull. He is merely a skeleton without the guts of feeling."[37]

Indeed, it is through the Ludovico Treatment that we see the most images of Nazism and World War II than in any Kubrick film before or since. Alex is forced to watch film footage of what Kubrick called "Nazi film," including "concentration camps," "hangings," "firing squads," and "brutal Nazi kickers and shooters." Alex's final session contains scenes from *Triumph of the Will* (1935) and German wartime newsreels. The device used to keep his eyelids open "resembled something from a torture chamber" according to Christiane. Overseen by Dr. Brodsky, played by the German actor Carl Duering (who previously played German and Nazi officers on film and television), he becomes a stand-in for Dr. Strangelove. The treatment itself evokes the notorious pseudoscientific medical experiments of Dr. Josef Mengele at Auschwitz. *Time* describes its adherent, the minister of the interior, as a "kind of well-tailored Goebbels, and unctuous fascist." And when the droogs convert to police officers and take Alex to a secluded rural area where they can do him in, it has resonances of Nazi special killing squads. Surely perceiving Stanley Kubrick's intentions, the *Jewish Chronicle* reviewer notes how the "continuous, mainly classical, background music serves, like the pyjama-clad orchestra in Hitler's death camps, to underline the horror rather than detract from it."[38]

Conclusion

Following his religious and spiritual turn in *2001*, in which he explored the origins and destiny of humanity, in *A Clockwork Orange* Kubrick produced a normatively Jewish answer to the question of what makes a man a mensch. Kubrick's everyman, Alex, might not be a mensch in the sense of a decent, upstanding, ethical, and responsible person who displays his virtues through gentility and kindness, someone to admire and emulate or of noble character, but he was one in being able to choose, and that is what makes him a human being and not an animal. The real violence was that produced by the state, particularly in its threat of dehumanization and the removal of the soul. *A Clockwork Orange* concluded Kubrick's science-fiction trilogy but augured his trilogy of family-centered films. Where *A Clockwork Orange* posed an arid and sterile, quasi-totalitarian future, in his next film Kubrick turned back to the era where civilized society was as its peak.

7

A Spatial Odyssey

In its depiction of social exclusion and isolation, critic Jonathan Rosenbaum called *Barry Lyndon* Stanley Kubrick's most Jewish movie. By dramatizing the social climbing odyssey of Redmond Barry, aka Barry Lyndon (Ryan O'Neal), a young, enterprising, and unscrupulous Irish parvenu who attempts to ingratiate himself to the British upper classes, whatever the cost and consequences, Kubrick certainly tapped into anxieties that have dogged Jews ever since their encounter with Western, gentile, "civilized" society. Such anxieties permeated the works of those writers Kubrick admired, including Sigmund Freud, Arthur Schnitzler, Franz Kafka, and Hannah Arendt. An alternative, yet still apt, title for the film may well have been *The Ordeal of Civility*, the name of a book about the Jewish struggle with Western civilization, published one year before *Barry Lyndon* was released. At the same time, *Barry Lyndon* was Kubrick's most complete, personal, and emotional meditation on paternity to date, on what it meant to be a mensch—a father, a husband, and a son—building on *A Clockwork Orange* and foreshadowing what was to occur in his next film, *The Shining*.[1]

Memoir to Movie

On April 16, 1972, only a few months after the release of *A Clockwork Orange*, *Variety* announced "Kubrick Keeping Next Pic a Secret, Even from Warner." The only information it had about the "New Stanley Kubrick Project" was that "it will star Ryan O'Neal." Given Kubrick's interests at the time, this could have been *Napoleon* or *Traumnovelle*. Adding to the mystery, Kubrick had submitted to Warner Bros. a draft screenplay in which the title, dates, and characters' names had been altered so as not to reveal the project's real identity, as well as "to protect the public-domain status of the source material against imitators." Ultimately, the project was *The Luck of Barry Lyndon*, based on William Makepeace Thackeray's 1856 novel, *The Memoirs of Barry Lyndon, Esq., of the Kingdom of Ireland*, adapted from his earlier serial, published in *Fraser's Magazine* in 1844, as *The Luck of Barry Lyndon: A Romance of the Last Century, edited by George Savage Fitz-Boodle*.[2]

Kubrick deeply admired Thackeray's writing. According to Ken Adam, *Barry Lyndon*'s production designer, "Stanley believed there were very few screenwriters as good as Thackeray. *Barry Lyndon* was, in his mind, like a screenplay. . . . He thought that Thackeray was better than any screenwriter alive." Kubrick told Michel Ciment, "I have had a complete set of Thackeray sitting on my bookshelf at home for years, and I had to read several of his novels before reading *Barry Lyndon*." Although impressed by Thackeray's *Vanity Fair*, he felt "the story could not be successfully compressed into the relatively short time-span of a feature film." By contrast, as soon as he read *Barry Lyndon*, he became "very excited": "I loved the story and the characters, and it seemed possible to make the transition from novel to screen without destroying it in the process." *Barry Lyndon*'s relative obscurity combined with its historical nature allowed Kubrick a measure of freedom in his adaptation. Critic Andrew Sarris suggests Kubrick's "strange choice of this particular project" tells us much about him: "Kubrick can virtually conceal his own personal obsessions in Thackeray's largely obscure literary persona."[3]

Another appeal was Thackeray's take on society. Barbara Hardy explains how "Thackeray is the great sociologist of nineteenth-century fiction, the great accumulator of social symbols, of class and money. To read him is to read a fictional form of Veblen's *The Theory of the Leisure Class* or Galbraith's *The Affluent Society*. Like these eloquent social scientists, he is not merely reporting or describing. Certain facts, if gathered together, unified, and shown in vivid particularly create a statement of horror, disgust, incredulity. This is what Thackeray's portrait of conspicuous consumption, mercenary marriage and self-indulgence creates." Kubrick admired his ability to see the severity and cruelty below the superficial artifice of the British aristocracy's elaborate codes of etiquette, which required the withholding of emotion during the eighteenth century, a period described, variously, as an age of gentility, sensibility, and enlightenment. This was a society of goyim naches par excellence and totally lacking in menschlikayt. Whereas others saw gentility, no doubt Kubrick saw goyishness; indeed, in French the term for gentile and genteel are the same.[4]

Thackeray's satire drew Kubrick. Willem Hesling explains, "In Thackeray, who liked to confront his contemporaries with their faults and shortcomings, Kubrick must have recognized a nineteenth-century kindred spirit. In contrast to Dickens, whose novels offered a comic-melodramatic panorama of the lower classes, Thackeray directed his attention to the pretentions and complacency of the middle and upper classes." Thackeray "never closed his eyes to the darker side of this 'glorious' period in European history."[5]

Some of Thackeray's caricatures and names were reminiscent of *Lolita*, *Dr. Strangelove*, and *A Clockwork Orange*. His hero alone adopts the monikers Barry Redmond, Barry of Barryogue, Captain Barry, and Redmond de Balibari. To these can be added Sir Huddleston Fuddleston, Lady Susan Capermore, Amelia Kiljoy, the Hon. Miss Flint Skinner, Lord Deuceace, the Earl of Crabs, Mr. Splint the timber dealer, Mr. Tapewell the solicitor, the Rev. Mr. Jowls, Count Pippi, Mr. Screw, Lady Jane Peckover, Miss Driver, and Rev. Mr. Runt. Incidentally, Kubrick retained only the latter name, to which can be added Potzdorf, translatable as "village prick."

Alexander Walker describes *Barry Lyndon* as a movie "born on the rebound," while production designer Ken Adam calls it a "dress rehearsal" for Kubrick's *Napoleon*. It may well have been Thackeray's interest in Napoleon that led Kubrick to the author. Walker surmises that "one of the academic historians signed up to consult on the aborted *Napoleon* pointed him toward this collateral source of inspiration about pre-Napoleonic manners and morality." Thackeray had incorporated the emperor's exploits as the backdrop to *Vanity Fair*—his antihero Becky Sharp was a female version of Napoleon—and he had written *The Second Funeral of Napoleon* in 1841. And portions of *Barry Lyndon* were "largely derived" from Baron de la Mothe-Langon's *L'empire, ou dix ans sous Napoléon* (1836). The result was a film that resonated with Napoleon's story.[6]

In addition to *Barry Lyndon*'s Napoleonic setting, Kubrick's interest in Nazi Germany also led him to the novel. "He was very intrigued by the Third Reich business," Andrew Birkin recalls. "There's a lot in common with Hitler and why he wanted to do 'Napoleon.'" For these reasons, Birkin sent Kubrick a screenplay he'd adapted from *Inside the Third Reich: The Secret Diaries* by Albert Speer, Hitler's architect. "And he was obviously interested. But he said, 'I'm Jewish. I can't get involved with this.'" Nevertheless, the bildungsroman of Speer's story resonated in *Barry Lyndon*, as did some of the locations and themes.[7]

In *Barry Lyndon* Kubrick engaged those themes that had emerged in his earliest works. By featuring what seems to be, on the surface, a Catholic protagonist, Kubrick was returning to his roots as a photographer and filmmaker. Catholicism had fascinated Kubrick since his days at *Look* and was at the heart of his first three documentary films. It cropped up with regularity since, often disguised by his signature misdirection.

As with *A Clockwork Orange*, Kubrick undertook to adapt the novel himself, which he began in the autumn of 1972. In so doing he continued his taste for such English writers as Peter George, Arthur C. Clarke, and Anthony Burgess. Kubrick spent almost a year on preproduction research, in pursuit of authentic costumes, furniture, props, architecture, carriages, hairstyles, and locations. He also wanted to shoot using available natural light, on location, preferably within a twenty-mile radius of his home. The lack of suitable locations forced him to look farther afield.

Barry Lyndon was filmed entirely on location, primarily in Ireland, and principal photography began September 17, 1973, and ran through to February 8, 1974, but with a break from October 31 to January 1. Filming recommenced in England on February 12 and ran through to July 24, 1974. Second-unit photography lasted from August 1 until September 24. It was Kubrick's first mature film to be shot entirely on location. He employed the largest number of crew to date—approximately 170—costing £11 million. The film opened on December 18, 1975.

Mr. Barry Kubrick

Kubrick identified with Barry, perceiving in him an avatar. As an American Jew living in an English country house in rural Hertfordshire, Kubrick surely felt removed from the society that enveloped him, as somewhat of a social pariah. When Thackeray writes, "You who have never been out of your country, know little what it is to hear a friendly voice in captivity." Kubrick surely empathized with the feeling of exile. "Clearly," B. F. Dick writes, "Kubrick saw something of himself in the novel: the boy from the Bronx, now London based, who compensated for his lack of university education by acquiring a knowledge of the arts that few academics could match." Norman Kagan adds, "Perhaps it was Stanley Kubrick's stately and beautiful eighteenth-century English manor home itself that eventually led to his choosing a novel of that period for his next film." Gavin Lambert feels, "There's a lot of that character in Stanley. Not the defeated Barry but the fuck-the-world Barry. That great moment after the marriage when they go into the coach and Marisa Berenson says something stupid, and he just blows smoke rings. Fabulous! It's very Kubrick-esque. A gesture I could very easily see him do. It's his wicked, humorous side coming out. It's a wonderful comment on her, and why he's married her, and this extraordinary cold indifference is there at the centre of him. It's a fable, not a realistic film in any sense. It's his Ophüls side." After all, O'Neal was the only American among a European cast, much resembling Kubrick's own position within a British film industry.[8]

Barry is an outsider, a theme that has distinct parallels with Kubrick's previous films. Kubrick, as we know, admired such types. Back in 1960 he had praised the "outsider who is passionately committed to action against the social order." He was referring to such criminals, maniacs, poets, lovers, and revolutionaries as Johnny Clay, Dax, Spartacus, and Humbert. To this list can be added Alex and Barry. All were "outsiders fighting to do some impossible thing."[9]

Kubrick communicated Barry's loneliness and isolation in spatial, color, and musical terms. Many critics complain that the film was cold, alienating, beautiful but empty. Pauline Kael describes it as "chilly," "an ice-pack of a movie," "a coffee-table movie; the stately tour of European high life is like a three-hour slide show for art-history majors." But they misunderstand that the medium is the message, as Kubrick surely intended us to feel this way. His glacial style in *Barry Lyndon* not only communicates Barry's estrangement from the surrounding society but also transmits Kubrick's feelings about it. This society is as empty as the void that envelops Bowman in *2001*. (And, anticipating Barry, Bowman ends up on Jupiter in a bedroom decorated in an eighteenth-century style.) Georg Friedrich Handel's mournful, slow, and sad sarabande accompanies Barry throughout the film at the same time as, in Frank Rich's words, "Kubrick's austere pictorial style emphasizes the lonely spaces and chilling desolation." Kubrick typically positioned Barry as a tiny figure in a large frame, often utterly alone in a cold and inhospitable world. The long shots stress his insignificance in this inhuman society, one that privileges the goyish nastiness of a well-born Lord Bullingdon (Leon Vitali) over the well-meaning menschlikayt of a lower-born Barry. The innovations in shooting, fitting a 50 mm Zeiss f/0.7 NASA-designed lens to a Mitchell BNC camera to film in low-level, namely natural and candle, light, had the effect of flattening the frame, creating a painterly aesthetic, underlining the characters' two-dimensionality. It also accentuated their lack of moral fiber and ethical substance. Against this backdrop Barry's multidimensionality as a character stands out. This style conveys Kubrick's view that, although externally ordered by ritual and propriety, the civilization beneath was hollow.[10]

Red-Mensch Barry

Thackeray wrote in *Barry Lyndon* how "a man is not a complete *Mensch* until he is the father of a family, to be which is a condition of his existence, and therefore a duty of his education." Surely spurred on by this line, *Barry Lyndon* continued Kubrick's investigation into the ethical and psychological nature of man, as a son, husband, and father, into what makes a man a mensch. *Barry Lyndon* is an oedipal drama of fatherhood and paternity, as Barry seeks to become a father, a man, and a mensch. It was also Kubrick's most emotional film to date.[11]

Barry's fatherless status is foregrounded immediately. As with the screenplay for *2001*, *Barry Lyndon* opens with the death of the protagonist's father. In a change from the novel, the film begins with a dramatization of the duel in which Barry's father is shot dead. We observe from a distance as the narrator explains how his death arose from a trivial dispute over the purchase of some horses. This is a significant change from the novel, in which Harry Barry dies of apparent natural causes during a visit to the races. Walker describes this as the "theme of the father, or father figure, as fate's fearsome agent." Barry's fate is determined by an absent father.[12]

Subsequently, Barry encounters a succession of replacement fathers. The first is the usurping captain Jack Quin (Leonard Rossiter) who competes for, and wins, the engagement of Barry's first love, Nora Brady (Gay Hamilton). Jealous, Barry challenges Quin to a duel. In an oedipal gesture, Barry kills Quin, whose death, unknown to Barry, is faked. Quin's given name echoes that of Kubrick's own father while his surname recalls that of Quilty. Rossiter, who had earlier appeared in *2001*, was compared by Jonathan Cecil, who played Lt. Jonathan Fakenham, to Peter Sellers, describing him as a "way-out, off-the-wall actor" whose performance was "extraordinary." Forced to flee, Barry is robbed by a highwayman, Capt. James [another Jack] Feeney (Arthur O'Sullivan), and his son (Billy Boyle). Now penniless, Barry enlists in the British army, where he meets Capt. Jack Grogan (Godfrey Quigley), a much more benevolent mensch-like figure who provides Barry with advice and protection and whose given name is also replete with oedipal allusion. Here Kubrick changed his surname from Fagan, possibly, suggests Geoffrey Cocks, "fearing a distracting association in viewers' minds with the old Jewish crook Fagin in Dickens's *Oliver Twist* (1838)." Grogan is played by Godfrey Quigley, the chaplain who befriends Alex in *A Clockwork Orange*. Grogan's death prompts Barry to desert, during which time he comes under the aegis of Captain Potzdorf (Hardy Kruger), through whom he meets the Chevalier de Balibari (Patrick Magee), played by the same actor who was the writer in *A Clockwork Orange*. Barry feels emotionally close to his fellow countryman, the chevalier, as hinted by the similarity of their surnames, and Barry's search for a replacement father figure is hence terminated until he usurps the place of Sir Charles Lyndon (Frank Middlemass).[13]

The film also privileges familial tensions. Upon marrying Lady Lyndon (Marisa Berenson), Barry becomes a stepfather through marriage, like Humbert and Kubrick himself. Barry's relationship with his stepson, Bullingdon, becomes as complicated as that of Humbert with Lolita. Kubrick deliberately magnified the oedipal antipathy between them, and Barry never feels he "belongs" to the family acquired through marriage, particularly as his stepson refuses to accept him. The binaries evident in the confrontation between Barry and Bullingdon are reminiscent of those in *Paths of Glory* and *Spartacus*: both figures represent the opposite ends of the social scale and physical type. To this end, Kubrick significantly redrew Thackeray's Bullingdon from the brave young man who fights in the American War of Independence and returns to have Barry sentenced to a London debtors' prison into an unhealthily pale, slight, effeminate, and effete English aristocrat who perhaps has never consummated a heterosexual relationship. He's the embodiment of goyim naches. By contrast, Barry is strong, virile, charming, sexually experienced, sympathetic, and a mensch.

But it is only when Barry becomes a biological father that he becomes a complete mensch. As a father, Barry reveals his humanity and inner compassion, that is, his menschlikayt. As our narrator (Michael Holdern) tells us, "Barry had his faults, but no man could say of him that he was not a good and tender father." Originally, this was to be spoken by Barry: "I may have had my faults, but no man shall dare to say of me that I was not a good and tender father. *I loved that boy passionately, perhaps with a blind partiality; I denied him nothing.*" Kubrick filled out this sketch by inserting various scenes highlighting the father-son relationship: a lavish birthday party and procession and a deathbed sequence that was, for Robert Kolker, "the most sentimental thing Kubrick has ever filmed." Kubrick constructed two highly emotional scenes—the mirrored deaths of Grogan and Bryan (David Morley)—as both lie dying, Barry is moved to tears (just as when he reveals his real identity to the chevalier).[14]

The birth of Bryan only serves to intensify the hostility between Barry and Bullingdon, which isn't assuaged by Bryan's death. It is this conflict that Kubrick uses to demonstrate Barry's inner menschlikayt. Although Barry's nature is ground down by the corrupting society around him, it doesn't disappear completely. In the culminating duel, one completely of Kubrick's invention, not appearing in the novel, Barry displays his inner menschlikayt while engaging in the obligatory goyim naches of a duel. Nervous, Bullingdon fires his pistol into the ground, leaving Barry the choice to shoot him, thus winning the duel, or to fire away—which he does, recalling his earlier action of spontaneous compassion by carrying Potzdorf out of a burning building amid a battle, despite the danger, while his comrades around him flee to save themselves. Here Kubrick reverts to the comforting binaries of his Douglas films, and Bill Krohn observes how it appears inspired by "the moment in *Spartacus* when Woody Strode refuses to put Douglas to death after winning their duel, choosing instead to die attacking the aristocratic spectators." By contrast, Bullingdon chooses to take advantage of Barry in this moment of weakness and vulnerability. He takes his second shot, highlighting his cowardly and vicious nature, and wounds Barry in the leg, resulting in its amputation, giving us Kubrick's comment on this society and its goyish codes of civility. By rigidly obeying convention, Bullingdon underscores Barry's menschlikayt, consolidating our sympathies for him.[15]

Rodney Hill describes Kubrick's protagonist as one of the "most fully and sympathetically drawn in the Kubrick canon." Frank Rich, in the *New York Post*, notes how Kubrick "warped the original texts to suit his own ends." Barry is much more sympathetic than Thackeray drew him in the novel, where he's a semicriminal mercenary rapist and murderer who brags, lies, emotionally abuses, intimidates, and beats his wife, who herself isn't the melancholic beauty of the film. Thackeray's Barry also narrates the novel, which highlights his unreliability. Kubrick told Ciment, "Barry is naïve and uneducated. He is driven by a relentless ambition for wealth and social position. This proves to be an unfortunate combination of qualities which eventually leads to great misfortune and unhappiness for himself and those around him. Your feelings about Barry are mixed but he has charm and courage, and it is impossible not to like him despite his vanity, his insensitivity, and his weaknesses. He is a very real character who is neither a conventional hero nor a conventional villain." By casting O'Neal, Kubrick immediately presented Barry as attractive. Speaking to Mimi Crossley of the *Houston Post*, O'Neal felt, "I think what happened was that Stanley fell in love with the character of Barry Lyndon, and that changed the movie somewhere, at some point. He ended up seeing him as a sympathetic, tragic figure when he came to editing the film, instead of the heel he started out to be." Judith Crist characterizes Kubrick's film as a "portrait of a rather decent young man corrupted by a corrupt society, a man who learned the ways of that world too well and was fool enough to put his trust in in the nobility of noblemen. But his mother loved him."[16]

Kubrick's changes emphasize Barry's victimized mensch status. His decision to discard the first-person voice-over and replace it with an omniscient nondiegetic observer makes us feel greater sympathy for Barry. He becomes much more mensch-like, amplified by the addition of scenes of Kubrick's invention—Barry and Nora playing cards, his confrontation with Feeney, both battle scenes when he carries off Grogan and Potzdorf, his meal with the lonely Lischen (Diana Koerner), his climactic duel with Bullingdon, the amputation of his leg, and Lady Lyndon and Bullingdon paying bills at the end. As Kubrick presents it, Barry liberates Lady

Lyndon from a constricting marriage to a crippled old man. Barry is also much more loving: he dotes on his son, and he seems to evince real remorse after cheating on his wife and genuine grief for the loss of Grogan and later Bryan. He's surrounded by men no better than him; Kubrick reveals them to be far worse, flawed hypocrites. Edward Connor concludes, "If there is any moral problem at all I think it's the fact that a basically unsympathetic character (being at all times a self-seeking opportunist) is presented in an altogether sympathetic manner."[17]

The Wandering Jew

Again, Kubrick erased from his screenplay the explicit references to Jews found in the source text. In the novel Barry encounters a series of "treacherous" Jewish goldsmiths, pawnbrokers, tradesmen, diamond merchants, moneylenders, businessmen, horse dealers, and lawyers. Interestingly, the novel's most "Jewish sections" were those based on Baron de la Mothe-Langon's *Napoléon*. But Jewishness was explicitly on Kubrick's mind as he was researching *Barry Lyndon*, as it had been for Thackeray when writing it. "For Barry Lyndon, Casanova is a role-model, one of the world's dedicated gamblers as well as lovers," Siegbert S. Prawer writes. "Indeed, both in form and content the memoirs Barry writes as an old and sick man appear consciously modelled on those of Casanova himself." Ken Adam recalls that Kubrick also borrowed material from *Casanova*. In Kubrick's historical research files for the film were annotated photocopies of *Histoire de Ma Vie* [*Story of My Life*] (1841) by Giacomo Casanova, the eighteenth-century Venetian adventurer and author. Kubrick had underlined various parts referring to Jews. While explicit references to Jews were ultimately erased from the finished film, their traces remained beneath its surface, nonetheless, in the Jewish actors Kubrick cast for various roles and also in the character of Barry himself.[18]

Thackeray had described Barry in terms that were historically associated with Jewishness. "I am very dark and swarthy in complexion, and was called by our fellows the 'Black Englander,' the 'Schwarzer Englander,' or the 'English devil.'" Thackeray also wrote, "But fate had determined that he [Barry] should leave none of his *race* behind him." And Barry has been called a female version of Thackeray's antihero, Becky Sharp, whose name, it has been suggested, hints at "racial astuteness."[19]

Kubrick's characterization of Barry, drawing on Thackeray, injected him with an allegorical Jewishness. In his signature misdirection, Kubrick cast a blond, gentile actor for the role—his initial choice was Robert Redford before O'Neal—seemingly and deliberately distancing himself from the Barry described by Thackeray. But, probably unknown to Kubrick, O'Neal has Jewish ancestry: his maternal grandmother, Mathilde Pius, was born in New York to a Jewish family; her father, Gustave Pius, was from Germany, and her mother, Rebecca/Regina Iglick, was from Schrimm (now Srem, Poland). Halachically, this meant O'Neal was Jewish. He had previously starred in *What's Up Doc?* (1972) alongside Barbra Streisand, as well as *Love Story*.[20]

Kubrick provided a series of clues. The first clue to Barry's allegorical Jewishness is his name. In his study of the representation of Jews and Judaism in Thackeray, Prawer observes how growing affluence, respectability, and assimilation to the British way of life among upper-class Jews brought with it name changes such as that which might lead Redmond Barry to become Barry Lyndon. The name "Redmond" also recalls Kafka's ape, Red Peter, and, like Kafka's ape, Barry is described as a "young monkey" and being in "captivity." Similarly, just as the ape is unable to speak, Barry lapses into silence in the latter half of the film.[21]

Scholar of Jewish names Benzion Kaganoff observes how those Jewish immigrants who chose such names as "Jack" for themselves and named their children "Stanley" were likely to have grandchildren called "Barry." In 1964 the prominent Republican presidential candidate, half-Jewish Barry Goldwater, prompted Lenny Bruce to wonder out loud about the possibility of electing a president of Jewish descent. He then turned on Goldwater's first name: "'Barry?' '*Barry!*' Are you kidding me with that? Mogen Dovid. Barry! Where is there one goy with the name of Barry? It's the most Jewishjewishjewish . . ." Arthur C. Clarke recalls discussing Goldwater with Kubrick while they worked on *2001*, and more than one critic of the film noticed the coincidence between the protagonist's name and those competing in the 1964 election (the Democratic candidate was Lyndon Johnson). A year earlier the cause célèbre television documentary *Citizen 63* had focused on the flamboyant Jewish music businessman Barry Langford.[22]

Jews and Irish have historically been viewed as synonymous. The poet Alan Grossman wrote in 1962 how "the Jew like the Irishman presents himself as a type of the sufferer in history." John Murray Cuddihy devotes a whole chapter to their similarities, describing them as "latecomers to modernity." Indeed, the notion that the Irish and the Jews possessed a shared cause was a common folkloric tradition with historical roots; it was even frequently suggested that the Irish Celts were descended from the lost tribes of Israel. Such ideas were taken up by James Joyce and embodied in Leopold Bloom in his 1922 novel *Ulysses*, who, like Barry, is a wandering Irishman. The product of a Jewish immigrant father and Irish Catholic mother, he is simultaneously, yet neither fully, Catholic nor Jewish. If Joyce recognized in the stereotype of the rootless diasporic Jew the fractures of Irish identity under British rule, then Kubrick saw in Thackeray's wandering Irish Barry the perfect emblem of the fractures of the diasporic Ostjude (eastern European Jew) in western Europe.[23]

A series of Hollywood films juxtaposed and mixed these conflicting identities. *Levy and Cohen: The Irish Comedians* (1902), *The Cohens and the Kellys* (1926), *Private Izzy Murphy* (1926), *The Jazz Singer* (1927), *Surrender* (1927), and *Abie's Irish Rose* (1928) typically featured visibly Jewish protagonists struggling either to assimilate or overcome institutional barriers and obstacles. *Abie's Irish Rose* was updated in 1972–1973, while Kubrick was working on *Barry Lyndon*, as *Bridget Loves Bernie*, focusing on the marriage between a Catholic teacher (Bridget) and a Jewish cab driver (Bernie). It also features Harold J. Stone, who'd played David the Jew in *Spartacus*. In each of these texts, the marker of final ascension into American life was intermarriage, just as the nominally Catholic Barry weds an openly Protestant woman. In *Killer's Kiss*, Kubrick had also focused on an image that similarly conflated Irish and Jews. A cartoon featured in that film depicts two men wearing clothing suggesting they are Irish, but their noses also suggest that they are Jewish.[24]

The nonspecific nature of Barry's religion also enables us to read him as Jewish. Thackeray "makes explicit the fact that Barry has descended from Catholic landowners who renounced their religion to retain their property under British rule." In a significant divergence, Kubrick downplays Barry's Catholicism to the effect that Catholic reviewers complained of the "lack of reference to Barry's religion throughout." "Being Irish," Edward Connor wrote, "he is presumed to be Catholic, yet he is never seen practicing or referring to it. He enters into a Protestant marriage with no seeming scruples—and his otherwise excellent Mother also seems to have no objections on that score." A change in the screenplay gives us a clue in this respect. Initially, Kubrick had scripted the words, "Barry's father had been bred, like many sons of a gentile family," recalling Quilty's eagerness to deny his Jewishness when encountering Humbert. But onscreen "gentile" becomes "genteel."[25]

Barry is an immigrant, an outsider, a colonized subject, and a pariah. Far from home, like Humbert, he's nomadic. As the narrator intones, "he was destined to be a wanderer." In *The Road to Xanadu*, a book Kubrick read and admired, John Livingston Lowes wrote of how Samuel Taylor Coleridge saw a farce called *The Wandering Jew; or, Love's Masquerade* by Andrew Franklin in 1797: "The Farce takes its title from the character of a young adventurer, who, failing in other expedients, assumes the garb of the Wandering Jew, attended by a brother fortune-hunter, dressed in a similar habit. The latter, who is an Irishman, gives some very curious descriptions of the exploits in their days of Julius Caesar, and other remote periods, blended with modern occurrences." Such a description befits Barry. He's also a social-climbing parvenu; in the Victorian era in which Thackeray wrote, it was suggested all social climbers were Jews, and all Jews were social climbers.[26]

Barry has Yiddische *kopf.* While seemingly not bright or very articulate, he's smart enough to keep his words to a minimum, to stay silent when required, and to maintain the required poise and facade. Largely living by his wits and resourcefulness until he marries Lady Lyndon, he's verbally adept, able to charm people. Capable of adapting to survive, he ingratiates himself with both men and women alike. In his narcissism and verbal adeptness, he's similar to Humbert and Alex, both of whom can be read, as we've seen, as Jewish.

Barry is like Zelig, a mimic, a chameleon who effortlessly shifts from one role after another. Like the protean Quilty, he adopts many names and facades during the course of the film, indicating his flexible personality. Born Redmond Barry, during the course of the film he plays many roles, from an innocent, naive, and enamored boy to a spurned lover, duelist, poor Irishman, runaway, English soldier, gay English officer, deserter, farmer, Prussian soldier, police informant, counterspy, Hungarian valet (named Lazlo Zilagy, curiously anticipating Zelig), the chevalier, gambler, cardsharp, fencer, game master, husband, lover, adulterer, ladies' man, stepfather, loving father, opportunist, English gentleman, and finally a poor but world weary Irishman again. B. F. Dick praises how O'Neal "unites the many faces of his character into one unforgettable portrait. Whether he is the ardent lover preparing to duel with his rival, an unwilling member of the Prussian army with his hair slicked down and speaking German with a disarming lilt, a white-wigged croupier, or a broken amputee escorted by his mother to the coach that will take him away from England forever: he is superb." As Maria Pramaggiore states, "Barry erases and rewrites his own identity on numerous occasions, at times to ensure his survival and at other times to secure social advantage . . . in palimpsestic fashion, his previous identity as Barry remaining in evidence linguistically."[27]

Barry even adopts some of the roles played by Quilty: boxer, womanizer, drunk, sybarite, police officer. When he assumes the identity of Fakenham, the first syllable highlights Barry's skill at mimicry, and the name sounds not unlike the Yiddish term for gay, *faygele*. The concluding duel, in bearing some resemblance to the Ping-Pong match between Quilty and Humbert, brims with similar sexual innuendo. Bullingdon seeks "satisfaction." He's told to "cock" his pistol. Barry is asked if he's ready "to receive." And Bullingdon fires his pistol prematurely into the ground.

Barry is another subtextual Jew in uniform, joining the ranks of Sidney, Dax, David, Spartacus, and Goldberg. But Kubrick's portrait is complex, for every positive trait is balanced by a more compromising one. Barry shoots the more obviously nervous Quin in a duel, but it is faked. He is then robbed by highwaymen. Barry is described as a "tall and proper soldier," and, like those earlier characters, Kubrick emphasizes his muscular physique. Shown topless, he's in good shape and easily wins a boxing match against a taller and heavier opponent. But this immediately proceeds the sequence in which Barry is mocked for his fussiness. And we never see him doing any fighting in the British army. While he marches in rank toward enemy fire, the injury to Grogan enables him to dodge the line of fire and hence avoid the fighting, so we do not yet see Barry prove himself in battle. We see him shooting from a protected vantage point when enlisted in the Prussian army, but, similarly, his action in rescuing Potzdorf allows him to avoid hand-to-hand combat.

Barry can box, a sport at which Jews excelled, particularly in the eighteenth century. This was the era of Daniel Mendoza (1763–1836), Peter Sellers's maternal ancestor, who rose to fame at precisely the same time as the film is set. Mendoza was admired for his technical prowess as a fighter. A star of his day, he styled himself "Mendoza the Jew." He was the first prizefighter to lay down some proper rules of boxing technique, fathering "scientific" boxing by writing its first-ever textbook, *The Art of Boxing* (1789), which stresses diet and training and teaches boxers how to sidestep and other ways of avoiding being hit. Mendoza's early victories were the first demonstrations that boxing had ever known of a smaller man defeating a larger one through quickness and finesse. In 1791 Mendoza toured Ireland, which brought him to the attention of Joyce, who mentioned him, by name, in *Ulysses*. Kubrick amplified Thackeray's one-paragraph description of a fight with cudgels aboard a ship into a two-and-a-half minute-long bare-knuckle boxing match, evoking both "Prizefighter" and *Day of the Fight*. Barry dances and skips, delivering his punches in a timely and tactical "scientific" manner, unlike Toole (Pat Roach) who relies simply on brute strength. In this way Barry's victory over Toole mirrors Mendoza's technique, further hinting at his subtextual Jewishness, as well as Kubrick's own love of boxing. Mendoza also admired fencing, at which Barry is also adept, and compared it to boxing for its "neatness, activity, and grace."

Barry bears comparison to another Jewish protagonist. In its parody, "Borey Lyndon," *Mad* compares *Barry Lyndon* to Budd Schulberg's 1941 novel *What Makes Sammy Run?* Andrew Sarris calls his review "What Makes Barry Run?" A. D. Murphy in *Variety* describes him as an eighteenth-century Sammy Glick. *What Makes Sammy Run?* is the story of the rise and fall of its eponymous Jewish hero who, born poor in New York

FIGURE 13 Barry (Ryan O'Neal) boxes in a "scientific" manner in *Barry Lyndon* (1975).

City's Lower East Side, determines to make it by social climbing through a combination of deception and betrayal.[28]

Barry demonstrates other physical tics historically stereotyped as Jewish. Like Quilty, he's sexually voracious; in his avid pursuit of sexual conquests and in his serial infidelities, he resembles Schnitzler. He smokes: not only does he refuse to give up the habit but he blows smoke in Lady Lyndon's face when she asks him to quit. He's left-handed, a trait emphasized in multiple scenes: when he throws the glass of wine in Quin's face, when he boxes, and when he duels (with pistols or swords). Similarly, the loss of his leg—his symbolic castration—at the hands of his stepson not only is a Kubrick innovation not found in the novel but also subtly invokes the notion of the "Jew's foot." Historically, Jewishness was coded in crudely stereotypical terms by a "clumsy, heavy-footed gait." This is yet another visual sign of his otherness.[29]

Barry is also banished from England and hence fulfills the requirements of a classical Jewish scapegoat. Broken, crippled, and outcast, he's a sacrificial victim, symbolized by the lamb that he steals early on in the film, connoting not only the innocence he'll lose but also the paschal sacrifice. He's also sacrificed by his Irish relatives for them to attain a better life.

Often Kubrick uses red to mark Barry's outsider status. Barry's given name is *Red*mond, and he wears the red coat of an English army officer in Prussia. Later, as Barry Lyndon, he wears a red jacket while a boat with a red sail passes behind him. Historically, red was another color used to demarcate Jewishness, including a circle cut out of red cloth, a red overskirt, a red tabard, and a red wheel in the fifteenth century.

Further compounding the suggestion that Barry is Jewish is the one constant in his life: his mother. In stereotypically Jewish fashion, Barry is a mama's boy. In contrast to the novel, Kubrick magnified the role of Mrs. Barry (Marie Kean). She becomes more prominent and dominant, shifting their relationship into more obviously oedipal territory. Following the death of Barry's father, she rejected all suitors and "lived for her son only," devoting her life to her son, whom she shelters and smothers. When he leaves home for the first time, Captain Grogan reprimands him for failing to write to his mother—a very stereotypical gesture. Kubrick makes her much pushier, trying to take over the Lyndon household and nudging Barry to try to acquire a title for himself, ultimately leading to his ruin and downfall, where he ends up alone with and completely dependent on her.

In stereotypically Jewish fashion, Barry is feminized. Kubrick emphasizes his passivity, as a figure whose best plans go awry; he is subject to circumstance, buffeted by the winds of fate and chance, rarely intervening to alter events. In this passivity and entrapment, Barry echoes Humbert and Alex in the second half of *A Clockwork Orange*. The opening section emphasizes Barry's youth, innocence, and hence sexual inadequacy. He's nervous with Nora and his repeated refusal to find the ribbon with the words "I cannot" highlight his lack of experience. In the sections that follow, this is stressed through the repeated use of the terms "boy," "brat," and "impudent young swine." When, in the British army, he complains about the grease in his cup, his prissy tastes are mocked for violating the tough goyish code. The leader of those mocking him is called Toole, a name hinting at his goyish hyperphallic properties, especially in contrast to the callow Barry. When his beloved Grogan dies, Barry kisses him passionately on the lips and then sobs uncontrollably. To escape this military regime, he masquerades as a gay English officer called Jonathan Fakenham, invoking the biblical Jonathan whom loved King David deeply. At his wedding to Lady Lyndon, he's wearing thick makeup and lipstick and has coiffed and powdered hair. Following the marriage, he takes her name, formerly that of her late incapacitated, wheelchair-bound husband. And by the end of the film he's frozen in a static, half-legged pose, as Kubrick terminates his story in a freeze frame.

Kubrick's other choices bear the palimpsestic trace of Thackeray's Jewish characters. He cast Jewish actor Steven Berkoff to play Lord Ludd, the noble who duels with Barry to resolve the matter of his gambling debt to the chevalier. Ludd is effete and in the duel, resembling that between Alex and the Catlady, he assumes the feminine position. He, too, is left-handed. Berkoff describes him as an "English fop. He was dressed with the white wig and beauty spots and lipstick." He recalled playing him with "foppishness, decadence, indulgence, and enormous wealth. Once I saw the costumes being designed and the effect of the makeup, I very easily got myself into that way of thinking and the role of that kind of elegant, rather sophisticated fop who loved the ladies and was a kind of Regency dandy."[30]

The casting of Marisa Berenson as Lady Lyndon adds a further layer of Jewishness to the film. Although brought up Catholic, she was of Lithuanian Jewish descent. Friends with Henry Kissinger, she had previously been engaged to David de Rothschild. It was her role as Natalia Landauer, the wealthy German Jewish department store heir, in Bob Fosse's *Cabaret* (1972), that attracted Kubrick's attention. Similarities can be seen between Natalia and Lady Lyndon, as both are somewhat naive women preyed on by seemingly gold-digging men. At least one reviewer picked up on this, observing, "she is, however, terrific at wearing elaborate hairdo's [*sic*] and at looking—I don't think this was intended—tragically Jewish." Parallels can also be drawn with the casting of Shelley Winters in *Lolita*, who had played the very same role in *I Am a Camera* (1955), which, like *Cabaret*, was based on Christopher Isherwood's *Berlin Stories* (1945) about the doomed intelligentsia in prewar Berlin. Peter Sellers had even photographed Berenson for the *Daily Mirror* in October 1973. Kubrick was so taken with Berenson that she never even auditioned for the role. She recalls, "I was sitting in my apartment in Paris one afternoon last February when the phone rang. It was Kubrick. He said he had seen my performance in *Cabaret* and asked me if I'd be available for a film later this year."[31]

The Unruly, Coarse (Y)id

Adding to the implicit Jewishness of Barry's character, *Barry Lyndon* very much codes the problematics of assimilation faced by Ostjuden in Western, civilized, Protestant society. In his *Beyond Good and Evil*, Friedrich Nietzsche wrote how the Jews "want and wish rather, even with some importunity, to be absorbed and assimilated by Europe; they long to be fixed, permitted, respected somewhere at long last, putting an end to the nomad's life, to the 'Wandering Jew.'" According to Cuddihy, this process of adaptation, which had taken hundreds of years in Europe, had to be learned very quickly by Jews who were dumped into modernity extremely suddenly. Civilized aristocratic eighteenth-century Christian society required the sublimation and domestication of the "unruly, coarse 'id'" beneath a complex system of social codes and conventions. Cuddihy explains how the "*Ostjude* is not admissible into the civil society of the Gentile unless he submits to social censorship, disguising his unruly importunity in socially acceptable ways." Without the preparation of the kind Norbert Elias details in his book, Jews were made to feel "primitive." Thus the "Jewish social parvenu who 'tried at a bound to bridge the gap between his aspiration and his real social status,'" Cuddihy notes, "was masked." Cuddihy's book is somewhat of an intellectual cause célèbre, reviewed in the *New York Times*, *Commentary*, *Encounter*, and panned and admired alike for its chutzpah. Surely, this very chutzpah drew Kubrick to it.[32]

For Hannah Arendt, the Jew "concealed his true nature wherever he went, and through every hole in this costume his old pariah existence could be detected."[33] Lenny Bruce's shtick specifically "played on [this] inherent problem of masking—the fear of being unmasked—a motif that applied all too well to assimilated Jews, and one that would reappear in many of his routines." Anxious to pass, Jews thus feared "the 'sudden havoc' that the involuntary eruption of Ostjude identity from beneath the skin of 'passing' exception-Jew can create in a public place." Such un/masking is also the backdrop to and literal theme of *Traumnovelle*, which was on Kubrick's mind through the 1970s. The neoclassical facades that pepper *Barry Lyndon*, as they were in vogue in the eighteenth century, underline this anxiety, for they are precisely that, facades, false fronts, imitations, or mimics of real temples, almost the same but not quite.[34]

This is precisely the challenge that Barry, as the allegorical Ostjude, undergoes. *Barry Lyndon* explores the British class system's highest echelons and Barry's attempts to become "civilized" by overcoming the disabilities of his lowly birth. Richard Schickel describes him as a young man "trying to find the clues and cues to what's right behavior. What's the behavior that's going to advance me in this society? So it's a movie really about a young man defining himself in a climate that's foreign to him." Parvenus, like Barry, consumed art to prove their cultivation. In Guy de Maupassant's *Bel-Ami* (1885), the Jewish social climber Walter carefully displays his acquisitions to demonstrate his taste, just as Barry does through his purchase of the *Adoration of the Magi*, by Ludovico Cardi. Barry, though, has foolishly stepped into a situation in which he is out of his league; Kubrick said, he "gets in over his head." As Walker puts it, *Barry Lyndon* "ends with its eponymous parvenu drummed out of the social class he'd attempted to gatecrash—short of one leg, too, as a permanent reminder of his presumptuousness in social climbing."[35]

In this world Barry stands as the untamed id or Yid encountered in *A Clockwork Orange*, adopting various dis/guises to pass. Such a situation, where this coarse unruly id emerges, is glimpsed at a key moment in *Barry Lyndon*, when Barry loses control and erupts into spontaneous emotion, rendering him unfit to pass within this overly civilized world. This occurs at the event at which Barry stages his quest for a peerage, hopefully passing as one of the "best people," a sophisticated member of the "civilized" upper class he desperately wishes to enter: a proper, stately, orderly, and civilized recital of highly structured harpsichord music perfectly reflecting the ordered state of eighteenth-century society. But the recital, wholly invented by Kubrick, erupts into violence, and Barry's inner, real self (his [Y]id) is revealed as he violently beats Bullingdon in an uncontrolled, impulsive, brutal attack. Barry displays his barely suppressed aggression, the eruption of his unruly coarse id within the composed, civilized world of the gentile superego. Completely out of control, Barry attacks Bullingdon's jugular. His loss of any sense of decorum, composure, order, pretense, and artifice reveal him for what he is, making it feel so exhilaratingly liberating. Kubrick's camerawork highlights "Barry's emotional instability and cultural difference." The use of handheld camera jars with the overwhelming stasis of the film and connects to one previous occasion—the boxing match. Kubrick depicts the violence as brutal, animalistic, even intimate, by contrast to the rest of the violence, which is conducted per strict rules and rituals. These are the moments when Barry is at his most Jewish, revealing his inner (Y)id, and hence Kubrick himself held the camera, revealing his shared ethnicity and empathy for Barry. Relinquishing all hope of becoming a peer, Barry is cast out, renouncing any hope of joining that private exclusive "club," ostracized by the very men he'd sought to cultivate. Bullingdon spits out the "shameful nature" of the "insolent Irish upstart" whose "lowly birth," explains the "general brutality of his manners" and "brutal and un-gentlemanlike behavior." Referring to him as "Mr. Redmond Barry," he implies that his underlying identity is ineradicable and that this coarse, importunate Yid cannot be domesticated.[36]

Kubrick's changes remove the Jewish particularities, transforming *Barry Lyndon* into a more universal allegory. Barry is depicted as an everyman. As B. F. Dick puts it, "There is something of a Barry Lyndon in all of us who aspire to be what we are not." Kubrick, it seems, also wants us to identify Barry with his previous everyman, Alex, to whom he bears great resemblance. The minister of the interior describes Alex as "enterprising, aggressive, outgoing. Young. Bold. Vicious." Such a description is just as fitting for Barry. When Barry cavorts with two topless women in the scene immediately following the birth of his son, it mirrors those sequences of Alex with two biblical handmaidens. Their adventures, emphasized by the symmetry in their respective plots, are not dissimilar. Both undergo a "civilizing process," and the Ludovico Technique is alluded to through a painting by "Ludovico Corday," which Barry admires. The similarities between the two films are announced almost from *Barry Lyndon*'s opening words. Nora Brady says "Now, what shall it be?" which almost duplicates Burgess's opening question of *A Clockwork Orange*, "What's it going to be then, eh?"

FIGURE 14 Barry (Ryan O'Neal) as the coarse, importunate (Y)id in *Barry Lyndon* (1975).

Both films are marked by an ironic tone and approach and both protagonists end up bed-bound.[37]

The characterization of Barry shows how far Kubrick had come in in his exploration of subtextual Jewish masculinity since his films of the fifties and sixties. Barry isn't wholly moral and infallible like Dax and Spartacus. No military leader, he is a reluctant, forced conscript and ultimately a deserter. Neither is he the victimized Humbert or completely dissolute Quilty. Although, like Quilty, he's chameleonic, vain, and ambitious, motivated purely by self-interest at times and blind to the needs and desires of others, at the same time, Barry performs heroic deeds and betrays his inner menschlikayt: he passionately sobs over Grogan's corpse, and he rescues Potzdorf, for which, as an inspiration to his comrades, he's rewarded. Against his own desires, he excels in uniform, dispelling notions that would arise subsequently that Jews were unfit for military service, particularly as foot soldiers in the infantries of the newly formed nation states that would emerge in the period following the film's ending. Barry also helps the chevalier to flee and ultimately elects to spare Bullingdon when given the chance to shoot him. Kubrick's earlier portraits have thus been molded into one of infinite more complexity in the social-climbing Barry who attempts to undergo the ordeal of civility or the civilizing process but fails and loses his leg in the process. As Jonathan Benair says of it, "it's

Kubrick's most Jewish film. Rise above your station and God will strike you down and cut off your leg!"[38]

From Enlightenment to Holocaust

Thackeray's *Barry Lyndon* was inspired by Enlightenment novels, allowing Kubrick the opportunity to consider the age of the Enlightenment, the birthplace of the modern. The ancien régime European society depicted in *Barry Lyndon* was Western civilization at its most formal stage of development. Conformity to its innumerable codes of ritualized social conduct was essential for entry to its higher echelons. Everything—war, courtship, card games, highway robbery, marriages, duels—was conducted through precisely enacted, meticulously stage-managed rituals and codified social interactions, which Kubrick presented in long, drawn-out, sequences. In vivid detail Kubrick also depicts its rotten decadence and spiritual corruption. The gambling, card-playing, fencing, and dueling all hint at Schnitzler's criticisms of the "great politicians who were either monomaniacs or great gamblers with human beings." Marcia Cavell Aufhauser points out how "The barbarity of civilized society, one of the themes of *A Clockwork Orange*, is a theme of *Barry Lyndon* as well. Scenes focusing on some monument of Western civilization—an ingenious palace or a Bach chamber concerto—alternate with revelations of human ugliness. The nobility, with their enormous false beauty spots, their rouged and powdered faces, look the like the painted devils of the earlier film. There the moral was explicit and facile: that the brutality of institutional power is not different from the brutality of thugs who rape and kill for pleasure." She concludes, "for Kubrick, evil and art spring from the same demonic impulse."[39]

The representatives of civilized society are, in *Barry Lyndon*, the descendants of Crassus (as mirrored in the taste for neoclassicism) and the ancestors of Mireau and Broulard in their baroque French chateau, the minister of the interior (reflected in the dress of the spectators in Alex's final fantasy), and the guests at the Overlook Hotel and Ziegler's party and orgy. They are, in the words of Lord Wendover (André Morel), "the best people. I don't mean that they're the most virtuous, or indeed the least virtuous, or the cleverest or the stupidest or the richest or the best born. But the best. In a word, people about whom there is no question."

The neoclassical facades in vogue in the eighteenth century, which pepper the film, are false. Kubrick's film is so curiously flattened that it barely reveals the inner world of the aristocracy, nor that which underpinned it. Those lower classes that service it and make such life possible are barely seen other than in brief glimpses of stable boys, attendants, servants, valets, butlers, maids, and the like. Only once does the narrator hint at the world propping up the one we see: "Gentlemen talk of the age of chivalry but remember the ploughmen, poachers and pickpockets they lead. It is with these sad instruments great warriors and kings have been doing their murderous work in the world." This civilization, at the height of its social, artistic, and philosophical refinement and enlightenment, lies atop a paper-thin surface of carnage and brutality. Kubrick exposed the moral and spiritual corruption underpinning "civilised" society, showing its superficiality that, beneath its beautiful exteriors, was void. As Frank Rich writes, "What Kubrick does in 'Barry Lyndon' is, quite simply, examine human civilization at the point when the ordinary underpinnings of this doomsday modern world were formalized—during the Age of Reason, a time when optimism ran high about the ability of man to conquer savagery, injustice and suffering through the powers of his rational mind."[40]

Dueling, which is at the heart of *Barry Lyndon*—two duels invented by Kubrick bookend the film—epitomized this world of eighteenth-century goyim naches. A privilege enjoyed by the upper social classes, being challenged to a duel involved social selection in which the participant was deemed worthy of satisfaction, as someone regarded as both honorable and equal. Often, while duelists' eyes and throat were protected, faces were not, to allow the intentional creation of scars, as a mark of the duel, and hence social status and manhood. Here we might usefully remember Mireau's scar in *Paths of Glory*. For centuries Jews were excluded from this practice, so when finally allowed to duel, many acculturated Jews, such as Schnitzler (and the founder of Zionism, Theodor Herzl), relished the test and adventure of the duel in the belief that it had a manly and edifying effect. Since scars were visual markers of integration into the wider culture, the more marginal the individual, the keener their desire to be scarred.[41]

Even the church offers no respite from this society, but instead is its pillar. John Driscoll describes the "cold, un-Christian cruelty that breathes subsiding life across this scene of events and people." The church administered the ritualized violence of the duel, as a form of legalized execution; the setting of the final duel, an abandoned church with cruciform slits in its walls, highlights the institution's hypocrisy. Its representative, Rev. Samuel Runt (Murray Melvin), is a sneaky self-serving, venal individual, looking out for his own interests but masking it by seeming to look out for Lady Lyndon's, engaged in his own machinations to preserve his own privileged sinecure. His mincing mannerisms undermine the morality of his character, as does his pontificating about "fornication" when officiating the Lyndons' marriage.[42]

This is the self-same society, at its height, that culminated in the Holocaust. In a chilling foreshadowing of the Nazi era, the emphasis on outward civility at all costs required the constant use of euphemisms. Everyone is extremely polite, and sinister terms are cloaked in doublespeak. As Sarah Kozloff points out, "civility covers the worst of misdeeds." Captain Feeney robs Barry in a polite fashion, exhibiting manners and good grace, while exchanging pleasantries. Introducing himself with the words "at your service," his meaning is the exact opposite. The narrator says "stormed and occupied" when he means "love" and "sex." Gambling is a "science," and its practitioners "professors." A duel is a "meeting" and "satisfaction" revenge. Even Barry submits to such language: when he asks, "will you excuse Lord Bullingdon and me for a few minutes; we have something to discuss in private," it's to remove him from the presence of company to viciously beat him. Bullingdon refers to Barry's "illustrious blood" when he means his lowly birth. Cementing the link was the location of some of the setting in Thackeray's novel at Berlin's Lake Wannsee. This location was filled with resonance, for at a villa by that lake, on January 20, 1942, fifteen high-ranking Nazi Party and German government officials gathered to discuss and coordinate the implementation of what, using one of the most murderous euphemisms ever, they called the "Final Solution of the Jewish Question." And the year *Barry Lyndon* was released, Kubrick asked his brother-in-law and *Barry Lyndon*'s executive producer, Jan Harlan, to read Raul Hilberg. As Aaron Schindler explains, "Barry is merely the vehicle for taking us on this tour through the Age of Reason—that time that shaped much of our present-day ideas and values." Underlining this is the change that Kubrick made to the end of the film, which ended in 1789 rather than Thackeray's 1811.[43]

Conclusion

Barry Lyndon is a film seemingly out of its time. Where Kubrick's previous films are topical, tapping into the major intellectual trends of their day, including existentialism, Freudianism, nuclear disarmament, the death of

God, Nietzschean ethics, Kabbalistic spiritualism, violence, and behavioral conditioning, *Barry Lyndon* seemingly ignores the burning issues of U.S. society and cinema in the mid-1970s, including Watergate, My Lai, the Pentagon papers, and the fall of Saigon. Kubrick had turned his back on his countercultural films of the 1960s and early 1970s, movies that so clearly anticipated and fed the zeitgeist. Instead, he made a period costume drama, a blend of his incomplete Napoleon and Schnitzler projects, with an innovative painterly style, but it was interpreted as cold and static and helmed by a blank for a star. This disconnect made it his least commercial film thus far. *Barry Lyndon* clearly meant much to Kubrick, a deeply personal movie pursued in the face of its costs and commercial risks. It is subconsciously autobiographical. The element of being an ethnic outsider in a privileged WASP society struck a chord, manifesting that unconscious Jewish desire, as social pariahs, to unmask the respectability of the European society that shut them out. Its closest parallels are films by two other American Jewish directors that same year, Joan Micklin Silver's fin de siècle *Hester Street* and Woody Allen's Napoleonic *Love and Death*, both of which present Jewish characters completely out of sync with the world around them.

8

Dream Interpretation

The Shining capped Stanley Kubrick's trilogy of family films, exploring the nature of a man, a mensch, a father, and a son. If *Barry Lyndon* was Kubrick's most complete, personal, and emotional meditation on paternity to date, *The Shining* extended the investigation even deeper. It also continued Kubrick's grappling with the nature of evil in a post-Holocaust world, mirroring *Barry Lyndon*'s grappling with it in a pre-Holocaust one. *The Shining* was Kubrick's most autobiographical, and Freudian, film to date. An autocase history, it compares to Freud's *Interpretation of Dreams* (1899)—in which, like Freud, Kubrick engaged with some of the deepest and most enduring myths of Western civilization, including the problems of fathers and sons, dreams, obedience, and the nature of evil. The result was a psychologically dense film, a multilayered palimpsest, one of Kubrick's few films where he openly admitted to "psychological misdirection."[1]

From King to Kubrick

Back in 1966 Kubrick had expressed his desire "to make the world's scariest movie." During the seventies he searched for an appropriate horror vehicle. He inquired after such novels as *Rosemary's Baby* and *The Exorcist* (1973), admiring the resulting film adaptations. When John Calley, Warner Bros.'s production chief, sent him galley proofs of Stephen King's *The Shining* (1977), he found his source. In the book Jack Torrance, an ex-teacher and aspiring writer, accepts a job as the winter caretaker at the Overlook Hotel, set high in the Rocky Mountains in Colorado, despite the hotel's history of violence and "cabin fever." Jack brings his wife, Wendy, and son, Danny, with him to the isolated hotel. Because of his ability to "shine"—his capacity to see events in the past and future—Danny fears the hotel. After several months Jack's mental state declines and he experiences delusions, leading him to seek to kill his family. Ultimately, Jack's family is saved, as the hotel's exploding boiler kills him. The book is manifestly a ghost story, pitting an innocent child against the evil of the hotel, with Jack caught in the middle. Although psychologically damaged by and angry at the abuse he suffered at the hands of his own father, he's a decent man (a mensch), overcome by supernatural forces rather than his own rage and alcoholism. It was, Kubrick explained, "very compulsive reading" and "the plot, ideas and structure were much more imaginative than anything I've ever read in the genre."[2]

Kubrick hired Diane Johnson to cowrite the screenplay. Her 1974 novel, *The Shadow Knows*, impressed him. He considered adapting it but found it unsuitable for his vision. Kubrick described her as an "ideal collaborator" in part because of her own writing but also because she was then teaching a course on the Gothic novel at the University of California at Berkeley. They began working together in June 1977. Kubrick and Johnson made significant alterations to the novel. They eliminated almost all of Jack's backstory, removing any obvious trace of his menschlikayt in the process. They also downplayed and deleted outright various supernatural phenomena, including animate fire hoses and topiary animals. Rather, they provided psychological motivation for the events, rendering the supernatural elements superfluous. The external conflict of the novel became an inner one waged within Jack. He is the source of his own undoing and his motivation for murder is never entirely clear.[3]

Kubrick's film is gloomier, darker, and more enigmatic and pessimistic in outlook, privileging ambiguity and confusion over certainty and morality. It doesn't end happily. "Very early on, I decided the novel's ending wouldn't do," Kubrick recalled. "I didn't want the conventional ending—the big bad places burns down." Kubrick annotated his copy of the novel with the words, "fuck the boiler," denying Jack (Jack Nicholson) the redemption he achieves in the novel through self-sacrifice. In a deliberate maneuver to stamp the film as his own, Kubrick devises a maze in which Jack freezes to death after Danny (Danny Lloyd) bamboozles him. Although there is a fight at the finish, evil is not definitively defeated nor do cheerful emotions ultimately dominate. There is no resolution, as the film ends on an enigmatic note, leaving the whole thing open to interpretation. Kubrick offered no uplifting codas. Unlike King's novel, there is no epilogue showing us what happened to Danny, Wendy (Shelley Duvall), or the hotel. Although Kubrick shot one in which hotel manager, Stuart Ullman (Barry Nelson) visits Wendy and Danny, who are recuperating in hospital, he scrapped it after test screenings. The image of Jack in a photograph on the hotel's wall dated 1921 (frozen in a frame just like Barry Lyndon) leaves us with a host of queries regarding what we've just seen, posing more questions than it answers. Shooting started in May 1978. Scheduled to last seventeen weeks, it went on for fourteen months. The film was released on May 23, 1980.[4]

Fathers and Sons

The Shining represents a form of Freudian introspection into the nature of paternity and the father-son relationship. Kubrick was drawn to King's novel because of its "psychological underpinnings," Johnson states. "A father threatening his child is compelling. It's an archetypal enactment of unconscious rages. Stephen King isn't Kafka, but the material of this novel is the rage and fear within families." She describes the film as an "underlying story of a father's hate for his child and his wife." She adds, "the murderous father, is a very very frightening one." She further recalls that Kubrick "wanted to know what the King novel was about, in the deepest psychological sense; he wanted to talk about that and to read theoretical works that might shed light on it, particularly works of psychology and especially those of Freud." And, she explains, "Family hate seemed quite important. We decided that in the case of *The Shining* this was a central element. I had the very strong impression that Kubrick was attracted to *The Shining* because of the father/son thing."[5]

That the film constitutes a form of internal auto- or self-reflection is suggested by Kubrick's fascination with those central European authors who haunt *The Shining* like the Overlook's ghostly presences. Kubrick was already a fan of Franz Kafka, Stefan Zweig, Joseph Conrad, and Arthur Schnitzler. In preparation for the film, he immersed himself in even more psychoanalytic reading, including Freud's "The Uncanny" (1899) and Bruno Bettelheim's *The Uses of Enchantment* (1976), along with writings by Freud's pupil Karen Horney and more contemporary Freudian thinker Simon O. Lesser. He also read Galician Jewish author, Bruno Schulz, considered to be the Polish Kafka, who translated Kafka's *The Trial* into Polish in 1936. Schulz's 1934 book *The Street of Crocodiles*, translated into English in 1963, features Schulz's father, who, like Freud's and Kubrick's, was named Jacob. Father-son relations and hostility, or fear, of the father pervades their work, all of whom influenced *The Shining*. In this way, Kubrick also suggests his own family history in the Austro-Hungarian Empire. Indeed, Kubrick's deliberate location of *The Shining* in the bourgeois spaces of the well-to-do hotel evokes the interwar milieu of central Europe, when Jews like his own ancestors and Kafka frequented such spas as Marienbad or Zweig's Summering. The hotel setting even acts as an allegory for central Europe. Clearly some of Kubrick's frustrated desire to adapt Zweig's *Burning Secret* was channeled into *The Shining*, not just in its setting in a summer holiday spa resort in the mountains but in the oedipal drama witnessed from a young boy's perspective, seeing things he shouldn't and desiring to protect his mother from his father's wrath.[6]

There are also clear echoes of *Traumnovelle*. Kubrick's "unfulfilled ambition" of adapting Schnitzler "found an outlet in *The Shining*," Michel Ciment writes. Freud's essay on the uncanny was written only a few years prior to *Traumnovelle* and was an influence on Schnitzler, who changed his working title (*"Doppelnovelle"* or "Story of Doubleness") to mirror Freud's *Interpretation of Dreams*. Similarly, Johnson's novel, *The Shadow Knows* is a psychological mystery inspired by *Traumnovelle*. Like Schnitzler's novella, *The Shining* features a father-mother–young child triad in which the husband undergoes a psychic odyssey, during which distinctions between delusion and reality are deliberately blurred, making us question whether what we are watching in the film is real or a projection from the protagonist's mind. Kubrick still intended to adapt Schnitzler's novella and worked on it through the 1970s. By this point, he wanted Woody Allen in the lead, playing a New York Jewish doctor, but he became dissatisfied with his screenplay and gave up, adapting King instead. Perhaps, though, it was his consideration of Allen that led him to cast Shelley Duvall as Wendy. Her previous role had been a cameo in Woody Allen's 1977 *Annie*

Hall. As Pam, one of Alvy Singer's lovers, she had told him "Sex with you is really a Kafka-esque experience." Three years later Duvall's character was suffering another Kafkaesque experience at the hands of a Jewish New York director.[7]

Kubrick clearly had *Traumnovelle* in mind when working on *The Shining*, as demonstrated by drafts of the screenplay. He wrote, "plant early on an innocent admission by Wendy that she has thoughts but never has and never would be unfaithful. What kind of thoughts. Sexy dreams. He could build on this in the hotel." Johnson envisaged a masked ball, as well as a ballroom orgy that interweaved Schnitzler's work with Edgar Allen Poe's "The Masque of the Red Death" (1842) referenced in King's novel. Such ideas were diluted to the naked lady in the bathtub and Wendy's glimpse of a man in an animal costume fellating another guest. Eventually, material omitted from *The Shining* was inserted into *Eyes Wide Shut*, including the Poe-inspired masked ball, orgy, and beautiful women. Making *The Shining*, therefore, was part of the process of adapting *Traumnovelle* into *Eyes Wide Shut*, ultimately Kubrick's most autobiographical and Freudian film.[8]

Kubrick explicitly identified Kafka as his template for the film. "The hotel's labyrinthine layout and huge rooms, I believed, would alone provide an eerie enough atmosphere. This realistic approach was also followed in the lighting, and in every aspect of the décor. It seemed to me that the perfect guide for this approach could be found in Kafka's writing style. His stories are fantastic and allegorical, but his writing is simple and straightforward, almost journalistic." He also told *Cahiers du Cinéma*, "I compare the mood of the film to the lucid style of Kafka's writing. . . . It is not overwrought, for the fantastic should be based on the ordinary." Kubrick explained to Alexander Walker, "It's the way a hotel would be lighted. You'd need illumination if you were a caretaker in the off-season—lights would be left on in the main rooms and corridors," Kubrick explained. He continued, "A simple naturalistic style is best. I'm sure it is. Kafka approached the same problem in the same way. . . . Conversely, the films based on Kafka's novels have never done themselves any good by using baroque lighting and sets that are half consciously 'Kafka-esque'. Kafka should be filmed like *Marty*, and acted that way, too. There isn't any dark at the top of the stairs in *The Shining* for the same reason—and it's well-lit at the bottom, too!"[9]

The introspective element is compounded by Kubrick's directorial decisions. The opening serpentine helicopter traveling shot and title sequence conceived by Kubrick mirrors the structure of Francis Ford Coppola's adaptation of Conrad's *Heart of Darkness*. Released the previous year, *Apocalypse Now* uses the device of a journey up a river as a means of exploring America's psyche. As Kubrick "was putting the finishing touches on *The Shining*, he asked me very specific questions about *Apocalypse Now*, a work print of which had just had its first screening on the Croissette," Ciment recalls. Kubrick signals that *The Shining* is a Freudian, metaphysical journey deep into the dark recesses of the human subconscious by Jack's long, winding drive up the mountain. It hints at an inward, psychological, rather than real, physical journey, a "fairy tale." As he told Nicholson, "what was going on in *The Shining* was largely going on in the head of the character he was playing."[10]

The hotel and its grounds are external physical representations of the interior of Jack's disordered mind and internal world. Ciment feels that it is "within Jack himself that the real battle is fought." As Alexander Walker puts it, Kubrick's set represents "the structure of the mind and the architecture of the soul" and compares it to Orson Welles's *War of the Worlds* broadcast in October 1938, which Kubrick could quote from memory. "Like the H.G. Wells novel, *The Shining* is a story of alien invasiveness, although the invaders are inside a man's mind, not a nation's." This explains Jack's sense of déjà vu and why it feels so "homey," "as though I know what was going to be around every corner." Of course he knows, for he was "home" inside his head, embedded in his own mental landscape. Gilles Deleuze famously suggests the hotel represented a brain, and it certainly appears to be a living, bleeding organism, full of cavities and pipes resembling arteries and veins. Jack's use of the term "homey" explicitly invokes Freud's notion of the "*Heimlich*" in his essay on "The Uncanny" and since the hotel is located on an Indian burial ground, it invokes Freud's comparison of the unconscious history of the individual to the buried, archaeological strata of historical sites, in what he called psycho-archaeology.[11]

To this end, Kubrick designed a deliberately labyrinthine layout, containing spatial defects, physical impossibilities, and inner recesses, constantly intersected by new angles. He said, "Most of the hotel set was built as a composite, so that you could go up a flight of stairs, turn down a corridor, travel its length and find your way to still another part of the hotel. It mirrored the kind of camera movements which took place in the maze." In fact, the rooms were designed to interconnect to facilitate the use of Steadicam. These blatant design anomalies and mistakes in the hotel layout translate into structural mind games in the film. The Overlook becomes a vast disorienting and bewildering maze of corridors and impossible windows and doorways. And this is only the surface. The elevator, stairwells, piping, and electrical cable all point to a similar yet unseen world within and beneath the hotel. On top of all this, Kubrick added a maze constructed of hedges thirteen-feet high, not found in the novel.

This introspective, internal element is further coded by the oedipal theme, which has marked Kubrick's work since *Lolita* but comes to the fore here. Johnson explained that "Kubrick and I thought that *The Shining* was really about family hate . . . the contact between the little boy and his father or the resentment by the father of the threatening little boy for the love of the mother." She jotted "Oedipal" alongside a draft scene in which Danny defeats Jack. She characterized Danny's relationship to his father as "Danny/Problem. Progressions = fear, disillusion, disobedience." The original Greek myth begins with parents abandoning their son, whose ankles are mutilated by his father, who pierces and ties his ankles together (hence the name Oedipus, which means "swollen foot"). But where Freud ignored or repressed this incident of paternal abuse, Kubrick includes it, dramatizing Jack's hostility toward Danny (and toward his wife). Reinforcing this reading is Jack's consumption of Jack Daniels bourbon, in the Gold Room (in the novel he liked martinis), the drink invoking his own and his son's given names. And, like Oedipus, Danny unwittingly causes the death of his father; attempted infanticide becomes successful parricide. Jack dies in retaliation for his filicidal efforts, and, ironically, it is he who's lamed. In the end, Danny is left alone with his mother, who kisses him on the lips.[12]

Self-Reflexivity and Autobiography

Underlining the interpretation of *The Shining* as an autobiographical, autocase history, in an avowedly and self-consciously Freudian mode, is the unprecedented amount of autobiography and self-reflexivity manifested in the film. Ciment, who interviewed Kubrick numerous times, suggests, "In many respects, *The Shining* is one of his most intimate works. Isolated, hemmed in, beset by a siege mentality, an intellectual (a former teacher) sees himself as an artist who cannot manage to create. . . . By choosing an artist for the first time as the protagonist of one his stories (a theme prefigured in *Lolita* by the character of Humbert) and making him a failure, Kubrick exorcises his own demons."[13]

The Shining was Kubrick's sole film for which he deliberately commissioned and allowed someone to make the only formal record of him at work, offering an unprecedented glimpse into his working methods. The person he trusted to document the production was his daughter Vivian. It remains the only Kubrick-sanctioned footage in which we meet his family, including Vivian, as well as his parents, who pay an on-set visit. It's revered by fans as an especially authentic, candid, revealing, and truthful piece of work, particularly in the absence of any other available footage of Kubrick at work or otherwise.

Walker, who was close to Kubrick, felt that the film "reveals much more about its maker than he may have intended." According to Johnson, there are, for example, many uncanny parallels between Kubrick and Jack, whose character Kubrick pretty much wrote. Like Jack, he let his beard and hair grow from a clean-shaven look, and he went from being smartly dressed to somewhat disheveled by the time he made *The Shining*. They both wore lumber jackets and were fans of baseball. Kubrick's high school baseball team was called the Golden Eagles, mirroring the Stovington Eagles T-shirt Jack wears.[14]

Both Kubrick and Jack move to secluded buildings to work. Anne Jackson recalls that Kubrick was a "preoccupied man with a lot of things on his mind." Walker suggests that, like Jack, "defiantly demanding nothing better than a long winter to get down to concentrated work, Kubrick 'dug in' on his St. Alban's estate: his communications base, workshop and family dwelling." Walker thus saw a parallel with the Overlook Hotel and the mazelike configuration of Elstree Studios, where the film was shot. The very set of the Overlook mirrors that of the hotel constructed within its walls. Just as the Torrances are trapped in the snowbound Overlook, encased by the Rockies, so Kubrick, his cast, and crew were enfolded within the walls of a protective soundstage, cutting them off from the outside world until he allowed them to go home.[15]

Both Kubrick and Jack were liberal, well-read, *New York Review of Books*–subscribing (copies can be seen in the Torrances' apartment), Marlboro-smoking Americans (Kubrick's preferred brand, which he puffed ubiquitously on set), aspiring to be writers. Johnson recalls that Kubrick's "approach was very literary and intellectual" and that he had a "strong literary sense. In all respects he thinks like a novelist." Kubrick himself compared his job to a writer's: "In terms of working with actors, a director's job more closely resembles that of a novelist," and it is "more or

less than a continuation of the writing." This may explain why he personally typed out the sheets that appear in Jack's typewriter on his own personal small yellow Adler model rather than delegating the task and why
Jack uses one of Kubrick's own typewriters on what became Kubrick's
own table.[16]

Maybe Kubrick identified with Jack's writer's block. Walker describes
Jack as a "self-tortured reclusive writer . . . whose creative juices simply
won't start flowing," leading some critics "to see a parallel between such
a crisis and the slowing of *The Shining*'s production tempo. Enhancing
this theme was the fact that, like Torrance, Kubrick had steadily retreated
into a secluded world of his own where, for all any outsider knew, there
might be demons." Kubrick was a writer manqué who never originated
his own screenplays, preferring to tinker with others' work. Eight years
before making *The Shining*, he said, "A great story is a kind of miracle.
I've never written a story myself, which is probably why I have so much
respect for it. I started out, before I became a film director, always thinking, you know, if I couldn't play on the Yankees I'd like to be a novelist. The people I first admired were not film directors but novelists.
Like Conrad." In a letter to Anthony Burgess, he confided, "I am not a
writer, merely an adapter, at best." Kirk Douglas recalls, "Stanley is not
a good writer. He has always functioned better if he got a good writer
and worked with him as an editor. . . . I have a copy of the terrible *Paths*

FIGURE 15 The Torrances subscribe to the *New York Review of Books* in *The Shining* (1980).

of Glory that he wrote to make it more commercial. If we had shot that script, Stanley might still be living in an apartment in Brooklyn instead of in a castle in England."[17]

Kubrick's directorial methods mirrored Jack's behavior in the film. After all, as Patrick McGilligan states, the director is the "father figure on any motion picture set." Walker points out how *Making the Shining* only serves to confirm the "impression at times of an almost sinister autocrat, muffled against a wintry cold on the back lot at MGM's British studio (where the Overlook Hotel's exteriors and ominous garden maze were constructed), exacting, tireless, and dispassionate. Kubrick is seen urging Nicholson into ever more inventive but taxing interpretations of a scene." This is most evident in terms of Kubrick's treatment of Duvall. Whereas he showed overt admiration for Nicholson, his behavior toward her, combined with his comments about her in interviews, was very negative. Gordon Stainforth, who assisted Vivian with the editing of the documentary, recalls that while Kubrick demanded many cuts, "he had no real problem with the scenes where he was harassing the lead actor Shelley Duvall to the point of a nervous breakdown." He allowed his daughter's documentary to depict him as being impatient, if not outright cruel, toward her, "venting his exasperation . . . for some alleged inattentiveness. Occasionally Kubrick seems to want to make his point the way Torrance does, with a fireman's ax. Some people, seeing Vivian Kubrick's short film on television, find it easy to conflate the menacing vision of Jack Nicholson in *The Shining* with his authoritarian director in the documentary."[18]

Yet this was surely part of Kubrick's trademark staging, manipulation, and misdirection. He presented a view to the world, which was ultimately swallowed with little critical digestion but which didn't reflect reality. Christiane recalls that he and Duvall "had a good working relationship and Stanley was delighted with Shelley's performance in this very demanding and difficult role." Duvall recalls how he spent a great deal of time teaching her about handling the camera, and she spent the last three months playing chess with him between takes. For Stainforth, "Stanley was one of the most demanding people in the business, but he could be agreeable and touching. He had two faces, but for reasons of his own only wanted to show one. He actually did not want to appear as a sympathetic character." That he played a heavy hand in editing the documentary indicates the final cut had his approval. He deliberately chose to present a public image that served to reinforce the parallels between him and Jack.[19]

This lends the performance and casting of Duvall its own intriguing resonances. When Vincent LoBrutto wrote, "Duvall felt she wasn't getting as much attention and wasn't given the same respect or consideration for her ideas and feelings," it echoed how Shelley Winters felt ignored on the set of *Lolita* two decades earlier. In terms that mirror Winters' description of playing Charlotte, Duvall recalls, "From May until October I was really in and out of ill health because the stress of the role was so great. Stanley pushed me and prodded me further than I've ever been pushed before. It's the most difficult role I've had to play." The experience of berating "Shelley" surely evoked some memories of *Lolita*, especially given the parallel oedipal themes. Both performances were described as "hysterical," and, in another nod to *Lolita*, Jack uses a line straight out of Vladimir Nabokov's novel when he calls Wendy "light of my life." There is even the coincidence of the actors' first names, and, given Duvall's surname, one might mistake her for Jewish, not least because her role immediately prior to *The Shining* had been a cameo as Woody Allen's lover in *Annie Hall*. In 1980 Winters had published her autobiography, and Kubrick requested a copy of it. There's also some resemblance to Lady Lyndon, played by the part-Jewish Marisa Berenson, whose life unravels as a result of her spouse's actions. One can also see echoes of Ruth Sobotka as Iris Kane in *Killer's Kiss*.[20]

Kubrick's casting for the role of Jack is similarly intriguing. The actor and role seemed a perfect fit. "Nicholson was his first—and immediate—choice on reading the Stephen King novel," Walker states. Born in 1937, he was only nine years younger than Kubrick and was friends with a photographer that Kubrick had known at *Look*. Kubrick had admired Nicholson ever since seeing him in *Easy Rider* (1969) and wanted to cast him as Napoleon in his never-to-be-made film. Many see a physical resemblance between them, and Michael Herr perceives a parallel between a picture of Kubrick taken when he was around twelve or thirteen and that of Jack which ends the movie. Walker feels, "No one could have anticipated how much Nicholson's physical appearance in the film resembled Kubrick's at the time. . . . As shooting progressed and the strong-browed Jack Nicholson, whose eyes seem to command and possess whatever his looking at, grew into the brooding, saturnine, and eventually intimidating character, people did see an affinity of manner and even appearance between him and his director."[21]

Kubrick bonded with Nicholson in the way he had with Sellers two decades earlier, allowing Nicholson to similarly improvise (the "Three

Little Pigs" is the most famous example). Nicholson produced a similarly over-the-top comical performance that, for some, bordered on the absurd, harking back to Sidney in *Fear and Desire*. *Mad*'s parody accused him of "some AWFUL CRIMES," including "over-acting!" When Jack says, "God, I'd give anything for a drink. I'd give my goddam soul for just a glass of beer," it uncannily recalls Quilty's utterance, "Gee, I'm just dying for a drink. I'm just dying to have a drinkie!" Earlier Ullman had described Grady (Philip Stone) as a "completely normal individual," recalling Quilty's overuse on the term to mask his abnormality. By this point, Kubrick's reputation increasingly resembled Nabokov's portrait of Quilty; as LoBrutto writes, "Face-to-face contact with Stanley Kubrick was becoming less frequent for anyone not directly working on one of his films or not within his well-found intimate sphere. The world began to see Stanley Kubrick as the Howard Hughes of cinema. He rarely left his home, except to work at a nearby studio. He almost never left England."[22]

Kubrick squeezed in other self-reflexive gestures. The twin girls in the film recall a photograph of two little girls, standing side by side, smiling, wearing similar dresses, arms fully extended downward as they hold hands and stare directly into the lens, that he took for *Look* (May 25, 1948). They also bear some resemblance to a famous photograph, "Identical Twins" (1967), by Diane Arbus, whom he knew from his Greenwich Village days. As the father of three daughters, he had spent years photographing them. And the black-and-white photographs that are a key part of the decor of the hotel, but on which Kubrick is careful to never focus on for too long, recall his early photojournalism. Vivian can be glimpsed as one of the crowd in the Gold Room sequence, and his daughter Katharina was a locations researcher. He even cameoed himself as a voice on the radio in the film. Wendy is shown reading *The Catcher in the Rye*, whose author, J. D. Salinger, was as famously reclusive as Kubrick was perceived to be (and a copy of *Catch-22* can be seen on the shelf behind her). And there's the coincidence of the initials of its author's given names and those of *The Shining*'s protagonist, Jack Daniel Torrance.

Jack the Jew

Reinforcing the Kubrick/Jack equation are the series of hints that allow us to read Jack as allegorically Jewish. His animated gesticulations are reminiscent of an immigrant's, suggests Mario Falsetto. He's an ex-teacher who is struggling to become a writer who lives in an apartment strewn with the *New York Review of Books* and books. King describes him as a "college fella" who talks "just like a book." Nelson describes him as a "model of liberal politics and education." Patrick Webster argues that even in the midst of his breakdown and contemplation of murder, "his liberal sensibilities were still shocked by the use of such politically incorrect and 'murderously' racist language" as "nigger." And for the role, Kubrick chose an actor whom he described as "intelligent and literate." Jack is defined by intellectual rather than physical activity, manifesting Yiddische *kopf*. Jack persuades Ullman to give him the job, and, in a display reminiscent of Quilty's death sequence, he uses his Jewish brains to attempt to wheedle his way out of the walk-in freezer, switching personalities from a hurt little boy to a screaming bully.[23]

But Jack is an outsider. Attempting to buy a drink at the bar, Lloyd the barman (Joe Turkel) ominously informs him, "Your money's no good here. Orders from the house," hinting at the restricted nature of such hotels as the Overlook in the 1920s. Such restrictions remained a feature of U.S. hotels well into the 1950s, afflicting Humbert in Nabokov's *Lolita*. And when Jack strolls through the ballroom, in full 1920s swing, wearing his modern-day and hence anachronistic clothes, it reinforces his lack of status and belonging and his failure to pass, just like Barry Lyndon.

The prominent use of color, specifically yellow, also marks Jack out as Jewish. For centuries, more than the red discussed in the previous chapter, yellow historically connoted Jewishness, particularly as accusations of blood libel and ritual slaughter morphed into racial anti-Semitism. In a change from King's novel, in which it's red, Jack's car is yellow. Nelson observes how, as the film moves closer to Jack's madness, yellow becomes increasingly prominent. Garrett Brown, the Steadicam operator, describes the set as "poisonly [*sic*] yellow-looking." The Gold Room chandeliers cast a yellow golden light; the Grady murder corridor is covered in faded yellow wallpaper; a yellow lamp next to Jack's typewriter gives the paper a yellow texture; his face and eyes turn yellow like the yellow bourbon in his glass; the hallway in the Torrance apartment is decorated with yellow-flowered wallpaper; Jack's face takes on a yellow hue while he stands outside the bathroom with an ax; as he pursues Hallorann (Scatman Crothers), the interior lighting transforms the walls into evening yellow; and both the Gold Room and gold corridor suggest yellow. And Grady spills the distinctively yellow drink Advocaat over Jack. "It tends to stain," Grady tells Jack, and the Advocaat becomes emblematic of Jewish origins, which are a blemish, a mark of shame, just as the yellow badge the Nazis forced Jews to wear was known in street slang as the "gelber fleck" or "yellow stain."[24]

Jack's imitation of the "Big Bad Wolf" of the Disney's 1933 *Three Little Pigs* also has Jewish resonances. Uttering the line, "little pigs, little pigs, let me come in," he chops down a door to get at Danny and Wendy. In the original Disney cartoon—and there are multiple references to cartoons peppering the film—the wolf is disguised as a stereotypical Jewish peddler, complete with large crooked proboscis, eyeglasses, black hat, thick Yiddish accent, and hand gestures. His hat is like that worn by the caricatures in the illustration in *Killer's Kiss*. Although the wolf's disguise was later changed to that of a Fuller Brush salesman, the unaltered soundtrack remained until it too was reedited. Nevertheless, the anti-Semitic stain was not rubbed away, and, similarly, in the Nazi version of *Red Riding Hood*, the wolf is Jewish.

Kubrick thrice inserted an explicitly Jewish product into the film, one not found in the novel. When Hallorann gives Wendy and Danny a guided tour of the kitchens, three cans of "Heinz Fresh Pack Thick Kosher Dill Pickle Slices" are clearly visible, with the label turned toward the camera. We see them again (twice) when Jack is shut into the food storeroom. Given Kubrick's eye for detail, as evidenced in this instance by a photograph by Christiane of him carefully arranging the cans and jars on the shelf of the storeroom, the cans can be interpreted as a sly nod and wink to Jack's (and Kubrick's own) ethnic origins (and culinary tastes). Christiane captioned the image, "Getting the positioning of the props just right for the scene where Jack is locked in the pantry in *The Shining*."[25]

Jack demonstrates other physical tics historically ascribed as Jewish. Like Barry and Quilty, he's left-handed. Wendy's crippling of his right leg heightens the ability of his left. This disability is emphasized in a twelve-second uncut sideways tracking shot of him dragging his limp foot as he pursues Danny. Like Barry, it is another visual marker of his Jewish otherness, which taps into the uniqueness of the Jew's foot, which was, in medieval times, linked to the cloven-hoofed devil. Jack is certainly represented as a satanic figure, and there are multiple comparisons between him and the Devil, alluding to classic Christian Judeophobia in which Jews were perceived as Satan's earthly mediators and hence possessing similar attributes.

FIGURE 16 A can of Heinz Kosher Dill Pickle Slices is clearly visible in the storeroom in *The Shining* (1980).

Ultimately, in becoming the sacrificial victim, Jack (like Alex and Barry before him), becomes the Jewish scapegoat.

Jack's limp also alludes to his biblical namesake and patriarch Jacob. The son of Isaac, who cheated his brother Esau out of his birthright by fooling his blind father, Jacob wrestled with an angel, damaging his thigh and causing him to limp, with a slow and weak gait. He was subsequently named Israel, and his sons were the ancestors of the Twelve Tribes, known as the Children of Israel. The name "Jack" can be read as the diminutive of Jacob. In one draft Wendy stabs Jack "in the thigh." Like Jacob, Jack awakes from a terrifying dream in which he murders his family and from which he awakens in a fright. The accompanying music is that of Krzysztof Penderecki's *The Awakening of Jacob* (sometimes translated as *The Dream of Jacob*), suggesting Jacob's dream of angels ascending and descending a heavenly stairway (Gen. 28:10–18, JSB). Kubrick's insertion of an elevator, which didn't appear in the novel, is none other than a mechanical ladder, gateway, or stairway to heaven.[26]

Jack and Wendy have named their son Daniel, another name replete with biblical allusion. Daniel translates from Hebrew as "God is my judge," "God judges," or "Judge of God." Daniel is the name of the biblical prophet and Babylonian royal courtier who, like Danny, is "terrified" by the "vision of my mind" (Dan. 7:15, JSB). Both are adept at divination and, like Freud, the interpretation of dreams, and they have "understanding of visions and dreams of all kinds" (1:17, JSB). "You wouldn't do anything to hurt us?" Danny asks Jack, in an act of premonition. When the king of Babylon, Nebuchadnezzar, dreams of strange writing on the wall, Daniel is the only one able to decipher it. Danny writes strangely on the wall when he scrawls "Redrum" on the bedroom door, its real meaning only discernable in the mirror.

Wendy and Jack call Danny "Doc," yet another name that bears Jewish traces. The use of this nickname explicitly references Warner Bros.'s cartoon rabbit, an image of whom Danny wears on his shirt in the beginning of the film. In fact, the postproduction script specifically states that "Doc" is "short for 'Doctor'—a character in Bugs Bunny cartoons." Voiced by Mel Blanc and "modeled on the urban, ethnic, Brooklyn type," Bugs is characterized by Jewish mannerisms, mimicry, voice, accent, and other tics historically ascribed to Jews. Because such types populated Barbra Streisand's youth, Bugs's street-lingo catchphrase, "What's up, Doc?" became the title of her screwball comedy film in 1972, which also starred Ryan O'Neal. The name "Doc" suggestively harks back to an early draft of *Dr. Strangelove*, in which Kubrick considered naming a character, "Lt. Irving 'Doc' Schwartz."[27]

"Doc" also has oedipal echoes, inviting us to consider Kubrick's physician father. Jacob Kubrick dropped his more Jewish name for the more cosmopolitan "Jack" or "Jacques." Various fatherly "Jacks" have cropped up in Kubrick's oeuvre, including Johnny Clay in *The Killing* and Jack D. Ripper in *Dr. Strangelove*. This last name deliberately echoes the allegedly Jewish Victorian serial killer and is directly invoked by Johnson in a draft screenplay: "Actually Ullman looks like he'd hire Jack the Ripper if he'd work for these wages." It's also uncanny that Kubrick chose to collaborate with a writer whose last name translates as "son of John" or "son of Jack." Similarly, he personally hired the actor Anne Jackson ("son of Jack") to play the doctor who examines Danny.[28]

The Banality of Evil

There remains another troubling dimension to the movie. Geoffrey Cocks presents a compelling argument that, although Kubrick never succeeded in making a film explicitly about the Shoah, *The Shining* was his Holocaust movie, albeit in an allegorical fashion. As we've seen, in one way or another, the Holocaust underpinned all of Kubrick's feature films, but evidence exists suggesting the Shoah was on his mind as he developed *The Shining*. During preproduction, the major landmark NBC television miniseries *The Holocaust* was broadcast on U.S. television in 1978, and a few weeks later President Jimmy Carter announced the U.S. government's intention to create a memorial "to the six million who were killed in the Holocaust." Not long before working on *The Shining*, in 1975 Kubrick had asked Jan Harlan to read Raul Hilberg. That same year Harlan approached Isaac Bashevis Singer to write a Holocaust screenplay, but he declined. In 1980—the same year as *The Shining*—Kubrick sent Hilberg's book to Michael Herr, describing it as *"monumental"*; Herr recalls how it "absorbed" Kubrick. Shortly thereafter Kubrick wrote to Hilberg, asking him to recommend a novel on which he could base a film about the Holocaust.[29]

While that film never came to fruition, *The Shining* bookended a decade, beginning with *Rosemary's Baby*, in which Jewish directors grappled with the nature of evil in a post-Holocaust world through a series of horror films in which the protagonists were often pointedly not Jewish. They include *The Exorcist* and *The Omen* (1976), both of which drew on the ur-subsurface Holocaust film *Psycho* (1960). Kubrick referenced all three films in *The Shining*. Their protagonists can be characterized by the moniker, popularized in the 1960s, as "the banality of evil." To recap, this phrase, introduced by Hannah Arendt observing the Eichmann Trial and built on the earlier observations of Hilberg, suggested that the Nazi perpetrators were ordinary, typically professional, often intellectual, individuals seeking career advancement. As Hilberg wrote, "Most were intellectuals. By and large, they were in their thirties, and undoubtedly they wanted a certain measure of power, fame, and success." For Arendt, Eichmann personifies the ambitious bureaucrat who was ordinary, even mediocre, but given opportunities to rise far beyond his station through a Faustian pact. She also argues that Eichmann operated within a radically new moral order, where the Kantian categorical imperative was turned upside-down. Most controversial was Hilberg's and Arendt's opinion that Jews cooperated in their own destruction, and, just as the Nazis used a euphemistic language to hide their actions and facilitate the process of killing, so their Jewish victims also internalized and deployed this mode of reference.[30]

Kubrick was insistent on "the appearance of being as realistic as possible. People should behave naturally in the mundane way they normally do." Initially, we are led to believe the Torrances are an all-American family. Jack is friendly and smiling, seemingly an affectionate father and husband, who engages in "Blondie-and-Dagwood banter" with his wife. He's seemingly liberal, intellectual, artistic, and professional—a family man, a former schoolteacher who reads the *New York Review of Books* and aims to become a writer. Jack's sartorial banality and undistinguished clothing make him the anonymous, inconspicuous, unobtrusive, and average everyman. And Wendy is a model of "wifely banality," as she engages in the many routines of housework and does her domestic and hotel duties and hobbies: preparing and serving meals, washing up, watching TV, exercising, checking the boiler, and looking after Danny. Kubrick emphasized the quotidian. *The Shining* is replete with miscellany and ephemera. It's punctuated by title cards, stating such mundane facts as "The Interview," "Closing Day," "One Month Later," "Tuesday," "Thursday," "Saturday," "Monday," "8 am," and "4 pm," which serve to remind the audience of everyday reality. Household brand names (Calumet, Heinz, Jack Daniels, 7-UP), popular culture such as magazines and journals (*Playgirl, New York Review of Books*), books (*The Catcher in the Rye*), television (Johnny Carson, TV news and weather, *I Love Lucy*), Disney cartoons (*Mickey Mouse, Bugs Bunny, Three Little Pigs, Roadrunner, Winnie the Pooh*), and films (*The Summer of '42*) are either seen or mentioned.[31]

Kubrick's insistence on authenticity and realism lent it a mundane, banal quality. He shot the film in what seems to be existing natural light rather than the low-key melodramatic effect characteristic of the horror genre. The hotel's design grew out of this same philosophy of realism. Kubrick told Ciment, "I wanted the hotel to look authentic rather than like the traditionally spooky movie hotel." He also explained, "Certainly, rather than have an art-director try to design a hotel for this, which I think is almost impossible without it looking like a stage set or an opera set, it was necessary to have something real. I think also because in order to make people believe the story is very important to place it in something that looks totally real, and to light it as if it were virtually a documentary film, with natural lighting, which one normally sees in a horror film . . . so that the fantastic is treated in a very everyday, ordinary way." Its interior, entirely fabricated on a studio set, was based on hundreds of photos of corridors, bedrooms, bathrooms, lounges, game rooms, signs, elevators, fireplaces, other fixtures, gift shops, Indian decorations, toilets, boards, and so on of existing hotels. The result was a grand hotel archetype (mirroring

Castle Lyndon), one for the moneyed classes (the more everyday motel was done in *Lolita*), a composite of several real hotels, whose murderousness was hidden behind a facade of normality.[32]

The banality of language is conspicuous. For an aspiring writer, Jack is particularly cliché-ridden (like his clothing). He talks of the "White Man's burden," "that bitch," and "the old sperm bank upstairs." When he chops through the bathroom door, all he can do is to parrot such pop cultural clichés as "Three Little Pigs," "Here's Johnny," and "Wendy, I'm home." His use of euphemism is especially striking. Kubrick noted, "Euphemism is more frightening" and "Euphemisms not 'kill, kill, kill.'" Jack dismisses Ullman's concern over the problem of "isolation," which takes on the chilling echo of a Nazi-era euphemism, as Jack seeks to isolate the family so he can murder them. It recalls the use of the term in *Lolita* when, after being told off, Lolita mimics a left-handed Hitler salute and says "Sieg Heil" to Charlotte. In response, Charlotte informs Humbert that she has been "too liberal" and is sending Lolita off "long-distance" to a "camp" for "isolation." Jack repeatedly refers to his "work" and the phrase he types obsessively is "All work and no play makes Jack a dull boy." Walker observes, when Jack recounts injuring Danny, "he cloaks his guilt in one of those self-exculpating euphemisms Kubrick makes a point of storing away for use in certain kinds of situations." It was not fatherly rage that made him hurt Danny: only a "momentary loss of muscular coordination." A similar "loss" will shortly lead him to swing an ax at his family. Wendy explains it away as "just one of those things . . . purely an accident." Such euphemisms deny reality. Jack denies that much of what he sees is the result of internal delusions and his own ability to shine. He even denies his violent nature to Wendy: "I'm not gonna hurt ya," he reassures her. "I'm just going to bash your brains in." At the same time, Wendy denies the reality of Jack's instance of paternal abuse and his breakdown and its severity.[33]

Kubrick was similarly insistent that Grady "should talk in aphorisms." He wrote, "Find some clichés about discipline, family." In one of Johnson's drafts, Grady urges Jack to "administer the necessary 'chastisement.'" With the outward civility, propriety, and reserve of a proper English butler, Grady politely orders Jack to "correct" his family, prompting him "to deal with this matter in the harshest possible way." Cloaked in the language of manners, Grady is ordering murder. As Johnson wrote, "Using ominously polite euphemisms for murder, Grady suggests to Jack that he must discipline and correct his family." Roger Luckhurst points out, "Philip Stone's crisp English accent, heavy on the hard 'c', gives Grady's euphemism a menacing twist, like a term Goebbels might have used to evade the realities of mass murder in the concentration camps." Significantly, Philip Stone had previously played Nazi war criminal Alfred Jodl in *Hitler: The Last Ten Days* (1973). Grady refers to "doing my duty," when speaking about murdering his daughters. Likewise, Jack picks up on this language and obsesses about his own "responsibilities," which he repeats five times in his exchange with Wendy. Jack dresses up his "responsibilities" (murder) as a moral and ethical principle. And the Overlook Hotel may be seen as precisely such a system in which the Kantian moral order had been turned upside down.[34]

In the language of the famous study of American character, *The Lonely Crowd*, Jack is an "other-directed" type. He seeks approval rather than autonomy and hence is susceptible to obeying orders in the mode of those who participated in Stanley Milgram's experiments. Milgram discovered that "almost two-thirds of the participants fall into the category of 'obedient' subjects. . . . They represented ordinary people drawn from working, managerial, and professional classes." He continued, "With numbing regularity good people were seen to knuckle under the demands of authority and perform actions that were callous and severe. Men who are in everyday life responsible and decent were seduced by the trappings of authority." Obsessed with his standing, status, and career, Jack is very susceptible to the influence of others when he senses a chance for progression. His self-serving ambition is revealed when he rejects Wendy's request to leave the hotel to find medical assistance and calls it a "problem" obstructing his "chance to accomplish something." In his agentic state Jack gives into the demands of conformism and submission. He's enticed into killing his family by apologetic, deferential, ingratiating, aggrandizing, and toadying comments that he is in charge. Grady obsequiously calls him "Mr. Torrance." In return, Jack willingly obeys the "orders from the house," a phrase uttered by Lloyd and parroted by Jack, but given a whole new and chilling dimension in this context, particularly when issued by men in "uniform," namely Grady and Lloyd. Although somewhat subservient to Jack, both hold positions of "authority," as a waiter and bartender respectively, which Jack acknowledges when he refers to the former as "Mr. Grady." Kubrick's use of color in these sequences is illuminating. Lloyd wears a red jacket, white shirt, and black bowtie, while Grady is dressed in a tuxedo but is located in a white and blood-red bathroom. Such colors invoke the Nazi flag (as well as Kubrick's and Jack's favorite brand of cigarette, Marlboro).[35]

The Akedah

There is one final aspect to *The Shining* that links all of these elements—Kafka, Freud, fathers, sons, autobiography, and the Holocaust—together, namely, the Akedah, or the "Binding of Isaac." As recounted in Genesis 22 (JSB), God instructs Abraham, "Take your son, your favored one, Isaac, whom you love, and go to the land of Moriah, and offer him there as a burnt offering [*olah*] on one of the heights that I will point out to you." Abraham and Isaac then journeyed for three days to a place called Mount Moriah. Abraham "saw the place from afar," and there, up on the mountain, he prepared Isaac as an offering by binding him tightly to a pile of wood, hence the name "binding" or "Akedah" for this event. As Abraham raises his knife to slaughter Isaac, an angel intervenes to stay his hand and draw his attention to a ram caught in a thicket by its horns. Isaac is unbound and the ram is substituted and sacrificed in his place. In Kabbalistic thought Isaac, the son of Abraham, represents the divine emanation of *din* (judgment), relating to Daniel.

The Akedah is central to Judaism. Robert Alter notes that it reflects "a 'Jewish' preoccupation with failed relationships between fathers and sons." It forms a key part of the New Year's Day service, when it is commemorated by being read aloud in synagogue and by the blowing of a ram's horn. Jewish (and Christian interpreters) have long struggled with the character of God as the deity is depicted in the Akedah. Given the deeply troubling nature of this story, more than one interpretation has grown up around it, and it has inspired generations of thinkers, theologians, intellectuals, artists, poets, writers, and musicians. Even those Jews who identify little with Judaism, are familiar with the story because it has become the focus of so much legend, myth, folklore, and popular culture. The Akedah underpins Freud's work, particularly his *Moses and Monotheism* (1939). There are many similarities between Isaac and the story of Oedipus: both are bound by theirs fathers, who attempt to kill them, and both become blind. Kafka was also obsessed with the story, as manifested in his 1912 story "The Judgment." In June 1921 (a month before the photograph of Jack, which ends the film, was taken), Kafka wrote to a friend, imagining Abraham's willingness to carry out the sacrifice "with the promptness of a waiter" who "would still never be able to perform the sacrifice." James Mason, before his role as Humbert, had played a teacher believing he was Abraham performing the sacrifice in the 1956 film, *Bigger Than Life*. George C. Scott played

Abraham in the 1966 film *The Bible: In the Beginning*. Eugene Burdick and Harvey Wheeler's 1962 novel *Fail-Safe*, with which Kubrick was very familiar, raised Genesis 22 to prevent nuclear holocaust. And as we've seen, Kubrick invoked the Akedah in his previous films.[36]

The Akedah also connects to the Holocaust. The Hebrew term *olah* means a sacrifice wholly consumed by fire or a whole burnt offering, which, when rendered into Greek, becomes *holokauston* or "Holocaust." Catholic Bibles continue to translate it in this way. Milgram's experiments especially link the two, as he explicitly invokes the Akedah as the prime example of the age-old problem of blind obedience to authority: "The situation in which one agent commands another to hurt a third turns up time and again as a significant theme in human relations. It is powerfully expressed in the story of Abraham, who is commanded by God to kill his son."[37]

In its central idea of a father seeking to murder or sacrifice his son at the bidding of a supernatural power, *The Shining* resembles the Akedah. Just as God instructed Abraham, a mysterious force draws Jack to the Overlook, which sits in a lofty, exalted position, just like Mount Moriah. The name "Overlook" itself suggests a Godlike higher power in its omniscience and omnipotence. *The Shining* focuses on a single day of judgment ("Wednesday"), and the film's opening music sets the religious tone—an electronic rendering of the thirteenth-century Latin hymn "Dies Irae" (Day of Wrath), which derives from the Hebrew prayer Unetaneh Tokef (Let Us Tell), recited as part of the Rosh Hashanah liturgy when Genesis 22 is also read aloud. "Dies Irae" had been used in 1967 by Penderecki for his "Auschwitz Oratorio," a musical memorial to the victims of Auschwitz, and in 1974 Leonard Cohen released "Who by Fire" (1974), whose melody and lyrics are similarly based on Unetaneh Tokef. Since the leaves on the mountains are just beginning to change color when Jack's car treks to the hotel, there's every possibility that Jack's interview occurred in conjunction with Rosh Hashanah.

Jack compares to Abraham, who, in turn, is intertextually linked with Jacob. Both receive a new name in addition to their given names at birth (Abram/Abraham; Jacob/Israel). Their descendants are blessed by God, who promises them that they will multiply. Where Jacob rested is identified, in Midrash, with Mount Moriah, the very same place where Abraham bound Isaac. In one interpretation Abraham argues with God to let him complete the sacrifice. Carried away, drunk with submission, he's obsessed with obeying God. In this respect, he compares to Jack, who is, in his mind anyway, drunk, as well as submissive to that higher power ordering the "correction" of his family. He also resembles the father in Kafka's "The Judgment" and to James Mason in *Bigger Than Life*, both of whom go in for the kill. "God was wrong!" the latter bellows. Ultimately, as Paul Miers states, despite Jack's obedience, he's left "bellowing in the maze like an Abraham just deprived of both the son and the ram."[38]

Kubrick provides hints as to Jack's fate. On the guided tour of the hotel's kitchens, Halloran's list of the contents of the store freezer includes "twenty legs of lamb." Wendy cripples and drags him, like a piece of meat, and locks him in the storeroom, where he rests on sacks of "Holly [Holy?] Salt," as if to be koshered. Ultimately, he's abandoned like a frozen lamb in the snowy maze. Given that this "snow" consisted of nine hundred tons of dendritic dairy salt, Jack is salted—a piece of kosher sacrificial meat. If Jack's metamorphosis means he can be compared to Kafka's Gregor, then it's notable that the term Kafka uses to describe him, *ungeheures Ungeziefer*, can be translated as "unclean animal not suited for sacrifice." Trapped in the maze, Jack himself becomes the proverbial ram caught in the thicket, the unclean offering for his obedience. In his willingness to slaughter his son, Jack has sacrificed his menschlikayt. If no longer a father, he is unfit to be a mensch.

Conclusion

The Shining stands out as an unusual film in the mature Kubrick canon. It is one of his few films, like *2001*, in which its source text contains no extant traces or footprints of Jewishness. Nevertheless, like *2001*, allusions to Judaism and Jewish history and culture fill the film in a fashion that is integral more than incidental (Kubrick specifically hired Ray Lovejoy, *2001*'s editor, to work on *The Shining*). *The Shining* bears traces of the Akedah, a trope Kubrick had deployed previously. By reading Jack allegorically, as the Abrahamic father figure obediently willing to murder his son at the bidding of a higher power, we can also see that same obedience in those who perpetrated the Holocaust. It's therefore also a meditation on the banality of evil in a post-Holocaust world, even though the Shoah is never mentioned. This then renders the implicit comparisons between Jack and Kubrick, and the coincidence in Jack Torrance's and Kubrick's father's given names, as very troubling. In *The Shining* there is a clear autobiographical element and introspection on Kubrick's own paternity, now that his children had entered their twenties, as Kubrick was clearly continuing his exploration into man's propensity toward evil, suggesting that no one is safe from its banality. As Kubrick said, "There's something inherently wrong with the human personality. There's an evil side to it. One of the things that horror stories can do is to show us the archetypes of the unconscious: we can see the dark side without having to confront it directly." Certainly, Kubrick continued to be struggling with his own inner Jewish conflicts and demons, which are never entirely resolved in *The Shining*, if they are even reconcilable.[39]

9

Men as Meat

Full Metal Jacket, a film about the training and conditioning of raw marine recruits subsequently sent to Vietnam during the height of the Tet Offensive in 1968—the year of *2001*'s release—ostensibly returned Kubrick to the theme of war of *Fear and Desire, Paths of Glory, Spartacus, Dr. Strangelove*, and *Barry Lyndon*. It continued his preoccupation with the nature of ordinary men and their transformation into willing executioners. It further inquired into the morality of war and the oxymoron inherent in making a bullet—designed to wound, kill, and maim—more humane. It also allowed him to redress the mistakes of his earliest war films.

Hello Vietnam

While making *The Shining*, Diane Johnson recalled that Kubrick was "thinking about a war movie, partly, perhaps, challenged by rumors of Francis Ford Coppola's *Apocalypse Now*, then underway, to be released in 1979, a little before *The Shining*." Jan Harlan adds, "Kubrick always wanted to make, basically, a stylized film about war. Not necessarily the Vietnam War. But the phenomenon of war." In the spring of 1980 Kubrick contacted Michael Herr with a view to making this movie. Herr had gone to Vietnam during 1967–1968 as *Esquire*'s foreign correspondent. He subsequently published his wartime experiences as *Dispatches* (1977) before working on the narration for *Apocalypse Now*. Kubrick admired both works and met Herr—who was then also living in England—in 1980. He immediately dismissed *Dispatches* as a source text because it lacked a story and was nonfiction, which Kubrick typically stayed away from (Napoleon aside), but a fair proportion of incidents and dialogue from that book made into the film anyway.[1]

In 1982 Kubrick discovered Gustav Hasford's 1979 novel *The Short-Timers*. Hasford had served as a marine military correspondent during the height of the Vietnam War in 1968 and wrote the book based on his experiences. Kubrick, was attracted to its "writing, the dialogue, and its sense of uncompromising truth. The book offered no easy moral or political answers; it was neither pro-war nor antiwar. It seemed only concerned with the way things are. There is a tremendous economy of statement in the book." He liked how it "was written in a very, very almost poetically spare way," an approach he sought to retain for the film. Hasford had dedicated his book to a combat photographer killed in action in Vietnam, a fate that Kubrick, the photographer, was all too aware he avoided. "I was very lucky. I slipped through the cracks each time. I was 17 when World War II ended and was married when the Korean War began. I wouldn't have volunteered." It also enabled Kubrick to film a war that he "must have been fighting inside his head for thirty-five years, ever since he had attempted a film about a 'lost patrol,' *Fear and Desire*." But now he had the skill, technical resources, and finances to do it properly and not to show his hand as clearly as he had with his first feature.[2]

Kubrick was also attracted to *The Short-Timers*'s absurdist treatment of war, as found in *Catch-22*, and for its vein of black, vulgar, scatological, comic humor reminiscent of *Lolita* and *Dr. Strangelove*. It had such characters as General Motors, Gomer Pyle, Animal Mother, Leonard Pratt, Hand Job, and Lieutenant Shortround. The comedy implicit in a group of freshly shaved "privates" being put through their paces was probably too hard to resist for the director who reveled in sexual puns. One line in particular line caught his attention: "I like you. You can come over to my house and fuck my sister."[3]

At the start of 1983, Kubrick absorbed himself in historical research. He watched a myriad of movies and documentaries, read contemporary newspapers, and studied hundreds of photographs. By 1985, having completed a detailed treatment of the novel, Kubrick formally approached Herr to work on the screenplay. For the first time since *Spartacus*, Kubrick collaborated with another American Jewish writer. Born in Syracuse, New York, in 1940, Herr described himself as a "nice, middle-class, educated Jewish boy who as a kid had every nervous tic and allergy possible." Like Kubrick, Herr had also lived in Greenwich Village, where he became influenced by Buddhism, before going to Vietnam, the subject of *Dispatches*. Emilio D'Alessandro recalls, "Stanley and Michael got on swimmingly. 'How come he never gets angry?' asked Stanley. 'Why doesn't he ever tell me off?' asked Michael. I'm convinced that along with Diane Johnson, Michael was the writer Stanley worked most productively with. Their meetings were prolific, and they freely exchanged ideas. They rarely disagreed and never to the point of spoiling the pleasant atmosphere, enjoyable lunches, and relaxing walks in the grounds of the house." Together they broke the treatment down into scenes from which Herr wrote a prose first-draft screenplay. Kubrick and Herr then worked together on the screenplay, with some involvement from Hasford. Kubrick altered the title from *The Short-Timers* to *Full Metal Jacket*, supposedly so audiences weren't fooled into thinking it was a film about part-time factory workers.[4]

Full Metal Jacket continued Kubrick's method of family-centered film-making. Harlan was again his executive producer. His new son-in-law, Philip Hobbs, was associate producer. His daughter Vivian, using the pseudonym Abigail Mead, composed the score. Vivian also appeared in the film as a camerawoman. Like *The Shining*, *Full Metal Jacket* was the only other film in which Kubrick allowed a documentary to be made about his work, again by Vivian. It was never released. Filming started at the end of August 1985 and lasted eleven months. It was released on June 17, 1987.

The Vietnam Mess

Kubrick's interest in Vietnam dated back to the origins of U.S. intervention in the region. In 1964 he wrote to Leo Jaffe at Columbia Pictures, "In view of the present situation in Viet-Nam, I would strongly advise that the picture [*Dr. Strangelove*] not be booked in that country at present." In the midsixties he monitored shortwave radio broadcasts from Moscow to learn the Russian perspective on Vietnam. He undoubtedly kept abreast of developments as reported in such journals as *Commentary*, *Encounter*, and the *New York Review of Books*. In 1966, for example, he requested a copy of S.L.A. Marshall's 1966 *New Leader* article "Press Failure in Vietnam." He continued to follow the war on television and shortwave radio, as well as through video cassettes sent from the United States.[5]

Kubrick was thinking about the conflict while making *2001*, which explored the nature of human violence and its effects. In 1968, in a long interview with *Playboy*, he referred to the "current mess in Vietnam" and believed that the "inherent irrationality in man that threatens to destroy him"—explored in *Dr. Strangelove*—"is with us as strongly today and must be conquered." He continued,

> Particularly acute is the possibility of war breaking out as the result of a sudden unanticipated flare-up in some part of the world, triggering a panic reaction and catapulting confused and frightened men into decisions they are incapable of making rationally. In addition, the serious threat remains that a psychotic figure somewhere in the modern command structure could start a war, or at the very least a limited exchange of nuclear weapons that could devastate wide areas and cause innumerable casualties. This, of course, was the theme of *Dr. Strangelove*; and I'm not entirely assured that somewhere in the Pentagon or the Red army upper echelons there does not exist the real-life prototype of General Jack D. Ripper.

He told Charlie Kohler in the same year, "It's great that anything that goes on long enough that's terrible and comes into the living room every night in vivid, sync-sound-dialogue newsreel form makes a big impression on people. It will produce a more active body politic." When Kohler asked him if he was glad if the United States was withdrawing from Vietnam, he replied, "Sure." No doubt the conflict, in some way, was on his mind as he made *A Clockwork Orange*, *Barry Lyndon*, and *The Shining*.[6]

Diane Johnson feels "he certainly wasn't a hawk on Vietnam." He was "like a lot of liberals who find themselves out of sympathy with public policy. He was now the father of teenage girls, and he had what I would called straitlaced ideas. He liked having guns in the house." Larry Smith, who worked on *Barry Lyndon* and *The Shining*, though, describes him as a "committed pacifist," whereas Gideon Stainforth, who edited *The Shining*, recalls, "He was slightly mysterious. I never could work out where he lay on the political spectrum. Bit of a mystery." Kubrick described himself as "typically dubious and critical of the Vietnam War in its day," and by 1987 he felt the war as "awful" and "evil, and the soldiers and civilians were its victims." He elaborated, "The Vietnam War was, of course, horribly wrong from the start, but I think it may have taught us something valuable. We would probably be fighting now in Nicaragua had it not been for Vietnam. I think the message has certainly gotten through that you don't even begin to think about fighting a war unless your survival depends upon it. Fancy theories about falling dominoes won't do in the future."[7]

Although Kubrick told Gene Siskel he "didn't set out to do a Vietnam film," surely he wanted to weigh in on the burning issue of 1960s and 1970s U.S. foreign policy, which was spilling over into the 1980s, just as he had with MAD and the space race. The revisionist approach to the war of the early eighties gave Kubrick his opportunity. Ronald Reagan had redefined the war as a "noble cause," and in 1982 Norman Podhoretz, erstwhile editor of *Commentary*, published *Why We Were in Vietnam* to dismiss views of the conflict as a "mistake" and a "crime." Kubrick had highlighted this book (along with *Dispatches*) in a "Marine Corps Association" brochure, and, like Podhoretz, sought to provide an answer to Norman Mailer's 1967 question, "Why are we in Vietnam?" a novel he'd read (a copy is in the archives) and whose scatological, homoerotic, anal, and sexual language arguably made its way into *Full Metal Jacket*.[8]

Apocalypse Now in 1979 had sparked a cycle of war films, stretching into the 1980s, which had begun to become much more militaristic and simplistic, culminating in the gung-ho *Rambo: First Blood Part II* (1985). Kubrick revealed to Dorian Harewood, who played Eightball, that *Full Metal Jacket* was "his answer to *Rambo*, to show what war was really like." As Kubrick's driver, Emilio D'Alessandro, puts it, "In the mid-eighties, the public was ready for a film about America's war in Asia, but seen from a different, more detached perspective compared to the films about the conflict made in the mid- to late seventies."[9]

Dispatching the Novel

On the surface the topic suggested that *Full Metal Jacket* would be Kubrick's most political film since *Dr. Strangelove*. Yet he characteristically refused to adopt an explicit point of view. "He didn't want to make an anti-war film," Herr recalls. "He just wanted to depict war. He wanted to show what war is like." Kubrick told Herr, "I want to make a war movie, just to consider the subject without a moral or political position but as a phenomenon." As with *Paths of Glory* and *Dr. Strangelove*, his approach was to attack the military, targeting his attention on the cynical establishment and the clear disconnect between the brass and the grunts, as well as their use of euphemism and media that backed the war. Like *The Shining*, it had a "very ambiguous" ending, privileging uncertainty over clarity and comfort. Star Matthew Modine, who played Joker in the film, feels it "gives no explanations, no excuses, and no justifications for the war in Southeast Asia. . . . When you watch it, you don't know who to cheer for." As Kubrick jotted, "We don't know if Joker gets out alive. . . . To be crude, there is no dramatic pay-off, not in plot, character or idea. It just ends." Herr predicted, "I know there's going to be a lot of outraged and offended responses to this movie. The political left will call him a fascist, and the right—well, who knows?"[10]

Full Metal Jacket's deliberately elliptical structure, reminiscent of *2001*, further confused simplistic readings. Like *The Shining* and *Fear and Desire* before it, *Full Metal Jacket* can be read as a fairy tale. Critics variously called it "unreal," "hallucinatory," and a "dreamscape." Harking back to *Fear and Desire*, it was similarly allegorical, occurring in the landscape of the mind. Its marketing campaign, in its focus on a solitary combat helmet, hinted it occurs inside someone's head, as in *Fear and Desire* and *The Shining*. Labyrinthine Hue city is a bombed-out version of the Overlook Hotel and its maze, as well as the depopulated streets of New York City in *Killer's Kiss*. Yet its very lack of narrative continuity, particularly the fracture between its two parts in how almost nothing from boot camp is referenced in Vietnam, perhaps indicates Kubrick's subsurface critique of the war. The film's collapsed structure reflects the muddled thinking that prompted U.S. intervention in Vietnam in the first place. This is metonymized in the film when the squad becomes lost. Eightball turns a map this way and that while his squad leader stands above him, uselessly consulting a compass.[11]

Any pro-Vietnam sentiments are further undermined by Kubrick's artistic choices. The opening forty-five minutes, as the raw recruits are brutalized, provides a dark experience of black comedy and humor reminiscent of *Dr. Strangelove*. Modine felt like he was in Heller's *Catch-22* and wondered if "Stanley is going to go into 'Dr. Strangelove' territory. Or maybe Mike Nichols's version of Heller's book." Gunnery Sgt. Hartman's (Lee Ermey) invective is a Vietnam-era version of Nadsat: "sound off like you got a pair" being a translation of "Come and get one in the yarbles, if ya have any yarbles, you eunuch jelly thou!" It also echoes the choreographed, balletic violence of *A Clockwork Orange*, what critic Rita Kempley calls a "boot camp opera, the Parris Island Follies, a drill instructor's aria sung to a chorus of grunts," in which "Marines chant like a chorus line in fatigues, jogging to the tattoo of macho doggerel." At the film's conclusion, Kubrick's grunts sing the *Mickey Mouse Club* theme tune, returning it to the musical genre. The final credits song, "Paint It Black" (1966), mirrors the use of "Singin' in the Rain" in *A Clockwork Orange* but replaces upbeat music with the downbeat lyrics of the Rolling Stones. While Kubrick excluded the typical protest songs of the 1960s—none of them, except Johnny Wright's "Hello Vietnam" (1965) even overtly mention the war or Vietnam—he included Nancy Sinatra's "These Boots Are Made for Walking," which had previously been used in Peter Gessner's antiwar documentary, *Time of the Locust* (1966), to accompany compiled footage of combat and atrocities.[12]

Yet, despite this unreal (or hyperreal) representation, coupled with its absurdist nature, accuracy was important to Kubrick. He consulted some 190 books, including memoirs, firsthand accounts, novels, military manuals, encyclopedias, and photobooks, as well as documentaries, video news footage from the 1960s, and newspapers. He asked advisers who had served in Vietnam (in addition to Herr and Hasford), including Lee Ermey, who had been a U.S. Marine Corps drill instructor. Kubrick told Ermey "I want it real." The set for the film's second half was shot at Beckton Gasworks, designed by the same French architects that did Hue's outer industrial areas. Based on thousands of photographs, Kubrick mimicked every detail, from Hue's 1930s European architecture to its signs and advertising billboards. He imported two hundred palm trees from Spain and a hundred thousand plastic tropical plants from Hong Kong. The only unrealistic set was the latrine with its rows of identical (British) toilets facing each other. Kubrick explained, "We did that as a kind of poetic license. It just seemed funny and grotesque."[13]

Much like Kafka, Kubrick aimed "to photograph things realistically." He told Siskel, he lit things "as they would be lit" because "I'm after a realistic, documentary-type look in the film, especially during the fighting. Even the Steadicam shots purposely aren't very steady. We wanted a newsreel effect." The results are "harshly lit barracks and urban daylight." The second and third sections are especially characterized by the realist, documentary style that distinguishes *Dr. Strangelove*'s battle sequences. Kubrick even wanted to cast eighteen year olds, reflecting the real average age of marine infantry but was forced to ditch this plan when the actors lacked the required maturity.[14]

Full Metal Jews

It is hard to conceive of a less Jewish topic than the training of marines for a subsequent tour of duty in Vietnam. Jews rarely joined the U.S. Marine Corps—Leon Uris, who was a rare exception, recalls "half a dozen Jews, or less" in his battalion of eight hundred men. In his taxonomy of what was Jewish or goyish, Lenny Bruce describes marines as "heavy *goyim*, dangerous." Yet, as with many of Kubrick's previous films, *Full Metal Jacket* possesses a complex, somewhat contradictory, relationship with Jewishness. Like *The Killing, Spartacus, Lolita, A Clockwork Orange*, and *Barry Lyndon*, Jews are explicit in the source text, only to be removed. Kubrick excised Hasford's deliberate killing with a hand grenade ("fragging") of the Jewish officer Shortround (who is described as "that little kike"), replacing him with a Polish Catholic called Walter J. Schinoski (Ed O'Ross). While *Full Metal Jacket* duplicates the "lost squad" motif of *Fear and Desire*, this time Kubrick omitted the explicitly Jewish character, as traditionally found in platoon movies and novels.[15]

Yet palimpsestic traces of Jewishness are evident in the adaptation process. Draft screenplays refer to Jews multiple times. Kubrick considered including such Jewish-sounding characters as "Rick Berg," "The Kid from Brooklyn," "Sgt. Blaustein," and "Kaminski." While none of these references made it into the final screenplay, *Full Metal Jacket* remains Kubrick's only film to contain a clearly spoken and explicit reference to Jews qua Jews. Significantly, the term deployed is derogatory—"kikes"—part of a list that included "niggers, wops, and greasers."[16]

Jewishness was reinserted in a subtextual fashion, producing an underlying Jewish sensibility. For example, nothing in the novel or draft screenplays indicates Joker is Jewish. Given no biography, he comes from nowhere, existing solely in the context of the war. Without any backstory, psychology, and little personal information other than his full name printed on the back of his sweatshirt, he is an enigma. As Modine recalls, "Joker doesn't have a name in the film. He's Private Joker from the get-go; he could be any soldier in any war." In characteristic misdirection, Kubrick cast Matthew Modine, who couldn't have been more different from the Jewish Kubrick. As Modine puts it, "A Jew from the Bronx and a Mormon from Utah." But it is this very blankness that allows us the possibility of reading him as Jewish.[17]

First, autobiographical traces can be detected in the character. Joker and Rafterman (Kevyn Major Howard) recall the writer-photographer pairings of *Look*, as well as Harris-Kubrick Pictures and screenplay partnerships responsible for *Full Metal Jacket* and his other movies. As correspondent and photographer for *Stars and Stripes*, respectively, Joker and Rafterman are in the business of turning the war into entertainment, just like Kubrick. Karen Ritzenhoff points out how *Full Metal Jacket* is uniwque among Kubrick's films in its representations of journalism and filmmaking, not just making explicit use of them but also questioning their role in the construction of (hyper)reality. At the mass-grave site, a television news crew is filming, and Vivian Kubrick plays the camerawoman, as she simultaneously shoots *The Making of Full Metal Jacket*. Later a TV news crew shoots footage before interviewing the marines. The camera lens and boom microphone both reach into the frame, explicitly signaling the use of this equipment. The TV cameraman in the film is played by John Ward, Kubrick's Steadicam operator.[18]

As our guide and narrator, Joker is the key to understanding *Full Metal Jacket*, which Kubrick acknowledged in interviews. He serves as Kubrick's mouthpiece in the film and is another Kubrick avatar. Identifying with Joker, Kubrick gives him the first point-of-view shot—from the same perspective as Alex when forced to lick the shoe—presumably shot by Kubrick himself. Joker sardonically articulates Kubrick's ideological sentiments. As a wry observer of the conflict, Joker questions the ethics of U.S. military journalism and its misinformation by distorting and inflating Vietnamese casualties. In the exchange at a *Stars and Stripes* editorial meeting, Joker voices his misgivings over the U.S. military's policy of deliberate deception exemplified by such directives referring to "search and destroy" as "sweep and clear." "Very catchy," he avers, articulating Kubrick's own sentiments about the reporting of the war: "Vietnam was such a phony war, in terms of the hawkish technocrats fine-tuning the facts like an ad agency, talking of 'kill ratios' and 'hamlet pacification' and encouraging men to falsify a body count or at least total up the 'blood trails' on the supposition they would lead to bodies anyhow."[19]

Kubrick and Herr repeated wartime and postwar tropes of representing Jews. In 1953 Leon Uris, whose epitaph is "American Marine/Jewish Writer," wrote *Battle Cry*, based on his own experiences as a marine in boot camp during World War II, which appears a direct influence on *Full Metal Jacket*. Some of Hartman's diatribes appear verbatim in Uris's novel: "Your soul may belong to Jesus, but your ass belongs to me" and "This is my rifle, / This is my gun, / This is for fighting, / This is for fun." In general, in World War II films and novels, the Jew in the platoon was typically an amusing street kid from New York. Mark Harris's 1957 *Something about a Soldier*, for instance, features a similar humorous, wisecracking, intellectual, eighteen-year-old Jew named Jacob "Epp" Epstein undergoing basic training in the Deep South in 1943. Joker is marked out, early on, for his wit—Hartman calls him a "fucking comedian." He has chutzpah: he's the first to assert his individuality in the face of Hartman's verbal assault. At the same time, as a universal everyman, Joker is a stand-in for all liberal-minded rebels challenging and subverting the conservative hierarchy. He performs the same role as Yossarian in Heller's *Catch-22*, another allegorically Jewish soldier. And like the conceptually Jewish Holden Caulfield in *The Catcher in the Rye* (of copy of which is glimpsed in *The Shining*), Joker unmasks and challenges the phoniness of the goyish WASP system.[20]

As an everyman, he bears similarities to Alex, Barry, and Jack, thus possessing some of those same traits in which we can detect subsurface Jewishness. Kubrick retained Joker's real name from the novel, which is only glimpsed on his sweatshirt in the film: James T. Davis. James is the long version of Jack or Jacob. His nickname sounds homophonous to Jack, as well as invoking the playing card, recalling both *One-Eyed Jacks* on which Kubrick worked, as well as the one-eyed-Jack playing card on which Davey rests face down in *Killer's Kiss*. His surname also recalls Davey, as well as David the Jew in *Spartacus*, and Bowman in *2001*.

A cerebral, verbal writer, Joker is smarter, more sensitive, streetwise, and sympathetic than those around him. His intelligence is denoted by his spectacles, outweighing any obvious physical characteristics. As Kubrick put it, "Joker is smart enough to have earned a student deferment." Like Quilty, he's a mimic, as his name suggesting the playing card implies, and he repeatedly impersonates John Wayne. In addition to his intellect, mimicry, and menschlikayt, he is an insubordinate, wisecracking smartass, who clearly delights in showing how much cleverer he is than his superior officers. This is clearly the case when he encounters the colonel (Bruce Boa), explaining his peace button, to the officer's clear confusion. He can't resist even when it harms him. Lieutenant Lockhart (John Terry) sends him to Phu Bai, an assignment that will be probably get him killed, for "being a smartass and questioning his authority."[21]

Kubrick also arguably remade Leonard "Gomer Pyle" Pratt into an allegorically Jewish character. By removing any suggestion that he is the redneck of the source text—on one preproduction card, he wrote, "He is not a dumb hillbilly"—Kubrick allowed the possibility of reading him as Jewish.

Kubrick retained the name "Leonard" possibly because interwar Jewish parents, like his own, chose such "regal-sounding names" in "trying to give their precious sons a boost towards upward mobility in America." Leonard was Kubrick's own father's middle name as well as the given name of the Jewish doctor, "Clam Fink," in Mailer's Vietnam War novel. Another was Leonard (Lenny) Bruce; as fellow stand-up Rodney Dangerfield (b. Jacob Cohen), who appeared briefly in *The Killing*, points out, "All you guys who try to get away from being Jewish by changing your last name always give the secret away for forgetting to change your *first* name. What kinda *goy* has the first name Lenny?" His nickname, "Gomer Pyle," references the homosexual actor who played that character on TV. Gomer is also a biblical name, while Pyle suggests disease (piles) and defecation. In the novel and draft screenplays, his surname is "Pratt," hinting at female genitalia, as well as the Nabokov character in *Lolita* replaced by Zemph. Kubrick changed it to the more sexually ambiguous Lawrence ("Lawrence is for faggots and sailors").²²

Pyle's symbolic Jewishness is conveyed through stereotypical traits. He is marked as different by his gluttony and inability to control his appetites. He chooses the anal foodstuff of a doughnut (a subtle switch from the novel's cookie). He wears yellow flip flops, a deliberately connotative color. In one draft screenplay, Sgt. Gerheim orders Pyle to nurse from a milk-filled canteen with a condom fitted over its spout. While removed from the film and replaced with just his thumb, the device fulfils the same function, infantilizing Pyle while implicitly suggesting fellatio, as does his final act of inserting his rifle—which bears the female version of the name Charles, Charlene—into his mouth and bringing it to a fatal orgasmic ejaculation, much like Major Kong at the end of *Dr. Strangelove*. And Pyle's suicide resembles the death of the Jewish soldier, Roth, in *The Naked and the Dead*.²³

Pyle's Jewishness is expanded through Pyle's visual characterization. Using his signature misdirection, Kubrick forsook the obvious route of casting a well-known or even moderately recognizably Jewish actor for the role, which he said "was the hardest part to cast in the whole movie." Wanting to find a new face, he cast Italian American Vincent D'Onofrio from some three thousand to four thousand audition tapes. In a departure from the novel, in which Pyle is "skinny," however, Kubrick asked D'Onofrio to gain nearly seventy pounds, transforming him into a zaftig Charlotte Haze–like recruit: fat, round-shouldered, and feminized. Pyle's soft plump physique emasculates him—in their first encounter Hartman calls him "numb nuts." Repeated close-ups of Pyle's fatness emphasize the lack of musculature required to be macho—Cowboy (Arliss Howard) calls him "fatboy." Pyle hence fails to complete the obstacle courses and other physical training exercises.[24]

Pyle is a "misfit." Like one of the doomed soldiers in *Paths of Glory*, he's the fall guy for the unit, the symbolic martyr sacrificed for the common good. Like Jack and Barry, he becomes the outcast and the crippled scapegoat, even talking to himself, as Jack does. And like Jack and Gregor Samsa, he undergoes a metamorphosis after awaking from a nightmare, becoming figurative vermin that must die. As Cowboy tells him after the "blanket party," in which he is brutally beaten by his comrades, "Remember, it's just a bad dream." He is the target of an obsessive, coordinated, and unrelenting campaign of physical and psychological humiliation and abuse, deliberately designed to eliminate him from the corps. In Hannah Arendt's term, Pyle is a pariah. As the weak link in the body politic, he must be either reformed into a useful body or eradicated for it to function effectively. Pyle is therefore victim to a disciplinary regime, under the watchful gaze of the overly surveillant drill instructor, subjected to a systematic crusade of violence directed against him. In reality, Hartman's violent practices were not tolerated in the U.S. Marine Corps and no drill instructor employed them, at least not openly. But Kubrick used artistic license to focus Hartman's attention on Pyle, even removing a suicide attempt by another recruit to highlight Pyle as the lone problem.

Because Pyle is fat, he becomes easy prey for Hartman. Kubrick allows Hartman to single Pyle out for "special treatment," suggesting the Nazi linkage of physical with mental abnormality. Pyle is oppressed at the hands of a racist drill instructor, whose Germanic-sounding name insinuates a member of the SS, a "hard man," echoing Hartman's mantra "it is the hard heart that kills." At one point, Hartman asks a recruit to give "one for the kommandant." In an echo of Nazi eugenicist policies, Hartman threatens to sterilize Pyle so that he "can't contaminate the rest of the world." Pyle is therefore reduced to a metaphorical "stain" on the platoon, one that must be scrubbed away in line with Hartman's fanaticism for obsessive cleanliness and immaculate orderliness. Hartman intones, "If your killer instincts are not clean and strong you will hesitate at the moment of truth," reflecting U.S. military policy in Vietnam, where killing was equated with neatness: "sweep and clear" meant "search and destroy." He also parrots Crassus, who declared, "I shall cleanse this Rome."[25]

Hartman wishes to purify the unit of this impurity. His recruits understand and in one sequence Pyle is "disinfected." Pinned to his bunk, he's beaten with bars of soap wrapped in towels. As soap is a cleaning agent, this ritual suggests disinfection, or what the Nazis euphemistically referred to as "special treatment" or "cleansing operation," for "the destruction of the Jews was represented as a 'hygienic' process against 'jewish [*sic*] vermin.'" The connection between soap and the Holocaust (both to fool the Jews as to their fate and of their eventual outcome) was such a strong one that Holocaust survivors in Israel were referred to as "soap." In deliberately duplicating a similar scene from *The Blue Angel* (1930), Kubrick hints at a Germanic background. Geoffrey Cocks relates it to the brutal discipline of the Prussian army and suggests "the celesta on the soundtrack revisits a major musical motif of *The Shining* tied directly to fascism in the 1930s." The cold cerulean blue lighting that swathes the scene and the eerie electronic score enhance the chilling effect, recalling Alex's forced licking of the actor's shoe. This portrait of Pyle is far removed from the good, allegorically Jewish, soldiering of *Paths of Glory* and *Spartacus*—even Sidney cut the mustard in *Fear and Desire*. And a topless Pyle compares most unfavorably with Mazursky, Kirk Douglas, and Tony Curtis.[26]

The Hard Father

According to Anya Kubrick, "War brings situations that expose the essence of someone's personality. What the driving forces are." Kubrick added, "If I am forced to suggest something about the deeper meaning of the story, I would have to stay that it has a lot do with the Jungian idea of the duality of man: altruism and cooperation on one hand, and aggression and xenophobia on the other. I suppose the single improvement one might hope for in the world, which would have the greatest effect for good, would be an appreciation and acceptance of this Jungian view of man by those who see themselves as good and externalize all evil." As Modine wrote, "if you scrape the veneer a little bit and get into man's psyche, he becomes an animal; there's a beast just beneath this thin façade of peace."[27]

Joker embodies this condition. "He has so many contradictions," Modine said. "His intelligence meant he could have avoided the draft, yet he's in Vietnam. In one moment, he can be exceedingly kind to the misfit trainee Pyle; later, he can be coerced into pummeling the poor slob along

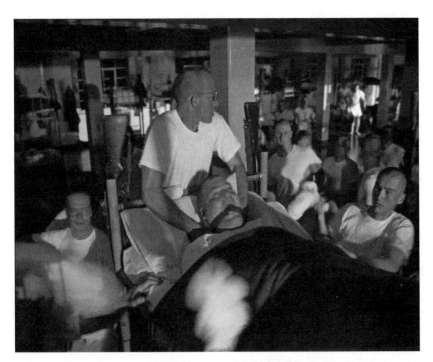

FIGURE 17 Pyle (Vincent D'Onforio), the "stain" on the platoon, is symbolically "cleansed" in *Full Metal Jacket* (1987).

with the rest of his company. He wears a peace button on his uniform, but his helmet reads 'Born to Kill.'" Expressed in other terms, this duality represents menschlikayt versus goyim naches. This mensch/goy or human/ animal opposition is stressed throughout the film, expressed by Joker as "the duality of man." In the novel Joker articulates the difference between the mensch and the marine: "I can't tell you what to do. If I was a human being instead of a Marine, maybe I'd know." This subtext, and the side favored by Kubrick, is signaled immediately by the very title of the film, in its reference to a type of bullet design that, as Kubrick pointed out in interviews, was "regarded as more *humane* by the Geneva Convention on Warfare."[28]

The mensch/goy binary is embodied by two figures in *Full Metal Jacket*. As Lenny Bruce avers, marines are the embodiment of goyim naches. Their teacher is Hartman, whose role is enlarged and much more colorful than in the novel, and he becomes the film's heart even when he's not present, like Quilty before him and anticipating Ziegler. And like Quilty his predecessor, Kubrick massively expanded his role, allowing ex-marine drill instructor

Lee Ermey to improvise approximately 50 percent of his dialogue. A fouler-mouthed Mireau, he's a Turdigson-Ripper-Quilty hybrid whose attitude is summed up by the phrase, "Here you are all equally worthless." His recruits are not even men, they are "pukes," "worms," "maggots," and "unorganized grabasstic pieces of amphibian shit." They are a "herd" of "animals" who "are not even human fucking beings!" And when the recruits have graduated to the infantry, they are no more than "grunts," the inarticulate snorting of a pig, apt, considering they join the Lusthog Squad, itself suggesting an unbridled goyish sexuality coupled with *treyf* meat.

Hartman, like Jack, is another terrifying, monstrous, murdering, nightmarish, and sadistic paternal caretaker. This time, though, the traditional family unit is replaced by the "mother green" of the U.S. Marine Corps. He encourages his "children" to "say good-bye" to the normative family unit, substituting it with the corps, where "every marine is your brother." At the film's close, the marines invite us to "join our family." Hartman is also the Abrahamic figure, preparing his "sons" as a sacrifice to be offered up on the altar of anticommunism in Southeast Asia. He readies them for the slaughter by shearing them like sacrificial rams, reinforced by the "bleating, beating, moaning" music.[29]

Hartman's name sums up his personality much better. Hartman's aim is to make his men metallic, to transform them from meat to metal, unsentimental, unfeeling killing machines impervious to human emotion and compassion. D'Alessandro describes Hartman as a "machine gun" and Thomas Allen Nelson observes how, "bent on shaping his offspring into his own 'hard' and mechanical likeness," he "dissembles his male children like an M-14 rifle and then puts them back together." While Joker says that the U.S. Marine Corps doesn't want "robots," Hartman is creating golems whose only choice is to kill everything they see. The film's title refers to this production line of clockwork oranges. The metallic ring of Abigail Mead's electronic music, composed on an inorganic Fairlight music computer, reinforces the psychological conditioning of hardening and dehumanization.[30]

Hartman lacks a moral core. Hasford calls Hartman "Gerheim," but Kubrick renamed him, possibly because the second syllable means "home" in Yiddish, as in *heimish*. Hartman may invoke Christianity, but, typically, it is coupled with profanity, never appearing genuine, making it hard to believe that someone who refers to God having a "hard-on" even believes in Him in the first place. Instead, he's a sadist who appears to revel in death.

"What makes the grass grow?" he asks. "Blood, blood, blood" is the answer. The marines' job is to "kill everything we see" to "keep Heaven packed with fresh souls," which surely includes innocents. A kill is a kill, regardless of the target, and Hartman praises civilian mass murderer Charles Whitman, and John F. Kennedy assassin Lee Harvey Oswald for their "outstanding" U.S. Marine Corps–taught marksmanship. So unsentimental, unfeeling, and impervious to human emotion and compassion he is that even when threatened with death he forgets how to be human and deliberately remains in character. Even Quilty put up more of a fight. Kubrick instructed Ermey not to let up and to put "all his considerable powers of intimidation into his best John-Wayne–on-Suribachi voice." By linking Hartman to Wayne's character in *Sands of Iwo Jima* (1949), Kubrick subverts and condemns the code of goyish toughness that both represent. And in killing him, it signals how Kubrick favors menschlikayt over goyim naches, reinforced throughout the film by Joker's mimicry and mocking of the John Wayne persona.[31]

Full Metal Mensch

The mensch, by contrast, is Joker. If *Full Metal Jacket* is about the duality of man, then Joker is the other side to Hartman's coin, mirroring Humbert/ Quilty, Dax/Mireau, and Spartacus/Crassus. Joker's empathy stands out as an incongruity against the violent impulses of those other men who've been conditioned into violence. He presents the only deliberately non-conformist exception to the nameless orderly green clones, "one of a few solid characters to emerge from the faceless body marine." He is one of the only recruits to express an opinion. When he informs Hartman that he doesn't believe in the Virgin Mary, it signals his rejection of the Christian goyish code of toughness.[32]

For these reasons, in creating Joker, a softening process between novel and film can be traced. In the novel Joker is not a mensch. When Hartman orders him to bunk with Pyle, he resists. He repeatedly turns away from Pyle, who fails to improve under his tutelage. He suffers no ethical qualms about faking or staging photographs for propaganda purposes (recalling Kubrick's staging of some of his *Look* photographs) and even engages in the sort of contrived misinformation that he opposes in the film. Kubrick deliberately sanded down Joker's rough edges. His friendliness motivates Pyle to respond, and Joker and Cowboy offer the only genuine friendship in the entire film. He also retains his normality despite the violence and psychopathy raging around him.[33]

Joker's menschlikayt is revealed in his relationship with Pyle. He nurtures Pyle in loco parentis. In a gentle, tender even, patient, kind, and calming manner, he teaches him how to clean and reassemble his rifle properly, lace his boots, make his bed, and perform the manual of arms. He addresses him by his given name, Leonard—the only person to do so—never calling him "Pyle," resisting Hartman's dehumanization. He encourages and reassures him. His words after Pyle has killed Hartman also recognize Pyle's inner humanity, "Easy, Leonard. Go easy, *man*."

The blanket party scene, Joker's seemingly betrayal of Pyle, in fact reinforces his humanity. Crucially, Joker hesitates, joining in only because Cowboy implicitly threatens him. Hitting Pyle harder and five more times than anyone else, as if to prove his lack of pity, his excess fails to convince as it fails to hide the fact that his heart has not yet hardened. Covering his ears to block out Pyle's screams, shame and remorse are written across his features. Talking for Joker, himself, or both, Modine recalls "tak[ing] no pleasure in this towel beating. Because [Pyle] cannot fight back. He cannot defend himself. What pleasure is there in beating the defenceless? Zero. It's shameful. I feel disgusted by the whole event." And Pyle recognizes this fact, sparing Joker's life.[34]

The death of Hartman, like that of HAL, allows Joker, as it did Bowman, to progress to the next stage of his evolution, continuing a journey into his personal heart of darkness. As a combat correspondent, he retains an air of ironic and ethical detachment. By deliberately choosing a desk job, in the protective environment of the field newsroom, he isn't required to deploy his weapon. It explains Hartman's disgust at Joker's choice of "Basic Military Journalism." Joker's reply ("A killer, yes, sir!") is unconvincing.

Joker can only posture as a marine. He is, in his words, "phony-tough." His "war face" fails to convince Hartman ("You don't scare me"), and his engagement in sexual banter fails as well. When he asks Cowboy, "I want to slip my tube steak into your sister. What'll you take in trade?" it is mere empty posturing. He does not respond to Cowboy's challenge, "What have you got?" When a Vietnamese thief steals Rafterman's camera and mimics Bruce Lee, Joker's ineffective response is a poor impersonation. Payback (Kirk Taylor) jeers that Joker lacks the "thousand-yard stare" of a true grunt. Although the North Vietnamese Army's attack on his base camp as part of the Tet Offensive forces him to stop observing and to participate, he confesses he "ain't ready for this shit." He witnesses firsthand a machine-gunner killing civilians, but only observes, as a passive bystander, either incapable or unwilling to intervene. The intelligent, wisecracking Joker can only mimic toughness, resorting to his John Wayne impression that marked him from the outset. He has not fully adopted the goyische marine mantle. His Campaign for Nuclear Disarmament "peace button" is more revealing of his actual nature. Although he wears a field jacket with grenades hanging from it like a real marine, it is unconvincing, particularly because of his spectacles. As if to cover up for his failure to mimic, he affects excess in the form of the legend "Born to Kill" scrawled on his helmet, but it lacks authenticity.

When Joker is knee-deep "in the shit," it reveals his inner menschlikayt even more starkly. He doesn't want Rafterman to accompany him to Phu Bai because he wishes to protect him ("If you get killed, your mom will find me after I rotate back to the world, and she'll beat the shit out of me"). His initial impulse is to question the door gunner's morality in such indiscriminate slaughter ("How can you kill women and children?"). When he encounters a mass grave of slaughtered Vietnamese civilians, he feels sick, his face betraying his menschlikayt, particularly in comparison to those surrounding him.

The contrast is even clearer when he encounters Animal Mother (Adam Baldwin). As his name implies, Animal is the very antithesis of the mensch, underscored by the knowledge, for those familiar with the novel, that, caught stealing a car, he was given a choice of prison or service in the marines. He's also suspected of raping and killing underage Vietnamese girls and is responsible for fragging his Jewish officer. Although Kubrick omits these details, their underlying traces remain in the film, where he becomes what Lenny Bruce imagined marines to be, a "heavy goy." Sheathed in bullets, thus literally encased in a full metal jacket, he is a parodic caricature of Sylvester Stallone's Rambo. Big, athletic, and lacking in eloquence, Arnold Schwarzenegger was reportedly envisaged for the role. Angry, bullying, and violent, Animal is the perfect product of the style of training given by Hartman, whom he resembles physically. He is a genuine and unrepentant racist, praising sickle cell disease because it kills African Americans. His theme tune, "Woolly Bully" (1965), by Sam the Sham and The Pharaohs, suggests he is the hairy beast of the song, which "Had two big horns and a woolly jaw," and in the proposed "*Vietnam, the Movie*," he's assigned the role of a "rabid buffalo."

When Joker finally does kill—the mortally wounded sniper—it's out of basic human decency to terminate her suffering. His exchange with Animal codes the mensch/goyische binary: Animal wants to "let her rot," while Joker feels "we can't leave her like this." It's the moment when Joker has to decide whether to intervene or not. As he fortifies himself, the emotional struggle is written across his features. Lasting about a minute, the close-up on his face reveals what Kubrick called his "humanity rearing its ugly head." Joker ultimately concludes that he cannot remained uninvolved, and he uses his own weapon to dispatch the sniper, acknowledging her inner humanity. He rejects the goyish grunt creed of revenge and reprisal or, in their parlance, "payback." Kubrick maintains the shot against the backdrop of the chorus of approval from his comrades. In his diary of the production, Modine describes Joker's feelings: "I have to murder the Sniper. It is agonising for me to imagine standing over another human being and deciding their fate. Even with that person begging to end it. This is the moment that so many writers have struggled with. Stephen Crane, Gus Hasford, Michael Herr. But this is different. She's not running. She's no threat. The scene makes me sick to my stomach. I have to go there. I look at the ground. I have to do this. She's in pain. She's suffering. My emotions blur. Fear. Anger. Fear. Resentment. Revenge. Fear. Horror. Horror. Horror. BANG! I'm dizzy. Underwater." The chaplain's credo of *A Clockwork Orange*—"When a man cannot choose, he ceases to be a man"—returns to haunt Joker here. Faced with a choice, his killing of the sniper reveals his menschlikayt.[35]

Having crossed the line, Joker undergoes a metamorphosis, or reincarnation. Modine recalls, "The others speak to me, but I do not understand. I am changed. I have climbed the wall and fallen to the other side. There's no going back." Rafterman quips, "We're gonna have to put you up for the Congressional Medal of . . . Ugly!" The emphasis on the last word echoes Kubrick's statements in interview. Donlon's (Gary Landon Mills) coda is apt: "Hard-core, man. Fucking hard-core," echoing Hartman's name and mantra that it is a hard heart that kills, as if Joker is now hard to his very core. Yet, in spite their words, Kubrick forces us to empathize with Joker here and takes no pleasure in the killing. There is no "money shot," as implied by the term "hard-core," and what we see is anything but a graphic depiction of the shot that kills the sniper. We see no shot of either Joker and the sniper. And we do not see the sniper die, as Kubrick shoots only the heads of the soldiers as the shot is heard offscreen. To emphasize the

FIGURE 18 A journey deep into Joker's (Matthew Modine) menschlikayt in *Full Metal Jacket* (1987).

gravity of Joker's act, Kubrick reduced the number of mercy killings performed by Joker in the novel to focus the dramatic climax on the shooting on the sniper.[36]

To preserve our vision of Joker as a mensch, Kubrick also altered the scripted ending. Initially, he insisted on Joker's death. According to Julian Senior, "Originally the film began at Joker's funeral. It was told in flashback. But he felt it was wrong, that he'd be telling the whole story before you got a chance to see it. What's important is Joker's affirmation of life." Kubrick made a further change. After Joker has shot the sniper, he narrates, "Your feet take you up . . . up . . . over the rubble up . . . up. . . . You're loving it. . . . You're not human, you're an animal, you feel like a god. . . . You scream: 'DIE! DIE! DIE, YOU MOTHERFUCKERS! DIE! DIE! DIE!'" Ending the film this way would have conveyed the wrong impression of Joker. That he leads the marines in a rendition of the *Mickey Mouse Club* theme tune highlights his rejection of the U.S. Marine Corps goyish code, for he resorts to a song remembered from his pre-Vietnam childhood rather than any of Hartman's cadences. The film concludes with the introspective song "Paint It Black," in which Mick Jagger sings, "I look inside myself, and see my heart is black." If the "I" here is Joker, than his heart has not been hardened by war. "I am alive, and I am not afraid" echoes Alex's "I was cured all right," as does his dreams of the "great Homecoming Fuck Fantasy." When placed in the wider filmic context of the 1980s, Kubrick's movie stands as a beacon of menschlikayt when compared to such fare as *Rambo*.[37]

Full Metal Evil

Like his previous films, *Full Metal Jacket* reflects on the nature of evil. Kubrick told Siskel, "I don't see the characters in the story in terms of good or evil, but in terms of good *and* evil. There is no question in my mind that their innocence and courage was misused. The war was evil, and the soldiers and civilians were its victims." The novel's back cover describes how in Vietnam "ordinary men are transformed into obsessive executioners." Kubrick was interested, John Calley explains, "in watching the transmutation of young men into killers, exploring the metamorphosis that occurs when you take young people and, in effect, brutalize them and inure them to a sense of right and wrong." The title's reference to a shell casing can be interpreted as a hollow cocoon from which high school graduates emerge as mass murderers. To this end, Kubrick's depiction of basic training, where the recruits are "born again hard," greatly expanded Hasford's brief descriptions. In rich detail Kubrick shows ordinary men being brainwashed to remove any trace of humanity and civility so they can kill. The training regime is so effective that even the most helpless, bumbling, and ineffective recruit as Pyle is transformed into a highly efficient killing machine, demonstrated in his burst of sudden murderous violence.[38]

As the Vietnam War intensified, comparisons between the Americans in Vietnam and the Nazis in Europe increased in frequency, particularly following the My Lai Massacre in 1968. In 1973 Robert Jay Lifton's *Home from the War: Vietnam Veterans; Neither Victims nor Executioners* sought to understand the Vietnam conflict through the prism of the Holocaust, by focusing on the Vietnam veteran as analogous to the Holocaust "survivor." A year later Stanley Milgram published his *Obedience to Authority*, which considered the problem of Nazi obedience during World War II and American war crimes in Vietnam. Milgram outlined how "a person who is decent, within the course of a few months finds himself killing other men with no limitations of conscience."[39]

Hasford's novel likewise implicitly compares Vietnam to World War II by explicit references to the Holocaust. He described Parris Island as "symmetrical but sinister like a suburban death camp." A marine is "as skinny as a death-camp survivor." There are also mentions of Adolf Hitler, "Arbeit Macht Frei," Joseph Goebbels, Hermann Göring, and "cattle-car buses." The American soldiers engage in similarly sadistic acts in Vietnam, including murdering civilians and mutilating corpses. Such comparisons were in his mind when Kubrick approached Herr. In 1980 he sent Herr a copy of Raul Hilberg's book, describing it as "*monumental*" and asking him to read it. Herr said Kubrick was "absorbed" by it and "what he most wanted to make was a film about the Holocaust, but good luck in putting all that into a two-hour movie." In August 1981 a bookseller provided him with a list of twenty "novels inspired by [the] Holocaust," apologizing for his failure to "find any diaries or reminiscences written by Nazi leaders or sympathizers." Kubrick's correspondence, circa 1982–1983, indicates he was simultaneously reading about Vietnam and World War II. In 1985 he was considering adapting Mike Zwerin's *Swing under the Nazis*, as *Dr. Jazz*.[40]

World War II is suggested from the film's opening images. In a sequence Kubrick invented, the recruits' hair is sheared. This familiar trope of the Holocaust evoked the mounds of human hair discovered at the Nazi death camps. This is compounded by Kubrick's presentation of Parris Island as a hard, antiseptic, sanitized, surgically clean, immaculate, functional environment, in which waste (however defined) is eliminated, what Gilbert Adair refers to as its "concentrationary symmetry," evoking the style of Leni Riefenstahl's *Triumph of the Will*. The *Nation*'s Terrence Rafferty compares it to a brightly and evenly lit surgical theater in a pristine medical facility in which the uniformly white surfaces have been scrubbed to an "antiseptic shine." These images recall Hasford's description of Parris Island as a suburban death camp, as does the systematic singling out and oppression of Pyle, the soap, and Hartman's use of collective punishment to discipline the platoon.[41]

The unusual location of the second half also evokes World War II. Unlike its immediate predecessors, *Apocalypse Now*, *The Deer Hunter* (1978), and *Platoon* (1986), which used jungle locations, Kubrick's Vietnam is urban, set in the bombed-out Hue city. Whereas those other films used Thailand and the Philippines, Kubrick filmed in London, a city bombed by the

Nazis, and Beckton gasworks' functionalist architecture was a holdover of the 1930s and 1940s. Kubrick's visual style, especially his shaky handheld camerawork, was redolent of World War II combat footage and films so that they appeared "like soldiers creeping into some tumbled city in West Germany." Presumably referencing those same films and documentaries he has watched on TV, Cowboy says, "when we're in Hue City . . . it's like a war. You know like what I thought about a war, what I thought a war was, was supposed to be."[42]

Other echoes are contained in further Kubrick additions. The legend "I am become death" scrawled on Animal's helmet was used by J. Robert Oppenheimer at the detonation of the first atom bomb during the Manhattan Project, and Ernest Taylor Pyle was a World War II journalist. The multiple references to John Wayne, forced prostitution (a Vietnamese hooker suggestively wears red, white, and black, while in the background a beer commercial features an eagle and the number "33"), a mass grave, and the unnecessary and sadistic killing of civilians, as well as such visual metaphors as a tall column of flaming and smoking concrete resembling a crematorium chimney and the clearly visible swastikas in the sniper sequence, all invoke Nazism.

The other clear comparison between Vietnam and World War II is the Nazi-like use of euphemism during the conflict. Milgram notes how in both Vietnam and the Holocaust, "frequent modification of language" allowed individuals to commit war crimes. He continues, "Euphemisms come to dominate language—not frivolously, but as a means of guarding the person against the full moral implications of his acts." Herr's *Dispatches*, which informed *Full Metal Jacket*'s dialogue, is full of examples. Kubrick told Siskel, "One of the notable things about the Vietnam war was that it was manipulated in Washington by hawk intellectuals who tried to fine-tune reality like an advertising agency, constantly inventing new jargon like 'Kill ratios,' 'Hamlets pacified,' and so forth." He elaborated to Penelope Gilliatt, "Vietnam was probably the first war that was run—certainly during the Kennedy era—as an advertising agency might run it." In preparation for the film, Kubrick had read Hannah Arendt's *Crises of the Republic* (1972). On a photocopied page from the chapter "Lying in Politics," he had highlighted the section dealing with "the phony body counts of the 'search-and-destroy' missions, the doctored after-damage reports of the air force, the 'progress' reports to Washington from the field written by subordinates who knew that their performance would be evaluated by their own reports."[43]

Full Metal Jacket, like *Dr. Strangelove* before it, is full of banal language in which characters frequently resort to empty clichés. A kill is a "happy ending" and "taking care of business." "Condition Red" and "rain" refers to incoming enemy fire. "Sweep and clear" means "search and destroy." No one is safe from using such military banalities—from the top brass, as the colonel who grills Joker about his peace button demonstrates, to even the ironically detached Joker. Unlike *A Clockwork Orange*, in which only youth speak Nadsat, in *Full Metal Jacket* everyone does. Gilliatt recognizes how its very title is yet another example of the "counterfeit language" or "specious wording" of military jargon that tries to hide the fact that the purpose of the bullet is, in fact, to kill. And Alexander Walker notes how the "subtext of virtually every scene is a merciless, often hilarious dissertation on how officialese was employed in Vietnam to hide folly and hypocrisy. Specialized jargon distorted the facts, concealed calamitous judgements, plastered cosmetic cover-ups onto moral wounds."[44]

Conclusion

Over the course of the production of *Full Metal Jacket*, Kubrick's personal life underwent some quite significant changes. Between 1980, when he began the film, and 1987, when he completed it, he became a father-in-law when Katharina married Philip Eugene Hobbs and subsequently a grandfather when their son, Alexander Philip Hobbs, was born on January 20, 1985. At the end of April that same year his mother died. About the same time, his father, Jack, became seriously ill, and Kubrick asked him to come to England so they could spend some time together. D'Alessandro recalls, "When Jack decided to go back to California, father and son embraced each other for a long time." Jack died in October. Folded into the film's title was a sly reference to his late father, following a pattern of placing references to this name in his films from *Killer's Kiss* onward. Such a pattern was continued in the film itself with the retention of a character named "Doc Jay," as in Dr. Jack Kubrick.[45]

In the end, *Full Metal Jacket* concludes that men are meat. The recruits are meat for the grinder of the Marine Corps, as well as the U.S. military in Vietnam. They become meat for the North Vietnamese Army, particularly the sniper who picks them off as if they were choice cuts. A dead lieutenant is described as a "meat bag," and "meat" stands as slang for male genitalia, a metonym for masculinity ("you black boys pack too much meat"), but also for women, specifically prostitutes ("don't get between a dog and his meat") and the sniper ("she's dead meat"). *Full Metal Jacket* neatly wraps up the theme of war that interested Kubrick since his first feature.

10

Kubrick's Coda

Stanley Kubrick described *Eyes Wide Shut* as "my best film ever." It was the culmination of a lifetime's work, the one project he had been desiring to make since he turned into a filmmaker. The result was his most personal, autobiographical, and complex movie, particularly in terms of its and his Jewishness. He based the film on Arthur Schnitzler's *Traumnovelle*, a novel set in fin de siècle Vienna that is awash with Jews and Jewishness, his most explicitly Jewish source novel since *Spartacus*. Yet he seemingly made a notably concerted effort to purge the story of its European and Jewish elements, possibly to give his film a broader and more universal appeal. But given that the source text is suffused with Jews and Jewishness to its very core, even the superficial whitewashing that Kubrick gave it could not remove its Jewish traces. And, paradoxically, Kubrick inserted a wholly invented, subtextual Jewish character not found in the novella. He further inserted a series of Jewish clues, but only for those able to decode them, wanting his audience to work hard. *Eyes Wide Shut*, then, provides the ur-text to understanding Kubrick's ambivalent, ambiguous, and paradoxical approach to his Jewish identity. It is also the summation of Kubrick's career as a New York Jewish intellectual, reflecting on what it is to be a man, mensch, father, lover, husband, and Jew in the post-Holocaust world, transposed to a deeply personal, microcosmic American setting. It therefore, stands as a fitting coda to the Kubrick oeuvre, bearing a similarity to what his hero, Sigmund Freud, tried to achieve in his final book, *Moses and Monotheism*: a reckoning and coming to terms with his Jewishness on the eve of his death.[1]

A Lifelong Affair

Arthur Schnitzler (1862–1931) was a Viennese Jew, born in the late nineteenth century in the Austro-Hungarian Empire. He bore many similarities to Kubrick. Both were Jewish, hailing from central Europe, and their fathers shared the same profession and supported their sons' respective pursuits. Both were family men: Schnitzler a husband and father, Kubrick surrounded by his wife, daughters, and extended family. Both were a similar age, in their early sixties, when they began working on *Traumnovelle* and *Eyes Wide Shut*, respectively, and died aged sixty-nine and seventy respectively. In his reading about Schnitzler, Kubrick discovered a startling fact: Schnitzler's daughter, Lili, committed suicide on the day of Kubrick's birth. Perhaps this helped to cement a connection between them.

Schnitzler, like Freud, was interested in psychosexual dynamics. Schnitzler's work intrigued Freud, who, on Schnitzler's fiftieth birthday, wrote to him as a "colleague" in the investigation of the "underestimated and much maligned erotic." His affinity to Schnitzler was so strong that he consciously avoided him as "his double" (*Doppelgänger*). The respect was mutual: during its years of composition, *Traumnovelle*'s working title was "*Doppelnovelle*" ("Story of Doubleness") but was changed, deliberately, to explicitly refer to Freud's *Interpretation of Dreams*.[2]

Traumnovelle was initially serialized in the Viennese magazine *Die Dame* between December 1925 and March 1926. It was subsequently published as a book, translated into English by Otto P. Schinnerer as *Rhapsody: A Dream Novel* in 1927 and reissued in 1955. It was on this version that Kubrick based his film, an erotic psychological thriller in which his doctor protagonist, spurred on by his wife's revelations of her fantasies concerning adultery, embarks on a psychosexual odyssey that may or may not be a dream.

Accounts of when Kubrick first discovered *Traumnovelle* are conflicting. Alexander Walker feels "Kubrick's hankering to make a film of Schnitzler's novel probably goes right back to his cinema beginnings." James Harris confirms that Kubrick had read it before they met in 1955. Kubrick most likely came across it in his well-read father's cosmopolitan library; through his second wife, Ruth Sobotka, herself Viennese; or from the films of Max Ophüls, whose *Liebelei* (1933) and *La Ronde* (1950) were adaptations of Schnitzler's *Liebelei* (1896) and *Reigen* (1900), respectively. Ophüls's *Letter from an Unknown Woman* (1948) was based on a short story by Stefan Zweig, another Viennese Jew, who shared similarities with Schnitzler. In 1956 Kubrick began to adapt Zweig's novella *Burning Secret*. It never reached fruition. Kubrick also saw parallels between Schnitzler and *Lolita*, and he first mooted the idea of a Schnitzler-style screenplay in 1958 when he approached Jules Feiffer as a possible screenwriter. Kirk Douglas claims Douglas's psychiatrist, Dr. Herbert Kupper, recommended *Traumnovelle* to Kubrick while they were having problems on *Spartacus*, and in 1959 Kubrick invited Schnitzler's grandson, Peter, to spend a day on the set, where they chatted about his grandfather's work. It was in 1960, according to Michael Herr, that Kubrick read *Traumnovelle*, and it was clear he was working up a project, for he mentioned his desire to adapt Schnitzler in interviews in 1960, presciently admitting, "it's probably going to be the hardest film to make."[3]

Nothing happened until the late sixties. Following *2001*, Kubrick's interest in the novella was renewed and he acquired the rights to it. The event that may have prompted this was the sudden and tragic death in June 1967 of Sobotka. Jay Cocks claims that shortly afterward, in 1968, around the time Kubrick was finishing editing *2001*, Kubrick asked Cocks to acquire the rights to the novel. A card in the archive appears to back this up. Christiane recalls Kubrick recommending it to her. She told Nick James of *Sight and Sound* that, around Christmas 1969, "he fell in love" with the novel. In 1970, states Jan Harlan, Kubrick began to "concentrate" on it, and Kubrick asked Harlan to acquire the rights to the novella, which Harlan subsequently translated. Kubrick then bought every single existing copy.[4]

Over the years Kubrick kept coming back to Schnitzler. In May 1971 Warners announced Kubrick's next project as "Rhapsody," an adaptation of *Traumnovelle*. But the novella's complexity defeated him, and, after failing to develop a satisfactory screenplay, he gave up, turning instead to *A Clockwork Orange*. The novella wasn't forgotten, though, and he worked on it, mulling various ideas, and talking about the project in interviews through the 1970s, expressing his admiration for it. It was certainly on his mind as he made both *Barry Lyndon* and *The Shining*. He considered casting Steve Martin or Woody Allen in the lead role and asked director Albert Brooks, whose recent *Modern Romance* (1981) Kubrick admired, for advice. Kubrick approached various possible screenwriters, including Anthony Burgess, Diane Johnson, Neil Simon, David Cornwell (aka John Le Carré), Michael Herr, and Terry Southern. The screenplay came to nothing, however, and he turned to *Full Metal Jacket*. When that wrapped, he told Daniele Heymann, "I would love to do another film about love. But to do that, first I'd have to find the story." Kubrick's attempts to adapt Louis Begley's 1991 Holocaust-era novel *Wartime Lies* (as "Aryan Papers") and Brian Aldiss's 1969 short story "Super-Toys Last All Summer Long" (as *A.I.*) then got in the way.[5]

When neither of those projects came to fruition in the early 1990s, Kubrick returned to *Traumnovelle*. Woody Allen released his New York–based marital drama *Husbands and Wives* in 1992, and its themes of marriage, divorce, and remarriage chimed with *Traumnovelle*. Kubrick considered hiring David Mamet before approaching Candia McWilliam and settling on Frederic Raphael in the summer of 1994. Raphael's *Who Were You with Last Night?* (1971) is, arguably, a contemporary adaptation of *Traumnovelle*, and his *Two for the Road* (1967) is a story about the trials of a modern marriage. Only three years younger than Kubrick, Raphael was another transplanted American Jew living in Britain, culminating Kubrick's attempts to hire other American Jewish writers for the screenwriting job (Simon, Mamet, Herr). Raphael delivered the first part of his screenplay in December 1994 and continued working on the screenplay until mid-1996, producing four drafts. Kubrick had a fraught relationship with Raphael, imploring him several times to stick much more closely to the novella, seeking "as faithful an adaptation as possible." Seeking an alternative voice, in late 1995 Kubrick approached Sara Maitland, who'd been working on *A.I.*, but she showed no interest.[6]

Finally, on December 15, 1995, Warners announced, "Stanley Kubrick's next film will be *Eyes Wide Shut*, a story of jealousy and sexual obsession, starring Tom Cruise and Nicole Kidman." It added, "Filming is planned to start in London in the summer of 1996." It actually began on November 4, 1996, lasting almost two years, during which time the script was constantly rewritten. By the end of February 1999, Kubrick had finished his cut. The work print with temporary music tracks was screened for Cruise and Kidman, as well as Terry Semel and Bob Daly, Warners's joint chiefs, on March 1. Six days later, on March 7, Kubrick died, and a small team was entrusted to finish the film in accordance with his wishes. It was eventually released on July 13, 1999. *Eyes Wide Shut* had been fifty years in the making.[7]

The Ultimate Tale

What was Schnitzler's appeal? In 1958 Kubrick singled out Schnitzler's mood and feeling of "gaiety and vitality and superficiality and gloss," coupled with "charm, humor and excitement on the surface, concealing a fundamentally cynical and ironic sense of tragedy beneath the surface." "The atmospheres," he added, "have charm and gaiety, as well as falseness." Two years later he described Schnitzler's work as "masterpieces of dramatic writing. It's difficult to find any writer who understood the human soul more truly and who had a more profound insight into the way people think, act, and really are, and who also had a somewhat all-seeing point of view—sympathetic if somewhat cynical." In 1972 he said, "All of Schnitzler's work is psychologically brilliant, and he was greatly admired by Freud."[8]

Kubrick often explained *Traumnovelle*'s attraction. "It explores the sexual ambivalence of a happy marriage, and it tries to equate the importance of sexual dreams and *might-have-beens* with reality." Elsewhere, Kubrick is quoted as saying, "The book opposes the real adventures of a husband and the fantasy adventures of his wife, and asks the question: is there a serious difference between dreaming a sexual adventure, and actually having one?" Christiane revealed they "both talked a great deal" about these themes. "He thought about it in many different ways. It used to come back over the years again and again, as you see friends getting divorced and remarried, and the topic would come up again, and it had so many variations and so much serious thought to it that he knew one day he was going to make it."[9]

Home

In transposing the story to New York City, Kubrick figuratively returned "home." By choosing to shoot "NYC" in and around London and at

Pinewood Studios, Kubrick overlaid the city of his birth with that of his death, peppering it with more autobiographical references than any other film. Kubrick signals this when the mysterious Hungarian partygoer, Sandor Szavost (Sky Dumont), quotes Ovid. As the author of the *Metamorphoses*, Ovid obliquely invokes Kubrick's beloved Kafka. Ovid also provides a sly element of self-reflexivity, in that he was a poet of exile whose fate paralleled Kubrick's; as Alice Harford (Nicole Kidman) points out, "Didn't he wind up . . . in some place with a very bad climate?"

Before moving to England, Kubrick lived in Greenwich Village and Central Park West, where the film was set. Like *Eyes Wide Shut*'s protagonist, his father was a doctor, presumably with many Jewish patients. Todd Field, who played Nick Nightingale, appeared as a crooner in *Radio Days*, a film Kubrick loved as an evocation of his childhood. He based the Harfords' apartment on his New York City one in the early sixties: the books were those he'd brought over from America and never taken out of their boxes and most of the furniture came from his home at Childwickbury. The Kubricks always celebrated Christmas, decorating their house with a huge tree, hundreds of tiny lights, and garlands of holly. Bill watches football on the television, as Kubrick liked to do. Christiane recalled how in New York City they "watched a lot of television—we sat glued to it." The Kubricks' house in Hertfordshire had a paneled billiards room with a big pool table, which served as his "office," just like Victor Ziegler's. The paintings that adorn the walls were by Christiane and Katharina. Both appeared as extras in the film as a café guest and mother of a patient, respectively. Katharina's son in the film was played by her real son, Alex. Alice's appearance in the domestic scenes, particularly her hairstyle and glasses, strongly resembles photographs of Christiane taken at the time the film was made. Alice wraps a boxed edition of Van Gogh's paintings like the one that Kubrick gave Raphael as he wrote the screenplay.[10]

While Kubrick refrained from appearing in *Eyes Wide Shut*, two characters bear a strong physical resemblance: Rade Sherbedgia, who played Milich; and a customer in the Sonata Café, whom IMDb suggests is Kubrick himself. Whatever the reality, Bill and Ziegler are Kubrick doubles, and Lou Nathanson's death uncannily augurs Kubrick's own. One of the street storefronts is named Vitali's, a reference to his erstwhile assistant Leon Vitali, who played Bullingdon and Red Cloak. Vitali's name also appears in a *New York Post* article reporting a prostitute's death. Brian Cook, assistant director on *Barry Lyndon*, *The Shining*, and *Eyes*

Wide Shut, played a butler. Kubrick's longtime driver and handyman, Emilio D'Alessandro, appears as a newsstand vendor and has a restaurant, Caffe da Emilio, named after him. A restaurant with the same name was located downstairs from Kubrick's parents' Los Angeles apartment. D'Alessandro's wife, Janette, and his daughter, Marisa, also appeared in the film.

Eyes Wide Shut is a palimpsest of Kubrick's previous works, whose traces are visible in the film. Footprints of Kubrick's photography can be seen in the locations, many of which recall those of his *Look* assignments. When Bill stands in front of a newspaper vendor, buying a tabloid with the headline "Lucky to Be Alive," he's standing where, in 1945, Kubrick's snap of a news vendor kick-started his professional career as a photographer. Alice's naked back mirrors his 1949 photograph of a nude woman modeling for Peter Arno. Similarly, the waltzing Alice and Sandor—whose nationality hints at Barry Lyndon's assumed Hungarian identity—echo a picture Kubrick took for *Look* of staged shots of models portraying a couple spicing up their marriage by blissfully dancing and dining, underneath the caption ("Don't Be Afraid of Middle Age," January 31, 1950): "Re-courting and second honeymoons often help prepare couples for happy and productive middle age—at the same time, check urge for a 'fling.'" This is, as Philippe D. Mather points out, precisely the conclusion reached by the film.[11]

The location of Greenwich Village returns us to "Prizefighter," *Day of the Fight*, and especially *Killer's Kiss*. Many aspects of *Eyes Wide Shut* recall *Killer's Kiss*: both are set in New York City over three days, featuring subsurface Jewish men undergoing personal odysseys and couples whose future relationship is unclear, blocked by menacing father figures, but in which both end optimistically. Nick is from Seattle, where Davey is heading. Additional references to Kubrick's other films include the name Bowman on the wall of a building, a possible glimpse of a copy of *Full Metal Jacket*, and the use of György Ligeti's music (previously used in *2001* and *The Shining*). Alice watches *Blume in Love* (1973), which starred Shelley Winters and whose director, Paul Mazursky, was in *Fear and Desire*. The plot of *Blume* provides a mirrorlike image of *Eyes Wide Shut*, as its protagonist, Stephen Blume (George Segal), like his two literary namesakes in Joyce's *Ulysses*, wanders the streets in search of human contact. Bill's nighttime roaming also recalls *Ulysses*, as well as Kubrick's own nocturnal wanderings when he lived in the Village. At one stage Kubrick even considered transposing *Traumnovelle* to Dublin.[12]

But, as Kubrick's *Ulysses/Odyssey, Eyes Wide Shut*'s evocation of "home" is complicated. Lucy Scholes and Richard Martin observe how Kubrick's New York City, "is a fantasy. It has little desire to replicate the city as it physically exists." Kubrick's key streets were entirely constructed from his design, resulting in a dreamlike look (many critics attacked the film for lacking realism and naturalism). The street names were made up: Wren, Miller, and Benton were part of the film's dream motif, since no such streets exist in Greenwich Village. The city in the film probably bore more resemblance to how Kubrick remembered it than to any accurate portrait, giving it a "nostalgic, even melancholy, historical texture." Back in 1972, he told a *New York Times* interviewer, "I love the city—at least I love the city that it used to be." Sydney Pollack, who also starred in the film, states, "I don't think there was much in *Eyes Wide Shut* that was realistic, or that was intended to be realistic." Cinematographer Larry Smith describes the results as having a "slightly surreal edge," giving the film the feel of an "expressionistic fantasy." Surely influenced by Albertine's description of the sky in her dream as "far bluer and more expansive than in the real world," Smith explains, the blue used "was 'over-the-top,' very saturated, much bluer than natural moonlight would be, but we didn't care about that." And, surprisingly, there is a noticeable absence of Jewish references in a city with such a high and conspicuous Jewish population, not even to the seasonally appropriate Chanukah.[13]

Except for one: A Jewish bakery two doors down from Domino's apartment, which Bill visits twice. Kubrick based it on the real-life Yonah Schimmel Knishery, established in 1910, on Houston Street in the Lower East Side. However, he changed its name to "Josef Kreibich." This detail was not merely incidental. Smith recalls, "Stanley didn't do take after take because he enjoyed it or wanted to drive everyone crazy—the scene was either right or it wasn't right, and whatever kept it from being right had to be eliminated. It might be something very subtle, like an ashtray facing the wrong way, but Stanley had a phenomenal eye for small details." This bakery was so important to Kubrick that he went to the expense and effort of having it reconstructed on the backlot set built for *Eyes Wide Shut*. There is even a folder in the archives containing photocopies of a knishery menu. As they were typically sold outside, knishes were a visible and visibly Jewish food. Kubrick surely remembered it from his days living in the Village, but strangely it is a Lower East Side landmark, specifically lower Second Avenue, which was nicknamed "knish alley." It stands as the only explicitly Jewish reference in the entire film and thus as a key autobiographical moment. It recalls a quip he made to Jeremy Bernstein, back in 1966, while he was working on *2001*, "I feel like the counterman at Katz's Delicatessen on Houston Street at lunch hour." Kubrick was always sending D'Alessandro out to central London for bagels that "he was convinced were identical to the ones he ate in New York when he was little." It also cross-references the kosher pickles in *The Shining*, Kubrick's most autobiographical film until *Eyes Wide Shut*. Finally, the placement of the knishery while Bill is talking to a prostitute can be read as yet another example of Kubrick's adolescent New York sense of humor, in the vein of *Lolita* and *Dr. Strangelove*, for a knish is also a vulgarism for vagina and hence is equated with sexual favors, as in "looking for some knish?"[14]

The faux New York City, reconstructed in and around London but standing in place of fin de siècle Vienna, blended Kubrick's birthplace and artistic home, as well as his central European roots in the Austro-Hungarian Empire. His choice of a story based in Vienna implicitly referred to the capital of the empire in which his forebears lived before emigrating to America in 1899, and Kubrick persistently reminded his audience of the Viennese setting of the original story through a series of musical, literary, and visual allusions. As Scholes and Martin point out, "traces of *Mitteleuropa*—an aristocratic Hungarian, a waltz, a thick accent,

FIGURE 19 A symbol for Kubrick's and Bill Harford's (Tom Cruise) Jewishness? Josef Kreibich's Knish Bakery in *Eyes Wide Shut* (1999).

dream analysis—litter *Eyes Wide Shut*." This includes the film's luxurious mise-en-scène, particularly its elegant and period interior sequences, which echo Egon Schiele and Gustav Klimt; in particular the curtain of lights in Ziegler's townhouse, Milich's costume shop, the golden glow of the Harfords' bedroom, and the dark wooden furnishings and fin de siècle artwork of Sharky's coffee shop mimic the Viennese cafes of the type Schnitzler frequented. The film ends in FAO Schwartz, whose German origin hints at German-speaking Vienna. The opening music, "Waltz No. 2" from Dmitri Shostakovich's *Jazz Suite*; the Beethoven opera *Fidelio*, which acts as the password to the orgy and which premiered in Vienna in 1805; and *Wien, Du Stadt meiner Träume*, by Rudolf Sieczynski, all evoke late nineteenth and turn-of-century Vienna. The recurring piano piece heard throughout the film, "Musica Ricercata II," was composed by the Hungarian Ligeti. Kate McQuiston has described the music in *Eyes Wide Shut* as Kubrick's greatest homage to the Vienna of Max Ophüls, whose graceful camerawork influenced Kubrick, especially apparent in *Eyes Wide Shut*'s Steadicam shots of characters walking through rooms or dancing around ballrooms. Although born in Germany, Ophüls was regarded as quintessentially Viennese and had filmed Schnitzler's *Reigen* as *La Ronde* (this was adapted in 1998 as the play *The Blue Room*, starring Kidman). The cast of Europeanized characters all serve to collapse Manhattan at the turn of the millennium into fin de siècle Vienna. Kubrick also slipped in references to his beloved Kafka. The costume shop scene "is a scene out of Kafka," says Brigitte Peucker, while Bill is put on "trial" at the orgy. The Josef Kreibich bakery incorporates the protagonist of Kafka's *The Trial*, Josef K. The men who follow Bill certainly aren't cops, but they represent the "authorities" and Kafka's officers of the court.[15]

Bill Harford, Unmanly Jew

Eyes Wide Shut is the culmination of a lifelong directorial style in which Jews in Kubrick's source texts were erased but replaced with an underpinning Jewish sensibility coupled with allegorical Jewish characters. As mentioned earlier, *Traumnovelle* was saturated with Jews and Jewishness, only to be removed from the final film. Raphael claims Kubrick "forbade any references to Jews" and that he was instructed to give the novel's Fridolin a "Harrison Fordish goy" name (which also recalled Gustav Hasford).

Critical and scholarly opinion has accepted the non-Jewishness of Bill Harford at face value. The casting of Tom Cruise in the role, his outward appearance and looks, as well as his oh-so-gentile name are adduced as evidence. But beneath the surface, Kubrick continued his exploration of Jewish masculinity and menschlikayt through the film's two central characters: Bill Harford (Cruise) and the wholly invented Victor Ziegler (Pollack).[16]

Palimpsestic traces of Bill's Jewishness are evident in the production process and finished film. Recall that during the 1970s and 1980s, Kubrick considered casting Woody Allen—who has made a career as an actor playing the nervous Jew trying to pass in the world of goyim—as the doctor. Initially Bill was to be named "Scheuer." During his nocturnal wonderings he encounters a junkie who calls him a "Levite," in reference to the story of the Good Samaritan and then "you cheap Jew sonofabitch." Eventually, the references were removed altogether, but their traces are still extant. Despite his insistence on changing the name from Scheuer to Harford, making Bill and Alice "vanilla" Americans, lacking any clues to arouse suspicions, Kubrick nevertheless adopted one that was a possible contraction of Harrison Ford, an actor with a Russian Jewish mother, a detail surely Kubrick knew. And the switch from a Jewish surname to a more gentile one was a typical Jewish practice in nineteenth- and twentieth-century Europe and America, as growing affluence, respectability, and assimilation to the Anglo way of life among upper-class Jews led to name changes such as "Hyam" becoming "Halford." Harford also sounds like the town of Hertford in England, near where Kubrick lived, and his home county of Hertfordshire, which, as he'd have known, has a high concentration of Jewish residents.[17]

Other circumstantial evidence can be gathered. In both location and profession, Bill upholds the stereotypical representation of Jews on (and off) screen. He lives in Central Park West; as Lenny Bruce said, "If you live in New York or any other big city, you are Jewish." He's a doctor and many Jews were and are physicians, including Kubrick's own father. We've seen how the image of the Jewish physician haunts the work of Schnitzler, as well as Kubrick's own films. Bill has many Jewish friends, colleagues, and patients, including "Dr. Sanders," "Mrs. Kaminsky" (recalling a character in *2001*), and "Mrs. Shapiro," as well as the Zieglers and Nathansons. We first meet Bill in the bathroom, a means of visually establishing, albeit on a submerged level, a character's Jewishness given, as I have shown elsewhere, the cinematic history of locating Jews there. As a "walker in the dream city," he evokes Jewish intellectual Alfred Kazin's memoir of growing up in New York, *A Walker in the City* (1951). Bill, as suggested by his diminutive, is the character most visually associated with money in *Eyes Wide Shut*. His first words are "Honey, have you seen my wallet?" and he spends more than $700 in cash over one night. And like many Jewish characters onscreen, Bill is approached by and attracted to a series of blond shiksas, but, although offered a myriad of potential sexual encounters, he consummates none. Cementing this link, Alice watches *Blume in Love* on TV, inviting comparisons between *Eyes Wide Shut* and Paul Marzursky's earlier film about a Jewish husband's sexual odyssey.[18]

Cruise's character links his previous roles and image to convey a weak, unmanly protagonist whose macho mask is a delicate and fragile veneer. Cruise played a series of roles as a superficially tough male whose manliness is ultimately undermined, including *Rain Man* (1988)—a brief glimpse of which can be seen playing on the VCR in the Harfords' bedroom—*Born on the Fourth of July* (1989), *Jerry Maguire* (1996), and *Magnolia* (1999). Accusations of homosexuality dogged Cruise throughout his career, as connoted by his very surname, which is replete with homosexual connotations (as in "to cruise"). Beneath his macho star persona lurked suggestions of sexual uncertainty, hinted at in such films as *Risky Business* (1983) and *Interview with the Vampire* (1994). Even his action film roles, such as *Top Gun* (1986), *Days of Thunder* (1990), and *Mission Impossible* (1996), failed to mask this ambiguity. Rumors that his marriage to Nicole Kidman was merely a facade to mask his ambiguous masculinity and sexuality based on their inability to conceive children abounded. This sexual ambivalence and lack of conventional male characteristics were stigmata long attached to Jewish men in Western Christian society, in which Jews and homosexuals have long been conflated.

Bill can only posture as manly. He is, in Joker's words in *Full Metal Jacket*, "phony-tough," and his macho face fails to convince, as a series of encounters serves to undermine his masculinity. He flirts with two sexually aggressive models but acts bashful and inexperienced, resorting to the same strategy when propositioned sexually by Domino (Vinessa Shaw). When he rents an outfit for the orgy, Milich's deliberately Lolita-esque daughter (Leelee Sobieski) whispers, "You should have a cloak lined with ermine," the suggested vaginal connotations of which are clear. It's also a sly reference to the fur coat that Fridolin wears in *Traumnovelle* but that is replaced with an overcoat not dissimilar to Humbert's. At the orgy he's a passive voyeur rather than active participant. The following day, as he searches for Nick (Todd Field) to explain the previous night's events, he enters a café where *I Want a Boy for Christmas* plays on the jukebox. The lyrics perfectly sum up Bill's situation: he wants Nick. A gay hotel clerk (Alan Cumming) flirts with him, recalling Quilty's similar encounter at the Enchanted Hunters, and the gay couple in *Barry Lyndon* (the hero of whom Bill resembles). Alice's revelation of her thoughts of infidelity present him as an unmanly cuckold and his failure to consummate his sexual encounters feminize and emasculate him in the same way as anti-Semitism feminized and emasculated Jewish men.

Kubrick's signature style of using color to convey meaning also suggests Bill's Jewishness. As we know, yellow has historically connoted Jewishness, and yellow shop fronts and cabs are visible in Bill's sequences. Red, as we've seen, is another color used to demarcate Jews, given its historical associations with the blood libel, and it is an omnipresent color throughout the film, appearing in nearly *every* scene, typically as part of the seasonal decorations. The Harfords' babysitter is called Roz, and the Nathansons' maid is named Rosa (also the name of a maid in Kafka's "The Country Doctor"). The use of red can also be read as a sly allusion to the switch from Vienna's red-light district to New York City's *Green*wich Village. (Surprisingly, for a film that on one level is about envy, green, other than in trees and plants, appears very little.) Christmas is systematically visible everywhere: trees, fairy lights, and wreaths populate every set. The pervasiveness of Christmas gives the film a superficially goyish sheen, which, in turn, precludes Jewishness. To quote the popular cartoon *South Park*, which aired a year and a half before *Eyes Wide Shut*'s release, "I'm a Jew / A lonely Jew / On Christmas." At Ziegler's party Alice asks Bill, "Do you know anyone here?" to which he responds, "Not a soul." It turns out that he does have an acquaintance, Nick, a hired musician, hence another outsider (and originally a Polish Jew in *Traumnovelle*), the only person Bill feels he can give a friendly slap on the back to. But if these signifiers seem arbitrary, tenuous, and circumstantial, then two sequences clearly suggest Bill as Jewish in spirit.[19]

The first is when Bill wanders at night in Greenwich Village. The Village was known for its large gay population in the 1970s (hence the name of well-known gay band, the Village People), suggesting that Bill is "cruising." As he strolls along the street, he passes a series of shops whose suggestive signs feminize and emasculate him. This includes the Pink Pussycat

Boutique, in the window of which is a headless male manikin, clad only in black briefs, displaying the stereotypical gay male gym body that Cruise showcased in *Top Gun*. It references as well the previous bedroom argument and confession sequence in which Bill wears only a pair of black boxers. Another store advertises "Ladies' Night." As he turns the corner, we see a Marlboro sign, a familiar Kubrickian motif from *The Shining* and *Full Metal Jacket*. Despite its rebranding as a manly smoke, Philip Morris had originally introduced Marlboro in 1924 as a women's cigarette. Advertised as "Mild as May," its filter had a printed red band around it to hide lipstick stains, giving it the reputation of being "something sissy."[20]

As Bill ambulates, he imagines Alice with the naval officer. The character is a key change from *Traumnovelle*, which mentions only an "extremely handsome youth." By branding him a naval officer, Kubrick draws on that service heavily associated with prostitution and homosexuality. The Village People, for example, sang "In the Navy." Bill contemplates and imagines Alice's infidelity, projecting in his head a pornographic movie of her making love to the naval officer, whose depiction echoes Kafka's description of a "huge German officer, hung with every kind of equipment. . . . His height and military bearing made him look stiff; it was almost surprising that he could move; the firmness of his waist, the breadth of his shoulders, the slimness of his body made one's eyes open wide in amazement in order to take it all in." Bill's imaginings position the naval officer as the fetishistic object of *his* gaze rather than Alice's, making his subsequent gesture of beating his fists in anger and his audible panting over his imagination even more ambiguous in its intensity.[21]

Bill is then jostled by a group of college boys, interrupting his fantasy. Reminiscent of the droogs, they insult him while one mimics fellatio and another anal sex, as if reading his mind. Their homophobic abuse effectively undermines Bill's heterosexuality and, by extension, his masculinity, already under question following his wife's revelations, as well as by the baggage that Cruise brought with him to the film (their ironic taunt of "macho man" seems to directly refer to it). If the film is indeed a dream, then perhaps these insults are manifestations of Bill's own psyche, confirming both the frat boys and Bill's own suspicions. Their references to tits, faggots, dumps, and butts recall Hartman's abuse of Pyle, another subsurface Jewish character. Like Pyle, Bill picks himself up and angrily stares at his tormentors as they go down the street shouting their insults. Finally, he turns and continues on his way, without having uttered a word. Where in

Traumnovelle, Fridolin *feels* emasculated by the encounter, Bill *is* emasculated. He is silent and, as Raphael described in an early draft of the screenplay, "The adrenalin rush in BILL fills him with rage and a fear that he has not been as manly as he would have liked, though he did pretty well. He is full of undischarged emotion."[22]

The detail in the sequence helps us to read Bill as the unmanly Jew. In the novella this scene was originally motivated by anti-Semitism. Raphael explained, "Fridolin is not declared to be a Jew, but his feelings of cowardice, for failing to challenge his aggressor, echo the uneasiness of Austrian Jews in the face of Gentile provocation." Early drafts of the screenplay identify the college boys as "Yaleys" who explicitly accuse Bill of being Jewish. While expunged from the final script, the anti-Semitic stain remains, as they wear Yale sweatshirts, a university that was known for its anti-Jewish prejudice. At the beginning of the twentieth century, Yale notoriously operated a *numerus clausus* designed to keep out too many Jews, which stayed in effect until the early 1960s. Those Jewish students who managed to slip past the quota system experienced social ostracism and were barred from clubs, positions on student newspapers, and fraternities.[23]

The scene also bears a deliberate resemblance to Freud's "cap in the mud" story in his *Interpretation of Dreams*. Freud recounted how his father, Jacob, told him that when walking one Saturday, "a Christian came up to me and with a single blow knocked off my cap into the mud and shouted: 'Jew! get off the pavement.'" When asked how he reacted, Freud's father answered, "I went into the roadway and picked up my cap." Jacob Freud had manifested the traditional Jewish reaction of controlling his anger, refusing to be provoked, sustaining his inner dignity and spiritual superiority over a thuggish Goy. Nevertheless, it prompted in Freud feelings of shame and embarrassment toward his father's "unheroic conduct." In failing to react, this "big, strong man" had shown weakness, castrating, emasculating, and feminizing him in his son's eyes. Schnitzler had read Freud, and Fridolin's reaction, or indeed lack of, clearly parallels that of Freud's father. Kubrick, too, had read Freud, and the parallel between the stories connected *Eyes Wide Shut* to the period in which *Traumnovelle* was set, suggesting Bill as an unmanly Jew.[24]

The second incidence is the orgy. It's the climax of *Eyes Wide Shut*'s depiction of social exclusion that led critic David Ehrenstein to call it Kubrick's most Jewish film. The orgy takes place at Somerton, a large country house, some distance from Manhattan. Somerton is a rural estate, literally an English pastoral idyll, complete with butler and servants of the type Jews didn't typically possess. The estate clearly resembles the seats of the landed gentry or the country clubs and golf clubs in Europe and America that excluded Jews. The long drive to Somerton, taking up almost ninety seconds of screen time, emphasizes Bill's distance from his urban heartland, as well as recalling Jack's drive to the Overlook (a similarly metaphysical journey deep into a man's psyche). Emphasizing Harford's sense of exclusion is the house's name. Somerton is Anglo-Saxon for "Summer dwelling," harking back to a premodern, preindustrial idyll in England, free of Jews, clearly coding that Bill doesn't belong and is trespassing in this WASP environment.[25]

Somerton also recalls the great houses of *Barry Lyndon*. The locations used for it—Mentmore Towers' exterior and Elveden Hall's interior—were built when Thackery wrote and set *Barry Lyndon*, respectively. Kubrick hired Larry Smith, who'd served as chief electrician on *Barry Lyndon* (and *The Shining*), to film *Eyes Wide Shut*. Raphael's ideas for the scene similarly echo *Barry Lyndon*, for he imagined the mansion "lit with candles only" while "Thirty or forty MEN and WOMEN, all lavishly cloaked, many of them in silken elegance, dancing some kind of Baroque minuet," as Bill wears "a 17th century military uniform coat, a cloak and a mask." Kubrick had shot a masked ball for *Barry Lyndon*, which, although abandoned, appears to have influenced the orgy in *Eyes Wide Shut*. The guests at Ziegler's party and orgy are the "best people," the spiritual descendants of Lord Wendover's friends and the Overlook's guests. Somerton and even Ziegler's library at his home are an extension of the settings in both films. Internet legend also says Bill's mask was modeled on Ryan O'Neal's face.[26]

A stranger in a strange land, Bill's Somerton odyssey resembles Barry's wanderings in Prussia. In this way, *Barry Lyndon* and *Eyes Wide Shut* form a coherent diptych. Everything about the setting serves to reinforce Bill's outsider status. The large iron gate, overhead lamps, and guards who "are most gracious and civilized in appearance" that protect Somerton ominously hint at a death camp, and Raphael suggested changing the masked attendants' costumes to "cloaks and black uniforms, and boots, whose manner and tailoring subtly suggest S.S. officers." Outside the house luxurious limousines are lined up, whereas Bill arrives in a yellow cab, which signals both his ethnicity and lower socioeconomic status in comparison to the other guests. He possesses enough cash to manipulate a costume shop proprietor and a cab driver, drawing attention to his parvenu-pariah status, but both are much lower in class than Bill, who is, in turn, clearly out of his depth in Somerton. Inside the house, purple, which has traditionally been utilized as a signifier of regal power and church authority, is dominant, and Walker, Sybil Taylor, and Ulrich Ruchti point out how a "palette reduced to stark crimsons and livid purples signals the danger of trespassing on forbidden territory."[27]

Bill seeks admission to a party to which he's not invited. In this way, he stands as a metaphor for the Ostjuden experience in Western Protestant civilized society as seen in *Barry Lyndon*. This was particularly true for Freud and Schnitzler, both of whom were assimilated, secular Jews whose ancestors came from Polish Galicia. Just as assimilation was the price for admission to Western society, to pass Bill is required to mimic by hiding his identity behind a mask and costume. As an unwanted guest, he's admitted by subterfuge into the WASP domain of Somerton, and the world it represents and that is denied to him. Of the other revelers at Somerton, Ziegler tells Bill, "Who do you think those people were? Those were not ordinary people there. If I told you their names—I'm not going to tell you their names, but if I did, you might not sleep so well." His words echo Wendover's about the "best people." Likewise, the unmasked portraits of European imperial nobility around Somerton represent and reflect those who are in attendance, further reinforcing the distance between them and Bill.

Once inside Bill witnesses a secret hermetic occult or satanic cultlike order composed of bizarre rituals and laws of the kind from which Jews were excluded. In a large cathedral-like chamber, a cardinal-like figure, waving a censer and holding a staff, presides over a highly ritualized, sacramental ceremony resembling a High Church Mass and Eucharist, or Black Mass. Guests wear the capes of cardinals, nuns, and priests while religious music plays, featuring a Romanian priest's voice running backward. Bill's costume is that of a monk's cowl.

But Bill fails in his mimicry. His deepest fear is realized as his attempt to pass fails, reflecting the Jewish experience through the centuries. Bill is revealed to be the figurative assimilated Yid hiding behind the mask of goyish civility. His waiting taxi, the rental ticket in his pocket, and his mask all identify him as an outsider. His mask is that of an unmanly man in stark contrast to the menacing, deformed, and animal-like masks of the other guests that, through their historical association with members of high society, project power. He's warned "you don't belong here" and "you can't fool them for much longer." Choosing to ignore these admonitions, Bill is delivered before an assembly and presided over by an imperious figure dressed in scarlet robes resembling those of Torquemada, the Grand Inquisitor of the Spanish Inquisition. (This color is a changed from the novella, in which the figure wears yellow.) A small cross adorns his throne. Just like those *conversos*—Spanish Jews forced to convert to Catholicism but who attempted and failed to hide their religion—so Bill is "exposed as an outsider, identified as the 'other,' and threatened with public undressing, rape, humiliation, and death—a modern auto-da-fé, the medieval ceremony of the public torture and burning of heretics." Lacking the strength and courage to resist, when ordered to remove his mask, Bill obeys, unlike Fridolin, who adamantly refuses to do so, challenging anyone who would try to remove it by force to a duel. Bill stands, symbolically naked, as the sole focus of attention before the gaze of the onlookers who have crowded in around him. Bill is then ordered to undress, with its echoes of the concentration camps and of Nazi methods of identifying Jews, as well as medieval Italian punishment in which Jews without their identifying badges might be stripped. In fact, in his first draft Raphael had written, "He is alone and then, shockingly, he is not: he has been bracketed, abruptly and menacingly, by two MEN in cloaks and black uniforms, and boots, whose manner and tailoring subtly suggest S.S. officers. . . . BILL stands at bay. Disgusted, somehow finding these people both *ridiculous*—as Nazis are ridiculous when one is not in their power and under their 'law'—and terrifying." Later Raphael wrote to Kubrick, "I am drawn to the idea of BILL being 'unfairly' accused of being the ultimate non-belonger, a J*w [*sic*]. . . . Can this be made to be our underlying accusation without it being stated?"²⁸

This humiliation ritual is like those endured by other subtextually Jewish Kubrick protagonists. Placed "on trial," Bill becomes the subject of a staged performance, recalling the unmasked Alex, who is literally put onstage, complete with a master of ceremonies. Bill's public unmasking and ejection from the house plays on the inherent problem of mimicry—the fear of being unmasked—an anxiety that gripped Jews in Western Protestant society, as developed in *Barry Lyndon*. His ordeal reveals him to be an imposter, a parvenu who becomes a pariah. And, like Barry, he has foolishly stepped into a situation that is out of his league, but while Barry can "'gate crash' high society for several years," Bill "cannot even manage it for one evening." As Ziegler growls, "You've been way out of your depth for the last twenty-four hours." Like Barry, Bill's attempt to mimic and hence pass fails and, surely not uncoincidentally, the man who expels Bill is played by the same actor who played the man who expels Barry—Leon Vitali. Bill then leaves, as he arrived, in a yellow taxi (just as Barry departs England in a stagecoach), the color of which clearly marks his Jewishness, and because he is the only guest to use such modest means of transport, it reinforces his otherness. As Raphael states in a manuscript note, "Bill [is] ejected from [the] party back into 'reality' with a warning not to mix outside his class again."[29]

Dark Father

Bill's double in the film is Victor Ziegler, a wholly invented character that doesn't exist in *Traumnovelle*. Ziegler stands as another Jewish Kubrick character. His casting suggests Kubrick always wanted an American Jewish actor-director for the part. In the 1980s, according to some reports, he wanted to cast Woody Allen in the role. By the time of shooting, he went with another Jewish actor-director, Harvey Keitel. Born in Brooklyn in 1939, like Kubrick, Keitel's parents were central European Jewish immigrants. Keitel, though, dropped out owing to clashing commitments. Serge Bokobza suggests because Keitel typically played thuggish gangsters and mobsters, the high point being his role in *Pulp Fiction* (1994), few were aware of his Jewishness, so he was replaced by Sydney Pollack, another American Jew, born in 1934, only six years younger than Kubrick. Pollack, by contrast, was clearly identified as Jewish, having been featured in a series of such roles, including *Tootsie* (1982) and *Husbands and Wives*.[30]

Pollack's career as a film director was surely a key element in his casting. In a sly nod, Helena (Madison Eginton) has a doll called Sabrina, to which she draws attention at the end of the film. *Sabrina* was a 1954 film by the Austro-Hungarian Billy Wilder, remade by Pollack in 1995, starring Harrison Ford. In 1993 Pollack directed Cruise in *The Firm*, in which a young ingenue lawyer discovers his outwardly respectable law firm is the sole legal representative for a Chicago crime family. The casting also resembles one which Kubrick's friend and contemporary Polanski did some thirty years earlier in *Rosemary's Baby*, when he cast fellow director John Cassavetes to play Guy Woodhouse. In this way, Kubrick, intentionally or otherwise, invokes the conspiratorial worlds of both *The Firm* and *Rosemary's Baby* and Bill compares to Rosemary, played by Mia Farrow, who later starred alongside Pollack in *Husbands and Wives*, as both characters are unable to draw a clear line between dream and reality.[31]

Other factors suggest Ziegler's Jewishness. Victor is phonetically related to the Hebrew Avigdor, which Midrash states is one of the names of Moses, while Ziegler is a variation of "Siegler," meaning an engraver of seals, a prominent Jewish occupation in eighteenth-century Germany. Rabbi Ignaz Ziegler was the chief rabbi of Carlsbad, a spa town resembling Zweig's Summering. Anna Ziegler was an American playwright. Raphael claims that the name originated from a former literary agent. Evarts Ziegler was an agent with whom Kubrick corresponded about the novel *Fail-Safe*. Ziegler might also be a corruption of Zweig, Zelig, or Lazlo Zilagy (Laszlo means "famous ruler" in Hungarian—somewhat like Victor). The exterior for Ziegler's mansion was shot at what the filming schedules describe as an "Israeli Bank," cementing a connection with Ziegler, Jews, and money. According to IMDb, the Consulate General of the Republic of Poland in New York City was used as the exterior for Ziegler's mansion, connecting *Eyes Wide Shut* both to the Austro-Hungarian Empire of Schnitzler as well as Kubrick's ancestors.[32]

Ziegler is a charming Quilty-like character whose representation draws on some of the oldest stereotypes of Jewish masculinity. Extremely wealthy, he treats other human beings, especially women, as servile objects. He's sexually deviant with little concern for the women he uses; he almost kills a prostitute but does not worry about her welfare. His bathroom is decorated with very explicit and, arguably, misogynistic artworks of nude women in various sexual poses. He's powerful, lying, hypocritical, hypersexual, and misogynistic, orchestrating and participating in the sexual corruption (and possible murder) of beautiful gentile women. He's even left-handed, demonstrated when he flexes his serving arm.

Ziegler's Jewishness is emphasized in the bathroom, for it is there that his real but concealed nature is revealed. We are first introduced to Ziegler when Bill and Alice attend an extravagant formal Christmas party he throws at his vast and opulent Midtown Manhattan mansion. Together with his wife, Ziegler appears as an outwardly respectable, decent, upstanding New York socialite of high social prominence. Some minutes later Bill is summoned to a bathroom, where that we learn that this pristine facade is a sham that, just like the bathroom, is hiding a proverbial underworld of human waste. This scene has parallels with Billy Wilder's *The Apartment* (1960), when the Jewish doctor is called to assist with an overdose, also on Christmas.

In *Eyes Wide Shut* Ziegler is exposed as debauched. Of all the rooms in his vast townhouse, of which there are presumably many, the bathroom is the place that Kubrick chose to situate Ziegler in order to drop his mask. In this bathroom many traits, stereotypically attached to the Jew, are depicted. Luxurious, ornate, and spacious, it's bigger and better furnished than most New York City apartments, containing a bathtub, toilet, bidet, sink, armchair, fireplace with a mantelpiece, and those sexually explicit artworks adorning the walls, a combination of the taste of Charlotte Haze and the Catlady. Only a stereotypically tasteless Jew has a bathroom as lavishly and decadently decorated, his idea of WASP taste. The bathroom location suggests the dirty Jew doing his business in the conceptually filthiest of places, upstairs and out of sight of the genteel (and gentile) guests downstairs, the culmination of Kubrick's signature use of bathrooms in his films.

The sequence is laden with anti-Semitic tropes. Half-naked and shirtless, Ziegler stands over a naked prostitute slumped in a chair, semiconscious from a drug overdose, clad only in high heels and a pearl necklace. As the very first item that he puts on while getting dressed is his oversized glasses, attention is drawn to them, as well as his nose, thus dominating our image of his face. This is closely aligned with the suggested reference toward his (Jewish) penis by the action of zipping up. He remains shirtless for several minutes, emphasizing his hirsuteness. Hence, the stereotypical phenotype elements (body hair, glasses, nose, and penis) dominate the image for most of the scene.

Our second image of Ziegler, following the brief introductory scene with his wife, is an immediate postcoital one, coupled with a vulnerable woman. That he mercilessly and callously corrupts a weak and powerless gentile woman, who's certainly much younger than him (Ziegler calls her "kiddo"), recalls Quilty's predatory subtextual Jewishness. Having exploited her, he certainly shows no respect for her, refusing to cover her up, and only once she regains consciousness and presents no threat or embarrassment does he show any concern for her. When Bill revives the woman, Ziegler tells him "You saved my ass," clearly indicating that her fate is irrelevant. Ziegler fetishizes, objectifies, and sexualizes women in a manner little different to the art on his walls.

Ziegler is seemingly responsible for orchestrating the orgy, which further underlines negative Jewish associations. Anti-Semites regularly pointed to Jewish cabals and satanic worship among Jews, who were the devil's earthly representatives. Since the exterior shots of Somerton are of Mentmore Towers in Buckinghamshire, built in 1855 for the Jewish Rothschild family

FIGURE 20 Victor Ziegler (Sydney Pollack) as the predatory, sinister, Quilty-like double in *Eyes Wide Shut* (1999).

(with whom Thackeray was particularly interested), the place invokes anti-Semitic notions of an all-powerful cabal serviced by covertly manipulative court Jews as embodied by the Rothschilds. But the ceremony is a form of mimicry; it has the quality of a *purimshpil*, a comic masked reenactment of the Book of Esther. Ziegler is mimicking his concept of a Christian Mass. Arguably, only Jews could conceive of such a Catholic ritual, and, of course, it was a product of the Jewish imagination: Schnitzler as refracted through Raphael and Kubrick's screenplay and ultimately the latter's research and lens.[33]

Kubrick's use of primary color also conveys Ziegler's Jewishness. Red, as a color to denote Jews, appears in the key sequences featuring Ziegler, including the bathroom where Mandy (Julienne Davis) is sprawled on a red chair, and the unusual, yet visually striking, decision to have a red table in the center of nearly every frame of the thirteen-minute billiards room sequence, situated between Ziegler and Harford as they confront each other over the previous evening's events. The entrance to Somerton is carpeted in red and leads through the heavy velvet drapes in a vast hall carved in white marble. Of course, a red-cloaked figure presides over the orgy, while those participating in the ritual stand on a prominent red carpet.

Menschlikayt versus Goyim Naches

The relationship between Bill and Ziegler mirrors many of Kubrick's previous couplings in which menschlikayt is compared with goyim naches: Dax/ Mireau and Broulard, Spartacus/Crassus, Humbert/Quilty, Mandrake/ Ripper Muffley/Turgidson, Barry/Bullingdon, Joker/Hartman. And like Spartacus, Bowman, Barry, and Joker, in *Eyes Wide Shut* Bill undergoes an odyssey that takes him into the heart of his manliness and humanity.

Bill is driven not just by his Hippocratic Oath but also by a code of menschlikayt, and throughout the film he reveals himself to be a mensch. Gayle (Louise Taylor) recalls how he was "very kind" and "such a gentleman." Bill refuses to give in to temptation. He never takes advantage of the numerous women offered to him (Marion, Gayle, Nuala, Domino, Sally, Milich's daughter, the women at the orgy). Although he is seemingly tempted to sleep with Domino, a phone call from Alice resets his moral compass, and he leaves before doing so but pays her nonetheless. Bill is surrounded by women: his family, colleagues, patients, and friends. Where Victor can refer to a prostitute only as a "hooker" or "junkie," Bill calls her "Mandy," recalling Joker's humane treatment of Pyle. He genuinely appears to care about Mandy, Nick, and Milich's daughter, returning to check on their status, as well as his family. Kubrick had originally slipped a phrase in from the *Bhagavad Gita*, which he'd quoted in *Full Metal Jacket*, to articulate this theme. At the orgy Red Cloak repeatedly intones, in Hindi, "For the protection of the virtuous, for the destruction of the evil and for the firm establishment of righteousness, I take birth and am incarnated on Earth, from age to age." While the lines remained in the U.S. theatrical release, they were removed from the United Kingdom and DVD releases to respect religious sensibilities. Their trace is still evident in Bill's underlying sensibility nonetheless.[34]

If Bill stands for menschlikayt, then Ziegler mimics goyim naches. Outwardly, Ziegler conveys the facade of a wise, fatherly mensch. At the orgy a masked man, whom we presume to be Ziegler, looks down from an upper level gallery and nods at Bill. His mask, devoid of a mouth, seems to frown, suggesting the reproachful look of a disapproving father. "No games," he tells Bill after the orgy. "I was there at the house, I saw everything that went on." "This statement carries a firm warning, yet a familiar love. It is dialogue that could easily be used in the context of a reprimanding father to his son, 'games' being what children play in 'the house' of the family home."[35]

Jonathan Rosenbaum, however, notes that Ziegler is the only thoroughly evil character in the film. His evil is "wrapped in impeccable manners," suggesting Hannah Arendt's banality of evil. If we consider other sources for his name, this notion is reinforced, as "Ziegler" invokes Sieg, as in Sieg Heil, and Adolf Ziegler was president of the Reich Chamber of Art. Kubrick knew this: his *A Clockwork Orange* research includes a photocopied page from William L. Shirer's *The Rise and Fall of the Third Reich* (1960) mentioning it. Despite his social standing and artistic taste (Victor owns the "best collection of Renaissance bronzes"), he's dissolute, lacking in empathy, compassion, and moral righteousness. He treats women, and men for that matter, as objects or servants to do his bidding, much like Crassus in *Spartacus*. Where Bill is a faithful husband, father, and family man, Victor's marriage is a sham; he cheats on his wife, and we don't know if he has children. His ugly and brutal sexual vulgarities recall Hartman's invective in *Full Metal Jacket*. As an adulterer, drug taker, and user of prostitutes, he's the embodiment of a sinister, dangerous, and depraved sexuality. Utterly corrupt and morally bankrupt, he has no higher morality than his own ego and self-interest. He describes a dead woman as merely a "hooker" with "great tits." Later, although we never actually see his face (he subsequently confirms his presence), Ziegler orchestrates and attends such mock goyim naches as the highly ritualized, quasi-religious masked orgy, during which hired prostitutes, dressed only in masks, G-strings, and high heels, participate in the cultlike ritual. And when an uninvited outsider infiltrates the orgy, he's concerned only with protecting the identity and reputation of its guests rather than the legality, morality, and ethics of the event itself. Ziegler is not a mensch.[36]

Ziegler is another patriarchal figure. Bill is young enough to be his son, and Ziegler's relationship with him is clearly paternal, especially since Bill's own father is never mentioned. He's charming, benevolent, and fatherly like the chevalier or Grogan, but as menacing as Jack and Hartman. When Victor confronts Bill, it echoes Dax and Broulard in the book-lined study of *Paths of Glory*, but in his servility Bill resembles Antoninus in *Spartacus*, and Somerton can be compared to Crassus's villa, connecting American with Roman decadence. Like *Spartacus*'s bathing sequence, the confrontation between Bill and Ziegler in the billiards room is replete with sexual innuendo, whether in speech or in the careful positioning of the balls and cue on the pool table. Kubrick decided that Ziegler should have sudden, Hartmanesque outbursts of vulgarity; he is the only character in the film to use such words as "cocksucker," "prick," and "asshole," all of which betray his homophobia and, given the gay subtext of the film, cast his relationship to Bill in more ambiguous, and menacing, light. Even the frat boys refrain from using such explicit language ("faggot" is the strongest term). "Doctor Bill," the name Alice gives him, invokes Danny's nickname "Doc" in *The Shining*, equating Bill with Danny and Ziegler as the threatening father figure of Jack.

Folding Pollack's offscreen persona as a recognizably Jewish director with his onscreen presence, we can read Ziegler as another Quilty, and hence, another Kubrick double, standing in for the Jewish director himself. Ziegler may be translated as brick maker, hinting at K*ubrick*. Ziegler, like Quilty and Kubrick, is aware of the narrative and plot far more than the lead protagonist and directs Bill, as Pollack had directed Cruise in *The Firm*. Bill allows Ziegler to narrate an unbelievable and unreliable story and provide its meaning, which he then accepts verbatim. Bill, like Humbert, Alex, and Barry, is passive as events happen to him. and he does little to intervene into, or change, the narrative. Victor is an agent, whereas Bill is only a subject, and, as his first name indicates, Victor wins. When Ziegler asks Bill, who represents the innocent, virtually childlike, witness to events around him, "suppose I said all of that was staged, that it was a kind of charade? That it was fake?" it stands as a summary of Kubrick's entire career of staging, misdirection, and manipulation, from his first photograph for *Look* through to this final film.

Conclusion

If *2001* was Kubrick's Amidah, the silent standing prayer, then *Eyes Wide Shut* was his Shema, the Jewish prayer uttered with one's eyes covered, when facing imminent death. Kubrick died only one week after *Eyes Wide Shut*'s first official screening, and so *Eyes Wide Shut* became his final film. It was a deeply personal project for Kubrick, perhaps more than any other. That he chose this project over the other unfinished ones—*Napoleon*, *A.I.*, *Aryan Papers*—is a testament to its importance and hence is the key to understanding Kubrick and his ethnicity. Given the autobiographical touches that returned him to his roots, it seems pertinent to consider *Eyes Wide Shut* as an introspective Freudian autocase history in a similar mold to *The Shining*. It reached back to his origins as a photographer and filmmaker and was an odyssey into his own heart of darkness. As his most personal film, it was his most Jewish film, albeit by deliberate misdirection. A clue is given in his use of Ligeti's "Musica Ricercata II," which translates as "to search for [a hidden meaning]." Kubrick took a deeply Jewish text (Hitler described Schnitzler as "Jewish filth") but only superficially cleaned it, to then use its palimpsestic Jewishness as a structuring absence in the film. He identified with Bill; after all, he'd met Christiane at a masked ball. Kubrick lived as the lone American, a stranger in a strange land, living in rural England, and *Eyes Wide Shut* tapped into themes that have dominated his films, that unconscious Jewish desire, as social pariahs, to unmask the respectability of European society by exposing its sordid, sexual goyim naches. But, at the same time, the person seemingly organizing this goyishness, is a Crypto-Jew, a matrix of anti-Semitic attitudes, who becomes a stand-in for the director himself. Kubrick, it seemed, remained ambivalent about his Jewishness to the end.

Epilogue

At the time of Kubrick's death, two unmade projects lingered: *Aryan Papers* and *A.I. Artificial Intelligence* Kubrick had begun considering a World War II film project around the late 1950s. Harris-Kubrick Pictures planned to adapt the World War II comedy *Operation Mad Ball* (1957) into a television series. They also developed a script titled *The German Lieutenant*, which focused on two German officers during the war's last days. It was never made. Nor did it make any reference to the Nazi genocide of the Jews. Around this time, however, Kubrick appears to have begun reading books on the Holocaust, whose traces are found in *Spartacus*. Shooting for *Spartacus* began on January 27, 1959, the anniversary of liberation of Auschwitz, and later that year Kirk Douglas and Kubrick watched a TV program about the rise of Nazism. *Spartacus*'s iconography invoked both fascist and Nazi motifs. Crassus institutes a "new order," in which undesirables are "cleansed." Individual scenes suggest the atrocities and horrors of the Shoah: the opening Libyan quarry, the branding at the *ludus*, the slaves bearing placards, the slitting of Draba's neck and subsequent display of his corpse, what Kubrick referred to as the "death march," and the refusal to identify Spartacus. But perhaps the most notable post-Holocaust sensibility was what reviewers referred to as the film's brutality, cruelty, and sadism, as particularly manifested in shots of the wholesale slaughter of men, women, and children whose bodies lie tightly packed next to and piled on top of one another. Crassus inspects the dead in a "professional,"

265

"clinical" manner, "scientifically interested," suggesting an SS officer like Josef Mengele.[1]

Around 1960, Kubrick began work on an untitled Holocaust project based on his wife's experiences during World War II. Set in 1943, it focuses principally around the experiences of non-Jewish German girl who moves to live with her parents in Amsterdam, where she gradually becomes aware of the anti-Semitic persecution. Again, while it was never made, its traces show in *Lolita*, particularly in the casting of Shelley Winters, who won an Oscar for her role in the *Diary of Anne Frank* (1959). The Holocaust continued to make its presence felt in his next four films, particularly *Dr. Strangelove* and *A Clockwork Orange*. Incidentally, Kubrick lent some raw stock from *Dr. Strangelove* to help complete a film imagining life in Nazi-occupied Britain, titled *It Happened Here* (1964). After *Barry Lyndon* Kubrick again picked up the idea of making a Holocaust film, contacting Isaac Bashevis Singer in 1976. Although Singer declined, Kubrick was undeterred and continued his search for appropriate material. Traces of this research are evident in *The Shining, Full Metal Jacket*, and even *Eyes Wide Shut*.

Eventually, in 1991, he alighted on Louis Begley's semiautobiographical novel, *Wartime Lies*, a personal account written from a child's perspective. It describes how young Maciek, the son of a Jewish doctor (like Kubrick), together with his aunt Tania, avoided capture and death by pretending to be Catholic. Deceit, lies, and mimicry are essential to their survival. Maciek, like many of Kubrick's subtextually Jewish protagonists, is constantly required to reinvent himself. Extensive preproduction research, including casting, location scouting, and screenplay development, was undertaken under the working title of *Aryan Papers*, but it never came to fruition. The reasons given for its failure negate the excuses given for not making *Aryan Papers*. Its similarity to *Schindler's List* (1993) or the inability to get the details right didn't prevent Kubrick from creating the details of Vietnam in London so soon after *Platoon*.

The question remains therefore why Kubrick was never able to tackle the Holocaust directly and what light this sheds on his Jewishness. Conscious avoidance seems to be at work here. Kubrick chose a story in which Jews hide behind gentile identities. *Wartime Lies* describes how a young Polish Jewish boy avoids extermination by masquerading as a Catholic, just as Barry passes using faked identity papers in *Barry Lyndon*. And, as Marat Grinberg has argued, successive iterations of the screenplay progressively diluted its Jewishness, almost entirely scrubbing it away by the final draft. In a 1992 draft, for example, Maciek and Tania emigrate to Palestine, but by 1993 the story closes somewhere in a Polish forest, recalling *Fear and Desire*. Maybe Kubrick didn't make his Holocaust film because direct references to Jews were necessary, something he consciously avoided throughout his filmmaking career. As Jan Harlan said, "If Kubrick was ever afraid of anything, it was to be carried away by those emotions. Maybe deep down that's why he took so long in his decision to make the film."[2]

Kubrick's failure to make a film explicitly about the Holocaust resembled the response of many American Jewish intellectuals of the forties and fifties who didn't explicitly address the Holocaust in their work. This silence, or absence, signified a response nevertheless. The impact of the Holocaust still registered and is apparent in his films. Topics such as Jewish identity, anti-Semitism, the ability to pass, social ostracism, power and its abuses, and the nature of evil, violence, and genocide are approached obliquely, often through analogies and metaphors, if not outright misdirection, sometimes by overt, albeit brief, moments, but these are the very same issues raised by Jewish history, in particular the Shoah.

But maybe it was the film released after his death that encompassed Kubrick's long-held interests in the Holocaust, the nature of evil and humanity, and what it is to be a man, menschlikayt, and *tikkun olam*. That film is *A.I.* and reaches back to his earliest concerns. Parenthood changed Kubrick. Up to that point his films had been ambivalent in their existentialism. When he met Christiane and instantly became a stepfather, followed by the birth of his two daughters, the promise of birth, rebirth, and new life began to characterize his subsequent films. *Paths of Glory*'s coda rehumanizes the troops. Lolita is settled, somewhat happily married, and pregnant. *Dr. Strangelove* envisages a postapocalyptic rebirth of humanity energized by a "spirit of bold curiosity for the adventure ahead." At the end of *2001*, the birth of the Star-Child heralds a messianic era. Alex is "cured alright," and *A Clockwork Orange* concludes with an image of publicly applauded, thus socially sanctioned, consensual lovemaking. The clear enjoyment of the woman's face, coupled with the virgin purity of the snow they romp in, contrasts with the brutality of the rape of the writer's wife. *Barry Lyndon* is hopeful in heralding the death of the decadent, elitist ancien régime and the advent of a brave new world that gave birth to the French Revolution and in which American democracy was already nurturing. *The Shining* ends on a positive note, as mother and child escape the murdering father; even Jack lives on in a photograph. Joker survives Vietnam with his menschlikayt intact. And *Eyes Wide Shut* ends with the words "there is something very important we need to do as soon as possible . . . fuck," as if invoking the first-ever biblical commandment, "Go forth and multiply." As Joker says, "The dead know only one thing: it is better to be alive," or perhaps we can rephrase that to "it is better to be born."

This was clearly the subject of *A.I.*, based on Brian Aldiss's 1969 short story, "Super-Toys Last All Summer Long." It depicts the family of Henry and Monica Swinton and their son, David, whose only companion is a teddy bear. His love for his mother is unrequited, no matter how hard he strives to please her. This is because he's revealed to be an android and her love for him is incomparable to that she will have for her birth child. Kubrick first showed his interest in the story in 1976 and he worked on it, intermittently, until the mid-1990s. Then *Eyes Wide Shut* absorbed his attention, but as that was wrapping he returned to "Super-Toys."

The story intrigued him for several reasons. It foregrounds such oedipal issues as a son's attachment to his mother, who is simultaneously distant from him, and it explores the nature of love, recalling Zweig's *Burning Secret*. The more vividly realized Monica is David's emotional core, in contrast to her husband, Henry, who is colder, distant, and largely absent, continuing the themes of Kubrick's earliest works. The story inquires into the nature of humanity, asking what is real and human versus android, continuing the theme of man's relationship with machines and technology. And Kubrick's drafts explore humanity's self-destructiveness but simultaneous ability to create, to produce robots that would outlive and, ultimately, resurrect them. Although humanity is destroyed, the robots are perhaps able to repair the world.

"Super-Toys" also considers such Jewish issues as identity, difference, otherness, the ability to pass, social ostracism, violence, and genocide. In retaining the name David, Kubrick's protagonist joins the ranks of other subtextually Jewish Davids in his oeuvre, reaching back to *Killer's Kiss*. David is a golem, the symbolic child of HAL (short for Henry?). He, like Quilty, Alex, Barry, and Joker, is a mimic. But because David is almost the same, but not quite, and his parents know his true identity, he's cast out just like them. He's able to pass effectively in the wider society, though, masquerading as human, mirroring Barry's and Bill's odysseys. In the future society posited by Kubrick, the binary oppositions of his earlier films are resurrected in the pairing of "orga" versus "mecha," or human masters versus robotic slaves. Mecha are hunted down and publicly tortured in gruesome spectacles, recalling the gladiatorial combats of *Spartacus*.

The draft screenplays betray a subtextual concern with the Holocaust, perhaps because of Kubrick's failure to make a Holocaust film. Harlan's approach to Singer about a Holocaust project approximately coincided with Kubrick's initial contact with Brian Aldiss. Returned to the android factory, David learns that "terrible things" are happening to androids. Escaping with an adult android named GI Joe, they flee to Tin Town, allegedly a haven for escaped androids. But on arrival they are forced to line up, where a "human is dividing them quietly into two files. . . . Battered ones go to the left and are told they will get a shower and polish." The shower is an "acid bath." Other drafts are even more explicit. Tin Town becomes "Paradise Konzentration Kamp" guarded by men "in SS uniforms." The treatment meted out to the Mecha precisely parallels that which awaited the Jews at Auschwitz. Although ultimately directed by Steven Spielberg and released in 2001, it stands a posthumous testament to Kubrick's deepest concerns.[3]

As demonstrated, indications in Kubrick's films show that he never fully abandoned the heritage, culture, and traditions of his forebears. While he may not have practiced any religion, he never repudiated his ethnicity. He may have lacked any Jewish faith, but he was certainly aware of his ethnic otherness. His given and family names marked him as different from the mainstream society. And this Jewish otherness bled into his films. Seemingly devoid of ethnic references, and where the deliberate suppression of the explicit allusion to Jewish culture and historical experience is evident, his films were nonetheless still informed by that very knowledge. Although not immediately noticeable or obvious, Kubrick's Jewishness was indelibly inscribed, forming the bedrock of his filmmaking, what George Steiner referred to as the "pride and the burden of the Jewish tradition." As Paula Hyman has observed, "Even secularized Jews were likely to retain a strong ethnic Jewish identification, generally internally and reinforced from without."[4]

Jewish meaning can be derived from Kubrick's films, much of which can be attributed to an upbringing and education that influenced his work, consciously or not. Therefore, they can be mined for their deeper biblical and Jewish religious, as well as secular, resonances. Whereas the previous scholarly tendency has been to interpret them within an overwhelmingly Christological framework, an alternative approach reveals a distinctly

Jewish understanding of the universe, especially in their use of imagery drawn from Hebrew scripture and Jewish liturgy, as well as other Jewish and modernist sources, particularly the writings of Sigmund Freud, Franz Kafka, Arthur Schnitzler, Bruno Schulz, Stefan Zweig, Harold Pinter, Joseph Conrad, James Joyce, among many others. His films engage with Jewish texts—albeit in an oblique way. A complete understanding of Kubrick's work is impossible without recognition of the debt it owes to Judaism and the way in which it engages Jewish themes and thought.

That Kubrick habitually wrote Jewish characters out of his films was in part due, as he himself indicated, to his desire to appeal to a majority non-Jewish movie audience, not to mention his own universalizing modernism. It also almost certainly had to do with his ambivalence and conflict over his own background, both familial and cultural, just like Kafka. Kubrick, it seems, could not bring himself to insert the word "Jew" in his films. The only certain instance emerges in the epithet "kike" in *Full Metal Jacket*. There is a story his daughter Vivian tells. She first chose "Moses Lumpkin" for her screen name as composer for *Full Metal Jacket*. It "horrified" Kubrick possibly because it sounded "too Jewish." Instead, she recalls, "I thought of the house our family used to live in, where we had many good times, and like many in England, it had a name: Abbot's Mead. *Abbot* became *Abigail* and then Stanley had someone look up the name's meaning. Its ancient meaning [in Hebrew] is 'a father rejoices.' He loves coincidences, and really loved this one." Abigail Mead became the name she used.[5]

Yet, like Kafka, Kubrick's characters, either by conduct or particularized portrayals, invite identification as Jews, particularly as he worked with many major and minor Jewish actors, including Paul Mazursky, Joe Turkel (thrice), Jacob Adler, Kirk Douglas (twice), Paul Tamarin, Tony Curtis, Peter Sellers (twice), Shelley Winters, Miriam Karlin, Steven Berkoff (twice), Harvey Keitel, and Sydney Pollack. This extends from Sidney, through to Davey, Leo, Dax, Spartacus, David, Antoninus, Humbert, the Hazes, Quilty, many of the characters in *Dr. Strangelove*, Bowman, Alex, the Catlady, the Lyndons, Lord Ludd, Jack, Joker, and Pyle, culminating in Bill and Victor. Kubrick's technique of encouraging actors to improvise around the script resembled, if only to a limited extent, the working method of another Jewish director whose work Kubrick admired, Mike Leigh, one of the few fellow film directors who was invited to Kubrick's funeral. Like Kubrick, Leigh did not tend to insert any Jewishness into his films in any direct or explicit fashion (*Hard Labour* [1973] being the conspicuous exception to this rule).

Frustratingly, however, unlike his American contemporaries, such as Woody Allen, Mel Brooks, and David Mamet, Kubrick did not publicly affirm his Jewish identity and thus offered us no easy way into ethnic identification in his work (but then he offered us no easy way into anything!). Stripped of overt, explicit Jewish references, his films appear severed from his ethnic and cultural roots, ostensibly the least Jewish of the twentieth century's Jewish filmmakers. But scrutiny of Kubrick's canon reveals that Jewish thought and values are not a digression but a vital element fundamental to understanding his artistic vision. When the development of Kubrick's work over his entire career is traced, a subtle link between the moral and intellectual vision that distinguishes his films and its foundation in Jewish thought, values, and cultural experience is discernible.

If Kubrick had a spiritual home, it was Jewish. He gained public attention in 1956, at roughly the same time as Allen Ginsberg, whose work has been described as angry, powerful social statements denouncing hypocrisy and demanding attention, in the Hebrew prophetic tradition. Kubrick, like Ginsberg, fits this template. And like the prophets Ezekiel and Isaiah, he created visions and visionary experiences. In 1967 theologian Vernard Eller detected a biblical morality lying beneath *Mad* magazine's surface: "*Mad* is every bit as preachy as that old codifier Moses. Beneath the pile of garbage that is *Mad*, there beats, I suspect, the heart of a rabbi." What was said about *Mad* in 1967 is just as apt for Kubrick. Beneath the surface of Kubrick's films beat the heart of a secular rabbi, consciously using his Jewishness to comment on the key intellectual issues that preoccupied Jews in the post-Holocaust era.[6]

It has not been my intention to reduce Kubrick to a single message or to suggest that he made "Jewish films" (whatever that means) with purely literal and exhaustive significance. While it's possible to see a certain kind of Jewish influence in Kubrick's films, I'm not labeling them as "Jewish." Kubrick, like Leigh, took the route of universalizing his Jewishness into the public sphere and retaining enough clues to invite specific identification. And, to be sure, his Jewishness was far from the only factor that determined the shape of his films. His work can be enjoyed without recourse to its Jewish ethics or vision. Yet to do so is to fail to read it backward, to understand the impact and sweep of history that inform his canon. Like the political and intellectual concerns that influenced him early in life, his ethnic and family background continued to play a significant role long after he rejected any ties to Judaism. Rather than diminish the universality that Kubrick achieved in his cinematic oeuvre, such an approach illuminates the sources and scope of his body of work in the hope of enhancing our understanding of his artistic expression by intensive and comprehensive (re)viewing of one of the foremost postwar filmmakers.

Acknowledgments

This project has its genesis in my job offer at the then University of Wales, Bangor, in 2005–2006. Asked if I would design a new module, I decided to run one on Stanley Kubrick. This soon developed into my most popular module, in student feedback terms at least: Stanley Kubrick: Auteur. It took five years of teaching the module before I finally came up with an original angle: Kubrick's Jewishness.

For a book that had its genesis over a decade ago, there are many people to thank. Because I have been silly enough not to keep a list of everybody, undoubtedly some people will be left out, and for that I wholeheartedly apologize. This includes my former students, both undergraduate and postgraduate, who have contributed ideas, as well as friends and colleagues at Bangor and elsewhere and participants in the many talks I have given over the years at Limmud, other universities, and a variety of venues. I particularly would like to thank those who have read drafts of my work and provided invaluable advice and criticism, both those whom I know and the anonymous ones.

Various individuals deserve singling out for their advice, insights, and support. Robert Kolker, my co-conspirator in Kubrick, has provided very close readings of my work and extremely useful comments, and I look forward to a long and fruitful collaboration. Geoffrey Cocks, Peter Kramer, and Ian Hunter have also been keen-eyed readers and referees, to whom I owe much. Indeed, it was Geoffrey who laid the archival, cultural, and historical groundwork for this study. Senior Kubrick archivist, Richard

Daniels, has patiently put up with my consistent queries, but I hope I have given him something back in return. Jan Harlan, Kubrick's brother-in-law and erstwhile producer, has been a font of knowledge, anecdotes, and confirmation where sorely needed. And thank you to Kubrick's former partner, James B. Harris.

Others who have provided assistance along the way include Jon Abrams, Saer Maty Ba, Michael Berkowitz, Costica Bradatan, Rhonda Burnette-Bletsch, Paul B. Cohen, Ned Comstock, James Fenwick, Kirsten Fermaglich, Danielle Friel, Marat Grinberg, Will Higbee, Llion Iwan, Dyfrig Jones, Jonathan Judaken, Tatjana Ljujić, Toby Manning, Rod Munday, Simone Odino, Gerwyn Owen, Kira-Ann Pelikan, Steve Price, Lawrence Ratna, Jenni Steele, Ceri Sullivan, Filippo Ulivieri, Camil Ungereanu, Laurent Vachaud, and Steve Whitfield. They have all provided assistance and advice of one kind or another. Pastoral support and babysitting have been given by many people, but in particular by our friends Kate and Rob Thomas and my ever-supportive parents-in-law, Trish and Dan Friel.

I would like to thank the staff at the various archives and libraries I have utilized over the years, of which there have been many. These include the Harry Ransom Humanities Research Center, University of Texas at Austin; Wisconsin Historical Society; Margaret Herrick Library of the Academy of Motion Picture Arts and Sciences, Los Angeles; the Manuscript Division, Library of Congress; Georgetown University Library Special Collections Research Center, Washington, DC; Brandeis University Libraries; Robert D. Farber University Archives and Special Collections Department; Yale University Library; Henry W. and Albert A. Berg Collection, New York Public Library; and Department/Office of Film and Broadcasting, American Catholic History Research Center and University Archives, Catholic University of America, Washington, DC. Many of them went beyond the call of duty to dig up materials for me, often with no charge. But, above all, I want to thank the Stanley Kubrick Archive, University of the Arts, London, without whom none of this would have been remotely possible.

Leslie Mitchener at Rutgers University Press saw the potential in this project and has nurtured it to fruition. Her comments have been insightful and have improved the text immeasurably. The team at Rutgers University Press, including Anne Hegeman, Lisa Banning, and Jennifer Blanc-Tel, deserves praise for producing such a handsome volume. Thank you to Susan Silver for her keen-eyed copyediting. Finally, I would like to thank the anonymous readers whose comments were invaluable. Needless to say, any errors in fact or matters of interpretation remain my own.

Writing this book has been somewhat of a Kubrickian odyssey. After five years of research, I have amassed a vast amount of material, much of which had to be cut to fit the word limit. This has given me an insight into the sort of tasks in terms of preproduction research and postproduction editing Kubrick faced. The necessity to trim the book has meant that I haven't been able to acknowledge and cite directly everyone who has had a hand in shaping this material, and there have been many. I hope, however, in lieu of this, that my bibliography will serve as a guide to those many voices. I have also not been able to follow the many paths down the rabbit warren as I would have liked.

The primary research for this book was made possible by grants from the Arts and Humanities Research Council, the British Academy, and the Harry Ransom Humanities Research Council at the University of Texas, Austin, as well as two periods of study leave granted to me by Bangor University. I would like to thank those colleagues who provided feedback on those applications, in particular Professor Carol Tully and Dr. Hazel Robbins.

Earlier versions of six chapters have been revised and expanded here. They are "Kubrick's Double: *Lolita*'s Hidden Heart of Jewishness," *Cinema Journal* 55, no. 3 (2016): 17–39; "Becoming a Macho Mensch: Stanley Kubrick, *Spartacus* and 1950s Jewish Masculinity," *Adaptation: The Journal of Literature on Screen Studies* 8, no. 3 (2015): 283–296; "A Hidden Heart of Jewishness and Englishness: Stanley Kubrick," *European Judaism* 47, no. 2 (2014): 69–76; "An Alternative New York Intellectual: Stanley Kubrick's Cultural Critique," in *New Perspectives on Stanley Kubrick*, edited by Tatjana Ljujić, Richard Daniels, and Peter Kramer, 62–81 (London: Black Dog, 2014); "The Banality of Evil: Polanski, Kubrick, and the Reinvention of Horror," in *Religion in Contemporary European Cinema*, edited by Costica Bradatan and Camil Ungereanu, 145–164 (New York: Routledge, 2014); and "'A Double Set of Glasses': Stanley Kubrick and the Midrashic Mode of Interpretation," in *De-Westernizing Film Studies*, edited by Saer Maty Ba and Will Higbee, 141–151 (London: Routledge, 2012). I am grateful to the publishers for giving me permission to reproduce them in part here.

I dedicate this book to my parents, Rosalind and Michael Abrams, and my family: my wife, Danielle; my children, Isabel Willow and Jacob Leon; my cats

Stanley (who came with that name) and Elwood and Pepper the dog—with all my love. In fact, Dani, Isabel, and Jacob have known no other partner and daddy other than the one who has been writing about Kubrick and who goes on "the holiday" because of Kubrick. My children have been brought up watching his films and listening to me talk about him. I hope my passion will be passed on to them.

Notes

Abbreviations

AB Anthony Burgess Papers

AMPAS Academy of Motion Picture Arts and Sciences

DJ Diane Johnson Papers

DM Dwight Macdonald Papers

DT Dalton Trumbo Papers

GU Georgetown University Library Special Collections Research Center

JF Jules Feiffer Papers

JH Joseph Heller Collection

KD Kirk Douglas Papers

LD Linwood G. Dunn Papers

LM *Look* Magazine Photograph Collection

PCA Production Code Administration

SKA Stanley Kubrick Archive

TS Terry Southern Papers

USCCBC United States Conference of Catholic Bishops Communications

VN Vladimir Nabokov Papers

Introduction

1 The scholarly literature on Stanley Kubrick is simply too voluminous to cite; however, an idea of its scope is given here: "Stanley Kubrick: A Bibliography of Materials in the UC Berkeley Library," accessed May 30, 2015, www.lib.berkeley.edu/MRC/kubrick.html; John Baxter, *Stanley Kubrick: A Biography* (London: HarperCollins, 1998); Vincent LoBrutto, *Stanley Kubrick: A Biography* (New York: Fine, 1998).

2 Geoffrey Cocks, *The Wolf at the Door: Stanley Kubrick, History, and the Holocaust* (New York: Lang, 2004); Cocks, "Indirected by Stanley Kubrick," *Post Script* 32, no. 2 (2013): 20–33.

3 Margaret Burton, "Performances of Jewish Identity: *Spartacus*," *Shofar: An Interdisciplinary Journal of Jewish Studies* 27, no. 1 (2008): 1–15; Frederic Raphael, *Eyes Wide Open: A Memoir of Stanley Kubrick* (London: Ballantine, 1999), 105.

4 Raphael, *Eyes Wide Open*, 105–106; Jan Harlan, e-mail to author, July 22, 2015.

5 Stanley Kubrick, interview with Michel Ciment, July 28, 1981, SK/1/2/8/7, SKA; Harlan, e-mail, December 31, 2015; Michael Herr, *Kubrick* (New York: Picador, 2000), 21.

6 Stanley Kubrick, qtd. in Jerome Agel, *The Making of Kubrick's 2001* (New York: Signet, 1970), 330; Hobbs, qtd. in Cocks, *Wolf at the Door*, 23; Emilio D'Alessandro, *Stanley Kubrick and Me: Thirty Years at His Side*, with Filippo Ulivieri, trans. Simon Marsh (New York: Arcade, 2016), 149; Harlan, e-mail, December 31, 2015.

7 Dalton Trumbo, "Notes," August 23, 1959, 24/8, DT; Raphael, *Eyes Wide Open*, 149.

8 Alexander Walker, *"It's Only a Movie, Ingrid": Encounters On and Off Screen* (London: Headline, 1988), 301.

9 Stanley Kubrick, qtd. in Jeremy Bernstein, "How about a Little Game?," *New Yorker*, November 12, 1966, 70; Brendan Gill, "To Die Laughing," *New Yorker*, February 1, 1964, 75.

10 Michael Herr, "Kubrick," *Vanity Fair*, April 21, 2010, www.vanityfair.com/hollywood/2010/04/kubrick-199908.

11 Robert Emmett Ginna, "The Artist Speaks for Himself," *Archivio Kubrick*, accessed May 30, 2017, www.archiviokubrick.it/english/words/interviews/1960ginna.html; Michel Ciment, *Kubrick* (London: Collins, 1983), 33; Stanley Kubrick to Roger Caras, November 22, 1966, SK/12/8/1/6i, SKA.

12 Herr, *Kubrick*, 11; Midge Decter, "The Kubrick Mystique," *Commentary* 108, no. 2 (1999): 55.

13 Irving Howe, "The New York Intellectuals: A Chronicle and a Critique," *Commentary* 46, no. 4 (1968): 29.

14 Dwight Macdonald, "No Art and No Box Office," *Encounter* 13 no. 1 (1959): 51; Dwight Macdonald to Stanley Kubrick, April 21, 1959, 26/693, MS 730, DM.

15 Penelope Gilliatt, "Mankind on the Late, Late Show," *Observer*, September 6, 1987, 20.

16 Alex Ross, "Stanley Kubrick Was My Friend, Too," *New Yorker*, August 2, 1999, 37; Herr, *Kubrick*, 55, 11, 26; Anthony Frewin, "Stanley Kubrick: Writers, Writing, Reading," in *The Stanley Kubrick Archives*, ed. Alison Castle (Cologne: Taschen, 2005), 514; Loudon Wainwright, "The View from Here: The Strange Case of Strangelove," *Life*, March 13, 1964, 15.

17 Leo Rosten, *The Joys of Yiddish* (London: Penguin, 1972), 240; Rebecca Alpert, "The Macho-Mensch: Modeling American Jewish Masculinity and the Heroes of Baseball," in *Muscling in on New Worlds: Jews, Sport, and the Making of the Americas*, ed. Raanan Rein and David M. K. Sheinin (Leiden, Netherlands: Brill, 2014), 109.

18 Stanley Kubrick, in Natalie Zemon Davis, *Slaves on Screen: Film and Historical Vision* (Toronto: Vintage Canada, 2000), 39–40; Kubrick, qtd. in Yann Tobin and Laurent Vachaud, "Brève rencontre: Christiane Kubrick et Jan Harlan," *Positif* 464 (October 1999): 43; Eric Nordern, "*Playboy* Interview (1968)," in *Stanley Kubrick: Interviews*, ed. Gene D. Phillips (Jackson: University Press of Mississippi, 2001), 67; William Makepeace Thackeray, *The Memoirs of Barry Lyndon, Esq.* (Oxford: Oxford University Press, 1999), 94; Harlan, qtd. in Ian Freer, "Strangelove," *Empire*, October 2001, 49; Barbara Kubrick, *Stanley Kubrick: A Life in Pictures* DVD (Harlan, 2001).

19 Christiane Kubrick, *Stanley Kubrick: A Life in Pictures* (London: Little, Brown, 2002), 23.

20 Lamm, in Anthony Frewin, ed., *Are We Alone? The Stanley Kubrick Extraterrestrial-Intelligence Interviews* (London: Elliot and Thompson, 2005), 135; Warren Rosenberg, *Legacy of Rage: Jewish Masculinity, Violence, and Culture* (Amherst: University of Massachusetts Press, 2001), 153; John Murray Cuddihy, *The Ordeal of Civility: Freud, Marx, Lévi-Strauss, and the Jewish Struggle with Modernity* (Boston: Beacon, 1978), 22; Irving Howe, *World of Our Fathers* (New York: Simon and Schuster, 1976), 645.

21 Laurence Roth, *Inspecting Jews: American Jewish Detective Stories* (New Brunswick, NJ: Rutgers University Press, 2004), 31; Jeffrey T. Sammons, *Beyond the Ring: The Role of Boxing in American Society* (Urbana: University of Illinois Press, 1990), 91; Daniel Boyarin, *Unheroic Conduct: The Rise of Heterosexuality and the Invention of the Jewish Man* (Berkeley: University of California Press, 1997), 23, 78.

22 Boyarin, *Unheroic Conduct*, 23, 78; Sammons, *Beyond the Ring*, 91; Sigmund Freud, *Moses and Monotheism* (New York: Vintage, 1967), 147; Jean-Paul Sartre, *Anti-Semite and Jew*, trans. George J. Becker (New York: Schocken, 1965), 117; Rosenberg, *Legacy of Rage*, 153–154.

23 Frederick Ahl, "*Spartacus, Exodus*, and Dalton Trumbo: Managing Ideologies of War," in *Spartacus: Film and History*, ed. Martin M. Winkler (Oxford: Blackwell, 2007), 78.

24 Stanley Kubrick, in Nordern, "*Playboy* Interview (1968)," 68; Stanley Kubrick, "Now Kubrick Fights Back," *New York Times*, February 27, 1972, sec. 2, p. 1; Stanley Kubrick, qtd. in Ciment, *Kubrick* (1983), 163.

25 Howard Morley Sacher, *The Course of Modern Jewish History* (New York: Dell, 1958), 400–401.

26 Stanley Kubrick to Penelope Gilliatt, in Castle, *Stanley Kubrick Archives*, 477; Sydney Pollack, *TV Guide*, January 1–7, 2000; Anya Kubrick, qtd. in Richard Schickel, "All Eyes on Them," *Time*, July 5, 1999, 70; Stanley Kubrick, notecard, SK/16/1/23, SKA.

27 Louis Blau, qtd. in Army Archerd, "Kubrick 'Memoir' Shocks Spielberg," *Variety*, June 18, 1999, http://variety.com/1999/voices/columns/kubrick-memoir-shocks-spielberg-1117503222/; Stanley Kubrick, qtd. in Ciment, *Kubrick* (1983), 156;

Raphael, *Eyes Wide Open*, 150; John Orr and Elżbieta Ostrowska, *The Cinema of Roman Polanski: Dark Spaces of the World* (London: Wallflower, 2006), 142.

28 Cocks, *Wolf at the Door*, 70; Kubrick, qtd. in Dalia Karpel, "The Real Stanley Kubrick," *Haaretz.com*, November 3, 2005, www.haaretz.com/the-real-stanley -kubrick-1.173194.

29 Cocks, "Indirected," 26–27, 31; Kubrick, qtd. in Jon Ronson, "After Stanley Kubrick," *Guardian*, August 19, 2010.

30 Arthur Miller, "Concerning Jews Who Write," *Jewish Life* 2, no. 5 (1948): 7–10.

31 Leslie Fiedler, "Jewish-Americans, Go Home!," in his *Waiting for the End: The American Literary Scene from Hemingway to Baldwin* (London: Penguin, 1967), 101, 107.

32 Rodger Kamenetz, *Burnt Books: Rabbi Nachman of Bratslav and Franz Kafka* (New York: Schocken, 2010), 222.

33 Maria Pramaggiore, *Making Time in Stanley Kubrick's Barry Lyndon: Art, History, and Empire* (New York: Bloomsbury, 2015), 92; Tony Pipolo, "Stanley Kubrick's History Lessons," *Cineaste*, Spring 2009, 7.

34 Ella Shohat, "Ethnicities-in-Relation: Toward a Multicultural Reading of American Cinema," in *Unspeakable Images: Ethnicity and the American Cinema*, ed. Lester D. Friedman (Urbana: University of Illinois Press, 1991), 220; Jon Stratton, *Coming Out Jewish* (London: Routledge, 2000), 300; Henry Bial, *Acting Jewish: Negotiating Ethnicity on the American Stage and Screen* (Ann Arbor: University of Michigan Press, 2005), 70.

35 Raphael, *Eyes Wide Open*, 58; Mamet, qtd. in Leslie Kane, *Weasels and Wisemen: Ethics and Ethnicity in the Work of David Mamet* (Basingstoke, UK: Macmillan, 1999), 362n40; Stanley Kubrick, "Words and Movies," *Sight and Sound* 30 (1960–1961): 14; Alexander Walker, Sybil Taylor, and Ulrich Ruchti, *Stanley Kubrick, Director: A Visual Analysis* (London: Weidenfeld and Nicolson, 1999), 38; Karen A. Ritzenhoff, "UK Frost Can Kill Palms: Layers of Reality in Stanley Kubrick's *Full Metal Jacket*," in *Stanley Kubrick: New Perspectives*, ed. Tatjana Ljujić, Peter Kramer, and Richard Daniels (London: Black Dog, 2015), 328; Modine, qtd. in Adam Feinstein, "Moves and Movies," *New in Chess* 4 (2014): 64; Wally Gentleman to Linwood G. Dunn, May 4, 1966, LD; Michael Henry, "What Stanley Wanted," *Positif*, September 1999, 18.

36 Raphael, *Eyes Wide Open*, 150; Matthew Modine, *Full Metal Jacket Diary* (New York: Rugged Land, 2005); Ginna, "Artist Speaks for Himself"; Michel Ciment, *Kubrick: The Definitive Edition* (New York: Faber and Faber, 2003), 59.

Chapter 1   Looking to Killing

1 Philippe D. Mather, "A Portrait of the Artist as a Young Man: The Influence of *Look* Magazine on Stanley Kubrick's Career as a Filmmaker," in Ljujić, Kramer, and Daniels, *Stanley Kubrick*, 22–23, 37–38; "Look Magazine, Articles," 1947–1950, SK/2/1, SKA.

2 Philippe D. Mather, "Stanley Kubrick and *Look* Magazine," in *Stanley Kubrick: Essays on His Films and Legacy*, ed. Gary D. Rhodes (Jefferson, NC: McFarland, 2008), 10–11, 12; Mather, *Stanley Kubrick at Look Magazine* (Bristol, UK: Intellect, 2013), 93.

3   Paul Duncan, *Stanley Kubrick: The Complete Films* (Cologne: Taschen, 2008), 15; Rainer Crone, "Kubrick's Epic Pictures as Parables," in *Stanley Kubrick: Drama and Shadows*, ed. Rainer Crone (London: Phaidon, 2005), 8.

4   Mather, *Stanley Kubrick at Look*, 128; Joanne Stang, "Film Fan to Film Maker," *New York Times Magazine*, October 12, 1958, 36.

5   Mather, *Stanley Kubrick at Look*, 31; "Woman Posing" contact sheets, SK/2/3/1/1, SKA.

6   Mather, *Stanley Kubrick at Look*, 82; *Look*, Job 47–1139, *Prints and Photographs*, accessed October 2015, www.loc.gov/pictures/item/lmc2000009041/PP/, LM.

7   Walker Taylor, and Ruchti, *Stanley Kubrick, Director*, 12.

8   Erica Fahr Campbell, "From Photography to Film: Stanley Kubrick Enters the Ring," *Time*, November 2012; LoBrutto, *Stanley Kubrick*, 63; Bernd Kiefer, "Chess Games in the Boxing Ring: Kubrick's Early Work," in *Stanley Kubrick* (Frankfurt: Deutsches Filmmuseum, 2004), 33; "*Day of the Fight* (1951): Trivia," accessed June 1, 2016, www.imdb.com/title/tt0042384/trivia?ref_=tt_ql_2; Singer, qtd. in Campbell, "From Photography to Film."

9   LoBrutto, *Stanley Kubrick*, 74.

10 Campbell, "From Photography to Film."

11 Thomas M. Pryor, "Young Man with Ideas and a Camera," *New York Times*, January 14, 1951.

12 Jerry McCulley, "Kubrick's Composers," *New Times* (Los Angeles), August 19, 1999, 56; Irene Thirer, "Another Boy Film Producer," *New York Post*, March 27, 1953.

13 Norman Kagan, *The Cinema of Stanley Kubrick* (New York: Continuum, 2000), 11; Thomas Allen Nelson, *Kubrick: Inside a Film Artist's Maze* (Bloomington: Indiana University Press, 2000), 22, 2.

14 Stanley Kubrick to Joseph Burstyn, November 16, 1952; *Modern Photography*, in Howard, *Kubrick*, 33.

15 Kubrick to Burstyn, November 16, 1952; Gene D. Phillips, *Stanley Kubrick: A Film Odyssey* (New York: Popular Library, 1975), 17.

16 Cocks, *Wolf at the Door*, 79.

17 *People Today*, April 8, 1953; James Naremore, *On Kubrick* (London: British Film Institute, 2007), 49.

18 Benzion Kaganoff, *A Dictionary of Jewish Names and Their History* (New York: Schocken, 1977), 62–63.

19 Cocks, *Wolf at the Door*, 78; Paul Mazursky, *Show Me the Magic: My Adventures in Life and Hollywood with. . . .* (New York: Simon and Schuster, 1999), 13; Singer, in Howard, *Stanley Kubrick Companion*, 58.

20 Curtis Harrington, qtd. in Baxter, *Stanley Kubrick*, 54.

21 Bill Krohn, *Fear and Desire*, commentary, DVD, dir. Stanley Kubrick, 1953.

22 Paolo Cherchi Usai, "Checkmating the General: Stanley Kubrick's *Fear and Desire*," *Image* 38, nos. 1–2 (1995): 27; Stanley Kubrick, interview with Robert Emmett Ginna, c. 1960, SK/1/2/8/2, SKA; Stanley Kubrick, qtd. in LoBrutto, *Stanley Kubrick*, 91; C. Kubrick, *Stanley Kubrick*, 44.

23 Irene Thirer, "Another Boy Film Producer," *New York Post*, March 27, 1953; Laura Lee, "More Action, Less Talking in Movies," *Sunday Bulletin*, July 26, 1953, 8, 10; Kubrick, interview with Ginna, SKA.

24 Eitan Kensky, e-mail to author, October 18, 2012; Ciment, *Kubrick* (1983), 117.

25 James Naremore, *More Than Night: Film Noir in Its Contexts* (Berkeley: University of California Press, 2008), 158.

26 Dana Polan, "Materiality and Sociality in *Killer's Kiss*," in *Perspectives on Stanley Kubrick*, ed. Mario Falsetto (New York: Hall, 1996), 92–93.

27 Cocks, *Wolf at the Door*, 83–87; Geoffrey M. Shurlock to Sol Konecoff, March 22, 1955, AMPAS.

28 Polan, "Materiality and Sociality," 93.

29 Stang, "Film Fan," 36; Robert Polito, *Savage Art: A Biography of Jim Thompson* (New York: Vintage, 1996), 394.

30 LoBrutto, *Stanley Kubrick*, 91; Robert Kolker, *A Cinema of Loneliness*, 4th ed. (New York: Oxford University Press, 2011), 110, 111; Jean-Paul Sartre, *Existentialism*, trans. Bernard Frechtman (New York: Philosophical Library, 1947), 37–38.

31 Lionel White, *Clean Break* (1955; repr., New York: Blackmask Online, 2005), 61, 94, 13–14, 15.

32 Rosenberg, *Legacy of Rage*, 84; White, *Clean Break*, 10; Gene D. Phillips and Rodney Hill, *The Encyclopedia of Stanley Kubrick* (New York: Checkmark, 2002), 65, 398, 185; "Bed of Fear: Synopsis," n.d., PCA.

33 Polito, *Savage Art*, 395; Naremore, *On Kubrick*, 77; Mario Falsetto, *Stanley Kubrick: A Narrative and Stylistic Analysis* (Westport, CT: Praeger, 2001), 107; Deborah Tresiman to Terry Southern, April 4, 1994, 119/ 26, TS.

34 Vincent Brook, *Driven to Darkness: Jewish Émigré Directors and the Rise of Film Noir* (New Brunswick, NJ: Rutgers University Press, 2009), 211.

Chapter 2   The Macho Mensch

1 Pauline Kael, *5001 Nights at the Movies* (London: Zenith, 1982), 459; Alpert, "Macho-Mensch," 109.

2 Jay Varela, "Conversation with Stanley Kubrick," *El Playano, Loyola Marymount University*, Spring 1958, repr. in Castle, *Stanley Kubrick Archives*, 312; Raymond Haine, "Good Morning Mr. Kubrick," *Cahiers du Cinema*, July 1957, repr. in Castle, *Stanley Kubrick Archives*, 303; Bernstein, "Little Game," 74; Kagan, *Cinema of Stanley Kubrick*, 64; Polito, *Savage Art*, 403.

3 Barry Mendel, "Calder Willingham," *The Literary Encyclopedia*, January 9, 2008, www.litencyc.com/php/speople.php?rec=true&UID=11815; Polito, *Savage Art*, 403–407; Kirk Douglas, *The Ragman's Son: An Autobiography* (Bath: Chivers, 1988), 321, 322.

4 LoBrutto, *Stanley Kubrick*, 133, 135.

5 Naremore, *On Kubrick*, 85.

6 Stanley Kubrick, qtd. in Andrew Kelly, "The Brutality of Military Incompetence: 'Paths of Glory' (1957)," *Historical Journal of Film, Radio and Television* 13, no. 2 (1993): 223.

7 Alpert, "Macho-Mensch," 109.

8 Wilfred Owen, "Parable of the Old Man and the Young" (1920), in his *Collected Poems* (Oxford: Oxford University Press, 1920), 42.

9 Adolphe Menjou, qtd. in *New York Times*, May 16, 1947, 1; Kolker, *Cinema of Loneliness*, 124.

10 Christiane Kubrick, broadcast, BBC Radio 4, May 1, 2014, www.bbc.co.uk/ programmes/b041yjy7; James B. Harris, telephone interview with the author, September 2, 2016; Douglas, *Ragman's Son*, 329.

11 Piers Paul Read, *The Dreyfus Affair: The Scandal That Tore France in Two* (New York: Bloomsbury, 2012), 46; Theodor Herzl, qtd. in "Schnitzler's Hidden Manuscripts Explored," May 20, 2008, www.cam.ac.uk/news/schnitzler%E2%80%99s -hidden-manuscripts-explored.

12 Humphrey Cobb, *Paths of Glory* (1935; repr., London: Penguin, 2010), 122, 123.

13 Naremore, *On Kubrick*, 95; Syd Stogel to Alfred H. Tamarin, March 30, 1957, 23/30, KD.

14 Hannah Arendt, *The Origins of Totalitarianism* (New York: Meridian, 1958), 45, 93; Elizabeth Greenhalgh, *The French Army and the First World War* (Cambridge: Cambridge University Press, 2014), 62.

15 Peter Ustinov, qtd. in Jan Harlan, *Stanley Kubrick: A Life in Pictures*, DVD.

16 LoBrutto, *Stanley Kubrick*, 147; untitled script, "Assorted Projects" box, n.d., SKA; Peter Ustinov, commentary, *Spartacus*, DVD, dir. Stanley Kubrick (Bryna Productions/Universal-International Pictures, 1960); Richard Adams and Stanley Kubrick, "The German Lieutenant," GU; Stanley Kubrick to Paul Botica, February 2, 1959, uncatalogued material, SKA.

17 Karpel, "Real Stanley Kubrick"; *Harlan: In the Shadow of Jew Süss*, dir. Felix Moeller (Germany: Blueprint Film, 2008).

18 Dalton Trumbo, "Notes," August 23, 1959, 24/8, DT.

19 Henry Popkin, "The Vanishing Jew of Our Popular Culture," *Commentary* 14 (1952): 51.

20 Paul Breines, *Tough Jews: Political Fantasies and the Moral Dilemma of American Jewry* (New York: Basic, 1990), 54–59.

21 Stanley Kubrick to Eddie Lewis and Dalton Trumbo, 24/6, DT; David E. Kaufman, *Jewhooing the Sixties: American Celebrity and Jewish Identity* (Waltham, MA: Brandeis University Press, 2012), 11; F.H.S., "High Life and Low Morals," *Jewish Chronicle*, December 9, 1960, 38.

22 Stanley Kubrick, qtd. in Eugene Archer, "'Spartacus': Hailed in Farewell," *New York Times*, October 2, 1960.

23 Stanley Kubrick, qtd. in *LA Mirror*, September 21, 1960; Stanley Kubrick, Biography file, AMPAS; Dalton Trumbo, "Report on *Spartacus*: The Two Conflicting Points of View," n.d., 24/6, KD; *LA Times*, September 29, 1960, C9; Larry Ceplair and Christopher Trumbo, *Dalton Trumbo: Blacklisted Hollywood Radical* (Lexington: University Press of Kentucky, 2015), 378.

24 Dalton Trumbo to Edward Lewis, September 21, 1960, 24/8, DT; Stanley Kubrick to Stan Margulies, October 21, 1959, 33/9, KD; Stanley Kubrick, qtd. in Phillips and Hill, *Encyclopedia of Stanley Kubrick*, 374; Kubrick, qtd. in *LA Times*, September 29, 1960, C9; Archer, "Spartacus."

25 Stan Margulies to Jeff Livingston, April 5, 1960, 33/15, KD.

26 Douglas, *Ragman's Son*, 370; Howard Fast, *Spartacus* (1951; repr., London: Bodley Head, 1979), 133–134.

27 Dalton Trumbo to Kirk Douglas, February 24, 1959, 6/4, KD; Douglas, *Ragman's Son*, 357.

28 Kael, *5001 Nights*, 547; Baxter, *Stanley Kubrick*, 133; Stan Margulies, *Spartacus: The Illustrated Story of the Motion Picture Production* (Saint Louis: Bryna Productions/ Universal Pictures, 1960); "'Spartacus' at-a-Glance," August 1960, USCCBC; Elizabeth Schmitt, n.d., USCCBC.

29 Arthur Koestler, *Gladiators*, Kindle ed. (1939; repr., New York: Vintage, 1999); Dalton Trumbo, "A Last General Note on *Spartacus*," 24/8, KD.

30 *LA Mirror*, September 21, 1960, Kubrick, Biography file, AMPAS; Ceplair and Trumbo, *Dalton Trumbo*, 391.

31 Ina Rae Hark, "Animals or Romans: Looking at Masculinity in *Spartacus*," in *Screening the Male: Exploring Masculinities in Hollywood Cinema*, ed. Steven Cohan and Ina Rae Hark (London: Routledge, 1994), 170n7; "The New Pictures, 1960," *Time*, October 24, 1960, 102; Russ Metty, qtd. in LoBrutto, *Stanley Kubrick*, 185.

32 Tony Curtis, qtd. in David Hughes, *The Complete Kubrick* (London: Virgin, 2001), 69; Tony Curtis, *The Autobiography* (London: Mandarin, 1995), 181; Stanley Kubrick, qtd. in Peter Bogdanovich, "What They Say about Stanley Kubrick," *New York Times Magazine*, July 4, 1999; Cocks, *Wolf at the Door*, 26; Fiona Radford, "Having His Cake and Eating It Too: Stanley Kubrick and *Spartacus*," in Ljujić, Kramer, and Daniels, *Stanley Kubrick*, 110.

33 Curtis, *Autobiography*, 186; Dalton Trumbo, commentary, *Spartacus*, DVD.

34 Trumbo, "Notes," DT; Stanley Kubrick to Eddie Lewis and Sam Jackson (Trumbo), November 20, 1959, 24/ 6, DT.

35 Edward Lewis and Trumbo, commentary, *Spartacus*, DVD.

36 Margulies, *Spartacus*; Monica Silveira Cyrino, *Big Screen Rome* (Malden, MA: Wiley-Blackwell, 2005), 116.

37 Phillips, *Stanley Kubrick*, 75.

38 Natalie Zemon Davis, "Trumbo and Kubrick Argue History," *Raritan* 22, no. 1 (2002): 184; Margulies, *Spartacus*.

39 Kubrick to Lewis and Jackson, DT; Dalton Trumbo, "General Broadcast," May 16, 1959, 24/6, KD; Trumbo, "Report on *Spartacus*," n.d., 27/6, DT.

40 Stanley Kubrick, qtd. in Davis, *Slaves on Screen*, 39–40.

Chapter 3   Kubrick's Double

1 Stanley Kubrick, qtd. in Jan Harlan, *Stanley Kubrick: A Life in Pictures*, DVD.

2 Frederick Wilcox Dupee, "Introduction," *Anchor Review* 2 (1957): 1–13; Helen Lawrenson, "The Man Who Scandalized the World," *Esquire*, August 1960, 71, 72; Dwight Macdonald to Stanley Kubrick, April 21, 1959, folder 693, box, 26, MS 730, DM; Kubrick to Macdonald, August 4, 1960, 26/693, Macdonald to Kubrick, December 7, 1960, folder 693, box, 26, MS 730, DM; Jack Kerouac, *Esquire* 54 (1960): 221.

3 Ginna, "Artist Speaks for Himself"; Ciment, *Kubrick* (1983), 146; Kubrick, qtd. in Jan Harlan, *Stanley Kubrick: A Life in Pictures,* DVD.

4 Lionel Trilling, "The Last Lover: Vladimir Nabokov's *Lolita*," *Encounter* 11, no. 4 (1958): 15, 19; Stanley Kubrick and Vladimir Nabokov, "Typed Sheet Entitled 'Nabokov,'" n.d., SK/10/8/2, SKA; Ginna, "Artist Speaks for Himself"; Stanley Kubrick to Peter Ustinov, May 20, 1960, SK/10/8/4, SKA; Terry Southern, interview with Stanley Kubrick, n.d., 128/8, TS.

5 Trilling, "Last Lover," 15.

6 Kubrick to Ustinov, SKA; Herr, *Kubrick*, 22; John Trevelyan to Stanley Kubrick, December 7, 1960, PCA;

7 Vladimir Nabokov, *Lolita* (1955; repr., London: Transworld, 1961), 267, 210.

8 *Hollywood Reporter*, October 3, 1958; Calder Willingham, "Lolita," screenplay, SK/10/1/1, SKA; Stanley Kubrick to Vladimir Nabokov, December 8, 1959,

Harris-Kubrick Pictures, Berg Coll MSS Nabokov, VN; James B. Harris, "The Five-O Interview," Fall 2002, www.hollywoodfiveo.com/archive/issue2/exclusive/harris/harris.htm.

9 Nabokov, *Lolita*, 9.

10 Ibid., 328; Trilling, "Last Lover," 19; Franz Kafka, "A Report for an Academy," *Jew*, November 1919, http://records.viu.ca/~johnstoi/kafka/reportforacademy.htm.

11 Nabokov, *Lolita*, 79, 83–84, 275; Alfred Appel Jr., ed., *The Annotated "Lolita"* (London: Penguin, 1971), 423.

12 Walter M. Abbott, SJ, to Monsignor Thomas F. Little, October 6, 1960, folders 27–29, box 27, USCCBC.

13 James Mason, narration, c. 1960, SK/10/1/9, SKA.

14 Naremore, *On Kubrick*, 109.

15 Ibid., 103; Alfred Appel Jr., *Nabokov's Dark Cinema* (New York: Oxford University Press, 1974), 245.

16 "Yet Another Face for Peter Sellers," *Jewish Chronicle*, November 20, 1959, 35; Miriam Karlin, *Some Sort of Life: My Autobiography* (London: Oberon, 2007), 91; Roger Lewis, *The Life and Death of Peter Sellers* (London: Arrow, 1994), 45–48.

17 Max Horkheimer and Theodor Adorno, *Dialectic of Enlightenment*, trans. John Cumming (London: Lane, 1973), 182; Cuddihy, *Ordeal of Civility*, 12–13; Lee Siegel, *Not Remotely Controlled: Notes on Television* (New York: Basic, 2007), 89.

18 James Mason, *Before I Forget* (London: Hamilton, 1981), 320, 318; C. Kubrick, *Stanley Kubrick*, 80; LoBrutto, *Stanley Kubrick*, 205.

19 Shelley Winters, *Shelley II: Best of Times, Worst of Times* (London: Muller, 1990), 349; Oswald Morris, qtd. in LoBrutto, *Stanley Kubrick*, 205.

20 Kubrick to Ustinov, SKA.

21 Ibid.; Andrea Pitzer, "'A Gentile's House': Lolita and the Holocaust," accessed June 6, 2017, http://cjmvoices.blogspot.co.uk/2016/08/a-gentiles-house-lolita-and-holocaust.html?m=1; Naremore, *On Kubrick*, 112; Phillips, *Stanley Kubrick*, 100; Richard Corliss, *Lolita* (London: British Film Institute, 2008), 47–48.

22 Nabokov, "Lolita: A Screenplay," n.d., Harris-Kubrick Pictures, Berg Coll MSS Nabokov, VN; Nabokov, part screenplay, c. 1959–1960, SK/10/1/3, SKA; Nabokov and Kubrick, *Lolita* screenplay, scene 47b-13, May 10, 1960, SK/10/1/22, SKA; Nabokov, "Lolita," VN; Susan L. Mizruchi, "*Lolita* in History," *American Literature* 75, no. 3 (2003): 639; Herr, *Kubrick*.

23 Bill Krohn, *Stanley Kubrick* (Paris: Cahiers du Cinéma, 2010), 44; Nabokov, *Lolita* screenplay, October 31, 1960, SK/10/1/26, SKA.

24 Michael Rogin, *Independence Day* (London: British Film Institute 1998), 49.

25 Phillips, *Stanley Kubrick* 88; Ed Sikov, *Mr. Strangelove: A Biography of Peter Sellers* (New York; Hyperion, 2002), 150, 4.

26 Robert Roper, *Nabokov in America: On the Road to Lolita* (New York: Bloomsbury, 2015), 240; "Lolita" dialogue continuity, labeled "S. Kubrick Corrected Copy" (containing notes to translators and dubbing directors), September 1961, SK/10/3/3, SKA.

27 Baxter, *Stanley Kubrick*, 158; Naremore, *On Kubrick*, 111; Corliss, *Lolita*, 47; *Lolita* daily continuity reports, January 5, 1961, SK/10/3/4, SKA.

28 Hannah Arendt, "The Jew as Pariah: A Hidden Tradition," *Jewish Social Studies* 6 (1944): 111; Stanley Kubrick, qtd. in Ronson, "After Stanley Kubrick"; Nabokov and Kubrick, "Annotated Screenplay," c. 1960, SK/10/1/4, SKA; Nabokov and Kubrick,

"Corrected Rough 1st Draft," c. September 9, 1959–October 31, 1960, SK/10/1/23, SKA; *Lolita*, breakdown copy, based on script, October 31, 1960, SK/10/1/25, SKA; Mason, *Before I Forget*, 318; Homi Bhabha, *The Location of Culture* (London: Routledge, 1994), 123.

29 Stanley Kubrick, qtd. in Ciment, *Kubrick* (1983), 156; Stanley Kubrick, "Outline of 'Lolita,'" May 20, 1960, SK/10/8/4, SKA.

30 Roper, *Nabokov in America*, 240; *New York Mirror*, June 14, 1960, 30; Cocks, *Wolf at the Door*, 102.

31 Sander L. Gilman, *Jewish Frontiers: Essays on Bodies, Histories, and Identities* (New York: Palgrave Macmillan, 2003), 146; Franz Kafka, "A Country Doctor," in his *A Country Doctor* (Leipzig: Wolff, 1919).

32 Gilman, *Jewish Frontiers*, 96–100.

33 Cocks, *Wolf at the Door*, 102; Patrick Webster, *Love and Death in Kubrick: A Critical Study of the Films from "Lolita" through "Eyes Wide Shut"* (Jefferson, NC: McFarland, 2011), 26.

34 Jan Harlan, *Stanley Kubrick: A Life in Pictures*, DVD.

35 Webster, *Love and Death*, 270n86; *London Evening News*, July 2, 1962, SK/10/6/3i, SKA.

36 "Corrected Rough 1st Draft," SKA; Nabokov, *Lolita*, 203; *Lolita* daily production progress report, February 3 and 6, 1961, SK/10/3/2, SKA; *Lolita* screenplay, SKA; Part screenplay, c. 1959–1960, SK10/1/3, SKA; James Harris, qtd. in Castle, *Stanley Kubrick Archives*, 333; Negatives, c. 1960–1961, SK/10/9/2, SKA.

37 "Artists Interviewed Re 'Lolita,'" October 13, 1960, SK/10/2/4, SKA; LoBrutto, *Stanley Kubrick*, 220.

38 Kubrick, "Outline of 'Lolita,'" SKA; Kubrick, "Sight and Sound," January 26, 1972, SK/13/8/3/69, SKA.

39 Roger Lewis, qtd. in Humphrey Carpenter, *Spike Milligan: The Biography* (London: Hodder and Stoughton, 2003), 93; Nabokov, *Lolita*, 269.

40 Rebecca Bell-Metereau, "The Three Faces of *Lolita*; or, How I Learned to Stop Worrying and Love the Adaptation," in *Authorship in Film Adaptation*, ed. Jack Boozer (Austin: University of Texas Press, 2008), 214, 216.

41 Terry Southern, "An Interview with Stanley Kubrick," New York City, 1962, accessed June 6, 2017, www.archiviokubrick.it/english/words/interviews/1962southern.html; Kubrick to Ustinov, SKA; Geoffrey Shurlock, memos, September 11, 1958, and March 18, 1959, PCA.

42 Shurlock, memo, September 11, 1958, PCA; Hollis Alpert, "The Bubble Gum Siren," *Saturday Review*, June 23, 1962, 40; Bosley Crowther, "Screen: *Lolita*, Vladimir Nabokov's Adaptation of His Novel," *New York Times*, June 14, 1962, 23; Trevelyan to Kubrick, PCA; James B. Harris to Martin Quigley, January 30, 1961, PCA.

43 Stanley Kauffman, "Humbug Humbug," *New Republic*, July 2, 1962, 29–30; Francis Russell, "Petronius Redivivus," *National Review*, September 11, 1962, 198–200; Shurlock, memo, PCA; Kubrick to Ustinov, SKA; Southern, interview with Stanley Kubrick, TS.

44 Ciment, *Kubrick* (2003), 92; Kael, *5001 Nights*, 335; Appel, *Annotated "Lolita,"* 323.

45 Jerold J. Abrams, "The Logic of *Lolita*: Kubrick, Nabokov, and Poe," in *The Philosophy of Stanley Kubrick*, ed. Jerold J. Abrams (Lexington: University of Kentucky Press, 2007), 125; Walker, *It's Only a Movie*, 291.

46 Nabokov, *Lolita*, 34; Christiane Kubrick, qtd. in Lewis Jones, "My Stanley Was Not Paranoid," *Telegraph*, October 9, 2002; "Stanley Kubrick: Trivia," accessed June 6, 2017, http://m.imdb.com/name/nm0000040/trivia.

47 C. Kubrick, *Stanley Kubrick*, 85; Mason, *Before I Forget*, 320.

48 "Stanley Kubrick: Trivia"; C. Kubrick, *Stanley Kubrick*, 82.

49 Naremore, *On Kubrick*, 111.

50 "*Lolita* (1962): Goofs," accessed June 6, 2017, www.imdb.com/title/tt0056193/trivia ?tab=gf; Krohn, *Stanley Kubrick*, 33; Dan Bates to Stanley Kubrick, August 7, 1966, SK/12/8/1/61, SKA.

51 Kaufman, *Jewhooing the Sixties*, 38; Jonathan Freedman, "Miller, Monroe, and the Remaking of Jewish Masculinity," in *Arthur Miller's America: Theater and Culture in a Time of Change*, ed. Enoch Brater (Ann Arbor: University of Michigan Press, 2005), 151.

52 Freedman, "Remaking of Jewish Masculinity," 151; Pauline Kael, "*Lolita*," accessed June 6, 2017, http://scrapsfromtheloft.com/2016/10/18/lolita-review-pauline-kael/; Kagan, *Cinema of Stanley Kubrick*, 104; Karyn Stuckey, "Re-writing Nabokov's *Lolita*: Kubrick, the Creative Adaptor," in Ljujić, Kramer, and Daniels, *Stanley Kubrick*, 118–135.

Chapter 4 Banality and the Bomb

1 LoBrutto, *Stanley Kubrick*, 227; Dwight Macdonald to Stanley Kubrick, September 4, 1962, 26/693, MS 730, DM.

2 Peter Krämer, "'To Prevent the Present Heat from Dissipating': Stanley Kubrick and the Marketing of *Dr. Strangelove* (1964)," *InMedia* 3 (2013), http://inmedia .revues.org/634, para. 18, n. 40; Stanley Kubrick, script, c. 1962, SK/11/1/7, SKA; Stanley Kubrick, handwritten note on letter from Donald Keys to Stanley Kubrick, July 9, 1964, SK/11/9/97/2/3, SKA; William Gaines, qtd. in Dwight R. Decker and Gary Groth, "An Interview with the Man behind EC," *Comics Journal* 81 (May 1983): 83.

3 Stanley Kubrick to Robert Murray, July 29, 1964, SK/11/9/1, SKA.

4 Kubrick, script, c. 1962, SKA; "*Lolita* Producer-Director Team Announces New Project," draft press release, n.d., SK/11/6/71, SKA; Terry Southern, typescript fragments, autobiography re: London and Kubrick, March 25, 1994, folder 10, box 123, TS.

5 Michael Broderick, *Reconstructing Strangelove: Inside Stanley Kubrick's "Nightmare Comedy"* (New York: Wallflower, 2016), 21; George Case, *Calling Dr. Strangelove: The Anatomy and Influence of the Kubrick Masterpiece* (Jefferson, NC: McFarland, 2014), 22; Stanley Kubrick to Jules Feiffer, December 16, 1958, box 8, MSS83993, JF; Stephen E. Kercher, *Revel with a Cause: Liberal Satire in Postwar America* (Chicago: University of Chicago Press, 2006), 331, 332; Grant B. Stillman, "Two of the MADdest Scientists: Where Strangelove Meets Dr. No; or, Unexpected Roots for Kubrick's Cold War Classic," *Film History: An International Journal* 20, no. 4 (2008): 487–500; Stanley Kubrick to Joseph Heller, July 30, 1962, I.ii.24, JH; David Seed, *American Science Fiction and the Cold War: Literature and Film* (Edinburgh: Edinburgh University Press, 1999), 148; Joseph Heller, qtd. in Castle, *Stanley Kubrick Archives*, 362; Peter George, letter to editor, *Life*, August 23, 1964, SK/11/9/94, SKA; LoBrutto, *Stanley Kubrick*, 249.

6   Kubrick, script, c. 1962, SKA; Theodore J. Flicker to Stanley Kubrick, December 16, 1962, SK/11/2/3, SKA; Stanley Kubrick, "Notes," SK/11/2/7, SKA.

7   Stephen E. Kercher, "Putting on the *Shpritz*: Postwar Jewish American Satire and Parody," in *Jews and American Popular Culture*, vol. 2, *Music, Theater, Popular Art, and Literature*, ed. Paul Buhle (Westport, CT: Praeger, 2007), 308.

8   Stanley Kubrick, interview with Terry Southern, n.d., 128/8, TS; Kubrick, script, c. 1962, SKA; Kubrick, qtd. in Castle, *Stanley Kubrick Archives*, 362; James Earl Jones, qtd. in Hughes, *Complete Kubrick*, 117.

9   Stanley Kubrick, script, August 31, 1962, SK/11/1/1i, SKA; Kubrick, script, c. 1962, SKA.

10 Rosten, *Joys of Yiddish*, 88, 365; LoBrutto, *Stanley Kubrick*, 155; Kaufman, *Jewhooing the Sixties*, 121; Kubrick, script, August 31, 1962, SKA; Stanley Kubrick, "Notes to Translators and Dubbing Directors," SK/11/4/1/2, SKA; Pat Ivens, "Comparison of the Two Endings," SK/11/9/68, SKA; Kubrick, script, c. 1962, SKA; "Intended Screen Play Revisions for the Novel 'Red Alert,'" October 25, 1961, SK/11/1/13, SKA.

11 Stanley Kubrick, qtd. in Nelson, *Kubrick*, 93; Kubrick, script, August 31, 1962, SKA; MPAA title registration for Polaris Productions, *Dr. Strangelove*, n.d., SK/11/9/124, SKA.

12 Gene D. Phillips, qtd. in Castle, *Stanley Kubrick Archives*, 348; LoBrutto, *Stanley Kubrick*, 239; C. Kubrick, qtd. in *Stanley Kubrick: A Life in Pictures*, DVD.

13 Pamela Carlton, qtd. in *Inside Dr. Strangelove*, dir. David Naylor, (United States: Columbia, 2000); Richard Corliss, *Talking Pictures: Screenwriters of Hollywood* (London: David and Charles, 1975), 350.

14 Lewis H. Rubman, letter to editor, *Commentary* 38, no. 4 (1964): 13; Bosley Crowther, "'Dr. Strangelove,' a Shattering Sick Joke," *New York Times*, January 30, 1964, 24; Lawrence J. Epstein, *The Haunted Smile: The Story of Jewish Comedians in America* (New York: Public Affairs, 2001), 169; Philip Hartung, *Commonweal*, May 3, 1968, USCCBC; Allen Ginsberg, "America," 1956, accessed June 6, 2017, www.writing.upenn.edu/~afilreis/88/america.html; Ginsberg *Howl*, 1955, accessed June 6, 2017, www.wussu.com/poems/agh.htm; J. D. Salinger, *The Catcher in the Rye* (1951; repr., London: Penguin, 1994), 127.

15 Kercher, *Revel with a Cause*, 106.

16 "*Characters*: Rough Delineation," SK/11/1/9, SKA; Robert Kolker, *The Extraordinary Image* (New Brunswick, NJ: Rutgers University Press, 2016), 177; Stanley Kubrick, qtd. in Castle, *Stanley Kubrick Archives*, 363.

17 Kubrick, "*Characters*," SKA; Penelope Gilliatt, qtd. in Walker, Taylor, and Ruchti, *Stanley Kubrick, Director*, 145.

18 Eric Rhode, "Second Coming," *Listener*, May 9, 1968, USCCBC; Peter Kramer, *Dr. Strangelove* (London: British Film Institute, 2014), 12; C. Kubrick, qtd. in "Dr. Strangelove 50th Anniversary Panel Discussion," YouTube video, 14:16, British Film Institute, January 31, 2014, www.youtube.com/watch?v=MM7wSNf_J08.

19 Kubrick, "Index Cards," c. 1963, SK/11/2/7, SKA; Kubrick, script, c. 1962, SKA.

20 Kramer, *Dr. Strangelove*, 10; Raul Hilberg, *Destruction of the European Jews* (New York: Quadrangle, 1967), 649, 189 (all quotations are taken from this edition).

21 Hannah Arendt, *Eichmann in Jerusalem: A Report on the Banality of Evil* (1963; repr., London: Penguin, 1994), 287, 125, 276, 48–49.

22 Stanley Kubrick, qtd. in Walker, Taylor, and Ruchti, *Stanley Kubrick, Director*, 184; Joseph Heller, qtd. in Castle, *Stanley Kubrick Archives*, 363.

23 Stanley Milgram, *Obedience to Authority: An Experimental View* (London: Tavistock, 1974), 7; Milgram, "Behavioral Study of Obedience," *Journal of Abnormal and Social Psychology* 67, no. 4 (1963): 371–378; Milgram, *New Haven Register*, May 21, 1963, 1; Milgram, *Yale Daily News*, October, 31, 1963, 1.

24 Peter Bryant, *Red Alert*, Kindle ed. (1958; repr., New York: RosettaBooks, 2014); Kubrick, "*Characters*," SKA; Script with cast list, January 1, 1963, SK/11/1/22, SKA; Stanley Kubrick to Peter George, February 19, 1963; George to Kubrick, February 28, 1963; Kubrick to George, March 4, 1963, all in SK/11/9/61, SKA; Flicker to Kubrick, SKA; Paul Igor Tamarin to Stanley Kubrick, January 7, 1965, SK/11/9/105, SKA.

25 Hilberg, *Destruction*, 668, 652, 658; Arendt, *Eichmann in Jerusalem*, 276, 48–49.

26 Kubrick, "Notes to Translators," SKA; Kramer, *Dr. Strangelove*, 89.

27 Eugen Sharin to Stanley Kubrick, September 7, 1965; Kubrick to Sharin, September 23, 1965; Kubrick to Leo Jaffe, September 23, 1965; Jaffe to Kubrick, October 14, 1965; Mo Rothman, memo to Jaffe, October 20, 1965; Kubrick to Jaffe, October 22, 1965, all in SK/11/9/35, SKA.

28 Dwight Macdonald, "A Theory of Mass Culture," *Diogenes* 3 (Summer 1953): 1–17, repr. in Bernard Rosenberg and David Manning White, eds., *Mass Culture: The Popular Arts in America* (New York: Free Press, 1957), 69; Jon Petrie, "The Secular Word Holocaust: Scholarly Myths, History, and 20th Century Meanings," *Journal of Genocide Research* 2, no. 1 (2000): 44; Bruno Bettelheim, "Comment," *Midstream* 7, no. 2 (1961): 86; Eugene Burdick and Harvey Wheeler, *Fail-Safe* (New York: McGraw-Hill, 1962), 230; Elie Wiesel, "Resistance in Hell," *New Leader*, August 5, 1963, 21; Lenny Bruce, qtd. in Kaufman, *Jewhooing the Sixties*, 136; Epstein, *Haunted Smile*, 171.

29 A. H. Weiler, "The East: Kubrick's and Sellers' New Film," *New York Times*, May 6, 1962, 149; Kubrick, "*Characters*," SKA; Kubrick, script, August 31, 1962, SKA; Peter George, *Dr. Strangelove; or, How I Learned to Stop Worrying and Love the Bomb* (1963; repr., London: Prion, 2000), 141, 35.

30 Kubrick to George, April 8, 1963, SK/11/9/61, SKA; Peter Sellers, qtd. in Lewis, *Life and Death*, 777; Sellers, qtd. in Mitchell Glazer, "The Strange World of Peter Sellers," *Rolling Stone*, April 17, 1980, 45.

31 Grant B. Stillman, "Two of the MADdest Scientists: Where Strangelove Meets Dr. No; or, Unexpected Roots for Kubrick's Cold War Classic," *Film History* 20 no. 4 (2008): 487–500; Ian Fleming, *Dr. No* (1958; repr., London: Penguin, 2002), 239.

32 Lewis Mumford, letter to the editor, *New York Times*, March 1, 1964, AMPAS; James A. Wechsler, "Strangelove," *New York Post*, February 25, 1964, 28; Gerald Forshey, "Review: *Dr. Strangelove*," *Christian Advocate*, July 30, 1964, 10; Joe Goldberg, "Dr. Kubrick," *Seventh Art*, Spring 1964, 26.

33 Max Lerner, "Folly on Film," *New York Post*, April 16, 1963, 33; Midge Decter, "The Strangely Polite 'Dr. Strangelove,'" *Commentary* 37, no. 5 (1964): 75–77.

34 C. Kubrick, *Stanley Kubrick*, 93, 95; Kubrick, "Intended Screen Play Revisions," SKA; Naremore, *On Kubrick*, 125; Glazer, "Strange World," 45–46; Walker, Taylor, and Ruchti, *Stanley Kubrick, Director*, 138; Arthur C. Clarke, draft of "Son of Dr. Strangelove; or, How I Learned to Stop Worrying and Love Stanley Kubrick,"

n.d., SK/12/8/1/10, SKA; Michael J. Neufeld, *Von Braun: Dreamer of Space, Engineer of War* (New York: Knopf, 2007), 406; Robert A. Levine to Stanley Kubrick, April 23, 1964, SK/11/7/17 3/3, SKA.

35 Stanley Kubrick, qtd. in Castle, *Stanley Kubrick Archives*, 364; Ciment, *Kubrick* (1983), 156; Roper, *Nabokov in America*, 240; Ivens, "Comparison," SKA.

36 Kubrick to George, April 8, 1963, SK/11/9/61, SKA.

37 Hughes, *Complete Kubrick*, 122; Eugene Burdick to Louis Blau, December 26, 1961, SK/11/9/14, SKA; Stanley Kubrick to Burdick and Harvey Wheeler, January 19, 1962, SK/11/1/13, SKA; Rebecca Raphael, "The Doomsday Body; or, Dr. Strangelove as Disabled Cyborg," *Golem: Journal of Religion and Monsters* 1, no. 1 (2006), http://lomibao.net/golem/article.php?id=1.

38 *Inside the Making of Dr. Strangelove*, dir. David Naylor (United States: Warner Bros., 2000); Ciment, *Kubrick* (1983), 50; Stanley Kubrick, qtd. in Castle, *Stanley Kubrick Archives*, 360; LoBrutto, *Stanley Kubrick*, 231; Goldberg, "Dr. Kubrick," 26; Pauline Kael, "*A Clockwork Orange*: Stanley Strangelove," *New Yorker*, January 1, 1972.

39 Ivens, "Comparison," SKA; Leslie Hodgson to Stanley Kubrick, October 29, 1961, SK/11/9/68 SKA; Decter, "Strangely Polite," 77.

40 Ciment, *Kubrick* (1983), 156.

Chapter 5   Kubrick and Kabbalah

1 Stanley Kubrick, qtd. in Eric Nordern, "*Playboy* Interview: Stanley Kubrick (1968)," in Phillips, *Stanley Kubrick Interviews*, 48.

2 Anthony Frewin, qtd. in Castle, *Stanley Kubrick Archives*, 378, 517; Walker, *It's Only a Movie*, 286; Madeline Church, letter to the editor, *Guardian*, April 3, 2004; *BBC Doctor Who Magazine, 50th Anniversary Souvenir Issue*, November 2013, 99; *Strangelove* script, August 31, 1962, SK/11/1/1i, SKA.

3 Stanley Kubrick to Arthur C. Clarke, March 31, 1964, SK/12/8/1/65, SKA; Stanley Kubrick and Arthur C. Clarke, "Journey beyond the Stars," SK/12/1/1/2, SKA.

4 Kubrick to Clarke, November 23, 1967, SK/12/8/1/11, SKA, Kubrick to Alex North, January 26, 1968, SK/12/8/1/50, SKA.

5 Stanley Kubrick, qtd. in Walker, Taylor, and Ruchti, *Stanley Kubrick, Director*, 184.

6 Stanley Kubrick, qtd. in Joseph Gelmis, *The Film Director as Superstar* (New York: Doubleday, 1970), 34; Nordern, "*Playboy* Interview," in Phillips, *Stanley Kubrick Interviews*, 48; Kubrick, handwritten note on letter from Clarke to Kubrick, August 25, 1965, SK/12/8/1/11, SKA; Piers Bizony, *2001: Filming the Future* (London: Aurum, 2000), 16.

7 Stanley Kubrick, qtd. in Baxter, *Stanley Kubrick*, 210; Gelmis, *Film Director as Superstar*, 397–398; C. Kubrick, interview with Charlie Rose, YouTube video, 2001, accessed June 8, 2017, www.youtube.com/watch?v=VrtJXH2hRGI; Arthur C. Clarke, qtd. in Jerome Agel, *The Making of Kubrick's 2001* (New York: Signet, 1970), 306.

8 Title registration for Polaris Productions, MPAA, SK/11/9/124, SKA; Arthur C. Clarke, qtd. in Hughes, *Complete Kubrick*, 135.

9 Robert Gluck, "Exhibition Looks Back on Kubrick, Legendary Director Who 'Knew He Looked Jewish,'" *Algemeiner*, March 22, 2013, www.algemeiner.com/2013/03/22/exhibition-looks-back-on-kubrick-legendary-director-who-knew-he-looked-jewish%E2%80%99/.

10 Bernstein, "Little Game," 85; LoBrutto, *Stanley Kubrick*, 257–258; Arthur C. Clarke, "Draft of 'Son of Dr. Strangelove; or, How I Learned to Stop Worrying and Love Stanley Kubrick,'" n.d., SK/12/8/1/10, SKA; Jan Harlan, qtd. in Gluck, "Exhibition Looks Back."

11 Arthur C. Clarke, *The Lost Worlds of 2001* (London: Sidgwick and Jackson, 1978), 35; Agel, *Making of Kubrick's 2001*, 304.

12 Barnett Newman, "Memorial Letter for Howard Putzel," 1945, qtd. in John O'Neill, ed., *Barnett Newman: Selected Writings and Interviews* (Berkeley: University of California Press, 1990), 97–98; Matthew Baigell, "Barnett Newman's Stripe Paintings and Kabbalah: A Jewish Take," *American Art* 8, no. 2 (1994): 32–43.

13 C. Kubrick, *Stanley Kubrick*, 129.

14 "Is God Dead?," *Time*, April 8, 1966.

15 Naomi Seidman, "Elie Wiesel and the Scandal of Jewish Rage," *Jewish Social Studies* 3, no. 1 (1996): 2; François Mauriac, qtd. in Petrie, "Secular Word Holocaust," 42; Richard L. Rubenstein, *After Auschwitz: Radical Theology and Contemporary Judaism* (Indianapolis: Bobbs-Merrill, 1966); Gershom Scholem "The Golem of Prague and the Golem of Rehovoth," *Commentary* 41, no. 1 (1966): 64; "The State of Jewish Belief," *Commentary* 42, no. 2 (1966): 71–160.

16 Henry Popkin, "The Vanishing Jew of Our Popular Culture: The Little Man Who Is No Longer There," *Commentary*, July 1, 1952, www.commentarymagazine.com/articles/the -vanishing-jew-of-our-popular-culturethe-little-man-who-is-no-longer-there/.

17 Clarke, *Lost Worlds of 2001*, 34; Stanley Kubrick to Roger Caras, February 6, 1967, SK/12/8/1/7ii, SKA; Alexander Walker, qtd. in Ciment, *Kubrick* (1983), 41; Fred Ordway, qtd. in Agel, *Making of Kubrick's 2001*, 300.

18 Stanley Kubrick and Marvin Minsky, correspondence, March 26, 1965–October 29, 1965, SK/12/8/1/34, SKA; Marvin Minsky, "Steps towards Artificial Intelligence," *Proceedings of the IRE* 49, no. 1 (1961): 369; Scholem "Golem of Prague," 64.

19 Stanley Kubrick, qtd. in Gene Siskel, "Kubrick: Director of the Decade," c. 1972–1979, SK/13/7/9, SKA; Carolyn Geduld, *2001: A Space Odyssey* (Bloomington: Indiana University Press, 1973), 34, 35, 54, 60, 62.

20 Robert Poole, "*2001: A Space Odyssey* and 'The Dawn of Man,'" in Ljujić, Kramer, and Daniels, *Stanley Kubrick*, 176.

21 Maryvonne Butcher, "Light Years Away," *Tablet*, May 4, 1968, folder 1, box 138, USCCBC; Joel Finler, *The Hollywood Story* (London: Wallflower, 2003), 156.

22 Clarke, *Lost Worlds of 2001*, 51–52; Fred Myers, "Sci-Fi Triumph," *Christian Century*, June 26, 1968, USCCBC.

23 Gelmis, *Film Director as Superstar*, 306; Arthur C. Clarke, "The Sentinel," in *The Best of Arthur C. Clarke, 1937–1971* (London: Sphere, 1973), 121; Joseph Dan, *Kabbalah: A Very Short Introduction* (Oxford: Oxford University Press, 2003), 6; LoBrutto, *Stanley Kubrick*, 284.

24 Harry M. Geduld, "Return to Melies: Reflections on the Science-Fiction Film," *Humanities* 28 (November–December 1968): 28; Willmon K. White, *Christian Advocate*, June 27, 1968; Penelope Gilliatt, "After Man," *New Yorker*, April 13, 1968, repr. in Agel, *Making of Kubrick's 2001*, 212; John Simon, *Tablet*, May 4, 1968, folder 1, box 138, USCCBC.

25 Hillel Halkin, "Law in the Desert," *Jewish Review of Books*, Spring 2011, 43; Mort Drucker and Dick De Bartolo, "201 Min. of a Space Idiocy," *Mad* 125 (March 1969), 10.

26 First draft outline, July 13, 1964, SK/12/1/1/1, SKA.
27 Clarke, *Lost Worlds of 2001*, 71; First draft outline, SKA.
28 Arthur C. Clarke, *Childhood's End* (1953; repr. New York: Del Ray, 1990), 85; Hollis Alpert, "Fantastic Journey," *Saturday Review*, April 20, 1968, 48; Kubrick, quoted in Franz Kafka, *Parables and Paradoxes* (New York: Schocken, 1961), 33; Agel, *Making of Kubrick's 2001*, 218; Geduld, *2001*, 41; Joseph Morgenstern, "Kubrick's Cosmos," *Newsweek*, April 15, 1968.
29 Arthur C. Clarke, *2001: A Space Odyssey* (New York: Signet, 1968), 135; Joseph Campbell, *The Hero with the Thousand Faces*, 3rd ed. (Novato, CA: New World Library, 2008), 131; LoBrutto, *Stanley Kubrick*, 278–279.
30 Mitchell P. Marcus, "Computer Science, the Informational, and Jewish Mysticism," *Technology in Society* 21 (1999): 368; Scholem "Golem of Prague," 63; Gershom G. Scholem, *On the Kabbalah and Its Symbolism*, trans. Ralph Manheim (New York: Schocken, 1965), 159; Clarke, *Lost Worlds of 2001*, 34, 39.
31 Bernstein, "Little Game," 92; Louis Blau to Stanley Kubrick, August 22, 1967, SKA; LoBrutto, Stanley Kubrick, 278.
32 Kubrick and Clarke, "Journey beyond the Stars," SKA.
33 Abraham Cahan, *The Rise of David Levinsky* (1917; repr., New York: Penguin, 1993), 501–502; Gary Lockwood, qtd. in David Konow, "A Look Back at Stanley Kubrick's *2001*," *Tech Guru Daily*, June 16, 2012, www.tgdaily.com/games-and-entertainment -features/64088-a-look-back-at-stanley-kubricks-2001#JX7vmLoVcxFodhZr.99.
34 Keir Dullea, qtd. in Agel, *Making of Kubrick's 2001*, 313.
35 *London Evening News*, July 2, 1962, Press Binder, SK/10/6/3i, SKA; John Livings-ton Lowes, *The Road to Xanadu: A Study in the Ways of the Imagination* (Boston: Houghton Mifflin 1964), 262, 224–227, 228, 238.
36 John Allen, *Christian Science Monitor*, qtd. in Agel, *Making of Kubrick's 2001*, 233; Clarke, qtd. in annotated copy of Agel, *Making of Kubrick's 2001*, SK/12/5/47/2, SKA.
37 Morgenstern, "Kubrick's Cosmos"; Bruno Bettelheim, *The Uses of Enchantment: The Meaning and Importance of Fairy Tales* (London: Peregrine, 1978), 53; Clarke, *Childhood's End*, 117–118.
38 Clarke, *Lost Worlds of 2001*, 36; "Other HAL Screenplay," October 4, 1965–February 25, 1966, SK/12/1/2/3, SKA; Rodger Kamanetz, *Burnt Books: Rabbi Nachman of Bratslav and Franz Kakfa* (New York: Nextbook/Schocken, 2010), 225; Scholem, *Kabbalah and Its Symbolism*, 12; Volker Fischer, "Designing the Future: On Pragmatic Forecasting in *2001: A Space Odyssey*," in Reichmann, *Stanley Kubrick*, 118.
39 Stanley Kubrick, qtd. in Gelmis, *Film Director as Superstar*, 304; Stuart Freeborn, "*2001: A Space Odyssey* Special," BBC Radio 4, November 30, 2014; John Simon, qtd. in Agel, *Making of Kubrick's 2001*, 244.
40 Incomplete novel text, July 1964, SK/12/1/1/2, SKA; Gelmis, *Film Director as Superstar*, 397.
41 Myers, "Sci-Fi Triumph"; LoBrutto, *Stanley Kubrick*, 312.

Chapter 6   A Mechanical Mensch

1 Anthony Burgess, *A Clockwork Orange* (London: Heinemann, 1962), 37.
2 C. Kubrick, qtd. in Nick James, "At Home with the Kubricks," *Sight and Sound* 9, no. 9 (1999): 12–18; Kubrick, qtd. in Penelope Houston, "Kubrick Country,"

Saturday Review, December 25, 1971, repr. in Phillips, ed., *Stanley Kubrick Interviews*, 109.

3   Kubrick, qtd. in Houston, "Kubrick Country," in Phillips, *Stanley Kubrick Interviews*, 109; Andrew Bailey, "Stanley Kubrick: A Clockwork Utopia," *Rolling Stone* 100 (January 20, 1972), www.rollingstone.com/movies/features/a-clockwork -utopia-19720120; Kubrick, qtd. in Ciment, *Kubrick* (2003), 163; Kubrick, qtd. in Kagan, *Cinema of Stanley Kubrick*, 181; Judith Crist, "A Feast, and about Time," *New York*, December 20, 1971; Bernard Weinraub, "Kubrick Tells What Makes *Clockwork Orange* Tick," *New York Times*, December 31, 1971.

4   "Kubrick Will Make 'Clockwork' or WB," *Variety*, February 3, 1970; A. H. Weiler, "Kubrick to Adapt *A Clockwork Orange*," *New York Times*, February 3, 1970; "Interview with a Grand Guy," *Write Stuff*, accessed June 9, 2017, www.altx .com/interviews/terry.southern.html; Michel Ciment, qtd. in Castle, *Stanley Kubrick Archives*, 411; Kubrick, loose script sections, February 1970–March 1971, SK/13/1/10, SKA; "Annotated Script: Final Version," 1970, SK/13/1/3, SKA; Kubrick, "'Master Script Copy for Duplication Purposes': Final Version," September 1, 1970, SK/13/1/2, SKA; Ciment, qtd. in Castle, *Stanley Kubrick Archives*, 411; Stanley Kubrick, "*A Clockwork Orange*: Shooting Script," September 7, 1970, SK/13/1/13, SKA.

5   Kirsten Fermaglich, *American Dreams and Nazi Nightmares: Early Holocaust Consciousness and Liberal America, 1957–1965* (Waltham, MA: University Press of New England, 2006), 84.

6   John Ashmead, "The Language of Movies and Kubrick's *Clockwork Orange*," *Alternative*, November 1972, 21; Stanley Kubrick to Gene Siskel, c. 1972, SK/13/7/9, SKA; Emanuel K. Schwartz, "A Psychiatric Analysis of Kubrick's *Clockwork Orange*," *Hollywood Reporter*, January 31, 1972, SK/13/7/11, SKA; Stanley Kubrick, drafts of interview for *Sight and Sound*, January 26, 1972, SK/13/8/3/69, SKA.

7   Edgar H. Schein, Inge Schneier, and Curtis H. Becker, *Coercive Persuasion* (New York: Norton 1961); Robert Jay Lifton, *Thought Reform and the Psychology of Totalism* (New York: Norton 1961); Jody Myers, *Kabbalah and the Spiritual Quest* (Westport, CT: Praeger, 2007), 42–44.

8   Christopher, Lehmann-Haupt, "It's a Wonderful Life," *New York Times*, March 26, 1976, 33.

9   Bailey, "Stanley Kubrick"; Stanley Kubrick, qtd. in Gene Siskel, "Kubrick: Director of the Decade," 1972, SK/13/7/9, SKA; Schwartz, "Psychiatric Analysis."

10 Craig McGregor, "Nice Boy from the Bronx?" *New York Times*, January 30, 1972; Final cast list, April 21, 1971, SK/13/2/9/9, SKA; Stanley Kubrick, qtd. in Gene Siskel, "Kubrick's Creative Concern," *Chicago Tribune*, February 13, 1972, repr. in Phillips, *Stanley Kubrick Interviews*, 122; Malcolm McDowell, qtd. in LoBrutto, *Stanley Kubrick*, 340; Jan Harlan, *Stanley Kubrick*; Hollis Alpert, "Milk-Plus and Ultra-Violence," *Saturday Review*, December 25, 1971, 40; Pauline Kael, "*A Clockwork Orange*: Stanley Strangelove," *New Yorker*, January 1, 1972; William S. Pechter, "Peckinpah and Kubrick: Fire and Ice," *Commentary* 53, no. 3 (1972): 81.

11 Stanley Kubrick, qtd. in Hughes, *Complete Kubrick*, 173; Houston, "Kubrick Country," in Phillips, *Stanley Kubrick Interviews*, 111.

12 John Weightman, "The Light and the Dark," *Encounter*, June 1972, 38; Alexander Walker, "The Case of the Vanishing Bloodstains," *Encounter*, March 1973, 43; Peter J. Rabinowitz, "A Bird of Like Rarest Spun Heavenmetal: Music in *A*

Clockwork Orange," in *Stanley Kubrick's "A Clockwork Orange*," ed. Stuart Y. McDougal (Cambridge: Cambridge University Press, 2003), 129n16; Falsetto, *Stanley Kubrick*, 150; Stephen Mamber, "*A Clockwork Orange*," in *Perspectives on Stanley Kubrick*, ed. Mario Falsetto (New York: Hall, 1996), 178.

13 Michel Ciment, qtd. in Castle, *Stanley Kubrick Archives*, 416; McGregor, "Nice Boy: Kubrick's 'A Clockwork Orange,'" *Playboy* 19, no. 1 (1972): 200–205; Kael, "*Clockwork Orange*."

14 Weinraub, "Kubrick Tells"; Stanley Kubrick, *Take One*, May–June 1971, 28, qtd. in Schwartz, "Psychiatric Analysis."

15 Anthony Burgess, "Clockwork Marmalade," *Listener* 87 (February 17, 1972), 198.

16 Ibid.; Norman Lamm, qtd. in Frewin, *Are We Alone?*, 136; Stanley Kubrick, qtd. in Ciment, *Kubrick* (1983), 149; Kubrick, qtd. in McGregor, "Nice Boy," *New York Times*, 1.

17 Jane Biberman, *Jewish Exponent*, n.d.; Kenneth Matheson, *Jewish Advocate*, February 17, 1972; Leighton Ford, *Kilgore Texas News Herald*, September 18, 1972; Frederic A. Brussat, *Lutheran Forum*, May 1972; John E. Fitzgerald, *New York Catholic News*, December 30, 1971, all in "US: Religious Press," SK/13/6/29/58, SKA.

18 Stanley Kubrick, qtd. in Ciment, *Kubrick* (1983), 149; Kubrick, qtd. in Siskel, "Kubrick's Creative Concern"; Naremore, *On Kubrick*, 161; Burgess, *Clockwork Orange*, 70.

19 Burgess, *Clockwork Orange*, 17, 76.

20 Kubrick, drafts of interview, SKA; Kubrick to Victor Davis, *Daily Express*, qtd. in LoBrutto, *Stanley Kubrick*, 356.

21 Biblical scenes research, c. 1970, SK/13/2/7/8, SKA; Hollis Alpert, "The Day of the Gladiator," *Saturday Review*, October 1, 1960, 32.

22 Scouting lists, August 15, 1970, SK/13/2/9/4, SKA; Jackson Burgess, "*A Clockwork Orange* by Stanley Kubrick," *Film Quarterly* 25, no. 3 (1972): 36; Benzion Kaganoff, *A Dictionary of Jewish Names and Their History* (New York: Schocken, 1977), 139.

23 Stanley Kubrick, "*A Clockwork Orange*: Stanley Kubrick Memorandum on Screenplays," August 18, 1971, SK/13/8/5/10, SKA; Burgess, *Clockwork Orange*, 51; *Albany New York Evangelist*, March, 16, 1972, "US: Religious Press," SK/13/6/29/58, SKA; Robert Hughes, "The Décor of Tomorrow's Hell," *Time*, December 27, 1971, 58.

24 Cocks, *Wolf at the Door*, 126–127; Karlin, *Some Sort of Life*, 42, 135, 81; Winters, *Shelley II*, 360.

25 Philip Strick and Penelope Houston, "Modern Times: An Interview with Stanley Kubrick," *Sight and Sound*, Spring 1972, repr. in Phillips, *Stanley Kubrick Interviews*, 129; Stanley Kubrick, qtd. in Weinraub, "Kubrick Tells"; Cuddihy, *Ordeal of Civility*, 18, 20.

26 Kaganoff, *Dictionary of Jewish Names*, 49; Julian Rice, *Kubrick's Hope: Discovering Optimism from 2001 to Eyes Wide Shut* (Lanham, MD: Scarecrow, 2008), 60.

27 Mamber, "*Clockwork Orange*," in Falsetto, *Perspectives on Stanley Kubrick*, 178; Burgess, "Clockwork Marmalade," 198.

28 Falsetto, *Stanley Kubrick*, 57; Jan Harlan, qtd. in *Stanley Kubrick: A Life in Pictures*, DVD.

29 Ashmead, "Language of Movies," 21.

30 Schwartz, "Psychiatric Analysis."

31 Cocks, *Wolf at the Door*, 127; John Clive, qtd. in Cocks, *Wolf at the Door*.

32 Weinraub, "Kubrick Tells"; Stanley Kubrick to Bernard Weinraub, December 1971, SK/13/8/3/87, SKA.

33 Norbert Elias, *The Civilizing Process: Sociogenetic and Psychogenetic Investigations*, rev. ed., trans. Edmund Jephcott (Malden, MA: Blackwell, 2000), 160.

34 Kubrick to Siskel, SKA; Kubrick, qtd. in LoBrutto, *Stanley Kubrick*, 339–340; *Albany New York Evangelist*, SKA.

35 Kubrick to Siskel, SKA; Kubrick, qtd. in LoBrutto, *Stanley Kubrick*, 339–340; Ciment, *Kubrick* (1983), 149; Kubrick, drafts of interview, SKA.

36 Sigmund Freud, "The Uncanny," 1899, in *An Infantile Neurosis and Other Works*, vol. 17 of *The Standard Edition of the Complete Psychological Works of Sigmund Freud* (London: Hogarth, 1956), 217–256.

37 Burgess, "Clockwork Marmalade," 198; Stanley Kubrick, qtd. in Strick and Houston, "Modern Times," in Phillips, *Stanley Kubrick Interviews*, 129; Vincent D. Foley, "*A Clockwork Orange*: Stanley Kubrick," January 12, 1972, folder 57, box 25, USCCBC.

38 C. Kubrick, *Stanley Kubrick*, 141; Gary Shepherd to Mrs. Baker, June 10, 1971, SK/13/3/12, SKA; Stanley Kubrick, "Annotated Script: 'The Ludovico Treatment' Version," May 1970, SK/13/1/2, SKA; "Kubrick: Degrees of Madness," *Time*, December 20, 1971, 80; Pamela Melnikoff, "Films," *Jewish Chronicle*, January 14, 1972.

Chapter 7   A Spatial Odyssey

1 Jonathan Rosenbaum, "In Dreams Begin Responsibilities," in Geoffrey Cocks, James Diedrick, and Glenn Perusek, eds., *Depth of Field: Stanley Kubrick, Film, and the Uses of History* (Madison: University of Wisconsin Press, 2006), 249.

2 "Kubrick Keeping Next Pic a Secret, Even from Warner," *Variety*, April 16, 1972; Walker, Taylor, and Ruchti, *Stanley Kubrick, Director*, 240; Stanley Kubrick, "Title Early Script-Opening Scene," November 29, 1972, SK/14/1/1, SKA.

3 Ken Adam, qtd. in Baxter, *Stanley Kubrick*, 287; Adam, qtd. in Christopher Frayling, *Ken Adam: The Art of Production Design* (London: Faber and Faber, 2005); Stanley Kubrick, qtd. in Ciment, *Kubrick* (2003), 167; Andrew Sarris, "What Makes Barry Run?," *Village Voice*, December 29, 1975.

4 Barbara Hardy, *Cultural Information Service*, January 1976, 12–13, SK/14/7/8/19, SKA.

5 Willem Hesling, "Kubrick, Thackeray, and *The Memoirs of Barry Lyndon, Esq.*," *Literature/Film Quarterly* 29, no. 4 (2001): 267.

6 Walker, Taylor, and Ruchti, *Stanley Kubrick, Director*, 234, 240; Ken Adam, qtd. in Frayling, *Ken Adam*, 123; Andrew Sanders, introd. to Thackeray, *Memoirs of Barry Lyndon*, xvi.

7 Andrew Birkin, qtd. in Baxter, *Stanley Kubrick*, 276, 278.

8 Thackeray, *Memoirs of Barry Lyndon*, 115; B. F. Dick, "Barry Lyndon," December 17, 1975, folder 66, box 9, USCCBC; Kagan, *Cinema of Stanley Kubrick*, 189; Gavin Lambert, qtd. in Baxter, *Stanley Kubrick*, 278; Sarah Kozloff, *Invisible Storytellers: Voice-Over Narration in American Fiction Film* (Berkeley: University of California Press, 1989), 121.

9 Archer, "Spartacus."

10   Frank Rich, "*Barry Lyndon*: A Kubrick Diamond," *New York Post*, December 19, 1975, 27, SK/14/7/8/19, SKA; Kael, *5001 Nights*, 42.
11   Thackeray, *Memoirs of Barry Lyndon*, 94.
12   Walker, Taylor, and Ruchti, *Stanley Kubrick, Director*, 264.
13   Jonathan Cecil, qtd. in LoBrutto, *Stanley Kubrick*, 395; Stanley Kubrick, "Waterford Script," n.d., SK/14/1/4, SKA; Cocks, *Wolf at the Door*, 130.
14   Stanley Kubrick, "Narrator's Voice," c. 1973, SK/14/1/26, SKA; Kolker, *Cinema of Loneliness*, 171.
15   Krohn, *Stanley Kubrick*, 69.
16   Rodney Hill, "*Barry Lyndon*," in Castle, *Stanley Kubrick Archives*, 430; Rich, "*Barry Lyndon*"; Stanley Kubrick, qtd. in Michel Ciment, "Interview with Stanley Kubrick," in Castle, *Stanley Kubrick Archives*, 441; Ryan O'Neal, qtd. in Mimi Crossley, "Chance of a Career," *Houston Post*, December 28, 1975, SK/14/6/17, SKA; Judith Crist, "Kubrick as Novelist," *Saturday Review*, January 10, 1976, folder 66, box 9, USCCBC.
17   Edward Connor, letter, December 13, 1975, folder 66, box 9, USCCBC.
18   Siegbert S. Prawer, *Israel at Vanity Fair: Jews and Judaism in the Writings of W. M. Thackeray* (Leiden, Netherlands: Brill, 1992), 133; Sanders, introd. to Thackeray, *Memoirs of Barry Lyndon*, xvi; Kathleen Tillotson, *Novels of the Eighteen-Forties* (Oxford: Oxford University Press, 1961), 236; Siegbert S. Prawer, *W. M. Thackeray's European Sketch Books: A Study of Literary and Graphic Portraiture* (Oxford: Lang, 2000), 136; Ken Adam, qtd. in Frayling, *Ken Adam*, 121; Giacomo Casanova, *Histoire de Ma Vie*, SK/14/2/3/3, SKA.
19   Thackeray, *Memoirs of Barry Lyndon*, 103; Baxter, *Stanley Kubrick*, 280.
20   "Ryan O'Neal: Biography," *IMDb*, accessed June 9, 2017, www.imdb.com/name/nm0641939/bio.
21   Prawer, *Israel at Vanity Fair*, 4.
22   Kaganoff, *Dictionary of Jewish Names*, 63; Lenny Bruce, qtd. in Kaufman, *Jewhooing the Sixties*, 114; LoBrutto, *Stanley Kubrick*, 261; Richard Corliss, "*Barry Lyndon*," *New York Times*, January 23, 1976, 56; Mort Drucker and Stan Hart, "Borey Lyndon," *Mad* 185 (September 1976): 4; Arthur C. Clarke, *Report on Planet Three* (1972; repr., London: Hachette UK, 1998), 261; "*Citizen 63* (1963)," *BFI*, June 9, 2017, www.screenonline.org.uk/tv/id/1351339/index.html.
23   Alan Grossman, "The Jew as American Poet," *Judaism* 11 (1962): 303; Cuddihy, *Ordeal of Civility*, 165; Ashel Grant, *The Nestorians; or, The Lost Tribes* (London: Clowes and Sons, 1843), 162.
24   Cocks, *Wolf at the Door*, 83.
25   Pramaggiore, *Making Time*, 87; Connor, letter, USCCBC; Stanley Kubrick, "Annotated Script," 1973–1974, SK/14/1/33, SKA.
26   Lowes, *Road to Xanadu*, 225.
27   Dick, "Barry Lyndon," USCCBC; Pramaggiore, *Making Time*, 102.
28   Drucker and Hart, "Borey Lyndon"; Sarris, "What Makes Barry Run?"; A. D. Murphy, "*Barry Lyndon*," *Variety*, December 17, 1975.
29   Muscat, qtd. in Sander Gilman, *The Jew's Body* (London: Routledge, 1991), 228.
30   Steven Berkoff, qtd. in LoBrutto, *Stanley Kubrick*, 402.
31   Roger Greenspun, "Not a Gainsborough," *New York Soho Weekly News*, December 25, 1975, SK/14/7/8/20, SKA; Marisa Berenson, qtd. in LoBrutto, *Stanley Kubrick*, 385.

32 Friedrich Nietzsche, *Beyond Good and Evil: Prelude to a Philosophy of the Future*, trans. Walter Kaufmann (New York: Random House, 1966), 188; Cuddihy, *Ordeal of Civility*, 17–19; Elias, *Civilizing Process*.

33 Hannah Arendt, *Rahel Varnhagen: The Life of a Jewess* (London: East and West Library, 1957), 183.

34 Cuddihy, *Ordeal of Civility*, 19.

35 Richard Schickel, qtd. in *Stanley Kubrick: A Life in Pictures*, DVD; Stanley Kubrick, qtd. in Richard Schickel, "Kubrick's Grandest Gamble: *Barry Lyndon*," *Time*, December 15, 1975, repr. in Phillips, *Stanley Kubrick Interviews*, 163; Walker, *It's Only a Movie*, 297.

36 Pramaggiore, *Making Time*, 136.

37 Dick, "Barry Lyndon," USCCBC; Burgess, *Clockwork Orange*, 1; Cocks, *Wolf at the Door*, 129.

38 Jonathan Benair, qtd. in Jason Bellamy and Ed Howard, "The Conversations: *Barry Lyndon*," *Slant*, October 21, 2011, www.slantmagazine.com/house/2011/10/the -conversations-barry-lyndon/.

39 Arthur Schnitzler, qtd. in Peter Gay, *Schnitzler's Century: The Making of Middle-Class Culture, 1815–1914* (New York: Norton, 2002), 22–23; Marcia Cavell Aufhauser, "The Genius of Kubrick," *New Leader*, January 19, 1976, 24.

40 Rich, "*Barry Lyndon*."

41 Sander L. Gilman, "Proust's Nose," *Social Research* 67, no. 1 (2000): 61–79.

42 Harold Rosenberg, "Notes on Seeing 'Barry Lyndon,'" *New York Times*, February 29, 1976; John Driscoll, December 15, 1975, folder 66, box 9, USCCBC.

43 Kozloff, *Invisible Storytellers*, 117; Stanley Kubrick, "New Kubrick Project," February 18, 1973, SK/14/1/5, SKA; Herr, *Kubrick*, 10; Aaron Schindler, *Family Circle*, n.d., SK/14/7/8/19, SKA.

Chapter 8   Dream Interpretation

1 Stanley Kubrick, qtd. in Castle, *Stanley Kubrick Archives*, 453.

2 Stanley Kubrick, qtd. in Baxter, *Stanley Kubrick*, 302; Kubrick, interview with Michel Ciment, July 28, 1981, SK/1/2/8/7, SKA; Kubrick to Roger Caras, February 6, 1967, SK/12/8/1/7ii, SKA; Kubrick, interview with Vincent Molina Foix, c. 1980, SK/1/2/8/1, SKA.

3 Kubrick, qtd. in Castle, *Stanley Kubrick Archives*, 448.

4 Stanley Kubrick, qtd. in LoBrutto, *Stanley Kubrick*, 415; Kubrick, incomplete annotated text from Stephen King's novel *The Shining*, August 26, 1977, SK/15/1/2, SKA.

5 Diane Johnson, qtd. in Kagan, *Cinema of Stanley Kubrick*, 203; Johnson, qtd. in *Visions of Kubrick*, dir. Gary Leva, DVD extra (United States: 2007); Johnson, "Writing *The Shining*," in Cocks, Diedrick, and Perusek, *Depth of Field*, 56; Johnson, qtd. in Baxter, *Stanley Kubrick*, 310.

6 Stanley Kubrick, handwritten notes on Stephen King's novel "The Shining," 1977, SK15/1/1, SKA; Poem cards, n.d., SK/15/3/4/8, SKA.

7 Ciment, *Kubrick* (1983), 144, 146.

8 Kubrick, "Incomplete annotated text," SKA; Stanley Kubrick, annotated text from Stephen King's novel *The Shining*, February 27 1977–April 12, 1977, SK/15/1/3, SKA; Diane Johnson, drafts, October 7 and 20, 1977, folder 1, box 23, DJ.

9   Kubrick, qtd. in Ciment, *Kubrick* (1983), 186; Kubrick to *Cahiers du Cinéma*, qtd. in Mark J. Madigan, "'Orders from the House': Kubrick's *The Shining* and Kafka's 'The Metamorphosis,'" in *The Shining Reader*, ed. Anthony Magistrale (Mercer Island, WA: Starmont House, 1991), 194; Kubrick, qtd. in Walker, *It's Only a Movie*, 299.

10 Ciment, *Kubrick* (1983), 308; Kubrick, interview with Ciment, SKA; Edward Douglas, *Jack: The Great Seducer* (New York: HarperEntertainment, 2004), 195.

11 Ciment, *Kubrick* (1983), 144; Walker, Taylor, and Ruchti, *Stanley Kubrick, Director*, 290, 283; Gilles Deleuze, *Cinema II* (New York: Continuum, 2005), 198; Freud, "Uncanny."

12 Kubrick, handwritten notes, SKA.

13 Ciment, *Kubrick* (2003), 146.

14 Walker, Taylor, and Ruchti, *Stanley Kubrick, Director*, 271, 278; Larry McCaffery and Diane Johnson, "Talking about 'The Shining' with Diane Johnson," *Chicago Review* 33, no. 1 (1981): 75.

15 Anne Jackson, qtd. in LoBrutto, *Stanley Kubrick*, 427; Walker, Taylor, and Ruchti, *Stanley Kubrick, Director*, 270–271, 91.

16 Diane Johnson, qtd. in Catriona McAvoy, "The Uncanny, the Gothic and the Loner: Intertextuality in the Adaptation Process of *The Shining*," *Adaptation* 8, no. 3 (2015): 350; LoBrutto, *Stanley Kubrick*, 413; Stanley Kubrick, qtd. in Bernard Weinraub, "Kubrick Tells What Makes *Clockwork Orange* Tick," *New York Times*, December 31, 1971; Kubrick, "Words and Movies," 14.

17 Walker, Taylor, and Ruchti, *Stanley Kubrick, Director*, 268; McGregor, "Nice Boy," 1; Stanley Kubrick to Anthony Burgess, October 15, 1976, 83/1, AB; Douglas, *Ragman's Son*, 395.

18 Patrick McGilligan, *Jack's Life: A Biography of Jack Nicholson* (London: Hutchinson, 1994), 309; Walker, Taylor, and Ruchti, *Stanley Kubrick, Director*, 273–274; Gordon Stainforth, qtd. in Laurent Vachaud, "Dans l'ombre de Kubrick," *Vanity Fair*, February 2015, 102.

19 C. Kubrick, *Stanley Kubrick*, 152; Shelley Duvall, qtd. in Ciment, *Kubrick* (2003), 301; Stainforth, qtd. in Vachaud, "Dans l'ombre," 102; Stanley Kubrick, "The *Rolling Stone* Interview, by Tim Cahill," accessed June 11, 2017, www.visual-memory.co.uk/amk/doc/0077.html.

20 LoBrutto, *Stanley Kubrick*, 442; Shelley Duvall, qtd. in Hughes, *Complete Kubrick*, 200.

21 Walker, Taylor, and Ruchti, *Stanley Kubrick, Director*, 271, 272, 273; LoBrutto, *Stanley Kubrick*, 329; Herr, *Kubrick*, 25.

22 Larry Siegel and Angelo Torres, "The Shiner," *Mad* 228 (April 1981): 12, SK/1/2/9/5, SKA; LoBrutto, *Stanley Kubrick*, 439.

23 Mario Falsetto, "The Mad and the Beautiful: A Look at Two Performances in the Films of Stanley Kubrick," in *Making Visible the Invisible: An Anthology of Original Essays on Film Acting*, ed. Carole Zucker (Lanham, MD: Scarecrow, 1990), 353; Stephen King, *The Shining* (New York: Signet, 1977), 97; Nelson, *Kubrick*, 213; Webster, *Love and Death*, 111; Kubrick, interview with Ciment, SKA.

24 Nelson, *Kubrick*, 216; Garrett Brown, qtd. in *Visions of Kubrick*.

25 C. Kubrick, *Stanley Kubrick*, 186.

26 Partial draft script, February 13 and 16, 1978, SK/15/1/22, SKA; Cocks, *Wolf at the Door*, 255.

27 Postproduction script, July 1980, SK/15/1/39, SKA; Kaufman, *Jewhooing the Sixties*, 228; Stanley Kubrick, "*Characters*: Rough Delineation," n.d., SK/11/1/9, SKA; Baxter, *Stanley Kubrick*, 16.

28 Diane Johnson, screenplay draft, October 18, 1977, 23/1, DJ; LoBrutto, *Stanley Kubrick*, 427.

29 Cocks, *Wolf at the Door*; Herr, *Kubrick*, 10.

30 Hilberg, *Destruction*, 189; Arendt, *Eichmann in Jerusalem*.

31 Kubrick, qtd. in Castle, *Stanley Kubrick Archives*, 453; Jack Kroll, "Stanley Kubrick's Horror Show," *Newsweek Magazine*, June 2, 1980.

32 "Location Research," 1977–1978, SK/15/2/1, SKA; Kubrick, interview with Ciment, SKA; Kubrick, interview with Foix, SKA.

33 Stanley Kubrick, annotated chapters from the novel, SK/15/1/2, SKA; Kubrick, copy of annotated novel text, *The Shine*, SK/15/1/3, SKA; Walker, Taylor, and Ruchti, *Stanley Kubrick, Director*, 300–301.

34 Kubrick, annotated chapters, SKA; Johnson, drafts, DJ; Roger Luckhurst, *The Shining* (London: British Film Institute, 2013), 69.

35 Walker, Taylor, and Ruchti, *Stanley Kubrick, Director*, 297; David Riesman, Reuel Denney, and Nathan Glazer, *The Lonely Crowd: A Study of the Changing American Culture* (New Haven: Yale University Press, 1950); Milgram, *Obedience to Authority*, 5; Stanley Milgram, "Some Conditions of Obedience and Disobedience to Authority," *Human Relations* 18 (1965): 57.

36 Robert Alter, "Jewish Dreams and Nightmares," *Commentary* 45, no. 1 (1968): 51; Kafka, "Letter to Richard Klopstock, June 1921," in his *Letters to Friends, Family and Editors*, trans. Richard Winston and Clara Winston (New York: Schocken, 1977), 285; Eugene Burdick and Harvey Wheeler, *Fail-Safe* (New York: McGraw-Hill, 1962).

37 Milgram, "Some Conditions," 57.

38 Kamenetz, *Burnt Books*, 134; Paul Miers, "The Black Maria Rides Again: Being a Reflection on the Present State of American Film with Special Respect to Stanley Kubrick's *The Shining*," *MLN* 95, no. 5 (1980): 1366.

39 Stanley Kubrick, qtd. in Kagan, *Cinema of Stanley Kubrick*, 203.

Chapter 9   Men as Meat

1 Diane Johnson, *Flyover Lives: A Memoir* (New York: Plume, 2014), 210; Jan Harlan, in *Full Metal Jacket: Between Good and Evil*, dir. Gary Leva (United States, 2007).

2 Stanley Kubrick, qtd. in Gene Siskel, "Candidly Kubrick," *Chicago Tribune*, June 21, 1987, repr. in Phillips, *Stanley Kubrick Interviews*, 180, 186; Kubrick, qtd. in Lloyd Rose, "Stanley Kubrick, at a Distance," *Washington Post*, June 28, 1987, F01; Walker, Taylor, and Ruchti, *Stanley Kubrick, Director*, 317.

3 Kubrick, qtd. in Siskel, "Candidly Kubrick," repr. in Phillips, *Stanley Kubrick Interviews*, 180; Gustav Hasford, *The Short-Timers* (London: Bantam, 1987), 4.

4 Paul Ciotti, "Michael Herr: A Man of Few Words," *Los Angeles Times*, April 15, 1990; D'Alessandro, *Stanley Kubrick and Me*, 172.

5 Stanly Kubrick to Leo Jaffe, August 20, 1964, SK/11/9/94, SKA; Bernstein, "Little Game," 85; Christine Mitchell to Bess Elkins, November 20, 1966, SK/12/8/1/6ii, SKA; Baxter, *Stanley Kubrick*, 333.

6   Stanley Kubrick, qtd. in Eric Nordern, "*Playboy* Interview: Stanley Kubrick (1968),"
    in Phillips, *Stanley Kubrick Interviews*, 70; Stanley Kubrick, qtd. in Charlie Kohler,
    "Stanley Kubrick Raps," *East Village Eye*, August 1968.
7   Diane Johnson and Gideon Stainforth, qtd. in Baxter, *Stanley Kubrick*, 333;
    "Cinematographer Larry Smith Helps Stanley Kubrick Craft a Unique Look for
    Eyes Wide Shut, a Dreamlike Coda to the Director's Brilliant Career," accessed
    June 11, 2017, www.theasc.com/magazine/oct99/sword/pg1.htm; Stanley Kubrick,
    interview with Daniele Heymann, in Castle, *Stanley Kubrick Archives*, 476; Francis
    Clines, "Stanley Kubrick's Vietnam War," *New York Times*, June 21, 1987, repr. in
    Phillips, *Stanley Kubrick Interviews*, 174; Siskel, "Candidly Kubrick," repr. in Phil-
    lips, *Stanley Kubrick Interviews*, 187, 185.
8   Siskel, "Candidly Kubrick," repr. in Phillips, *Stanley Kubrick Interviews*, 180; Nor-
    man Mailer, "Marine Corps Association," n.d., SK/16/2/1/2/8, SKA.
9   Dorian Harewood, qtd. in *Full Metal Jacket*; D'Alessandro, *Stanley Kubrick and Me*,
    188.
10 Michael Herr, qtd. in Ed Vulliamy, "It Ain't Over Till It's Over," *Observer*, July 16,
    2000; Herr, qtd. in, *Stanley Kubrick: A Life in Pictures*; LoBrutto, *Stanley Kubrick*,
    460; Harlan, *Full Metal Jacket*; Matthew Modine, *Full Metal Jacket Diary* (New
    York: Rugged Land, 2005); Stanley Kubrick, handwritten notes on Hasford, *Short-
    Timers*; Michael Herr, qtd. in LoBrutto, *Stanley Kubrick*, 486.
11 Walker, Taylor, and Ruchti, *Stanley Kubrick, Director*, 295.
12 Modine, *Full Metal Jacket Diary*, n.p.; Rita Kempley, "*Full Metal Jacket*," *Washing-
    ton Post*, June 26, 1987, SK/16/9/6, SKA.
13 Lee Ermey, qtd. in Walker, Taylor, and Ruchti, *Stanley Kubrick, Director*, 319;
    Kubrick, qtd. in Rose, "Stanley Kubrick," F01.
14 Siskel, "Candidly Kubrick," repr. in Phillips, *Stanley Kubrick Interviews*, 182.
15 Lenny Bruce, qtd. in Kaufman, *Jewhooing the Sixties*, 123; Leon Uris, in Matthew
    M. Silver, *Our Exodus: Leon Uris and the Americanization of Israel's Founding Story*
    (Detroit: Wayne State University Press, 2010), 53; Hasford, *Short-Timers*, 121.
16 Planning c. 1984–1985, May 25, 1984, SK/16/1/16, SKA; Script portions, unan-
    notated, c. 1985, SK/16/1/11, SKA; Stanley Kubrick, "Story," c. October 1982,
    SK/16/1/1, SKA; Script amendments, April 9, 1984, SK/16/2/5/13, SKA.
17 Modine, *Full Metal Jacket Diary*, n.p.; Matthew Modine, qtd. in LoBrutto, *Stanley
    Kubrick*, 464.
18 Ritzenhoff, "UK Frost," in Ljujić, Kramer, and Daniels, *Stanley Kubrick*, 336.
19 Walker, Taylor, and Ruchti, *Stanley Kubrick, Director*, 334; Stanley Kubrick, qtd. in
    LoBrutto, *Stanley Kubrick*, 460.
20 Leon Uris, *Battle Cry* (New York: HarperCollins, 1953), 43, 75.
21 Modine, *Full Metal Jacket Diary*, n.p.
22 Stanley Kubrick, scene cards, c. December 1985, SK/16/1/4, SKA; Kaufman, *Jew-
    hooing the Sixties*, 107.
23 "Manuscript Full Metal Jacket," May 3, 1985, SK/16/1/2/1; Script amendments,
    April 9, 1984, SK/16/2/5/13, SKA.
24 Stanley Kubrick, qtd. in LoBrutto, *Stanley Kubrick*, 465; Hasford, *Short-Timers*, 3.
25 Gilbert Adair, *Hollywood's Vietnam: From the Green Berets to Full Metal Jacket*
    (London: Heinemann, 1989), 178.
26 Milgram, *Obedience to Authority*, 187; Hilberg, *Destruction*, 658; Cocks, *Wolf at the
    Door*, 137.

27 Nick James, "At Home with the Kubricks," *Sight and Sound*, September 1999, 18; Siskel, "Candidly Kubrick," repr. in Phillips, *Stanley Kubrick Interviews*, 183; Matthew Modine, qtd. in LoBrutto, *Stanley Kubrick*, 464.

28 Matthew Modine, qtd. in LoBrutto, *Stanley Kubrick*, 464; Siskel, "Candidly Kubrick," repr. in Phillips, *Stanley Kubrick Interviews*, 183; Hasford, *Short-Timers*, 110; Siskel, "Candidly Kubrick," repr. in Phillips, *Stanley Kubrick Interviews*, 182–183 (my emphasis).

29 Kempley, "*Full Metal Jacket.*"

30 D'Alessandro, *Stanley Kubrick and Me*, 289; Nelson, *Kubrick*, 242.

31 Stanley Kubrick, Gustav Hasford, and Michael Herr, *Full Metal Jacket: The Screenplay* (London: Secker and Warburg, 1987), 46.

32 Kempley, "*Full Metal Jacket.*"

33 Hasford, *Short-Timers*, 10, 127, 59–60.

34 Modine, *Full Metal Jacket Diary*, n.p.

35 Kubrick, qtd. in Gilliatt, "Mankind," 20; Modine, *Full Metal Jacket Diary*, n.p.

36 Modine, *Full Metal Jacket Diary*, n.p.

37 Julian Senior, qtd. in LoBrutto, *Stanley Kubrick*, 483; Modine, *Full Metal Jacket Diary*; "Manuscript Full Metal Jacket," SKA.

38 Siskel, "Candidly Kubrick," repr. in Phillips, *Stanley Kubrick Interviews*, 187; John Calley, qtd. in *Full Metal Jacket*.

39 Milgram, *Obedience to Authority*, 180, 181–182.

40 Hasford, *Short-Timers*, 3, 41, 60, 144, 26; Herr, *Kubrick*, 7–8, 10; Geoffrey Cocks, "Death by Typewriter: Stanley Kubrick, the Holocaust, and *The Shining*," in Cocks, Diedrick, and Perusek, *Stanley Kubrick*, 196.

41 Adair, *Hollywood's Vietnam*, 176, 177; Terrence Rafferty, "*Full Metal Jacket*," *Nation*, August 1, 1987.

42 Kempley, "*Full Metal Jacket.*"

43 Milgram, *Obedience to Authority*, 187; Stanley Kubrick, qtd. in Siskel, "Candidly Kubrick," repr. in Phillips, *Stanley Kubrick Interviews*, 181; Kubrick, qtd. in Gilliatt, "Mankind," 20; Stanley Kubrick, "12-10-83 Hot Notes," October 12, 1983, SK/16/1/23, SKA.

44 Penelope Gilliatt, "Heavy Metal," *American Film*, May 1988, 39; Walker, Taylor, and Ruchti, *Stanley Kubrick, Director*, 332, 334.

45 D'Alessandro, *Stanley Kubrick and Me*, 182.

Chapter 10   Kubrick's Coda

1 Stanley Kubrick, qtd. in Bernard Weinraub, "All Eyes for a Peek at Kubrick's Final Film," *New York Times*, March 10, 1999; Freud, *Moses and Monotheism*.

2 Carl E. Schorske, *Fin-de-Siècle Vienna: Politics and Culture* (New York: Vintage, 1981), 11; Serge Bokobza, "Stanley Kubrick's *Eyes Wide Shut*: Decadent Europe and American Myth," in *Films with Legs: Crossing Borders with Foreign Language Films*, ed. Rosemary A. Peters and Veronique Maisier (Newcastle, UK: Cambridge Scholars, 2014), 175.

3 Walker, Taylor, and Ruchti, *Stanley Kubrick, Director*, 306; James Harris, telephone interview with the author, September 2, 2016; Stanley Kubrick to Jules Feiffer, January 2, 1958, MSS83993, box 8, JF; Kirk Douglas, *I Am Spartacus! Making a Film, Breaking the Blacklist* (New York: Open Road, 2012), 170–171; Peter A. Schnitzler

to Kubrick, May 27, 1959, SK/9/4/1, SKA; Herr, *Kubrick*, 7; Ginna, "Artist Speaks for Himself"; Kubrick, "Director's Notes," *Observer*, December 4, 1960, repr. in Castle, *Stanley Kubrick Archives*, 324.

4 Jay Cocks, qtd. in Castle, *Stanley Kubrick Archives*, 482; Stanley Kubrick, qtd. in Hughes, *Complete Kubrick*, 161; Jan Harlan, qtd. in Castle, *Stanley Kubrick Archives*, 512; Herr, *Kubrick*, 7.

5 "Kubrick Drama," *Kine Weekly*, May 8, 1971, in Castle, *Stanley Kubrick Archives*, 482; "Kubrick Sets Traumnovelle," *Los Angeles Herald Examiner*, May 11, 1971, unpaginated clipping on Stanley Kubrick fiche, AMPAS; Stanley Kubrick to Daniele Heymann, in Castle, *Stanley Kubrick Archives*, 477.

6 Raphael, *Eyes Wide Open*, 92.

7 "*Eyes Wide Shut* at 15: Inside the Epic, Secretive Film Shoot That Pushed Tom Cruise and Nicole Kidman to Their Limits," *Vanity Fair*, July 17, 2014, www .vanityfair.com/hollywood/2014/07/eyes-wide-shut-tom-cruise-nicole-kidman.

8 Stanley Kubrick, interview with Robert Emmett Ginna, 1960, SK/1/2/8, SKA; Kubrick, interview with Vincent Molina Foix, c. 1980, SK/1/2/8/1, SKA; Kubrick to Feiffer, JF; Kubrick, qtd. in Castle, *Stanley Kubrick Archives*, 483.

9 Kubrick, qtd. in Ciment, *Kubrick* (1983), 156; Kubrick, qtd. in Dan Glaister, "He Finished with His Life Less Than a Week after He Finished with His Movie," *Guardian*, March 9, 1999, www.theguardian.com/film/1999/mar/09/features; C. Kubrick, qtd. in *Stanley Kubrick: A Life in Pictures*, DVD.

10 D'Alessandro, *Stanley Kubrick and Me*, 148, 149, 295; Kubrick, qtd. in LoBrutto, *Stanley Kubrick*, 373.

11 Mather, *Stanley Kubrick at "Look,"* 254, 197.

12 Harlan, qtd. in Castle, *Stanley Kubrick Archives*, 512.

13 Lucy Scholes and Richard Martin, "Archived Desires: *Eyes Wide Shut*," in Ljujić, Kramer, and Daniels, *Stanley Kubrick*, 350; Weinraub, "Kubrick Tells"; Scorsese, qtd. on *Stanley Kubrick: A Life in Pictures*, DVD; Sydney Pollack and Larry Smith, qtd. in Castle, *Stanley Kubrick Archives*, 486, 488; Arthur Schnitzler, *Traumnovelle: Dream Story*, trans. J.M.Q. Davis (1926; repr., London: Penguin, 1999), 63.

14 "Cinematographer Larry Smith"; "Oversized Materials about Prop Research and Set Plans," folder 8, SK/17/2/22, SKA; Bernstein, "Little Game," 108; D'Alessandro, *Stanley Kubrick and Me*, 148, 149.

15 Scholes and Martin, "Archived Desires," in Ljujić, Kramer, and Daniels, *Stanley Kubrick*, 344; Kate McQuiston, *We'll Meet Again: Musical Design in the Films of Stanley Kubrick* (New York: Oxford University Press, 2013), 191; Brigitte Peucker, "Kubrick and Kafka: The Corporeal Uncanny," *Modernism/Modernity* 8, no. 4 (2001): 670; Richard T. Jameson, "Ghost Sonata: *Eyes Wide Shut*," *Film Comment*, September–October 1999, www.filmcomment.com/article/ghost-sonata-eyes-wide -shut.

16 Raphael, *Eyes Wide Open*, 59, 57.

17 Frederic Raphael, "Traumnovelle–F. Raphael Draft–William Morris," 1995, SK/17/1/2, SKA.

18 Kolker, *Cinema of Loneliness*, 173; Nathan Abrams, *The New Jew in Film: Exploring Jewishness and Judaism in Contemporary Cinema* (New Brunswick, NJ: Rutgers University Press, 2012).

19 "Mr. Hankey, the Christmas Poo," episode 9, season 1, *South Park*, December 17, 1997.

20 Michael E. Starr, "The Marlboro Man: Cigarette Smoking and Masculinity in America," *Journal of Popular Culture* 17, no. 4 (1984): 54.

21 Kafka, qtd. in Saul Friedlander, *Franz Kafka: The Poet of Shame and Guilt* (New Haven, CT: Yale University Press, 2013), 144.

22 Frederic Raphael, draft, June 6, 1995, SK/17/1/5, SKA.

23 Fredric Raphael, introd. to Schnitzler, *Traumnovelle*, xiii; Frederic Raphael, "Raphael First Draft," 1995, SK/17/1/1, SKA.

24 Sigmund Freud, *The Interpretation of Dreams* (1911; repr., Harmondsworth, UK: Penguin, 1977), 197.

25 David Ehrenstein, qtd. in Jonathan Rosenbaum, "In Dreams Begin Responsibilities," in Cocks, Diedrick, and Perusek, *Depth of Field*, 249.

26 Frederic Raphael, draft, January 24, 1995, SK/17/1/3, SKA; "Masked Ball," SK/14/2/3/5, SKA; "*Eyes Wide Shut*: Trivia," *IMDb*, www.imdb.com/title/tt0120663/trivia.

27 Randy L. Rasmussen, *Stanley Kubrick: Seven Films Analyzed* (Jefferson, NC: McFarland, 2001), 346; Raphael, "Raphael First Draft," SKA; Walker, Taylor, and Ruchti, *Stanley Kubrick, Director*, 230.

28 Schnitzler, *Traumnovelle*, 228–229; Peter Loewenberg, "Freud, Schnitzler, and *Eyes Wide Shut*," in Cocks, Diedrick, and Perusek, *Depth of Field*, 285; Frederic Raphael to Stanley Kubrick, January 1, 1995, SK/17/1/4, SKA.

29 Rodney Hill, qtd. in Castle, *Stanley Kubrick Archives*, 437; Raphael, "Raphael First Draft," SKA; Raphael to Kubrick, January 31, 1995, SK/17/1/4, SKA.

30 Bokobza, "Kubrick's *Eyes Wide Shut*," in Peters and Maisier, *Films with Legs*, 181

31 Rice, *Kubrick's Hope*, 229–230.

32 Raphael, *Eyes Wide Open*, 116; Stanley Kubrick to Eugene Burdick and Harvey Wheeler, January 19, 1962, SK/11/1/13, SKA; "Filming Schedules," SK/17/3/4, SKA.

33 Breakdown sheets, September 20, 1996–February 7, 1997, SK/17/3/3, SKA.

34 Ajay Shah Convenor to Warner Bros., August 3, 1999, cited in Christine Lee Gengaro, *Listening to Stanley Kubrick: The Music in His Films* (Lanham, MD: Rowman and Littlefield, 2012), 227; Rice, *Kubrick's Hope*, 192.

35 Bryn Vaughan Young-Roberts, "Gripping Kubrick's Phallus: The Oedipal Odyssey of *Eyes Wide Shut*" (Draft MA essay: Bangor University, 2010), in the author's possession.

36 Rosenbaum, "In Dreams Begin Responsibilities," in Cocks, Diedrick, and Perusek, *Depth of Field*, 249; Bokobza, "Kubrick's *Eyes Wide Shut*," in Peters and Maisier, *Films with Legs*, 180; "*Clockwork Orange*, Detroit," March–April 1972, SK/13/8/3/22, SKA.

Epilogue

1 Kirk Douglas to Stan Margulies, April 13, 1959, SK/9/4/5ii, SKA; Stanley Kubrick to Edward Lewis, November 7, 1959, 33/10, KD.

2 Jan Harlan, qtd. in Freer, "Strangelove," 49; Marat Grinberg, "Jewish Perspectives on Kubrick," a panel held at the Contemporary Jewish Museum, San Francisco, July 14, 2016.

3   Ian Watson, drafts, July 16, 1990, uncatalogued material, SKA; Ian Watson, "Meet-
    ing Notes," June 11, 1990, uncatalogued material, SKA.
4   George Steiner, *The Death of Tragedy* (New Haven, CT: Yale University Press, 1961),
    4; Paula Hyman, *Gender and Assimilation in Modern Jewish History: The Roles and
    Representation of Women* (Seattle: University of Washington Press, 1995), 91.
5   Vivian Kubrick, qtd. in LoBrutto, *Stanley Kubrick*, 481.
6   Vernard Eller, "The 'MAD' Morality: An Exposé," *Christian Century*, December 27,
    1967, 1647.

Select Bibliography

Archives

Burgess, Anthony. Papers. Harry Ransom Humanities Research Center. University of Texas at Austin. (AB)

Department/Office of Film and Broadcasting. United States Conference of Catholic Bishops Communications. American Catholic History Research Center and University Archives. Catholic University of America, Washington, DC. (USCCBC)

Douglas, Kirk. Papers. Wisconsin Historical Society, Madison. (KD)

Dunn, Linwood G., Papers. Margaret Herrick Library of the Academy of Motion Picture Arts and Sciences, Los Angeles. (LD)

Feiffer, Jules. Papers. Manuscript Division. Library of Congress, Washington, DC. (JF)

Georgetown University Library Special Collections Research Center, Washington, DC. (GU)

Heller, Joseph. Collection. Brandeis University Libraries. Robert D. Farber University Archives and Special Collections Department, Waltham, MA. (JH)

Johnson, Diane. Papers. Harry Ransom Humanities Research Center. University of Texas at Austin. (DJ)

Kubrick, Stanley. Archive. University of the Arts, London. (SKA)

Look Magazine Photograph Collection. Library of Congress, Washington, DC. (LM)

Macdonald, Dwight. Papers. Yale University Library, New Haven, CT. (DM)

Margaret Herrick Library of the Academy of Motion Picture Arts and Sciences, Los Angeles. (AMPAS).

Nabokov, Vladimir. Papers, Henry W. and Albert A. Berg Collection. New York Public Library. (VN)

Production Code Administration. Margaret Herrick Library of the Academy of Motion Picture Arts and Sciences, Los Angeles. (PCA)

Southern, Terry. Papers. Henry W. and Albert A. Berg Collection. New York Public Library. (TS)

Trumbo, Dalton. Papers. Wisconsin Historical Society, Madison. (DT)

Books

Abrams, Jerold J., ed. *The Philosophy of Stanley Kubrick*. Lexington: University of Kentucky Press, 2007.

Adair, Gilbert. *Hollywood's Vietnam: From the Green Berets to Full Metal Jacket*. London: Heinemann, 1989.

Agel, Jerome. *The Making of Kubrick's 2001*. New York: Signet, 1970.

Appel, Alfred, Jr., ed. *The Annotated "Lolita."* London: Penguin, 1971.

———. *Nabokov's Dark Cinema*. New York: Oxford University Press, 1974.

Arendt, Hannah. *Eichmann in Jerusalem: A Report on the Banality of Evil*. 1963. Reprint, London: Penguin, 1994.

———. *The Origins of Totalitarianism*. New York: Meridian, 1958.

Baxter, John. *Stanley Kubrick: A Biography*. London: HarperCollins, 1998.

Begley, Louis. *Wartime Lies*. New York: Fawcett Columbine, 1991.

Bettelheim, Bruno. *The Uses of Enchantment: The Meaning and Importance of Fairy Tales*. London: Peregrine, 1978.

Bhabha, Homi. *The Location of Culture*. London: Routledge, 1994.

Bial, Henry. *Acting Jewish: Negotiating Ethnicity on the American Stage and Screen*. Ann Arbor: University of Michigan Press, 2005.

Bizony, Piers. *2001: Filming the Future*. London: Aurum, 2000.

Boyarin, Daniel. *Unheroic Conduct: The Rise of Heterosexuality and the Invention of the Jewish Man*. Berkeley: University of California Press, 1997.

Breines, Paul. *Tough Jews: Political Fantasies and the Moral Dilemma of American Jewry*. New York: Basic, 1990.

Broderick, Michael. *Reconstructing Strangelove: Inside Stanley Kubrick's "Nightmare Comedy."* New York: Wallflower, 2016.

Brook, Vincent. *Driven to Darkness: Jewish Émigré Directors and the Rise of Film Noir*. New Brunswick, NJ: Rutgers University Press, 2009.

Burdick, Eugene, and Harvey Wheeler. *Fail-Safe*. New York: McGraw-Hill, 1962.

Burgess, Anthony. *A Clockwork Orange*. London: Heinemann, 1962.

Bryant, Peter. *Red Alert*. 1958. Kindle ed. Reprint, New York: RosettaBooks, 2014.

Campbell, Joseph. *The Hero with the Thousand Faces*. 3rd ed. Novato, CA: New World Library, 2008.

Case, George. *Calling Dr. Strangelove: The Anatomy and Influence of the Kubrick Masterpiece*. Jefferson, NC: McFarland, 2014.

Castle, Alison, ed. *The Stanley Kubrick Archives*. Cologne: Taschen, 2005.

Ceplair, Larry, and Christopher Trumbo. *Dalton Trumbo: Blacklisted Hollywood Radical*. Lexington: University Press of Kentucky, 2015.

Chion, Michel. *Eyes Wide Shut*. London: British Film Institute, 2002.

———. *Kubrick's Cinema Odyssey*. Translated by Claudia Gorbman. London: British Film Institute, 2001.

Ciment, Michel. *Kubrick*. London: Collins, 1983.

———. *Kubrick: The Definitive Edition*. New York: Faber and Faber, 2003.

Clarke, Arthur C. *The Lost Worlds of 2001*. London: Sidgwick and Jackson, 1978.

Cobb, Humphrey. *Paths of Glory*. 1935. Reprint, London: Penguin, 2010.

Cocks, Geoffrey. *The Wolf at the Door: Stanley Kubrick, History, and the Holocaust*. New York: Lang, 2004.

Cocks, Geoffrey, James Diedrick, and Glenn Perusek, eds. *Depth of Field: Stanley Kubrick, Film, and the Uses of History*. Madison: University of Wisconsin Press, 2006.

Corliss, Richard. *Lolita*. London: British Film Institute, 2008.

———. *Talking Pictures: Screenwriters of Hollywood*. London: David and Charles, 1975.

Crone, Rainer, ed. *Stanley Kubrick: Drama and Shadows*. London: Phaidon, 2005.

Cuddihy, John Murray. *The Ordeal of Civility: Freud, Marx, Lévi-Strauss, and the Jewish Struggle with Modernity*. Boston: Beacon, 1978.

Curtis, Tony. *The Autobiography*. London: Mandarin, 1995.

Cyrino, Monica Silveira. *Big Screen Rome*. Malden, MA: Wiley-Blackwell, 2005.

D'Alessandro, Emilio. *Stanley Kubrick and Me: Thirty Years at His Side*. With Filippo Ulivieri. Translated by Simon Marsh. New York: Arcade, 2016.

Davis, Natalie Zemon. *Slaves on Screen: Film and Historical Vision*. Toronto: Vintage Canada, 2000.

Deleuze, Gilles. *Cinema II*. New York: Continuum, 2005.

Douglas, Edward. *Jack: The Great Seducer*. New York: HarperEntertainment, 2004.

Douglas, Kirk. *I Am Spartacus! Making a Film, Breaking the Blacklist*. New York: Open Road, 2012.

———. *The Ragman's Son: An Autobiography*. Bath: Chivers, 1988.

Duncan, Paul. *Stanley Kubrick: The Complete Films*. Cologne: Taschen, 2008.

Elias, Norbert. *The Civilizing Process: Sociogenetic and Psychogenetic Investigations*. Rev. ed. Translated by Edmund Jephcott. Malden, MA: Blackwell, 2000.

Epstein, Lawrence J. *The Haunted Smile: The Story of Jewish Comedians in America*. New York: Public Affairs, 2001.

Falsetto, Mario, ed. *Perspectives on Stanley Kubrick*. New York: Hall, 1996.

———. *Stanley Kubrick: A Narrative and Stylistic Analysis*. Westport, CT: Praeger, 2001.

Fast, Howard. *Spartacus*. 1951. Reprint, London: Bodley Head, 1979.

Fermaglich, Kirsten. *American Dreams and Nazi Nightmares: Early Holocaust Consciousness and Liberal America, 1957–1965*. Waltham, MA: University Press of New England, 2006.

Fiedler, Leslie. *Waiting for the End: The American Literary Scene from Hemingway to Baldwin*. London: Penguin, 1967.

Fleming, Ian. *Dr. No*. 1958. Reprint, London: Penguin, 2002.

Frayling, Christopher. *Ken Adam: The Art of Production Design*. London: Faber and Faber, 2005.

Freud, Sigmund. *The Interpretation of Dreams*. 1911. Reprint, Harmondsworth, UK: Penguin, 1977.

———. *Moses and Monotheism*. New York: Vintage, 1967.

Frewin, Anthony, ed. *Are We Alone? The Stanley Kubrick Extraterrestrial-Intelligence Interviews*. London: Elliot and Thompson, 2005.

Friedlander, Saul. *Franz Kafka: The Poet of Shame and Guilt*. New Haven, CT: Yale University Press, 2013.

Gay, Peter. *Schnitzler's Century: The Making of Middle-Class Culture, 1815–1914*. New York: Norton, 2002.

Geduld, Carolyn. *2001: A Space Odyssey*. Bloomington: Indiana University Press, 1973.

Gelmis, Joseph. *The Film Director as Superstar*. New York: Doubleday, 1970.

George, Peter. *Dr. Strangelove; or, How I Learned to Stop Worrying and Love the Bomb*. 1963. Reprint, London: Prion, 2000.

Gilman, Sander L. *Jewish Frontiers: Essays on Bodies, Histories, and Identities*. New York: Palgrave Macmillan, 2003.

———. *The Jew's Body*. London: Routledge, 1991.

Greenhalgh, Elizabeth. *The French Army and the First World War*. Cambridge: Cambridge University Press, 2014.

Hasford, Gustav. *The Short-Timers*. London: Bantam, 1987.

Herr, Michael. *Kubrick*. London: Picador, 2000.

Hilberg, Raul. *Destruction of the European Jews*. New York: Quadrangle, 1967.

Horkheimer, Max, and Theodor Adorno. *Dialectic of Enlightenment*. Translated by John Cumming. London: Lane, 1973.

Howard, James. *The Stanley Kubrick Companion*. London: Batsford, 1999.

Howe, Irving. *World of Our Fathers*. New York: Simon and Schuster, 1976.

Hughes, David. *The Complete Kubrick*. London: Virgin, 2001.

Hyman, Paula. *Gender and Assimilation in Modern Jewish History: The Roles and Representation of Women*. Seattle: University of Washington Press, 1995.

Jenkins, Greg. *Stanley Kubrick and the Art of Adaptation: Three Novels, Three Films*. Jefferson, NC: McFarland, 1997.

Johnson, Diane. *Flyover Lives: A Memoir*. New York: Plume, 2014.

Kael, Pauline. *5001 Nights at the Movies*. London: Zenith, 1982.

Kafka, Franz. *Letters to Friends, Family and Editors*. Translated by Richard Winston and Clara Winston. New York: Schocken, 1977.

Kagan, Norman. *The Cinema of Stanley Kubrick*. New York: Continuum, 2000.

Kaganoff, Benzion. *A Dictionary of Jewish Names and Their History*. New York: Schocken, 1977.

Kamenetz, Rodger. *Burnt Books: Rabbi Nachman of Bratslav and Franz Kafka*. New York: Schocken, 2010.

Kane, Leslie. *Weasels and Wisemen: Ethics and Ethnicity in the Work of David Mamet*. Basingstoke, UK: Macmillan, 1999.

Karlin, Miriam. *Some Sort of Life: My Autobiography*. London: Oberon, 2007.

Kaufman, David E. *Jewhooing the Sixties: American Celebrity and Jewish Identity*. Waltham, MA: Brandeis University Press, 2012.

Kercher, Stephen E. *Revel with a Cause: Liberal Satire in Postwar America*. Chicago: University of Chicago Press, 2006.

King, Stephen. *The Shining*. New York: Signet, 1977.

Koestler, Arthur. *The Gladiators*. 1939. Kindle ed. Reprint, New York: Vintage, 1999.

Kolker, Robert. *A Cinema of Loneliness*. 4th ed. New York: Oxford University Press, 2011.

———. *The Extraordinary Image*. New Brunswick, NJ: Rutgers University Press, 2016.

Kozloff, Sarah. *Invisible Storytellers: Voice-Over Narration in American Fiction Film*. Berkeley: University of California Press, 1989.

Kramer, Peter. *2001: A Space Odyssey*. London: British Film Institute, 2010.

———. *A Clockwork Orange (Controversies)*. Basingstoke, UK: Palgrave Macmillan, 2011.

———. *Dr. Strangelove*. London: British Film Institute, 2014.

Krohn, Bill. *Stanley Kubrick*. Paris: Cahiers du Cinéma, 2010.

Kuberski, Philip. *Kubrick's Total Cinema: Philosophical Themes and Formal Qualities*. London: Continuum, 2012.

Kubrick, Christiane. *Stanley Kubrick: A Life in Pictures*. London: Little, Brown, 2002.

Lewis, Roger. *The Life and Death of Peter Sellers*. London: Arrow, 1994.

Lifton, Robert Jay. *Thought Reform and the Psychology of Totalism*. New York: Norton, 1961.

Ljujić, Tatjana, Peter Kramer, and Richard Daniels, eds. *Stanley Kubrick: New Perspectives*. London: Black Dog, 2015.

LoBrutto, Vincent. *Stanley Kubrick: A Biography*. New York: Fine, 1998.

Lowes, John Livingston. *The Road to Xanadu: A Study in the Ways of the Imagination*. Boston: Houghton Mifflin, 1964.

Luckhurst, Roger. *The Shining*. London: British Film Institute, 2013.

Magistrale, Anthony, ed. *The Shining Reader*. Mercer Island, WA: Starmont House, 1991.

Margulies, Stan. *Spartacus: The Illustrated Story of the Motion Picture Production*. Saint Louis: Bryna Productions/Universal Pictures, 1960.

Mason, James. *Before I Forget*. London: Hamilton, 1981

Mather, Philippe D. *Stanley Kubrick at "Look" Magazine*. Bristol, UK: Intellect, 2013.

Mazursky, Paul. *Show Me the Magic: My Adventures in Life and Hollywood with . . . .* New York: Simon and Schuster, 1999.

McDougal, Stuart Y., ed. *Stanley Kubrick's "A Clockwork Orange."* Cambridge: Cambridge University Press, 2003.

McGilligan, Patrick. *Jack's Life: A Biography of Jack Nicholson*. London: Hutchinson, 1994.

Milgram, Stanley. *Obedience to Authority: An Experimental View*. London: Tavistock, 1974.

Modine, Matthew. *Full Metal Jacket Diary*. New York: Rugged Land, 2005.

Myers, Jody. *Kabbalah and the Spiritual Quest*. Westport, CT: Praeger, 2007.

Nabokov, Vladimir. *Lolita*. 1955. Reprint, London: Transworld, 1961.

Naremore, James. *More Than Night: Film Noir in Its Contexts*. Berkeley: University of California Press, 2008.

———. *On Kubrick*. London: British Film Institute, 2007.

Nietzsche, Friedrich. *Beyond Good and Evil: Prelude to a Philosophy of the Future*. Translated by Walter Kaufmann. New York: Random House, 1966.

Nelson, Thomas Allen. *Kubrick: Inside a Film Artist's Maze*. Bloomington: Indiana University Press, 2000.

Neufeld, Michael J. *Von Braun: Dreamer of Space, Engineer of War*. New York: Knopf, 2007.

Olson, Daniel, ed. *Stanley Kubrick's The Shining: Studies in the Horror Film*. Lakewood, CO: Centipede, 2015.

Pezzotta, Elisa. *Stanley Kubrick: Adapting the Sublime*. Jackson: University Press of Mississippi, 2013.

Phillips, Gene D. *Stanley Kubrick: A Film Odyssey*. New York: Popular Library, 1975.

———, ed. *Stanley Kubrick Interviews*. Jackson: University Press of Mississippi, 2001.

Phillips, Gene D., and Rodney Hill. *The Encyclopedia of Stanley Kubrick*. New York: Checkmark, 2002.

Polito, Robert. *Savage Art: A Biography of Jim Thompson*. New York: Vintage, 1996.

Pramaggiore, Maria. *Making Time in Stanley Kubrick's Barry Lyndon: Art, History, and Empire*. New York: Bloomsbury, 2015.

Prawer, Siegbert S. *Israel at Vanity Fair: Jews and Judaism in the Writings of W. M. Thackeray*. Leiden, Netherlands: Brill, 1992.

———. *W. M. Thackeray's European Sketch Books: A Study of Literary and Graphic Portraiture*. Oxford: Lang, 2000.

Raphael, Frederic. *Eyes Wide Open: A Memoir of Stanley Kubrick*. London: Ballantine, 1999.

Rasmussen, Randy L. *Stanley Kubrick: Seven Films Analyzed*. Jefferson, NC: McFarland, 2001.

Read, Piers Paul. *The Dreyfus Affair: The Scandal That Tore France in Two*. New York: Bloomsbury, 2012.

Reichmann, Hans-Peter, ed. *Stanley Kubrick*. Frankfurt: Deutsches Filmmuseum, 2007.

Rhodes, Gary D., ed. *Stanley Kubrick: Essays on His Films and Legacy*. Jefferson, NC: McFarland, 2008.

Rice, Julian. *Kubrick's Hope: Discovering Optimism from 2001 to Eyes Wide Shut.* Lanham, MD: Scarecrow, 2008.

Riesman, David, Reuel Denney, and Nathan Glazer. *The Lonely Crowd: A Study of the Changing American Culture.* New Haven, CT: Yale University Press, 1950.

Roper, Robert. *Nabokov in America: On the Road to Lolita.* New York: Bloomsbury, 2015.

Rosenberg, Warren. *Legacy of Rage: Jewish Masculinity, Violence, and Culture.* Amherst: University of Massachusetts Press, 2001.

Rosten, Leo. *The Joys of Yiddish.* London: Penguin, 1972.

Roth, Laurence. *Inspecting Jews: American Jewish Detective Stories.* New Brunswick, NJ: Rutgers University Press, 2004.

Sacher, Howard Morley. *The Course of Modern Jewish History.* New York: Dell, 1958.

Salinger, J. D. *The Catcher in the Rye.* 1951. Reprint, London: Penguin, 1994.

Sammons, Jeffrey T. *Beyond the Ring: The Role of Boxing in American Society.* Urbana: University of Illinois Press, 1990.

Sartre, Jean-Paul. *Anti-Semite and Jew.* Translated by George J. Becker. New York: Schocken, 1965.

———. *Existentialism.* Translated by Bernard Frechtman. New York: Philosophical Library, 1947.

Schein, Edgar H., Inge Schneier, and Curtis H. Becker. *Coercive Persuasion.* New York: Norton, 1961.

Schnitzler, Arthur. *Traumnovelle: Dream Story.* Translated by J.M.Q. Davis. 1926. Reprint, London: Penguin, 1999.

Scholem, Gershom G. *On the Kabbalah and Its Symbolism.* Translated by Ralph Manheim. New York: Schocken, 1965.

Schorske, Carl E. *Fin-de-Siècle Vienna: Politics and Culture.* New York: Vintage, 1981.

Seed, David. *American Science Fiction and the Cold War: Literature and Film.* Edinburgh: Edinburgh University Press, 1999.

Siegel, Lee. *Not Remotely Controlled: Notes on Television.* New York: Basic, 2007.

Sikov, Ed. *Mr. Strangelove: A Biography of Peter Sellers.* New York: Hyperion, 2002.

Silver, Matthew M. *Our Exodus: Leon Uris and the Americanization of Israel's Founding Story.* Detroit: Wayne State University Press, 2010.

Steiner, George. *The Death of Tragedy.* New Haven, CT: Yale University Press, 1961.

Stratton, Jon. *Coming Out Jewish.* London: Routledge, 2000.

Thackeray, William Makepeace. *The Memoirs of Barry Lyndon, Esq.* Oxford: Oxford University Press, 1999.

Walker, Alexander. *"It's Only a Movie, Ingrid": Encounters On and Off Screen.* London: Headline, 1988.

Walker, Alexander, Sybil Taylor, and Ulrich Ruchti. *Stanley Kubrick, Director: A Visual Analysis.* London: Weidenfeld and Nicholson, 1999.

Webster, Patrick. *Love and Death in Kubrick: A Critical Study of the Films from "Lolita" through "Eyes Wide Shut."* Jefferson, NC: McFarland, 2011.

White, Lionel. *Clean Break.* 1955. Reprint, New York: Blackmask Online, 2005.

Winkler, Martin M., ed. *Spartacus: Film and History.* Oxford: Blackwell, 2007.

Winters, Shelley. *Shelley II: Best of Times, Worst of Times.* London: Muller, 1990.

Chapters and Journal Articles

Alpert, Rebecca. "The Macho-Mensch: Modeling American Jewish Masculinity and the Heroes of Baseball." In *Muscling in on New Worlds: Jews, Sport, and the Making of the Americas*, edited by Raanan Rein and David M. K. Sheinin, 101–120. Leiden, Netherlands: Brill, 2014.

Baigell, Matthew. "Barnett Newman's Stripe Paintings and Kabbalah: A Jewish Take." *American Art* 8, no. 2 (1994): 32–43.

Bell-Metereau, Rebecca. "The Three Faces of *Lolita*; or, How I Learned to Stop Worrying and Love the Adaptation." In *Authorship in Film Adaptation*, edited by Jack Boozer, 203–228. Austin: University of Texas Press, 2008.

Bokobza, Serge. "Stanley Kubrick's *Eyes Wide Shut*: Decadent Europe and American Myth." In *Films with Legs: Crossing Borders with Foreign Language Films*, edited by Rosemary A. Peters and Veronique Maisier, 174–186. Newcastle, UK: Cambridge Scholars, 2014.

Burton, Margaret. "Performances of Jewish Identity: *Spartacus*." *Shofar: An Interdisciplinary Journal of Jewish Studies* 27, no. 1 (2008): 1–15.

Freedman, Jonathan. "Miller, Monroe and the Remaking of Jewish Masculinity." In *Arthur Miller's America: Theater and Culture in a Time of Change*, edited by Enoch Brater, 135–152. Ann Arbor: University of Michigan Press, 2005.

Gilman, Sander L. "Proust's Nose." *Social Research* 67, no. 1 (2000): 61–79.

Hark, Ina Rae. "Animals or Romans: Looking at Masculinity in *Spartacus*." In *Screening the Male: Exploring Masculinities in Hollywood Cinema*, edited by Steven Cohan and Ina Rae Hark, 151–172. London: Routledge, 1994.

Kelly, Andrew. "The Brutality of Military Incompetence: 'Paths of Glory' (1957)." *Historical Journal of Film, Radio and Television* 13, no. 2 (1993): 215–227.

Krämer, Peter. "'To Prevent the Present Heat from Dissipating': Stanley Kubrick and the Marketing of *Dr. Strangelove* (1964)." *InMedia* 3 (2013), http://inmedia.revues.org/634.

Kubrick, Stanley. "Words and Movies." *Sight and Sound* 30 (1960–1961): 14.

McAvoy, Catriona. "The Uncanny, the Gothic and the Loner: Intertextuality in the Adaptation Process of *The Shining*." *Adaptation* 8, no. 3 (2015): 345–360.

Mizruchi, Susan L. "*Lolita* in History." *American Literature* 75, no. 3 (2003): 629–652.

Peucker, Brigitte. "Kubrick and Kafka: The Corporeal Uncanny." *Modernism/Modernity* 8, no. 4 (2001): 663–674.

Popkin, Henry. "The Vanishing Jew of Our Popular Culture." *Commentary* 14 (1952): 46–55.

Raphael, Rebecca. "The Doomsday Body; or, Dr. Strangelove as Disabled Cyborg." *Golem: Journal of Religion and Monsters* 1, no. 1 (2006), http://lomibao.net/golem/article.php?id=1.

Ritzenhoff, Karen A. "UK Frost Can Kill Palms: Layers of Reality in Stanley Kubrick's *Full Metal Jacket*." In Ljujić, Kramer, and Daniels, *Stanley Kubrick*, 326–341.

Shohat, Ella. "Ethnicities-in-Relation: Toward a Multicultural Reading of American Cinema." In *Unspeakable Images: Ethnicity and the American Cinema*, edited by Lester D. Friedman, 215–250. Urbana: University of Illinois Press, 1991.

Stillman, Grant B. "Two of the MADdest Scientists: Where Strangelove Meets Dr. No; or, Unexpected Roots for Kubrick's Cold War Classic." *Film History: An International Journal* 20, no. 4 (2008): 487–500.

Usai, Paolo Cherchi. "Checkmating the General: Stanley Kubrick's *Fear and Desire*." *Image* 38, nos. 1–2 (1995): 3–27.

Other

Bernstein, Jeremy. "How about a Little Game?" *New Yorker*, November 12, 1966.

Bogdanovich, Peter. "What They Say about Stanley Kubrick." *New York Times Magazine*, July 4, 1999.

Campbell, Erica Fahr. "From Photography to Film: Stanley Kubrick Enters the Ring." *Time*, November 2012.

Freer, Ian. "Strangelove." *Empire*, October 2001.

Gilliatt, Penelope. "Mankind on the Late, Late Show." *Observer*, September 6, 1987.

Ginna, Robert Emmett. "The Artist Speaks for Himself." *Archivio Kubrick*. Accessed May 30, 2017. www.archiviokubrick.it/english/words/interviews/1960ginna.html.

Gluck, Robert. "Exhibition Looks Back on Kubrick, Legendary Director Who 'Knew He Looked Jewish.'" *Algemeiner*, March 22, 2013.

Jameson, Richard T. "Ghost Sonata: *Eyes Wide Shut*." *Film Comment*, September–October 1999. www.filmcomment.com/article/ghost-sonata-eyes-wide-shut.

Karpel, Dalia. "The Real Stanley Kubrick." *Haaretz.com*. November 3, 2005. www.haaretz .com/the-real-stanley-kubrick-1.173194.

Vaughan Young-Roberts, Bryn. "Gripping Kubrick's Phallus: The Oedipal Odyssey of *Eyes Wide Shut*." Draft MA essay, Bangor University, 2010. In the author's possession.

Films

2001: A Space Odyssey. Directed by Stanley Kubrick. United Kingdom: MGM, 1968.

A.I. Artificial Intelligence. Directed by Steven Spielberg. United States: Warner Bros., 2001.

Annie Hall. Directed by Woody Allen. United States: MGM, 1977.

The Apartment. Directed by Billy Wilder. United States: Mirisch Corporation, 1960.

Apocalypse Now. Directed by Francis Ford Coppola. United States: Zoetrope, 1979.

Barry Lyndon. Directed by Stanley Kubrick. United Kingdom: Warner Bros., 1975.

Ben-Hur. Directed by William Wyler. United States: MGM, 1959.

Blume in Love. Directed by Paul Marzursky. United States: Warner Bros., 1973.

Body and Soul. Directed by Robert Rossen. United States: Enterprise Productions, 1947.

Cabaret. Directed by Bob Fosse. United States: Allied Artists Pictures, 1972.

Champion. Directed by Mark Robson. United States: Kramer Productions, 1949.

A Clockwork Orange. Directed by Stanley Kubrick. United Kingdom: Warner Bros., 1971.

Crossfire. Directed by Edward Dmytryk. United States: RKO, 1947.

Day of the Fight. Directed by Stanley Kubrick. United States: RKO, 1951.

Dr. Strangelove; or, How I Learned to Stop Worrying and Love the Bomb. Directed by Stanley Kubrick. United Kingdom: Columbia Pictures, 1964.

Exodus. Directed by Otto Preminger. United States: Otto Preminger Films, 1960.

Eyes Wide Shut. Directed by Stanley Kubrick. United Kingdom: Warner Bros., 1999.

Fear and Desire. Directed by Stanley Kubrick. United States: Distributed by Joseph Burstyn, 1953.

The Firm. Directed by Sydney Pollack. United States: Paramount, 1993.

The Flying Padre. Directed by Stanley Kubrick. United States: RKO, 1951.

Full Metal Jacket. Directed by Stanley Kubrick. United Kingdom: Warner Bros., 1987.

Full Metal Jacket: Between Good and Evil. Directed by Gary Leva. United States: Warner Bros., 2007.

Harlan: In the Shadow of Jew Süss. Directed by Felix Moeller. Germany: Blueprint Film, 2008.

Husbands and Wives. Directed by Woody Allen. United States: TriStar, 1992.

Inside Dr. Strangelove. Directed by David Naylor. United States: Columbia Pictures, 2000.

Jud Süss. Directed by Veit Harlan. Germany: Terra-Filmkunst, 1940.

The Juggler. Directed by Edward Dmytryk. United States: Kramer Productions, 1953.

Killer's Kiss. Directed by Stanley Kubrick. United States: Minotaur Productions, 1955.

The Killing. Directed by Stanley Kubrick. United States: Harris-Kubrick Productions, 1956.

Letter from an Unknown Woman. Directed by Max Ophüls. United States: Rampart Productions, 1948.

Liebelei. Directed by Max Ophüls. Germany: Elite-Tonfilm-Produktion, 1933.

A Life in Pictures. Directed by Jan Harlan. United States: Warner Bros., 2001.

Lolita. Directed by Stanley Kubrick. United Kingdom: Seven Arts, 1962.

Love and Death. Directed by Woody Allen. United States: Rollins and Joffe Productions, 1975.

Modern Romance. Directed by Albert Brooks. United States: Columbia Pictures, 1981.

Paths of Glory. Directed by Stanley Kubrick. United States: Bryna Productions, 1957.

Radio Days. Directed by Woody Allen. United States: Orion, 1987.

La Ronde. Directed by Max Ophüls. France: Films Sacha Gordine, 1950.

Rosemary's Baby. Directed by Roman Polanski. United States: Castle Productions, 1968.

Sabrina. Directed by Billy Wilder. United States: Paramount Pictures, 1954.

Sabrina. Directed by Sydney Pollack. United States: Constellation Entertainment, 1995.

Scarlet Street. Directed by Fritz Lang. United States: Wanger Productions, 1945.

The Seafarers. Directed by Stanley Kubrick. United States: Cooper Productions, 1953.

The Set Up. Directed by Robert Wise. United States: RKO, 1949.

The Shining. Directed by Stanley Kubrick. United Kingdom: Warner Bros., 1980.

Spartacus. Directed by Stanley Kubrick. United States: Bryna Productions/Universal-International Pictures, 1960.

Zelig. Directed by Woody Allen. United States: Orion Pictures, 1983.

Index

About the Author

NATHAN ABRAMS is a professor of film studies at Bangor University in Wales. He is the author of *The New Jew in Film: Exploring Jewishness and Judaism in Contemporary Cinema* (2012) and editor of *Hidden in Plain Sight: Jews and Jewishness in British Film, Television, and Popular Culture* (2016). He is also the founding coeditor of *Jewish Film and New Media: An International Journal*.